PENGUIN BOOKS

INSIDE JAPAN

Peter Tasker has lived and worked in Japan for six years and is a fluent speaker of the language. Educated at Clifton, he won a scholarship to Balliol College, Oxford, in 1973. After graduating he spent two years working at the head office of a Japanese multinational, including a one-year stint in the company dormitory. A financial specialist, he is currently Head of Japanese Research at a major British securities house and divides his time between Tokyo and London.

INSIDE JAPAN

Wealth, Work and Power
in the New Japanese Empire

Peter Tasker

PENGUIN BOOKS

For my mother and father

PENGUIN BOOKS

Published by the Penguin Group
27 Wrights Lane, London w8 5tz, England
Viking Penguin Inc., 40 West 23rd Street, New York, New York 10010, USA
Penguin Books Australia Ltd, Ringwood, Victoria, Australia
Penguin Books Canada Ltd, 2801 John Street, Markham, Ontario, Canada l3r 1b4
Penguin Books (NZ) Ltd, 182–190 Wairau Road, Auckland 10, New Zealand

Penguin Books Ltd, Registered Offices: Harmondsworth, Middlesex, England

First published in Great Britain by Sidgwick & Jackson 1987
Published in Penguin Books 1989
1 3 5 7 9 10 8 6 4 2

Copyright © Peter Tasker, 1987
All rights reserved

Made and printed in Great Britain by
Richard Clay Ltd, Bungay, Suffolk
Filmset in Monophoto Bembo

Contents

15.99

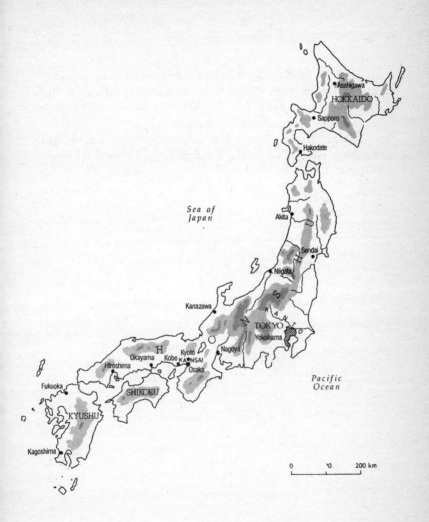

Acknowledgements

I am very grateful to the many people who have contributed ideas and information to this book, particularly Martin Roth, Simon Smithson, Jurek Martin, Makoto Ishimitsu, Yasuhisa Sokawa, and most of all, to Kuniko Usui, who provided special research and support. For the photographs I am obliged to Barbara Huss, Kyodo, the Foreign Press Centre in Tokyo, and Camera Press in London.

Prologue

Some time during 1985 an event of great historical significance occurred within the ceaseless electronic exchange of pluses and minuses that makes up the international financial system. Japan, a debtor nation for most of her modern history, became the world's largest creditor nation. At roughly the same time the United States, the previous holder of that distinction, became the world's largest debtor. There was no coincidence involved, for most of Japan's overseas assets were in the United States, and most of the United States' liabilities were owed to Japan.

Foreign perceptions of Japan have always lagged well behind the reality. Because the Japanese are modest in the geopolitical and diplomatic postures they adopt, the world has tended to underestimate their rapidly increasing power. Even the Japanese themselves seem bemused by the results of their economic success. After all, no industrialized nation has ever grown so rich so fast as Japan, nor has any superpower ever been so dependent on other countries for her continued wealth and security. Yet both foreigners and Japanese had better accustom themselves to the situation. Barring war and natural calamities, by the year 1995 Japan's overseas assets will have quintupled to $500 billion, making her the largest provider of capital that has ever existed. The poorer countries will look first to Japan to fund their development needs. Some of the richer countries will be relying on her to preserve employment. As the major supplier of finance and technology to the fast-developing East Asian countries, she will be the prime mover in the coming shift of economic power to the Pacific Basin region.

The sole natural resource which Japan has at her disposal is her people. With just 2.6 per cent of the world's population and 0.1 per cent of its inhabitable area, she generates 10 per cent of world economic value. She is the only non-Western country to have taken on the West at its own game and, on most measures, beaten it. Almost every industry that has faced the Japanese challenge has ended up smaller and poorer. Even Silicon Valley, the symbol of America's high-technology sunrise, has thrown in the towel and appealed for protectionist help. Meanwhile, Japanese corporations are building up powerful manufacturing bases in Europe and the US, often revolutionizing local work practices. By 1990 Japanese auto production within the US will exceed total British production. Already, the four largest banks in the world are Japanese, and the largest private-sector recruiter of Oxbridge graduates is a Japanese company.

Despite the large and increasing influence the Japanese have over our lives, much about their society and institutions remains unknown, hidden behind screens of misunderstanding and cliché. What lies behind the screens is quite different – but usually no less baffling. All foreign cultures seem paradoxical at first sight, but in Japan's case, even after close acquaintance many of the paradoxes remain intact. Indeed, dynamic contradiction – between preservation and transformation, between conflict and consensus – is at the heart of the Japanese experience.

In the centre of Shinjuku, the largest and most bustling of Tokyo's new business centres, stands the Sumitomo Building, a forty-two-storey, triple-sided, hollow-cored edifice which houses several of Japan's most famous corporations. Skyscrapers are still rare in Tokyo, a city where the average height of construction is under three storeys, and the Sumitomo Building towers over the jumble of smallness. Only recently have advances in anti-earthquake engineering made it possible to build to this height. The trick, successful so far, lies in the lightweight tensile structure which is supposed to move with any vibrations rather than resist them. The Sumitomo Building may appear monolithic, but it can be flexible when it must.

From a top-storey vantage point you might, on an exceptionally clear day, be able to make out the outline of Mount Fuji oscillating gently in the haze. Such days, however, are few and far between. Instead, you are more likely to be regaled with a vista unappealing to the eye but, on consideration, just as extraordinary as the shape of that barren, broken-headed volcano.

To the east lies Tokyo Bay, where forty years ago the deeds of surrender were signed aboard the USS *Missouri*. At that time, almost impossible to imagine, central Tokyo was a heap of charred rubble and her defeated people lice-infested and starving. For much of the city that was the second devastation in a generation, the first having being caused by the Great Earthquake of 1923. Today the space between the bay and the Imperial Palace contains the Marunouchi financial district, the most expensive piece of real estate in the world. It is populated by sharp-suited bankers and the best-dressed women outside Paris.

Directly to your right is Shinjuku Station, used by three million people every day. Twenty railway lines meet here, twelve belonging to the national railway, six to private companies, and two to the underground system. Altogether they handle 3000 train departures daily. On the circle line between eight and nine in the morning trains leave every three minutes. Even so, the human traffic reaches levels of congestion that elsewhere can only be experienced in soccer grounds or stock exchanges. Inside the carriages the distance between people simply disappears, leaving a single compressed body of flesh.

Looking to the west you have a panoramic view of the Kanto Plain, the industrial heartland of modern Japan, where thirty-five million people live and work. Here are their factories, homes, dormitories, offices and schools, all jam-packed together, competing for space and survival. Buddhist temples stand shoulder to shoulder with gaudy love hotels. Ramshackle wooden houses back up against great ferro-concrete apartment blocks, *futon* bed-rolls hanging like tongues from their every window. Any piece of land that could be built upon has been built upon. Even the occasional roof has been assigned a function, as a laundry area, or a beer garden, or a golf driving range where shirt-sleeved salarymen can tee off into the netting and dream of Gleneagles.

The streets – nameless, like all Japanese streets – thread through a puzzle of flyovers and railway tracks. The buildings that line them are cats-cradled in power and communication wires, apparently slung at random like washing lines in a Naples back alley. The bright new cars that fill them nudge forward patiently, conveying busy people from one place of busyness to the next. The whole cityscape is a jungle of messages, telling of new products, services, methods of contributing to GNP. Here and there slant-jibbed cranes peck away at orange scaffoldings, prefiguring further movement in the endless cycle of demolition and construction, obliteration and rebirth.

To those of us accustomed to intervals between our cities, this vast clot of phenomena presents an awesome prospect: Tokyo, Kawasaki, Yokohama, Hiratsuka – all one great conurbation, stretching on and on to the smog-blurred horizon. And yet it is inhabited by a people whose fastidiousness and devotion to order, as expressed in their language, in their customs, in their manufacturing techniques, almost approaches the fanatical.

Here they come now, streaming out of the station and across a six-lane interchange of zebra crossings. Here come the people who brought you the Walkman, the Watchman, the 1 Megabit Dynamic RAM, Zen Buddhism, Pearl Harbor, the tea ceremony, the no-panty coffee bar, the capsule hotel, the world's longest tunnel, fastest train, worst air disaster, and largest collection (eight million) of gods.

Here come the people who produce 50 per cent of the world's ships, 25 per cent of its cars, 90 per cent of its videos and 40 per cent of its integrated circuits. They are the most innovative imitators, the hardest-working hedonists, the lewdest prudes, the most courteous and cruellest and kindest of people. Rich and yet wealthless, confident but confused, they have just staged one of the greatest comebacks in history.

They are a people so conservative that they have let the same party rule them for thirty-five years. Simultaneously they have ridden a wave of economic change such as the world has rarely seen. They claim to be unreligious, but have their factories and offices consecrated by priests. They have the lowest crime rate in the developed world, and organized crime syndicates five times as large as the American mafia. They have voted convicted criminals into positions of power, yet will travel hundreds of miles to return a dropped wallet. They love to hear foreigners' opinions of their country, but would not dream of taking them seriously.

Their children go through one of the most rigorous educational systems in the world. Middle-class adults devour cartoon books and spend their mornings in pinball arcades. Famously sensitive to the glories of Nature, they have despoiled almost every beach and beauty spot they possess. They are convinced of their own culture's supremacy, yet suffer from an inferiority complex that makes all others look simple. They hold their traditions precious. They adapt.

Here come the Japanese. Once they've started, they take some stopping.

I

Place: The Edge of the Map

'Pat! Get Houston,' shouted the commander, staring at the screen. 'Tell them that Japan is going under.'

While the Pacific coast slid away into the deep, the Japan Sea coast rose up for a brief moment, like one side of a capsizing vessel. But then the same blind force took hold of it too and plunged it down into the sea.

Sakyo Komatsu, *Japan Sinks*

The word 'Japan' is a Portuguese mishearing of a Malay corruption of the Cantonese pronunciation of the Chinese term for the country known by its inhabitants as 'Nippon', or 'Nihon'. The characters used to write Nippon mean 'source of the sun', which accurately describes the country's position relative to the rest of the world. Further east than Japan there is only west.

The Japanese archipelago is a long crescent-shaped group of 5000 islands situated off the north-eastern flank of the Asian mainland. Its northernmost point is on a latitude with Belgrade and Montreal; its southernmost with Riyadh and Miami. The Japan Sea, never less than 200 miles across, separates Japan from her mainland neighbours, the expanse of the Pacific from America. It is a location that has had a profound influence on the country's historical development.

Until the coming of modern warships Japan's geographical position kept her well protected from invasion, the only serious attempt, that of Kubla Khan's fleet in the thirteenth century, being thwarted by the *kamikaze* wind of the gods. Yet, although insulated from the movement and conflict of peoples, the Japanese were close enough to the continent to absorb the benefits of the great Asian cultures. Priests and merchants could make the risky voyage across the Japan Sea and bring back new knowledge and crafts to be adapted to Japanese needs. Uniquely, Japan was able to take the best elements of Chinese culture without falling under China's economic and political domination. When the Western powers began to extend their colonization of East Asia, Japan's remoteness again helped her to maintain independence. Being one of the last Asian countries to be confronted with the Western challenge, she could learn from the fate of the others.

In the world of satellite communications, floating currencies and SS 20s, Japan's geographical location no longer affords much protection of any sort. On the contrary, it can only add to her feelings of insecurity. The nearest democracy is the Philippines, as far away from Tokyo as Morocco is from London. Immediately to the north is the Soviet Union, which has just built an air base on one of the small islands filched from Japan at the end of the Second World War. To the west the two Koreas glare at each other across the demilitarized zone. To the south Taiwan and China are still loosing off propaganda barrages across the Formosan Straits. Forty years ago they seemed suitable areas for colonization, and the Japanese empire was 40 per cent larger in area than modern Japan. Now, the Japanese could be excused for wishing their country towed several hundred miles further out to sea.

Modern Japan is in Asia, yet not of Asia. All the cultural elements which her people think most typically Japanese were imported from the mainland. Yet Japan's main markets and resource suppliers are on the other side of the world. The military alliance on which her security is based is with the leader of the Western bloc. In standard of living and political structure she is closer to America and Europe than to any of her neighbours, and it is with the people of those remote countries which the Japanese automatically compare themselves when they ask themselves the all-important question: 'How are we doing – have we caught up yet?' Periodically the Japanese rediscover their Asian identity – the justification for the Great East Asian War was the liberation of their fellow Asians – but for the most part they are suffused by a strong sense of geographic anomaly.

Japan's latitudinal stretch, reaching further than that of much larger countries, has created a great variety of climatic conditions. Hokkaido, the most northerly of the four main islands, is under snow for five months of the year. There are also heavy falls on the west coast of Honshu, where the inhabitants of small villages have to shovel the snow from their roofs to avert cave-ins. Far to the south lies semi-tropical Okinawa, where pineapples and bananas are cultivated. Thus the Tokyo inhabitant can spend his 'golden week' spring holiday either skiiing or snorkelling. The climate in Tokyo itself and the other major cities of the industrial belt is pleasantly mild, with average temperatures ranging from 40°F in January to 78°F in July.

The cycle of nature, from which much of Japanese art takes its inspiration, is reassuringly regular and well defined. The northward sweep of the 'cherry-blossom front' in April is as reliable as a Toyota. It moves one degree in latitude every two days, one hundred metres in altitude every three. As a result Japanese weathermen have an easier time of it than their British equivalents. They are able to announce the official beginning and end of the rainy season with masterful confidence. In return for their usually accurate prognostications they are given a generous benefit of the doubt. Thus any rain falling after the officially defined dry season commences is considered to be an entirely separate matter. Instead of cursing the authorities for getting it wrong, people congratulate themselves on the start of summer and hurry to work under their umbrellas.

The Japanese are justifiably proud of their four seasons, whose progress they mark by a number of traditional ceremonies and observances – saké under the cherry trees, saké under the autumn moon, snow-viewing and saké, et cetera. However, Nature has its darker side as well. It is a rare year indeed when human lives are not claimed by typhoon, tidal wave, avalanche, flood or volcanic eruption. The Japanese islands are themselves volcanic in origin, and about forty volcanoes remain active. Once every ten years or so a new island appears, thrusting itself naked and steaming into the sunlight. The birth takes only a matter of days, as does the process of mapping, measurement and incorporation into the appropriate administrative unit. Thus all history and pre-history – from the myth time, when creation sprang from Izanagi-no-Mikoto's Heavenly Jewelled Spear, down to the present, when roads and bridges spring from the pens of politicians – is compressed into less than a week.

In addition to the various volcanic gushings, hissings and eructations, there are far more destructive seismic phenomena to contend with. Japan lies close to two major fault lines, a situation which gives her an unenviable 10 per cent share of world earthquake energy. According to another legend the entire country rests on a gigantic catfish, whose periodic twitchings bring chaos and destruction to her unlucky inhabitants. In the eastern region earth tremors occur almost every day, most of them imperceptibly weak. However, more powerful shudders, strong enough to slop drinks and set lights swinging, are felt several times a year. The onset of such a quake is always a testing experience, inevitably provoking the unvoiceable fear: 'Could this be the Big One?'

The Big One, according to the Kawasumi theory, recurs at an average interval of sixty-nine years. Its last visit, in 1923, resulted in 100,000 deaths, the destruction of two-thirds of all dwellings in Tokyo, and a panic massacre of Korean immigrants. Most of the damage to property was done by the fires which raged out of control for several days. Today the city works on the assumption that newly developed systems and technologies will prevent a similar disaster. In the circumstances that is the only assumption possible. None the less all the technology in the world cannot drive away the atavistic dread of cataclysm which has been nurtured by centuries of terrible experience. It is there at its most bizarre and explicit in Sakyo Komatsu's best-selling SF novel, *Japan Sinks*. It can also be identified at work in some of the financial policies followed by the economic ministries. Who is to say that they are wrong?

In Japan earthquakes are usually discussed in terms of their intensity, not their magnitude. That is to say in terms of the vibration experienced, which varies from place to place, rather than the absolute quantity of energy released at the epicentre. Intensity is measured on a scale of seven, not by instruments, but by different categories of observable event. At intensity five gravestones are supposed to topple and windows smash. At intensity six roofs fall in and roads fissure. Since no one at the Meteorological Agency has had professional experience of intensity six (the last example was in 1929), classification of the stronger quakes can be somewhat ambiguous, with a natural enough tendency to boost the level of what has been successfully withstood. This preference for the vague and the subjective crops up repeatedly in more important contexts. In all sorts of aesthetic and ethical judgements the Japanese consistently favour intensity over magnitude.

Many Japanese believe their country to be pitifully small, even weak. Certainly she may appear so in comparison with the three resource-rich superpowers with whose fate she is so intimately involved. However, by most other standards Japan is large. She has roughly double the population of West Germany, the most populous West European country, and more land area than all save France, Spain and Sweden. Although Japanese is hardly spoken at all outside Japan, it is the sixth most widely spoken language in the world.

Structure, not scale, gives substance to the Japanese sense of insecurity. Until this century Japan was entirely self-supporting. When the Tokugawa Shogunate cut off contact with the outside world for 200 years, the result was an era of unprecedented prosperity and economic development. Modern industrial Japan is the least self-sufficient of the major powers. She must rely on foreign countries for her oil, her ores, her timber, her meat and grain. Even her most traditional foods are manufactured from American farm produce. When Richard Nixon's administration briefly embargoed the export of soya beans in June 1971 the awful prospect was raised of *suki-yaki* and *shabu-shabu* with no *tofu*, no soy sauce. The Japanese, however, are well acquainted with the unpleasant truth that they need the rest of the world much more than the rest of the world needs them. They have schooled themselves to act accordingly.

The geography of the islands is equally unaccommodating. Only 15 per cent of the total land area is arable, only 4 per cent pasture and grassland. This compares with figures of 30 per cent and 50 per cent for the United Kingdom. Roughly four-fifths of Japan is mountainous, consisting of steep, densely forested volcanic ridges, impenetrable valleys and soaring peaks, several of them over 5000 feet from sea level. This hinterland the bears, monkeys and other wild creatures have to themselves. The Japanese people inhabit the edges of their country, the narrow coastal strip which contains nearly all cultivable land. Since the time of Ieyasu, first of the Tokugawa Shoguns, the Japanese have laboured to secure and expand this area. The centre of modern Tokyo, including Ginza and Marunouchi, lies on land reclaimed by Ieyasu in the early seventeenth century – a mighty engineering project which took ten thousand men five years to complete. Now, more than 40 per cent of the Japanese coastline is artificial, as much a product of human endeavour as the cargoes of goods that leave it every day.

In the early years of this century Japanese emigrants streamed into the United States, Brazil and Hawaii in search of land and livelihood. After the Second World War, as domestic living standards rose, emigration slowed to a trickle, but the *Lebensraum* problem remained unsolved. Now grandiose schemes are being proposed to increase the supply of land. Over the next few decades the Japanese will begin the construction of several artificial islands, the first of which will bear airports and fuel dumps. Further in the future, there are powerfully backed plans to build a multi-level population centre 100 miles offshore – a project as ambitious in its time as Ieyasu's was in his. It would be ironic if the Japanese, who still consider themselves closer to Nature than any of the

Western peoples, were to be the first to create a wholly artificial habitat.

Nominally Japan's population density is less than that of its neighbour South Korea, less even than that of Belgium and Luxembourg. However, with 120 million Japanese crammed into just one-fifth of its land area, Japan's effective density is far higher than obtains in all except the single-city nations. In consequence land has come to occupy the same position in the Japanese consciousness as gold does in the French. *Nouveaux riches* individuals and companies buy land at the first opportunity and will part with it only on the brink of financial ruin. This has contributed to the notoriously high prices of Japanese real estate. According to official figures, the market value of Japan's total land area is double that of the United States, a country twenty-five times larger.

At the outbreak of the Second World War half of the Japanese population still worked on the land. Today only 9 per cent – still a high ratio by Western standards – is employed in the primary sector. The past forty years have seen a massive influx of population to the cities, particularly to the Tokyo–Nagoya–Osaka industrial belt. Just as an overwhelming proportion of the Japanese are now, by their own description, middle class, so a large majority have chosen to live in the geographical middle of their country. This is where the most characteristic images of modern Japan – the seething crowds and the jammed trains – are to be found. This is where the cultural conjunctions and disjunctions are at their most startling, and where the dynamism of the Japanese economy has its source. Perhaps it is not surprising that the Japanese have excelled at the production of semiconductor chips. In urban Japan the social and economic circuitry is more highly integrated than anywhere else, and people flow through it like charged particles.

Conformity and consensus – these are not matters of courtesy, but techniques of group survival. The Japanese city-dweller has no choice but to tolerate his fellow humans. The thin, poorly soundproofed walls of his apartment ensure that they know all about him, and he about them, even without being introduced. On the morning tube train their sweat drips down his back. They enclose him, pushing and squeezing, and if he dozes off to sleep, their comforting pressure will hold him upright. Everywhere he goes they are already there in mass. Overcrowding is a fact of life, and soon to be a fact of death. According to the Ministry of Health, by 1995 all Tokyo's cemeteries will be chock-a-block. That means that family urns will probably have to be kept in special 'columbariums' containing rows of cubicles, a dismal thought for the ancestor-worshipping Japanese. Even now Tokyo municipal cemeteries have twelve applicants for every available place, roughly the same ratio as for Japan's most prestigious universities.

Not all Japan has the same problems. The Japanese began the settlement of Hokkaido just 120 years ago, and its population density is still only one-quarter the UK's. Despite the hard winters it provides the only suitable pasture for Japan's growing dairy herds. The combination of cattle and wide open spaces even prompted film companies to use Hokkaido as the setting for the bizarre genre of Japanese Westerns, complete with gunfights, schoolmarms and noodle-slurping men in black hats. Some of the remote areas of Honshu are now suffering from serious depopulation, victims of the same modernization process which opened up the large island to the north. Their young farmers have to advertise far and wide, even in foreign countries, for willing brides. Over the past decade several small islands which had supported communities for centuries were deserted as the few inhabitants remaining became unable to support themselves any longer.

Such, then, is the physical condition of the Japanese islands: isolated, yet not isolated enough, blessed by a placid climate, but with an unfortunate tendency to erupt without warning. While much is moderate and well-blended, irreconcilable extremes still exist – of temperature, of population density, of geological pedigree. The comparison with the disposition of the Japanese themselves is hackneyed, but irresistible.

2

People: The Japanese
and the Rest

A perfectly paternal government; a perfectly filial people; a
community entirely self-supporting; peace within and without; no want; no ill will between classes. This is what I find
in Japan in the year 1858, after one hundred years' exclusion
of foreign trade and foreigners. Twenty years hence, what
will be the contrast?

Letters of Lord Elgin

'Meanwhile back in Penny Lane the barber shaves another
coostomer . . .'

The accent is deepest Liverpool, the hairstyle a shaggy
sixties fringe. Yet this is Tokyo 1989, and the singer a young
Japanese. He may bear a strong physical resemblance to Paul
McCartney, but in fact he speaks hardly any English – except
for the lyrics of every song the Beatles ever recorded. These
he and his friends pump out night after night, faithfully
reproducing the voice inflections, the guitar breaks, even the
bad notes of the originals. Little doubt, they can copy Beatles
recordings better than the Beatles ever could.

The fabulous four perform in an establishment called the
Cavern Club, which is to be found on the third floor of a
neon-splattered disco-infested building in Roppongi, the most
cosmopolitan of Japan's entertainment districts. Roppongi is a
place of flows – of faces, voices, signs, styles, money. It is
completely unreal, which is why it is so popular. Here,
amongst the polite pandemonium of a Friday night, people of
all origins and types mill around in search of energy and
excitement – diplomats, bankers, strippers, 'new humans' (see

p. 113), rivers of salarymen, oceans of office girls. Besides the eternal sixties, there is a selection of ersatz experiences to savour. At the country and western bar Hank Yamamoto warbles plaintively of the blue-ridged mountains he has never seen. The counter staff of the ubiquitous McDonald's outlets relay instructions to one another in a brand of English heard nowhere else on earth. In the Indian restaurant Japanese waiters wear orange turbans and Hindi-inscribed medallions, and the customers are entertained by a red-headed belly dancer from Wolverhampton.

A few minutes away from the main crossing stands Ark Hills, a complex of 'intelligent buildings' that has replaced the former huddle of *yakitori* bars and mom-and-pop stores. It contains an international hotel, a concert hall whose prime tickets cost £500 each, restaurants, apartments and high-technology open-plan offices – two-thirds of which are occupied by foreign firms. The parabolic antenna on the roof catches a constant stream of information from similar buildings on other continents. You could stay in there for years and never need to come out. Like the rest of Roppongi, it is everywhere and nowhere.

That is one side of modern Japan: the dynamic mix of influences and ideas. Few cultures have been as porous, as thirstily absorbent of the foreign and the new. Indeed, so supremely successful have the Japanese been in taking what they need from abroad and adapting it to their own purposes that they have often been accused, quite unfairly, of lacking creativity. Break-dancing, spoon-bending, gene-splicing – no sooner have the ideas been thought up than skilled exponents appear in Japan. The modern Japanese experience has been a process of enrichment through borrowing, with the greatest prizes going to those individuals and institutions who have shown the most receptivity to foreign influence.

Another side of Japan was epitomized in a trivial but extremely revealing incident which took place in September 1986. Prime Minister Yasuhiro Nakasone, brimming with the confidence of his recent landslide victory, made an off-the-cuff comment to his factional seminar: 'The level of knowledge in the United States is lower than in Japan due to the considerable number of blacks, Puerto Ricans and Mexicans.' The Japanese press, seeing nothing remarkable, gave the episode only cursory treatment, but foreign agencies instantly recognized its aggravation value and splashed it over the world's front pages. The result was instant uproar, with fulminations from the congressional black caucus, threatened boycotts of Japanese goods, and full-page advertisements in *The New York Times*. Every American columnist worth his salt suddenly had something to say about Japanese arrogance and unfairness, and the hapless bureaucrats of the Foreign Ministry were forced to scuttle around frantically in vain attempts to prevent all their hard work going up in smoke.

Matters were not helped by Nakasone's subsequent 'clarification'. Claiming that his words had been taken out of context, he explained that he had only meant to point out the remarkable nature of America's achievement in putting men on the moon, et cetera, despite the existence of so many troublesome minorities. More uproar. Explosives were planted in a Japanese-owned building in Los Angeles, and the Japanese ambassador was refused entry to a Washington party. Finally the shame-faced Nakasone managed to retrieve the situation through the transmission of an unprecedented Yasu-to-Ron national apology, but lasting damage had been done. Midterm congressional elections were due in six weeks' time, and the Reagan administration was forced to look on in silent mortification as the protectionist Democrats exploited the issue to the full. The degree of causality is impossible to assess, but the Republicans did lose their six-seat majority in the Senate, and trade negotiations grew even more acrimonious.

Nakasone is the foreigners' favourite Japanese politician, a man who is constantly reminding the public of the need for Japan to 'internationalize', and who secured unprecedented levels of electoral support through his self-proclaimed expertise in diplomacy. The incident served to demonstrate how far there is to go, for it is hard to imagine the leader of any other nation showing such massive disregard for the most basic sensitivities of a major ally. Equally significant were the speed and extent of the response. Nakasone had voiced similar opinions innumerable times before in his career, indeed was noted as something of a bore on the subject. Prominent Japanese in politics, business and the media had regularly expressed even more chauvinistic sentiments without international crisis developing.

The reason for the contrast was simple. Previously, few people outside academic circles cared what any Japanese was thinking about anything. Now, however, Japan was rich, powerful, and therefore big news. Nakasone had become a victim of his own and his country's success. He had made his name by demanding to be taken seriously, to be afforded the political respect that matched Japan's new economic might. He did not appear to understand the natural corollary – that the pronouncements of Japanese leaders would now be scrutinized not just by an apathetic domestic public but by concerned people all over the world. Many other Japanese who favour an abstract 'internationalization', which is usually interpreted as no more than the advancement of Japan's national interests overseas, may be equally unaware of the challenge to their deepest assumptions that will inevitably result.

In the parliamentary debate on the subject the leader of the Japan Socialist Party showed more honesty than political acumen when she pointed out that the prime minister had merely expressed what most Japanese were thinking. Nakasone had meant no particular offence to Americans of any race, creed or colour by his comments. He had been alluding to two beliefs as fundamental to the Japanese as personal liberty is to an American. Firstly, that the Japanese are a 'unique' people, entirely different from all the other peoples of the world. Secondly, that their extraordinary progress over the past 120 years is a direct result of this uniqueness. The Japanese are highly conscious of being misunderstood by foreigners, but do not consider it the unfortunate result of insufficient contact between peoples. Rather, it is a sign of Japanese success in preserving a homogeneity and separateness that is perceived in racial terms.

If the Japanese were indeed as homogeneous as they claim,

Japan would be one of the most tedious places on earth. Fortunately that is very far from being the case. Japanese society is filled with surprising and diverse characters, riddled with conflicts between opposing factions and interest groups. Where else do companies and ministries and even school-children compete amongst themselves with such unrelenting ferocity: could a dispute about the siting of an airport provoke a whole decade of violent protest; could two politicians of indistinguishable beliefs spend their careers plotting to destroy each other? In fact some sort of contact with the foreigner, or the outsider, may be necessary to create the sense of ethnic solidarity which prevents the whole social structure from collapsing under the strain.

Nakasone's comments were not just the musings of a crusty conservative, but part of a syndrome that has been reinforced by centuries of historical experience. To a Japanese, being Japanese is the primary fact in life. To be Japanese means to bear one of the names in the official register of Japanese names; to celebrate the yearly Festival of the Dead, when the spirits of all the other Japanese who have ever existed return to their native places. It means to be for ever an inside man – inside a family, inside a village, inside a company, inside the Japanese islands surrounded by sea.

In anthropological – as opposed to psychological – terms, the Japanese race does not exist. The Japanese belong to the Mongoloid group of peoples, which also includes the Koreans and the Han Chinese. All Mongoloid babies are born with a blue spot on their backs. As a cursory examination of the contents of any tube train will confirm, there is a wide range of physical and facial types on offer. According to folk anthropology the two main ones are the fox (slender, with a high nose and brow) and the racoon (broad in the waist, short-legged and flat of feature). Less picturesquely, one could identify Polynesian, Chinese and South-East Asian character-istics. Skin colour varies considerably, and naturally wavy or brown-tinged hair and brown eyes can crop up without any outside agency.

How the Japanese came to Japan and where they came from remain shrouded in mystery. According to legend they are descended from Amaterasu Omikami, the bashful sun goddess who could only be enticed from her cave by the noise of a party staged for her benefit outside. Thus not only the Imperial family but also the common people of Japan are divine in origin. Until the defeat of 1945 many people were prepared to take this fairly literally. Today the theory is frowned upon. Instead, Japanese scholars of anthropology and comparative linguistics have travelled the ends of the earth to study tribes who use Japanese-style tools or utter Japanese-style words. Their researches usually receive considerable attention in the media, for there are few topics which excite the Japanese quite as much as their own culture and history. So far, however, results have been inconclusive. The most likely solution remains the most obvious: that the Japanese people were formed by waves of immigration from the Asian continent, spread over thousands of years.

The Japanese have been in Japan a good long time, certainly since the period 18,000 years ago when land bridges existed between Hokkaido and Siberia and between Kyushu and Korea. Archaeologists have unearthed what are said to be Stone Age tools dating at least as far back as 30,000 BC, and perhaps from the last Ice Age. However, sceptics maintain that these are merely Stone Age tool-like stones. The first distinctive culture, called Jomon after the markings on the pottery it produced, is generally thought to have appeared at around 10,000 BC. The Jomon Japanese were hunters and shellfish gatherers, and makers of startling clay figurines probably used in fertility ceremonies. Their subsistence economy was transformed by the introduction of wet-paddy cultivation from China in 300 BC.

The group of indigenous Japanese that gained military ascendancy in the second and third centuries AD was known as the Yamato, after the area of west Japan it inhabited. Its leaders were the progenitors of the Imperial family. In modern Japanese, Yamato (written with the characters 'great peace') is used as a synonym for the Japanese nation, usually with a strongly patriotic resonance. However, some historians believe that the Yamato were the latest and most successful of the immigrant groups, their more recent contact with continental culture giving them a decisive edge in military techniques. Be that as it may, once the Yamato had pacified their competitors the basic composition of the Japanese nation was established.

The Yamato-led Japanese did not have Japan to themselves. The Ainu, an aboriginal Caucasian people, inhabited present-day Hokkaido and, probably, the northern regions of the main island. These simple bear-worshipping people were, over the course of the centuries, the object of various 'barbarian subjugation' campaigns which resulted in considerable depletion of their numbers and territory. In fact the original title and job description of Shogun was 'General-in-charge-of-barbarian-repression', the Ainu being the barbarians. There has subsequently been steady assimilation of the Ainu into the racial stock – which is why Japanese from the northern prefectures are generally more hirsute than their southern compatriots. Today only 12,000 pure-blooded Ainu remain, mostly in the special reservations established in central Hokkaido.

From the fifth century the Yamato-controlled Japanese court came into contact with T'ang-dynasty China, probably the most highly developed culture in the world at that time. Envoys were exchanged, and the Japanese liked what they saw. They decided to import, amongst other things, a religion, a written language, a cuisine and an administrative system, despite the fact that there wasn't much to administer. Many of the most traditional items of Japanese culture, such as the kimono and the *tatami* mat, are based on Chinese borrowings from this period which have long since vanished from their country of origin. However, in a striking prefigurement of the eager synthesis with the West twelve centuries later, existing Japanese forms refused to be overwhelmed by the foreign influence. In religion, for example, Buddhism and native Shinto began a symbiotic relationship that continues today. The spoken language managed to absorb its new vocabulary just as readily as English did the profusion of neologisms thrown up by the Renaissance. In course of time the written language developed in a way that would make it incomprehensible to a native Chinese.

Despite her cultural and economic might China presented no military danger – her rulers did not consider the world outside the Middle Kingdom worth the trouble of invading. From the ninth century, Chinese power ebbed and contacts between the two countries fell away. The Japanese were left to absorb and modify what they had learnt. Contacts with Korea were maintained, including the occasional immigration of craftsmen. The only real threat from the continent was the storm-thwarted offensive by Kubla Khan's armada in 1281.

When the West's merchants and missionaries arrived on the scene in the sixteenth century they found a comparatively prosperous martial society in which several warlords were competing for supreme power. Initially they were welcomed. Soon the Japanese were manufacturing high-quality rosaries and wearing them as fashion accessories, rather like the domestically produced Gucci handbags of today. However, apart from firearms and navigational technique, Westeners had little of obvious use to offer the Japanese this time round. The short fifty years in which their presence was tolerated happened to coincide with a resolution of the centuries-old state of conflict and the unification of the country under a centralized government. The Tokugawa Shogunate took an increasingly dim view of foreigners in general and their fast-spreading religion in particular. The activity of the missionaries, who taught a loyalty to Rome greater than the bond between man and master, was correctly seen as a destabilizing influence. The authorities decided on drastic remedies. The foreigners, both missionaries and traders, were thrown out, the native Christians extirpated, and the country closed to foreign contact. Japanese already outside were not let back in, and the building of ocean-going ships became a capital offence.

That was just part of the far-reaching system of social control established by the Shogunate. The populace was divided into four social classes – in order of descending merit:

the samurai, farmers, craftsmen and merchants. For each, the smallest details of everyday life, such as what kinds of food might be eaten and what kinds of clothes might be worn, were strictly regulated. In addition there were two classes of outcaste, composed of mendicant entertainers and leather-workers (*burakumin*), which were considered barely human, being referred to by the counter-word for animal and living in villages unmarked on any map. They were forbidden to have sexual relations with ordinary people or to eat or sit down in their company. Utter conformity was enforced on all sections of the population, as is illustrated by the following famous decree of Ieyasu Tokugawa:

Farmers, craftsmen and merchants may not behave in a rude manner towards samurai. The word for a rude man is 'other-than-expected-fellow' and a samurai is not to be interfered with in cutting down a fellow who has behaved to him in a manner other than is expected.

Thus courtesy is not just a matter of good manners. It is essential to personal survival. The samurai, who made up some 10 per cent of the population, had their own rigid codes of conduct, whose infringement might require atonement through ritual suicide. In theory, at least, there was no mobility between the classes or, for that matter, geographically. The performance of local administrations in preserving stability was monitored by an elaborate spy network maintained by the central government. In order to prevent the emergence of any rival power centre the Shogunate required the *daimyo* (regional lords) to spend one year in two at Edo (modern Tokyo), a practice which cost them much money and kept them out of touch with developments in their own power bases. The result of these arrangements was 200 years of political peace, a remarkable achievement after the centuries of strife which had gone before. Various channels were left open which kept Japan informed about developments in the West, but the Western nations had very little idea of what was happening in Japan – an imbalance in the flow of information that has yet to be corrected.

Commander Perry's black ships steamed into Yokohama

Bay in 1853. The Shogunate, lacking the capacity to fulfil its barbarian-suppressing responsibilities, was forced to conclude treaties with first the Americans, then the British and French. The 'outer *daimyo*', long restless with their exclusion from power, began to scheme against the Edo government, using the rallying cry 'respect the Emperor and expel the barbarians'. The first part was easier to manage than the second. After a spell of intriguing the Shogun was defeated in battle, and his job abolished. The Emperor was moved up from Kyoto to the Shogun's palace in Edo, which was renamed Tokyo. This by no means bloodless revolution has since been referred to as the Meiji Restoration, on the grounds that it restored the Emperor to his rightful position. In fact Japan's new leaders had no intention of handing over power to an inexperienced autocrat. Instead, they decided to wield it themselves.

What was to be done about those awkward foreigners? 'Expelling the barbarians' had a nice sort of ring to it, but nobody had the slightest idea of how to transform words into deeds. It was quite obvious that traditional Japanese techniques of warfare did not stand a chance against the armed might of the West – in the civil war, both sides had relied heavily on foreign weapons and military advice. An 'expulsion' of the type that had proved so effective 250 years before was simply not a realistic option. The only way to prevent the foreigners doing to Japan what they had done to the rest of the Far East was to match their military strength. That could not be accomplished without matching their technology and industrial structure, which in turn required copying some of their forms of social organization and even modes of thought. Not many years after the restoration/revolution, the instigators of the 'expel the barbarian' movement, who had previously resorted to the assassination of foreign merchants and diplomats, were sending fact-finding delegations to Europe and inviting foreign experts to come and teach Japan how the whole enlightenment and progress trick was performed. The course they chose deviated little from the principles suggested in 1857 by Masayoshi Hotta, one of the leading figures behind the despised accommodationism of the Shogunate:

I am therefore convinced that our policy should be to stake everything on the present opportunity, to conclude friendly alliances, to send ships to foreign countries everywhere and conduct trade, to copy the foreigners where they are at their best, and so repair our shortcomings, to foster our national strength and complete our armaments, and so gradually subject the foreigners to our influence until in the end all the countries of the world know the blessings of perfect tranquillity and our hegemony is acknowledged throughout the globe.

Perfect tranquillity is still a long way off, but the course of events generally followed Hotta's plans. The Japanese went to Britain for their navy, France for their army, America for their universities, and – fateful decision – Germany for their constitution. Just thirty years later they had transformed their country into a highly industrialized modern nation with a navy powerful enough to dispatch the Russian fleet to the bottom of the sea and an education system that was probably, even then, the most efficient in the world. Forty years further on Japan was the world's fifth-largest military power and, having swept the Europeans out of South-East Asia, was engaged in a struggle to the death with the sender of the original black ships. On the outbreak of the Pacific War she had an army of two million men and a navy that was the equal of the United States' in number of ships. In aero-engineering and shipbuilding her technology was a match for any in the world.

Some of the great figures of Meiji, such as the educator Yukichi Fukuzawa, admired Western institutions for what they were. On the other hand, reactionaries such as Takamori Saigo distrusted them. The group of oligarchs who controlled the government recognized the power of the West, while wishing to preserve traditional Japanese virtues. Then, as in modern times, the authorities understood the value of slogans in encouraging unified patterns of thought. The catchphrase they chose to express the desired synthesis was *wakon yosai*: 'Japanese spirit and Western knowledge'. The result was a decontextualizing process which allowed the rapid assimilation of Western techniques bereft of the cultural background which had created them. Steel manufacture, railway engineering, the administrative system – these were developed at a pace which made Britain's Industrial Revolution look leisurely. Parliamentarianism, individualism, liberal humanism and the other various isms were kept at arm's length. Christianity, which had made such a worrying impact in the late sixteenth century, failed to make significant inroads despite the strenuous efforts of missionaries far more numerous and better equipped than Xavier's Jesuits had been.

There was one major exception to the rejection of Western isms – imperialism. Apart from a few ill-fated forays into Korea the Japanese had never shown much enthusiasm for overseas expansion. Until the Tokugawa Shogunate bolted the door, Japanese pirates had ruled the China Sea, even establishing small empires in Burma, but that had been strictly private enterprise. Japan's rulers had been busy enough trying to impose control over their own territories. From the Meiji era onwards the West's aptest pupil developed a strong fascination with what was the most basic expression of national strength – domination over others. It seemed easy enough at first. China was defeated, the Russian fleet sunk, Korea and Taiwan annexed. Military power had been the main aim of the modernizing process and, backed by a resurgence of xenophobic nationalism, it acquired an irresistible momentum that took Japan to the edge of destruction. The series of decisions which brought the country into total war with the Western powers represented, if nothing else, a staggering miscalculation of relative military and economic strengths. Japanese ignorance of foreign conditions was bolstered by the cult of homogeneity at its most extreme and narcissistic – in the words of the propaganda songs, 'one hundred million spirits moving as one'. However firm their democratic principles, the men who rule Japan today cannot entirely rid themselves of the attitudes inculcated during their formative years.

After the surrender, Japan was fabricated once more; clipped and clamped into a different shape. The occupation authorities equipped her with a new constitution, new political, educational, and social systems, and a new set of values and assumptions. The Japanese, recognizing a successful formula when they saw it, accepted the new dispensation with as little protest as they had accepted the old one. Instead of 'rich country, strong army' it was now 'rich country, someone else's army'. *Wakon yosai*, having being tried and found wanting, was discarded in favour of democracy, pacifism and business as usual. It worked like a dream. The samurai allowed themselves to be crammed into trains by the JNR pushers and sternly strap-hung their way to the office.

The four great turning points in Japanese history – the infusion of Chinese culture, the establishment of the Shogunate, the Meiji Restoration, the occupation reforms – were all intimately connected with Japan's response to the intrusion of foreign influence. At the risk of considerable simplification it may be said that Japan's history is the story of a dialogue between the Japanese and foreigners, in which the foreigners have usually played the role of initiator. Chinese traders came to Japan before Japanese envoys went to the Chinese court. The West forced its attentions on Japan in the sixteenth and nineteenth centuries. The occupation stimulated the final and most drastic reorientation. In each case the appliers of foreign influence could have had little idea of the consequences of their action, the series of dynamic transformations that their intervention would catalyse. In the last case, the effects have yet to be fully experienced.

Despite her trade surplus and bulging portfolio of overseas assets Japan still remains a nation apart, not least in the consciousness of her inhabitants. Just 10 per cent of those assets are the fruit of 'direct investment' in property, factories and companies, the great mass being 'indirect investments' in foreign bonds. To maintain them requires skilled analysis of financial conditions, but no involvement with or commitment to the country concerned. Japan has a huge economy, only a small, specially cultivated part of which interacts with the rest of the world. Western newspaper readers tend to identify her with trade friction above all else, but only 15 per cent of her GNP is exported, much less than Britain's 29 per cent or West Germany's 31 per cent. In addition the largest Japanese companies typically have around 5 per cent of their production overseas, which compares with 15–20 per cent for their European and American rivals.

As with the movement of goods, so with the movement of people. It may seem as if the world's capitals are being overrun by crowds of Japanese tourists, but that is an optical illusion caused by the Japanese penchant for group tours which 'do' all Europe in less than a week. In fact the number of Japanese who travel abroad each year is small compared to the usual pattern in the rich Western countries – only one Japanese in twenty-five, versus one Briton in three. Thanks to the astronomical cost of accommodation and entertainment, the number of foreigners who visit Japan is even smaller – equivalent to 2 per cent of the native population, which compares with 25 per cent in Britain and 60 per cent in France. For the great mass of Japanese, direct contact with foreigners is still an extremely rare experience.

By the standards of the other developed countries there is remarkably little ethnic diversity within Japan's resident population. Only 900,000 foreigners live in Japan, or just 0.75 per cent of the total population. Of these over 80 per cent are Koreans – men and women and their families who emigrated to Japan or were brought as forced labour during the forty years of annexation. A much smaller number of people of Korean birth have subsequently been naturalized. After Korea regained her independence in 1945 Korean residents of Japan were automatically deprived of their Japanese citizenship. As their own country was in a state of turmoil unresolved for a decade, many decided to stay in Japan as resident aliens. Thus the unhappy situation has arisen in which people born in Japan and who speak no language but Japanese are nominally the citizens of a neighbouring country and have to confirm their resident status every five years. The regular fingerprinting of alien residents and the legal requirement to carry ID cards at all times are just the most obvious examples of the unsympathetic attitude of the Japanese authorities towards this problem of their own devising. Overt discrimination in employment and marriage has been successfully challenged in court, but the kind that leaves no trace is still a fact of Japanese life. In a survey taken in 1986 by Mindan, the pro-Seoul Korean Residents' Union, 80 per cent of respondents answered 'yes' when asked whether the Japanese have a keen sense of superiority towards them.

It will take a revolution in the attitudes of the Japanese towards their own identity for the Korean minority to be fully accepted. None the less its presence has put little strain on Japan's much-prized social stability. There have been no inner-city race riots, no demands for affirmative action, no instances of anti-immigrant thuggery or racist abuse at sports matches. Policy-makers in many Western countries would gladly swap Japan's minority problems for those they have to confront. Firstly, the numbers are low and not increasing. Secondly, Korean residents in Japan are culturally, if not socially, fairly well integrated already – 75 per cent of them speaking Japanese in their homes. Blue-chip companies maintain discriminatory hiring practices, but there are many examples of successful Korean entrepreneurs in the restaurant, food manufacture and entertainment industries. Of Japan's trinity of baseball greats, one is of Korean and one of Taiwanese origin. In the 1986 general election, for the first time ever, a politician of Korean descent was elected to the Diet, a clear sign of a softening in attitudes.

There are other minority groups within the native population, the most significant being that of the *burakumin* outcastes, ethnically indistinguishable from ordinary Japanese, but still subject to continued discrimination. Although full legal rights were granted them on the Meiji Restoration, many have remained within the ghetto districts, engaging in the trades, such as leatherwork, to which Buddhist taboos had originally restricted them. Socially they are still off the map, their existence rarely mentioned by the authorities or the media or even in private conversation. Amongst the violently prejudiced the four-finger sign (=four legs=non-human) is used, much as the vocabulary of racial hatred is in the West. There are believed to be about two million members of the various *burakumin* communities, many of them concentrated in the Osaka region. The *Koseki* Family Register, which gives a complete history of every Japanese family, is no longer open to public inspection, but parties in arranged marriage negotiations and prospective employers can make suitable investigations through the use of lawyers or private detectives. Various unofficial copies of the register are in circulation amongst Japan's top companies. *Burakumin* origins, like illegitimacy and foreign blood, can be easily detected and acted on.

The geographical entity known as Japan has, after centuries of stability, undergone some rapid transformations in the modern period. Hokkaido and its population of Ainu were incorporated into Japan in the early nineteenth century. Okinawa, which had been under Japanese sway for centuries, was absorbed in 1860. In the first forty years of the twentieth century the Japanese created and lost an empire half the size of their own islands. Millions of emigrants began new lives in the colonies, then were forced back to Japan. After the surrender, Okinawa remained under American jurisdiction until 1972, when it reverted to Japanese ownership. The one million Okinawans are another sizeable minority, speaking a variant of Japanese and possessing a quite distinct cultural heritage. Although there has never been the suggestion of an independence movement, Okinawans have a deep suspicion of the Tokyo government, the result of bitter experience. In the closing stages of the Pacific War Japan's leaders decided to use Okinawa as a strategic bulwark for the protection of the 'home islands', and the savage battle fought there was the only one that took place on Japanese soil. Today even the most nationalistic of Japan's politicians attend closely to Okinawan sensitivities on such powerful symbolic issues as the use of the rising-sun flag at school ceremonies.

Despite the fact that some four to five million out of the 120 million people residing in the Japanese islands belong to distinct minority groups, the concept of ethnic homogeneity has taken deep root in the national psyche. The Japanese are not as homogeneous as they like to believe, but certainly more so than the peoples of most other sizeable nations. This awareness, deliberately fostered by business leaders and politicians, has contributed much to the social cohesion and sense of shared purpose which are among the country's greatest strengths. Unsurprisingly, the Japanese authorities are anxious to preserve the status quo. Between 1980 and 1985 only 37,000 people were naturalized as Japanese citizens, less than the number naturalized in the United States every month. The process they underwent is hardly designed to make things easy. All prospective immigrants must place their entire families on the Japanese Family Register, and dual nationality is not allowed. Since ethnic diversity is to be avoided at all costs, applicants are strongly encouraged to adopt a name from the approved list of Japanese surnames.

It is sometimes suggested that Japan will one day have to liberalize her stringent immigration and naturalization regulations. As her own people grow richer, economic efficiency will require the importation of cheap labour to perform the varous menial and unpleasant jobs. It is not a convincing thesis, since a surplus of workers, not a shortage, is likely to be the main problem facing Japan in the years ahead. The moral obligation argument cuts no ice at all. Although Japan is one of the largest dispensers of development aid, she has shown extreme reluctance to offer the most direct type of succour. Since 1975 the United States has accepted one million refugees and France 160,000. Meanwhile Japan, enjoying unparalleled prosperity and accelerating economic advantage, has taken just 5000. Looking at the strains afflicting Western countries with sizeable racial minorities, the Japanese see more risk than profit in altering their present exclusionist policy.

The Japanese sense of isolation has been reinforced by language as well as by history and geography. Of all the world's major languages, Japanese has the closest identification with a particular ethnic group. English, Spanish, Hindi, Russian and Portuguese are spread across continents and disparate peoples. Even Mandarin – which to teach to a foreign devil was once considered treason – is now diffused through China's minority races, as well as being first language for millions of overseas Chinese. In Japan's case linguistic identity relates closely to cultural and political identity. They are not the same, but they are more nearly the same than is the case elsewhere and, what is more important, they are believed to be the same.

When the Western powers arrived on the scene in the middle of the last century, negotiations had to be carried out through a cumbersome system of Japanese-to-Dutch-to-English double translation. Due to the success of the isolationist policy there were no Japanese who knew any other European languages, nor any Europeans who knew Japanese. Despite the massive change in Japan's importance to the world since then, foreign expertise in her language has remained comparatively weak. Even now the subject is taught in only four British universities, with a combined course membership of less than one hundred. America has taken Japanese more seriously, first from military and now from commercial necessity, and a huge learning programme is under way in China. None the less the overwhelming majority of foreign executives working in Japan have insufficient command of the language to command their business affairs, and some, even after years of residence, are still unable to manage any but the most basic conversation. Only a select few of the media folk who describe Japan to the rest of the world have any idea of what her inhabitants are actually reading, writing and saying – so often completely different from what is served up in translation.

In speaking foreign languages, Japanese ineptitude equals that of the British and Americans. It is not unusual to meet graduates of top-flight universities who, after years of study, cannot string two sentences of English together. Unless posted overseas, they will probably never have the need. The Japanese have developed an extremely efficient translation industry, which makes up in speed and volume for what it lacks in finesse. The Japanese rarely laugh at foreign film comedies, not because their sense of humour is radically different but because the writers of subtitles leave out most of the jokes.

The Japanese language, like the culture which has created it, is simultaneously receptive and restrictive of foreign influence. There is no equivalent of the French Academy attempting to defend linguistic purity. Tens of thousands of loan words have flowed freely into common usage, where they are often bent into unrecognizable new shapes and meanings. Thus, for example, *avec* means a courting couple; *haitaku* a hired taxi; and *baito*, from *arbeit*, a part-time job. Foreign languages, English especially, are high fashion – appropriate adornment for T-shirts and shopping bags. Companies and government agencies merrily turn out wince-inducing Janglish slogans – such as 'lonesome carboy', 'snowtopia', 'humanification', and the unforgettable 'My Life, My Gas'. Pretentious intellectuals season their opuses with a liberal sprinkling of imported words and phrases – 'paradigm shift', 'the moratorium generation', and the like. To similar effect the Southern All Stars, Japan's favourite rock band, bellows out its blues refrains in a strange mixture of Japanese-accented English and American-accented Japanese, satisfactorily incomprehensible to more or less everyone.

The restrictive mechanism is the written language. Loan words are set down not in characters, but in *katakana* – a special syllabic script otherwise used for emphasis. Until the modern era the Japanese, as the Chinese do today, employed existing characters either to translate the meaning of any foreign term they wished to adopt, or to approximate its sound. That method of procedure had the advantage of preserving the dominance of native forms, but was cumbersome and inhibited the ready assimilation of new ideas. Japan's modernization required something much more porous, and several progressive thinkers suggested scrapping the traditional writing system altogether in favour of Roman script. *Katakana* is a less radical solution. It allows foreign words to pass straight into the language, new sounds bearing new information. At the same time they are kept for ever separate from the linguistic DNA in which centuries of tradition are encoded.

Characters hold their meaning. Together, they make up a complex, highly stable system of cross-signification. *Katakana* is a necessary tool for handling the various noises that slip in and out of the lexis. Modern Japan is largely a *katakana* construct. People wear *katakana* clothes (*nekutai, koto, shatsu*); fill their houses with *katakana* objects (*rajio, beddo, katen*); perform *katakana* tasks (*copi, taipu*) in *katakana*-filled offices, and pass their spare time with *katakana* hobbies (*gorufu, haikingu*). Emotions, relationships, the natural world, other Japanese people – all these exist in the deeper, character-based reality.

Although the Japanese are extremely well informed about the latest Western developments in business and technology, the countries that produce them are but hazily defined, ill-differentiated components of a single giant entity. It was symptomatic that when the Austrian 'tainted wine' scandal broke, many worried imbibers directed their inquiries to the Australian Embassy. The Japanese describe all other countries as *muko* – a somewhat vague term, meaning 'over there'. The people who come from *muko* are *gaijin* – literally, outside people. In normal usage *gaijin* refers to Caucasians, the descendants of the people who came first in the galleons and then returned in the steamships. Chinese, Koreans, Filipinos – these are not proper *gaijin*, not sufficiently different.

From the first contact the Japanese were fascinated by the 'southern barbarians', as is revealed by the contemporary paintings of huge sausage-nosed sailors in balloon-like trousers. In the early nineteenth century Japanese scholars were seriously debating whether the Dutch, who were available for inspection in Nagasaki, raised one leg in the air in order to urinate. Foreigners in Japan today are not taxed on that point, but they may find themselves the subject of some fairly unusual queries. Outside Tokyo *gaijin* still have enough novelty value to earn themselves blank stares of astonishment, free saké and noodles, requests for autographs, fervent declarations of international friendship, detailed interrogation about their sex lives, absolute rebuffs from the owners of half-empty inns and, most disconcerting of all, sudden fits of giggles from shop-girls. Children who watch foreigners on television every day seem amazed to be confronted by the real thing, and bellow out their single, completely useless sentence of English – 'This is a pen.' Their parents have different conversational gambits – 'Can you use chopsticks?' and 'Which Japanese foods can't you eat?' are particular favourites. The subtext of the statement is the same: 'I am a Japanese, you are a foreigner, and that distinction is of over-whelming importance.'

Public-opinion surveys show that the overwhelming major-ity of Japanese have no desire to mix with foreigners at all. None the less the response that the traveller in Japan meets most often from ordinary people is a powerful mixture of generosity, curiosity and shock. Perhaps every Japanese secretly wants to sample the national experience of those early historical contacts. Certainly the physical presence of a white foreigner can evoke a reaction that is difficult to explain in rational terms. The disembodied image does almost as much. Advertising agencies, who probably read the national tempera-ment better than any pundits, make heavy use of Western models and actors in television commercials. Foreigners appear in about one-third of all commercials shown during the evening 'golden hour'. Showroom dummies are given obvi-ously Western features – sharp noses, narrow jaw lines, thin lips. The cartoon books devoured by adolescent females of all ages depict a strange intermediate world, where lissom blonde heroines fall in and out of languid love with sharp-profiled, Porsche-driving men – all characters speaking perfect colloquial Japanese.

The complex, ambivalent attitude to foreign influence, both threatener and confirmer of the Japanese sense of identity, can be found in most areas of life and culture. Sport is an interesting example because it presents a magnification of everyday conflicts, and because the Japanese take it in such deadly earnest. Even eight-year-old boys playing catchball in a park will be kitted out with the most expensive and correct equipment. Anything less would risk serious loss of face.

Traditional Japanese sports have little connection with relaxation or fun. They derive from personal combat, and are pursued in order to 'forge' the body and spirit, a philosophy which usually carries over into modern sporting contests. In international competition tricky issues of national prestige are involved – the Tokyo Olympics having symbolized Japan's return to international respectability. When members of the female volleyball team burst into tears after an important defeat, they are not being bad losers, but giving expression to a profound sense of shame. As in the communist countries the government always takes an active interest in the performance of the national teams. When South Korea won more medals than Japan at the Asian Games, top officials of the Ministry of Education expressed public dismay and held urgent meetings to propose remedies. 'It's only a game' is not a sentiment which has much appeal.

The Japanese are genuinely proud of the transformation of judo into a world sport, although chagrined by any losses suffered in international tournaments. Karate and kendo have also, thanks to vigorous promotion, achieved widespread popularity abroad. In sumo wrestling, which originated with the fertility rites performed before the imperial court back in the mists of time, matters are not quite so simple. The powers-that-be were extremely disconcerted by the arrival of Konishiki, a thirty-three-stone Hawaiian wrestler who measures six foot around the waist. After he had bowled over a succession of champions and grand champions in one of his early tournaments, there were even dark mutterings about banning foreigners from the sport altogether. However, his strict regard for the formal dignities of sumo, coupled with his exciting style, succeeded in winning over the general public and he soon became one of the most popular wrestlers, making a great contribution to the revival of interest in the sport.

In baseball, which the Japanese treat like a kind of martial art, sensibilities are equally tender. For many years foreign journalists were not permitted entry to the high-school baseball tournament, a ritual glorification of youth and innocent strength which excites something close to national hysteria every August. Japan is the only country in the world to have developed a real enthusiasm for baseball outside the context of American cultural and political domination: the sport was already Japan's most popular before the Pacific War. During the war the enemy's language was expunged – Sino-Japanese locutions being found for batter, pitcher, two-base hit, et cetera – but there was no attempt to stifle the sport's popularity. One of the cinematic successes of 1984, *The Inland Sea Baseball Club*, gives a light-hearted version of what baseball has meant to the Japanese. It depicts the adventures of a group of village children in the wake of the surrender. The father of one is hauled away for execution as a war criminal, but her pals exact a kind of symbolic revenge by improbably outplaying a team of G Is in a baseball game.

Japan's professional baseball is modelled closely on the U S system. Although there are no vast distances to traverse, two separate leagues of equal standing are maintained, the component teams having names like the Buffaloes and the Braves and the Tigers. Over five hundred foreigners have played in the Japanese game, most of them has-beens or never-wases from the U S leagues. Their position is tricky, since they have to perform well enough to keep their teams afloat, but must be careful not to eclipse the local heroes. When one import came dangerously close to beating the home run record of Sadaharu Oh, a godlike figure in Japanese baseball, he found himself being repeatedly 'four-balled' by Japanese pitchers. In the last game of the season, against a team managed by the selfsame Oh, the frustrated *gaijin* was not allowed to face a single pitch in any of his four times at bat.

Japanese professional wrestling was started in the fifties by an ex-sumo wrestler who, according to legend, was drummed out of the sport because of his Korean origins. In Japan enthusiasm for *pro resu* is not confined to the terminally gormless, but is well distributed amongst all walks of life, including the higher echelons of business and the professions. The most popular fights are those pantomimes of barbarian expulsion which match a plucky Japanese against a huge and terrifying foreigner, such as André the Giant or Abdullah the Butcher. There are usually three phases to a bout. Firstly, a display of brute power and ill intent by the foreigner, in which the Japanese is hurled about in unmerciful style. Then an interlude outside the ring during which the two contestants belabour each other with steel chairs. Finally, back inside the ring for the dispatch of the foreigner and the triumph of right over might. It is a simple and satisfying process, close in spirit to the devil-chasing ceremonies which Japanese households still perform in the first week of February.

Japan's favourite exponent of the art is Antonio Inoki, the largest and most formidable of her three world heavyweight champions. For over a decade Inoki has been a hero to schoolboys, his large shoe-shaped face prominent on television commercials and advertising hoardings. In 1976 he even achieved a measure of international fame by going the distance with Mohammed Ali. Being a sensible fellow, he spent the entire fight crawling around the ring floor like a crab. However, not all foreigners can be trusted to play the game properly. Tempers flared in a battle with a brutishly powerful American called Hulk Hogan and, suddenly, Inoki was flung clean out of the ring. As the stretcher-bearers lowered his unconscious form into the ambulance, the arm of the shame-faced Hogan was raised in victory. Fortunately Inoki, who had landed on his head, was not seriously injured and soon resumed his career as world champion. Hogan, on the other hand, lost his name entirely.

How to prove yourself in the Big Leagues? How to let massively built foreigners into your own games without letting them spoil the fun? How to go international and stay Japanese at the same time? The same questions arise in the management of political and economic affairs, and have yet to be satisfactorily resolved.

The Japanese have a greater collective knowledge of their own doings and opinions than any other people in the world. Information is gathered, processed and disseminated with the sort of enjoyment that once would have been reserved for village gossip. There can be few Japanese who do not know which nation is most disliked by the Japanese (Russia, followed by Korea), and what is the most common cause of death amongst the Japanese (cancer, followed by heart disease). Every day government agencies and the mass media churn out reams of data about all aspects of Japanese life, explaining to the Japanese people what they believe, eat, earn and desire. One of the publishing successes of recent years was a book called *The Average*, which is nothing more than a compendium of official and private surveys, designed to help readers ascertain by how much they deviate from the norm. It contains such useful insights as that the average Japanese salaryman owns fourteen ties, cuts his toenails once a week, and leaves his office at 6.49 p.m. To most people 500 pages of that kind of information might seem stupefyingly dull. The Japanese find in it vital signals for living.

In addition to the raw data, various interpretations of it are avidly consumed. Bookstores have large sections devoted to *Nihonjin-ron* (Japan theory), a category of book which has an undying popularity. Authors catalogue, usually in pseudo-scientific terms, the special attributes of the Japanese, both positive and negative, which distinguish them from every other people on earth. To be marketable the work must start from the premise that the Japanese are unique in character and incomprehensible to foreigners. At a pinch, comparisons can be made with other highly distinctive and successful ethnic groups, such as the Jews. Most educated Japanese seem to have read several examples of the *Nihonjin-ron* genre, and are able to reproduce the main arguments with ease. The contributions of foreign writers are particularly valued since they invariably focus on the great difference, of as much fascination to the Japanese as that other difference celebrated by the French. In private conversations with foreigners, Japanese people return incessantly to the subject of Japaneseness, the difference between Japanese ways of thinking and living and those prevalent in the West. Indeed it is extremely difficult to have a conversation with a new Japanese acquaintance that does not cling obsessively to the topic. The formulaic phrase 'We Japanese think/like/dislike . . .' is announced with uncanny confidence, as if some form of telepathy is being employed. Foreign observers should be forgiven their predilection for generalizing about the Japanese, since the Japanese are so insistent on doing the same themselves.

The Japanese do not just consider themselves to be culturally distinct. It is almost an article of faith that they are physically distinct as well, that the Japanese body is the particular property of the Japanese people and no one else. Many of the older generation apparently believe that their intestines are longer than those of Westerners, and therefore unsuitable for the ingestion of meat. This argument was used in all seriousness by an ex-minister of agriculture to justify trade barriers against imported beef! Intelligent Japanese often maintain that they and their countrymen think with a different side of their brain from the rest of the world. According to the popular theory this accounts for the divergent responses to insect chirpings – the Japanese find the sound aesthetically pleasing, while Westerners associate it with creepy-crawliness and itches in embarrassing places. A celebrated Japanese scientist has devoted himself to proving this proposition through a complicated series of practical experiments. Again, it is the West–Japan contrast that is being invoked, the one which has supplied the motive force to the nation's entire modern history. An amusing example of the unassailable assumpton in action is provided by the following excerpt from an article on lingerie in the *Japan Times*, a newspaper read mainly by foreign residents:

Wacoal, Japan's leading lingerie maker, recently held a seminar on the changes in women's hips according to age . . . Kanji Kasei, doctor of obstetrics and gynaecology, said that Japanese women's hips are flatter than foreign women's and that this kind of hip is good for easy birth.

Thus there are two sorts of hips in the world – Japanese hips, nicely designed for childbirth, and foreign hips, Laotian, Eskimo, Zulu, et cetera, which are not. In fact the Japanese claim to physical distinctiveness rests on shaky grounds. There

39

are certain characteristics which are typically Japanese, just as there are characteristics that are typically Scandinavian, but there are none that are exclusive to the set of Japanese. Most of the signals that enable the Japanese to identify each other are culture-derived. For example it is frequently commented that the Japanese war orphans brought up in China 'do not look Japanese'. Dressed in Chinese clothes, speaking the Chinese language and using facial expressions learned from Chinese foster parents, they transmit none of the usual identifying signals. Conversely, the Japanese are unable to distinguish members of the Korean minority group resident in Japan.

Less controversial is the fact that the Japanese body is changing shape at a remarkable rate. The average height of a male university student is now six inches above what it was before the war, and it is not uncommon for a boy of fifteen to tower a full head above his parents. Furthermore the increase is not proportional, coming mainly in the legs. The factors responsible are Western nutritional patterns and the Western lifestyle, with its tables and chairs. Many young Japanese cannot sit for long in the legs-folded *seiza* position without suffering circulatory cut-offs. Expensive Japanese restaurants often provide wells under the tables so that diners can squat on the floor in traditional fashion while dangling their legs in comfort. The idea was originally devised to suit ungainly foreigners, but now provides a fine example of the Japanese talent for living two lifestyles simultaneously.

Height is only the most obvious example of physical change. The shape of the jawline and set of the mouth have been softened by improvements in dentistry. Bulging calf muscles ('radish legs'), the heritage of hard work in the paddies, are becoming less common. Breasts are swelling and waists narrowing – much to the detriment of the natural line of a kimono. The rapid influx to the cities has made skin tone much paler, and the boom in American-style fast food has created the first generation of obese children. The Japanese also make frequent recourse to artificial appearance-changing techniques. Tough guys boast 'punch perms', which turn their naturally straight hair into a close frizz. Delinquent high-school students of both sexes dye their hair brown. There was even once a craze for beach-use chest wigs. At almost every suburban station, placards can be found advertising quick plastic surgery – Western eyes and noses going cheap. The standard-issue Japanese eyelid (a single downward flap) is considered unattractive. Girls who cannot afford the permanent remedy can purchase small tabs of flesh-coloured adhesive paper which will do the job almost as well. Japanese ladies also use more orthodox methods of enhancing their attractions, being probably the most highly-skilled users of cosmetics in the world. It is the art that conceals art, noticeable only when it isn't there.

A samurai from pre-Meiji times transported to modern Japan would probably conclude that the country had been completely taken over by the *gaijin*. Even modern Japanese sometimes waver in their sense of physical identity. In 1983 a Japanese marriage fraudster was arrested for passing himself off as the nephew of the Queen of England. After applying a suitably blond tint to his hair, eyebrows and eyelashes, and investing in a little facial restructuring, Kazuo Suzuki managed to convince a succession of rich spinsters that he was in fact a foreigner. That he spoke no language other than Japanese mattered not at all, for the good ladies were lost in the cartoon-book world where image and language are patterned according to one's desires.

Given the historical vortex that Japan has passed through – the dizzying series of economic, cultural, and even physical transformations – some degree of disorientation is hardly surprising. Nor is the fact that the Japanese often seem uncertain how to evaluate what they have become. The national mood can veer from hubristic elation to dark moods of despair in which all institutions and traditions are decried as unworthy. In recent years the former tendency has been the more noticeable, as the Japanese congratulate themselves on their rise to fortune and power. Even the nominally anti-government sections of the press are constantly reminding their readers of Japanese superiority in various fields of endeavour, from semiconductor chip manufacture to human longevity. The *Japan Quarterly*, an English-language publication run by the left-leaning *Asahi Shimbun*, gave the following opinion:

The nation's confidence in its economic strength sagged during the years following the oil shock in the autumn of 1973, but since the end of the 1970s, with Japan's victory over the United States in the highly competitive field of high technology, the Japanese people came to realise their superiority.

Ezra Vogel's book *Japan as Number One* became an instant best-seller in Japanese translation. No doubt many readers fervently wanted to believe that Japan had finally ascended to the top of the international merit table. Yet beneath all the confident assertions of superiority and cataloguing of achievements there lurks a deep-seated feeling of inadequacy. According to a survey taken by NHK, the national broadcasting organization, 80 per cent of the Japanese do not believe that they are living in a 'first-class country', whatever that means. In the 1985 Gallup survey on international values 30 per cent of the Japanese sampled described themselves as 'not very proud' or 'not proud at all' of their nationality, against 11 per cent of the Britons and 3 per cent of the Americans. In the mid seventies the depths of masochism were plumbed by another best-selling book, written by a former diplomat, which claimed that the Japanese were physically the ugliest people in the world. There is also the ever-present suspicion that, despite all Japan's financial and economic power, foreign countries are still not taking her seriously. The *Yomiuri* newspaper can end a perfectly sensible leader on the international debt crisis with the following curious sentence: 'It is important for Japan to consult closely with other countries involved in order to avoid being the only country to be made a fool of in the long run.'

Being laughed at, being made a fool of – these are among the direst consequences with which a Japanese mother can threaten an errant child. Japan is still insecure about her place in the world, haunted by fears of isolation and betrayal. The

Japanese right blames the occupation-imposed education system for failing to cultivate a proper sense of national worth. More likely it is a natural result of the modernization process that the Japanese have chosen. Repeated comparisons with the West, constant soul-searching, constant self-improvement – these are the methods that Japan has used to spur herself to greater efforts. If the Japanese had a stronger sense of self-worth, they could not have achieved anything like as much.

By most standards Japan has now caught up with the West. The great 120-year forced march has been completed. In her economic management and business acumen she has become the object of admiring imitation. Influential commentators, both at home and abroad, have been discussing the need for a 'Japanese Marshall Plan' through which Japanese money can be efficiently channelled into the developing countries. Yet the main challenge that Japan must face over the years ahead is not financial or technological, but cultural. If the Japanese are to fulfil the role which their industrial success is forcing on them they must be prepared to redefine their relationship with the outside world.

3

Manufacturing Miracles

In Nagasaki, I was pleased to see that business was at a low
ebb. The Japanese should stay away from business.

Rudyard Kipling

The Japanese do not consider work a form of economic
activity. Rather, believing that there can be no work
which is not a form of religious devotion, they approach
everything as a discipline akin to the practice of Zen.

Shichihei Yamamoto, economic commentator

In 1973 Eiichi Hiki returned to his native land after forty
years spent in a remote Brazilian village. It was his first sight
of Japan since emigrating at the age of twenty-five.

'Banzai,' he cried on disembarking at Haneda airport. 'We
couldn't have lost the war. The Emperor is alive and the
country is prosperous.'

They reasoned with him, but in vain. They showed him a
US army base.

'The Americans must be here to work,' responded Hiki.
'That's why all the roads are in such good condition.'

Hiki belonged to the *kachi-gumi* (victory group) of Japanese
settlers, adamant ultra-nationalists who dismissed all reports
of Japan's defeat as enemy propaganda. On his return to
Japan, despite the protestations of relatives, Hiki continued to
believe what he liked, now apparently confirmed by the
evidence of his own eyes. Indeed, the vision of industrial
might which confronted him on stepping off the plane must
have been such as to make Japan's war aims seem very
modest. So much for securing markets and raw-material
sources in North-East Asia. Today Japan takes her resources

from Australasia, North and South America, the Middle East, Russia and South-East Asia. In output per head of population she now far exceeds her industrial competitors, being bested only by Switzerland. Her surplus of exports over imports has grown so huge that it threatens the stability of the global trading system. With the funds it generates she finances one-third of America's huge budget deficit. Of the world's top fifty banks, four are British, five American, seven German, and twenty, including the seven largest, Japanese.

As a nation Japan is massively rich. The living standards of her people have risen too. When Hiki left Japan the average worker earned less than in any other industrialized country. Today Japanese wage rates have risen close to American levels, and houses are crammed with high-tech consumer gadgets. It is not unusual to see pre-teens toting the latest video kit, young office-girls swathed in designer fashions that would have cost a pre-war farming village a month's output. Japanese lay waste whole counters at Harrods, bid away one-third of the impressionist masterpieces up for auction, sign up the New York and Los Angeles cityscapes. In the bay next to Pearl Harbor, a Japanese construction company is building a resort twice the size of Waikiki, a luxury playground where future generations will clink their drinks and wonder what the fuss was about.

So much in so little time. If the Japanese had not done it, nobody would have believed it possible. Their example has turned conventional wisdom on its head. It has shown developing nations that industrial success can be accomplished without massive injections of foreign capital, without state control, without social turmoil. It has defeated the centuries-old assumption, embedded deep in the psychologies of both communist and capitalist countries, that modernization equals Westernization.

Outside Japan ordinary people have grown used to the fact of Japanese economic power. They see the evidence in high-street windows, on hoardings at football grounds, even emblazoned on the players' shirts. They know that products like the compact disc player, the video tape recorder and the auto-focus camera are more or less monopolized by Japanese companies. The days when mothers deterred their children from buying cheap Japanese toys and when squat, tinny Datsuns could be mistaken for Ladas seem to belong to another era. That was only twenty years ago, but now Japanese economic success seems quite natural, inevitable even. Our appreciation of the remarkable quality of the transformation has, unlike Hiki's, been dulled by the gradualism of history.

At the end of the Second World War Japan had been defeated as few countries have ever been defeated. After fourteen years of conflict she had suffered three and a half million casualties, the destruction of 25 per cent of her physical capital stock and 25 per cent of all dwellings. Most major cities were bombed flat, two had been demolished by atom bombs, and ten million people had fled to the countryside. The raw material supply bases of Manchuria, Korea and Taiwan – in all, 45 per cent of the land area of the pre-war empire – had passed from her hands for ever. Towards the end of the war all non-strategic industries had been run down, reducing the civilian economy to a subsistence level. Into this shambles flowed six million repatriated soldiers and civilians.

Just as important as the physical damage was the spiritual shock. A proud nation unconquered for thousands of years had not only been defeated in war but was now to be governed by foreign soldiers while her own leaders were arraigned as criminals. Japan's long drive to be treated as an equal by the Western nations had ended in ignominy. Worst of all, the sacred belief that *Yamato damashi*, the Japanese spirit, was destined to triumph over any material disadvantage had been empirically disproven. This was equivalent to the Children of Israel being told that they had been deselected.

Japan had avoided partition, and was fortunate in being occupied by a power that soon became convinced of the need to build up her economic strength. Reparations were minimal, and food aid alleviated the most urgent problem of all. Until the start of the Korean War, US government programmes paid for over half of all Japanese imports. The occupation authorities instituted a series of radical reforms aimed not just at preventing a resurgence of militarism but also at creating a modern, dynamic economy. The land reforms of 1946 effectively abolished absentee landlordism, and the monetarist Dodge Line cut into rampant inflation.

Inevitably, recovery was slow. Manufacturing output did not return to mid thirties levels until 1951, and incomes took longer. However, Japan had several latent advantages which were soon to stand her in good stead. She had an ample supply of youthful, well-educated labour, an accumulation of technology developed for military purposes, and a domestic market that was potentially the second largest in the world. Furthermore she knew what she was about, having accomplished an astoundingly rapid industrialization just seventy years previously. And, just as then, for a short and crucial period she had a completely malleable socio-economic structure in which anonymous men of talent could start from the same level as everyone else.

The Korean War, more particularly the special procurements it required, supplied the catalyst for full-scale economic growth. In 1951–3 Japan supplied billions of dollars of production to the UN forces, equivalent to about half her exports for the period. After the war ended she continued to supply materials for the reconstruction of South Korea. As output rose, money was ploughed back into capital formation, setting off a virtuous growth circle that survived more or less intact for twenty years. From 1951 to 1955 GNP grew at an average of 8.6 per cent; from 1956 to 1960 at 9.1 per cent; from 1960 to 1965 at 9.7 per cent; and from 1965 to 1970 at 13.1 per cent. In every case the rate of growth was well above the target set by the government in its five-year plans. It was a well-balanced performance, with private-sector capital formation supplying most of the growth momentum, at first through the textile industry – Japan's pre-war success story – then through the development of heavier and more technologically advanced sectors.

By 1973 the Japanese economic revival was already a fact

of life, a 'miracle' to rank with the West German version. Prime Minister Ikeda's plan to double the national income by the end of the sixties had been achieved by 1967. Consumer goods such as televisions, washing machines and refrigerators were close to maximum levels of ownership. Japanese heavy industries – particularly shipbuilding and steel – were the most competitive in the world, her automobile exports were increasing dramatically, and her TVs, watches and stereos were gobbling market share at a frantic pace. None the less, serious underlying problems remained to be solved.

Most important of all, on the eve of the oil shock Japan was dangerously dependent on foreign imports, particularly energy – and particularly oil from the Middle East. Cheap energy was the foundation on which her rapid industrial expansion had been built. Meanwhile, although the drive for growth had fulfilled immediate material aspirations, much had been sacrificed and much remained to be done. Pollution levels were notoriously high, and children went to school wearing face-masks for protection against the ubiquitous photo-chemical smog. Social security benefits were negligible, health insurance non-existent. Inevitably the conviction grew, both amongst ordinary people and amongst business and government leaders, that growth at all costs was no longer a sensible objective. In addition, the Japanese corporate structure hardly seemed fitted for the turmoil ahead. The lifetime employment system adopted by most large enterprises made it extremely difficult to lay off workers in periods of slack demand. Furthermore companies had only slim internal financial resources, having piled up levels of debt that Western businessmen would have considered intolerable.

At the opening of the eighties, after a decade which had seen the price of Japan's key energy import rise 1200 per cent, she emerged with lower inflation, lower unemployment, lower interest rates and higher growth than any other developed country. From having the largest current account deficit amongst the major economies, she was on her way to chalking up 'structural' surpluses that would set off long and acrimonious trade disputes. Although her heavy industry, like heavy industry the world over, was mired in recession, she had developed overwhelming competitive strength in a range of vital new electronic products that were creating massive markets both domestically and overseas. Furthermore she had succeeded in building up a welfare system that provided pension and medical insurance benefits of a reasonable quality. Pollution, while not vanquished, had been substantially reduced by strict emission controls. Japan was no longer an extraordinarily apt pupil, but quite simply the most successful economy in the world. Her industrial policies and business methods, most of which had originally been adapted from Western models, were suddenly the topic of intense foreign interest. If imitation is the sincerest form of flattery, then she received the ultimate accolade when developing countries such as Singapore and Malaysia began their 'look East' campaigns.

This post-oil shock transformation was a greater miracle than the heady growth of the previous decade. After all, in the sixties circumstances had looked kindly upon Japan. The world economy was enjoying one of its longest periods of stable growth. Overseas markets were open to Japan's exports, but lagging perceptions of Japanese economic strength, coupled with skilful prevarication by the relevant ministries, enabled her to maintain quotas on imports while encouraging key exports through price cartels and credit incentives. Additionally, the yen rate was fixed at 360 to the dollar, which may have been an appropriate measure of relative strength in 1949, but took no account of the wide divergence in inflation rates and productivity growth that had taken place since. Consequently Japanese companies, after developing their home market, were able to undercut their rivals overseas more or less as they chose. And at this stage, superior price competitiveness was pretty well all the Japanese had to offer.

After 1972 these fortunate circumstances were reversed. World trade took a battering and the system of fixed exchange rates collapsed. Japan was asked to impose 'voluntary' restraints on a range of exports, starting with synthetic textiles and TVs and finally extending to passenger cars, the most important category of all. Simultaneously she was forced to dismantle her most obvious protectionist barriers. The series of unconsulted decisions that the Japanese call the Nixon *shokku* served notice that the United States would favour economic self-interest over the previous paternal relationship between the two countries. Suddenly Japan was on her own.

The odds were re-stacked, but there was no change in Japan's outperformance. Admittedly the response of her industrial competitors to that turbulent period of economic and technological change was woefully inadequate. None the less the Japanese must have been doing something remarkably right, as most observers of her progress have recognized. Conspiracies hammered out in the bowels of the Ministry of International Trade and Industry (MITI), Zen Buddhist management techniques, *The Book of Five Rings* – whatever the secret ingredient may be, it seems to work wonders. The truth is less exotic, but provides more food for thought. Japan has succeeded because she is structured for success. The main components of the structure are described elsewhere in this book. Here, it is sufficient to note the main principles.

The maximization of economic advantage is an objective agreed at nearly all levels of Japanese society, from the great industrial groups down to the corner shop that stays open all hours. The shapers of policy – the bureaucrats, politicians and business leaders – have suggested strategies and dreamed up slogans, but they have never been troubled by disputes about fundamental priorities. The role of government, now performed with practised ease, has been to set the conditions for growth, not to interfere with the mechanism. Foreign commentators are apt to take its various noises of encouragement and warning as control. In fact, economic activity usually creates its own imperatives, a process that the authorities have been wise enough to leave alone.

The framework that has been established can be characterized as low tax, low interest rate, high saving, high capital formation. In other words, industry first. Direct intervention is kept to a minimum. No major companies are nationalized, and of the utilities only water remains in public ownership.

When government does hold the reins, the results belie all the claims made for Japanese business skills. Just before its break-up and privatization by the Nakasone administration, the Japan National Railways sported long-term debts of Y23,000,000,000,000, more than the debts of Mexico and Argentina put together. The level of overmanning was spectacular, and 80,000 of the 300,000 workers were designated 'excess to requirements' – more than the entire work-force of Hitachi. The trains, however, did run on time.

Japanese salarymen do not take kindly to the proposition that they are lightly taxed, and indeed have demonstrated unwonted electoral cussedness when the spectre of higher taxes has been raised. None the less, on an international comparison they are doing quite nicely. The average rate of income tax is 16 per cent, commodity taxes are low and capital gains tax nonexistent. Government has yet to develop into a major business in its own right. Only 24 per cent of the national income is swallowed up by the tax office, less than the 28 per cent of the United States and well below the 40–50 per cent standard in Europe.

Investment by industry regularly accounts for double the percentage of GNP usual in Western countries, government expenditure for half. Given that sort of weighting of resources, it is hardly surprising that Japan's growth in productivity has outstripped the other developed economies by so much. In the auto industry, for example, the value of capital equipment per worker is more than double that in the United States, in the steel industry roughly treble.

What distinguishes the Japanese system from the consumption-driven American model is the high savings ratio, without which the gung-ho investment policy of the corporate sector would result in inflation and soaring interest rates. Japanese households save about 16 per cent of their income, which compares with 5 per cent in the United States and 9 per cent in Britain. Since that income now is generated by the world's second-largest economy and denominated in the world's strongest currency, the effect is considerable – enough to finance not just Japanese roads and schools, but also factories in Britain, presidential palaces in South America, and missile systems in the United States. When the diligent Japanese salaryman hands his pay packet over to his wife, he is setting off a chain of events beyond all his imagining.

Why do the Japanese save so much? Partly, because they must. About half of all household savings are 'contracted' in the form of life insurance and mortgage payments, and large-expenditure items like weddings, school fees and down payments on houses have to be provided for well in advance. The other reason is cultural. The Confucianist ideology which permeates Japanese thinking accords the same exalted status to thriftiness as did the religion of Knox and Calvin. Borrowing is shameful, a sign of desperation, while saving is prudent, patriotic and, nowadays, fashionable. Japanese in their early twenties have the same interest in the workings of the financial markets as the British do in house improvements and internal combustion engines. Housewives are ever eager to increase the yield on the family portfolio, and study the dozens of glossy magazines that offer financial advice. They start young, as well. According to a survey by Sanwa Bank, one twelve-year-old boy in five is stacking away his pocket money, with the standard nest-egg over Y20,000 in size. Two-thirds of the junior savers had in mind a specific purchase, such as a bike or a personal computer. The remainder were doing it because they enjoyed the feeling.

A stable, investment-conducive financial structure has provided the Japanese with the ideal context to indulge their favourite occupation – planning long term. Japanese companies operate on a different time-scale from their Western competitors. They are marathon men against milers, in a race where the finishing-tape is never in sight. In recruitment, investment and marketing they make their decisions, not according to the short-term effect on profitability, but for the long-term health of the corporate organism. Due to the peculiarities of the Japanese financial system they can pay the same dividend year after year without paying much attention to the speculative convulsions of the Tokyo stock market. Whatever the performance of their share price, they will be shielded from takeovers by the stable shareholder system, which keeps suitable portions of their equity away from unfriendly hands. The people whose opinions do matter are the large financial institutions whose perspectives are similarly long term and who are eager to do business in insurance, pension schemes and loans. The line of priorities is first of all customers, then main banks, then employees, then shareholders – almost the reverse of modern business psychology in the West.

In consequence Japanese companies have been able to invest aggressively even in periods of slack demand. When the semiconductor slump finally hit Japan in 1985, Fujitsu, NEC and the rest were forced to cut capacity, just like American firms. Simultaneously, however, they stepped up their R&D commitment, preparing the way for the next generation of devices. The great electronic companies are now pouring money into development projects that will not yield fruit until well into the next decade. In human investment the policy is the same. The Japanese prefer to train their people on the job, even if years of patient understudy are necessary, rather than buy in ready-made expertise. Retraining and skill enhancement are taken seriously, co-ordinated by large, well-equipped personnel departments.

In the development and marketing of products, Japanese companies are able to take a long-term strategic attitude. Western businesses concentrate on the immediate maximization of profit, to be achieved by charging whatever prices the market can bear. That is what brings soaring stock prices and big bonuses. The Japanese are equally concerned with profitability, but construe it over the long haul. The overriding priority is market share, which is best secured by undercutting rival producers. Indeed, Japanese companies are so obsessed by their position in the market that they often seem unconcerned whether they are making any money at all. As a result conventional performance measures, such as sales margin and return on capital, are miserable for even the best-quality Japanese firms. However, market dominance eventually brings its rewards in terms of customer acceptance, economies of scale and the gradual, inexorable squeezing of competitors.

Ex-employees of foreign motorbike, camera and audio firms can testify to that.

Companies take the long-term view because that is the view of the people who work in them. The identification of employees with the aims of the enterprise is one of the Japanese economy's most valuable assets. Lifetime employment and payment-by-seniority, the most famous characteristics of the Japanese system, cover only a tiny proportion of the work-force: males between twenty-two and fifty in large, 'name' companies. However, their influence spreads through most of the economy, symbols of the co-operative ideal aspired to by workers and managements everywhere. As a result money does not flow out of the firm in unearned wage increases – meaning those unmatched by productivity increases – any more than through dividend payments. Workers are prepared to accept the introduction of labour-saving technology without worrying about job security. That Toyota has not experienced a strike since 1953 does not just give it a tremendous advantage over foreign auto makers. It means that it is a completely different type of entity.

The quality of a work-force is best measured by results, and Japan's speak for themselves. Japanese workers are well educated, highly receptive to new ideas and technologies. They are diligent and industrious, putting in 10–15 per cent more hours per year than Europeans and Americans. However, the most complex and critical factor in Japan's success is the set of attitudes that the Japanese bring to the economic process. The ability to agree is the basic Japanese talent, honed by centuries of communal living in rice-farming villages. Almost as strong is the legacy of the samurai: the taste for quarrelling ferociously in groups. Together they make a blend formidably well suited to modern capitalism.

That the Japanese are expert at functioning within the ambit of shared values should be obvious to anyone who has experienced the morning rush hour or viewed a group of tourists in action. It is more difficult than it looks, requiring scrupulous attention to the behaviour of others and constant adjustments to one's own. At the political level it has led to one party holding a monopoly of power throughout the long climb to prosperity. At the level of individual consciousness it has led to the condition in which 90 per cent of the population considers itself to be middle class. In economic terms that belief is hard to justify. Although income differentials are low, wealth differentials, caused by rocketing land prices, have expanded rapidly. However, the strength of the consensus model is not attributable to purely financial factors. It is a habit of thought shared by households, bureaucrats, managements and workers, confirmed by the systems and customs by which the social group functions.

Japanese government, in the broadest sense of the word, is the rule of politicians, bureaucrats and industrialists, incorporating the opinions of interest groups, scholars, media people and even opposition figures. Major decisions are taken only after all affected parties have been consulted and their opinions sought. This makes policy-making a slow business, but once a direction has been fixed, far-reaching measures can be implemented with little resistance. Within the company a similar process takes place. New strategies are usually developed by middle-managers, adjusted in discussion with the people involved most closely, then taken to the top for approval and official adoption. Those who disagree or have been disadvantaged can expect compensation the next time round. It is an effective method of procedure, conducive to good morale and the creation of a whole greater than the sum of its parts. Its value was recognized as far back as the seventh century, when Prince Shotoku wrote it into his constitution, easily the wisest of the three that Japan has had. 'In order to achieve harmony,' he counselled, 'individual judgements and actions should be forbidden, and discussion at all levels should be respected.'

The Japanese consensus process is well known and has been subjected to much painstaking exegesis. What is not so clearly appreciated is the special dynamic of the Japanese business world, the vital competitive instinct that prevents all the group-think and the favour-swapping from collapsing into stagnation and inefficiency. The reason that Japanese companies are able to display such devastating competitive power in overseas markets is that their own is the toughest, most hotly contested in the world. Electronics, where Japanese dominance is greatest, is the most competitive sector of all.

The VTR was the most important consumer product since the colour television, fulfilling a completely new need and leading the electronics industry into a new era of growth. Since the launch of the first home-use models in 1975 over one hundred million units have been sold, 95 per cent of them of Japanese manufacture. The VTR is historically significant because it was the first major product, though it will certainly not be the last, dominated *from the outset* by non-Western companies. VTR technology was originally commercialized by an American company, Ampex, which produced a machine for professional use. However, no European or American company, with the exception of Philips and its ill-fated VC2000 format, even tried to compete in the mass market. Since 1985, Korean companies have moved into the lower end of the market, using technology licensed from Japan and large proportions of Japanese components. Some Western companies assemble and sell Japanese-made machines on OEM (Original Equipment Manufacture) contract, a process sometimes referred to by the Japanese as *tempura* (batter-fried) production.

The reasons that the Japanese have been able to make the video market their own are not very different from those which created their other successes. Since there never were any foreign competitors of substance, accusations of dumping or other unfair practices can be immediately dismissed. Skill in adapting existing technology to a new purpose; business flair in spotting the huge market potential; the ability to manufacture cheap, highly reliable machines – all these played important roles. However, the spur to success was the competitive mechanism. A dozen Japanese companies launched VTRs on the domestic market, and scrapped furiously for share by cutting prices, improving design and adding the extra capabilities that make Japanese products so acceptable to consumers everywhere.

The split into two rival camps – the non-compatible Beta and VHS formats – served only to intensify the conflict. After nearly a decade the marketing power and manufacturing technology of the Matsushita group triumphed, and the Sony-led Beta format, commonly acknowledged as the better product, was squeezed out of the picture. With profits tumbling and its reputation at stake, Sony struck back with the eight-millimetre video, a super-compact digital system. That introduced the 'camcorder', an innovation which made video-shooting as simple and accessible as holiday photography. Within months the VHS group had stolen Sony's thunder by launching a smaller, lighter camcorder that was fully compatible with all the millions of VHS video recorders that had already been sold. With scarcely time to pause for breath, battle was joined anew.

As the Beta-group manufacturers found to their cost, it is not enough for a product to be stylish, technologically sophisticated and directed towards a new growth market. It must also beat the competition. In compact disc players Sony took the initiative, bringing prices down from Y200,000 to Y50,000 in two dramatic leaps. On the production levels current at the time, that couldn't have been a paying proposition, but Sony's faith in the potential of digital audio technology was amply justified. The previously sluggish consumer response was completely transformed, and production had to be doubled to meet the new demand. Within three years Japan's audio industry was turning out more compact disc players than conventional decks, all the major companies having low-priced models on the market. It was then that they decided to introduce the digital audio tape player, the first major electronics product of purely Japanese origin. The technology was so fearsomely perfect that it had to be degraded. A vital circuit was vasectomized, thus rendering impossible the digital-to-digital recording that would have devastated the sales of other media, and compact discs most of all.

Memory chips are the tiny brains inside nearly all modern

electronic equipment, from digital watches to missile guidance systems. Without them there would be no personal computers or communication satellites, and household products would lack the sophisticated functions now taken for granted. The Japanese refer to this vital device as 'the rice of industry'. In its production they have established a position almost as commanding as in video and audio, with a world market share of 80 per cent and rising.

The first memory chip, the one-kilobit random-access memory, was developed at Texas Instruments in 1970. Since then the product has turned into a commodity ideally suited to the particular virtues and strengths of Japanese industry. Massive capital investment is required, favouring companies with easy access to funds. The R&D burden is also heavy, but the results desired are already known, which means no need for shot-in-the-dark basic research, which the Japanese find difficult. Since the product is completely standardized, and variable costs are insignificant, economies of scale work to dramatic effect. The more you make, the cheaper you can sell. Production technology is all-important. Apparently minor improvements in quality control lead to major increases in yield, meaning the proportion of usable product to total output. That in turn creates a sharp decline in unit costs, providing the opportunity to force down prices and expand market share. Finally, the Japanese integrated electronics makers, unlike their specialist American rivals, have large in-house markets in the form of their consumer and office-products divisions.

The Japanese did not target the memory market in the sense of secretly combining to do down foreign competition. From 1976 to 1980 the Ministry of International Trade and Industry did sponsor an intra-industry research programme which succeeded in fixing the technological parameters, but the funding was modest and the purpose limited. The decisive period came between 1981 and 1985 when Japanese companies conquered the world market simply by going for it hell for leather. Eight of Japan's most powerful, technologically advanced companies poured all the money they could lay their hands on, which was a considerable amount, into IC (Integrated Circuit) manufacture. Capacity was doubled and trebled, until the leaders were each pumping out over ten million chips per month.

In the delicate, highly complex processes of chip-making – crystal-pulling, dry-etching, photo-lithography, doping, bonding, and sealing – the presence of dust specks one thousandth of the width of a human hair can ruin whole batches. Cleanliness is a Japanese national obsession, manifested in such diverse phenomena as the custom of bathing daily and the purification rituals of the Shinto religion. Thanks to the scrupulous attentions of employees and suppliers, Japanese companies were able to achieve yield levels three times those of their American rivals. At the same time their frantic competition for market share was creating a massive oversupply. In 1985 the wholesale price of the 64K DRAM, the mainline memory product, plunged by 60 per cent, and the price of the 256K DRAM, its replacement, by 80 per cent. At these levels even the most efficient companies were barely breaking even. The result was the severest recession ever in the chip-making business. Most of the American competition was driven into loss, lay-offs and drastic rationalization, and the second tier of Japanese producers rapidly fell away. For the chip-users, however, it was a godsend, setting off a new wave of innovation and growth. Suddenly, makers of computers, cameras and audio equipment were able to offer smaller, cheaper, more complex products than ever before. It all happened just as the business textbooks say, but at breakneck speed and a vertiginous ratio of risk to reward.

To the Japanese, making IC chips or videos or cars is not a pastime pursued between nine and five in order to keep body and soul together. It is the central activity in the individual's endless struggle to assert the power of his own group against all others. As a perusal of Japanese business magazines will confirm, it is war by other means. Each week the great battles of Japanese and European history are refought in print, the tactics and errors of the various commanders being examined

in careful detail. In cover pictures, the industrialists and politicians who lead modern Japan are shown in the guise of
samurai: stern-faced, kimono-clad, sword at the ready. The
Nikkei newspaper, Japan's equivalent of the *Wall Street Journal*,
regularly carries advertisements for histories and fictionalized
versions of human conflict: 'Businessmen, let's learn from the
annals of war!' The world of work is considered the right
setting for romance, intrigue and deeds of derring-do. On the
morning train salarymen read 'corporate novels' which give
glamorized accounts of the goings-on at Japan's best-known
companies. The gossip magazines offer titillating glimpses of
the behind-the-scenes manoeuvring. Even the ubiquitous
comic books describe the daily routine of the office worker in
terms pregnant with drama and mystique.

The frame of mind revealed is the most important of all
reasons for the success of the Japanese: they have taken the
whole thing so seriously.

Honda Motor, provider of design technology to Austin
Rover, and motorcycles to the world, now produces a bike
that replicates the heavy, dignified outlines of the classic
British models – with upstanding headlight, bulbous tank and
black and silver finish. True enthusiasts of the genre can equip
themselves with the goggles and sheepskin-lined jackets that
the company thoughtfully supplies. The engine, however, is
somewhat different from the original. The GB 250 does not
rattle, leak or require any maintenance. In any other country
it might be considered an ironic tribute, but irony and
tributes are not what the Japanese are in business for. It sells
well, and that is what counts.

The sight of this magnificent machine racing along a
mountain road or, more likely, farting its disconsolate way
through a Tokyo traffic jam, is bound to provoke reflection
on one of the most enduring myths about the Japanese – that
they are copycats, unable to generate any ideas of their own.
Like most myths it is not without a kernel of truth. Japan has
only ever won three Nobel Prizes for science. That does not
measure well against Australia's eight or Switzerland's nine,

let alone the sixty-three bagged by Britain and the one hundred and thirty-three by the United States. Furthermore, both of her last two laureates won their prizes several years after leaving Japan for the less restrictive atmosphere of American research institutes. Dr Tonegawa, winner in 1987 for his work on immunology, made it plain that he considered the hierarchy and formalism of academic Japan inimical to the spirit of free inquiry. Certainly Japan's rigid corporate structure and fact-stuffing education system are not ideal breeding grounds for the great intuitive leaps by which the frontiers of human knowledge are advanced.

In the trade in technology, as opposed to that in goods, Japan is heavily in the red. In 1984 she paid out $2.3 billion for imported designs, patents and production licences, receiving just $0.7 billion for her own exports of the same. Both the scale of the deficit and the ratio of payments to receipts make Japan easily the largest user of other people's ideas among the major economies. About 40 per cent of the imported know-how comes from Europe and 50 per cent from the United States, which runs a multilateral surplus in technology of over $8 billion. In contrast, Japanese receipts are mainly from the developing countries, in the form of plant exports and joint ventures in the basic material and processing industries.

During the sixties the Ministry of International Trade and Industry used a range of subsidies and incentives to promote technology imports. Since the plethora of trade barriers then in force made direct marketing difficult, foreign companies were happy to fall into line. They grossly underestimated Japanese potential, with the result that many Western chemical, electronic and machinery makers gave crucial aid to the very companies now gobbling up their home markets. Gradually, however, the Japanese are emerging from their dependence on foreign sources. In new contracts, which give a much better indication of current strength, she has been in the black since 1970. It will take time for the backlog of old contracts to be worked through, but progress is being made. The number of import contracts signed each year levelled off in the early eighties.

Where the Japanese have already proven themselves supreme is in the development and adaptation of ideas that translate into money-making products. That itself is no mean accomplishment. Shape-changing titanium alloys had been around for ages, but it took a Japanese company to realize that they would make the perfect frame for brassières. The same goes for water-absorbent resins, now used in nappies all over the world. At a higher level of technology Japanese achievements in opto-electronics, rocketry and ceramics are evidence of an ability that goes far beyond mere imitation – an ability to analyse, synthesize and envisage new possibilities. Once the initial breakthrough has been made and the dominant technology established, the Japanese are fast into the breach with variations and improvements of all sorts. Every day the *Nikkei* newspaper announces dozens of new products and processes, most of which are described as 'epoch-making'. Indeed, if readers were to be given Y1000 for every epoch the *Nikkei* has made, they would be very comfortably off. No matter. More often than not, the subjects described are ingeniously conceived, useful and highly profitable.

The fertility of the Japanese business world is indicated by the number of domestic patents registered each year – more than in the United States and Britain combined. Even within the United States, about one-fifth of all patents granted go to the Japanese. In 1987, the companies which took the largest number of American patents were not IBM or GE, but, in order, Canon, Hitachi, and Mitsubishi. Moreover, the quality of Japanese patents is high and increasing. A study carried out by the National Science Foundation, a US government agency, shows that existing Japanese patents are now cited as precedents in new applications more frequently than American ones. Innovation, not invention, is how Japanese creativity manifests itself. And innovation, not invention, is where the profits are.

The problem with the Japanese approach is its reliance on someone else to furnish the dominant technology. The invention of the random access memory required not only a different concept of scientific inquiry from goal-oriented Japanese R & D. It also required a massive commitment of money, time and talent – in one sense all wasted, in another absolutely vital – to the thousands of failures and dead-end projects that went before. That is a cost which the Japanese have yet to bear. Their success in all the other areas of business means that the challenge is drawing closer.

Japan's prosperity has been built on her mastery of manufacture, her ability to turn out large quantities of high-quality products at reasonable cost. The principle does not vary whether the product be steel or V T Rs or memory chips, and neither does Japanese success. Indeed, the Japanese are so advanced in manufacturing technology that they have developed a fully automated factory where robots build robots twenty-four hours a day. That raised an important question. If manufacturing becomes standardized, will Japan be able to maintain her competitive edge? However dedicated, quality-conscious and skilled Japanese workers may be, they cannot compete with robots. Any company anywhere can buy Fanuc's flexible manufacturing system, install it (unions permitting), and achieve the same superior efficiencies.

Within the rich economies the shift away from manufacturing is already well under way. Service industries are occupying increasingly large slices of employment and gross national product, with the United States leading the trend. Meanwhile developing countries like Taiwan and South Korea are moving up the skill hierarchy at an astounding pace. In communications and data-processing the value of the manufactured part of the product – the hardware – is steeply declining as a proportion of the whole. The highest growth and the highest value added is in the software, the knowledge-intensive element that no machine can provide. In the new industrial order now taking shape, the winners, amongst both companies and countries, will be those who control the software market. So far, Japanese achievements in this area have been relatively undistinguished.

Japan is the only sizeable computer market in the world where I B M does not command top position. Domestic companies such as Fujitsu and Hitachi have bravely held the fort.

However, no Japanese company has ever developed its own operating system for a mainframe computer. Fujitsu and Hitachi both market 'IBM-compatible' machines, relying on price, marketing power and incremental improvements to attract customers. In micro-processors the American lead is just as telling. Although Japanese companies have captured the market for memory chips they have made little headway in the development of the more complex 'logic elements' that do the actual thinking. Nearly all the logics made in Japan and used in Japanese-made products are 'second-sourced' (licensed) from American companies. In computer-aided manufacturing systems, the software tool now vital to the design process in industries ranging from apparel to autos, American companies hold 80 per cent of the Japanese market.

The most knowledge-intensive of all the traditional industries is pharmaceuticals, and here too the Japanese have yet to show much form. The structure of the market has not helped. Instead of the oligopolies found in most countries, Japan has several dozen companies all scrabbling for a piece of the pie. Not one features in the world top ten either in sales or, more importantly, in the scale of R&D expenditure. Japan is also unusual in the dispensing system she maintains. Japanese GPs give out medicines directly to their patients. The difference between the price charged by the pharmaceutical companies and the amount reimbursed by the government goes straight into their pockets. Discounts on drugs are believed to make up about 30 per cent of the average doctor's income, and Japanese doctors are extremely rich individuals. This method of proceeding is good for business relations between pharmaceutical companies and doctors, but bad for the national budget. The effect on patients is a matter of opinion. They certainly get the chance to try lots of new medicines. When expertly treated, even the mildest sniffle requires several bags of brightly coloured pills and powders. The highest margins of all are carried by injections, which explains why Japanese doctors are the world's quickest on the needle.

The pharmaceutical market has been just as competitive as the other sectors of the Japanese economy, but its great aim has always been to create increasingly expensive drugs for the treatment of the most common diseases – thus, the concentration on cephalosporin antibiotics and anti-cancer nostrums of negligible efficacy. There has been no incentive for innovation or diversity. Consequently Japanese companies have failed to develop into forces on the international market. Less than 5 per cent of the pharmaceutical industry's revenues are derived from foreign countries, which compares with 40–60 per cent for the Western majors, and over 50 per cent for the Japanese auto and electronic industries. Recently, however, there have been signs that the Japanese pharmaceutical industry is shifting up a gear. New compounds have been discovered for the treatment of ulcers, arthritis and senile dementia, Japan's fastest-growing diseases. Japanese companies have invested heavily in biotechnology, and progress in complex areas such as prostaglandins has won world-wide attention. In 1986 new contracts for exports of pharmaceutical technology exceeded those for imports for the first time ever, thus repeating the 1970 experience of Japanese industry as a whole.

The Japanese have to make a go of pharmaceuticals. It is too early to judge their chances, but the opposition from Europe and America will be more formidable than any faced so far. Japanese drug companies do, however, have one important advantage – which applies equally to all the new strategic sectors. They are extraordinarily rich. Thanks to the revaluation of the yen, Japan has the chance to buy into the creativity and talent that she cannot yet generate at home. After the Second World War, the best scientific brains in Europe gravitated towards the economic power of the United States. In a world far more complex, both financially and technologically, the money comes looking for the brains. Through tie-ups and direct takeovers, Japanese companies can absorb the best of what Europe and the United States have to offer.

How long before the Japanese start to make their own breakthroughs? It will not be easy. Free-ranging experimentation accords ill with the conformist, homogeneous ideology needed to justify the sublimation of individual interests to those of the group. Yet if new service businesses are to be created then some of Prince Shotoku's wise words will have to be forgotten. If the Japanese software industry is to compete, Japanese hackers are needed. If biotechnology is to be mastered, then the value of accident and aberration must be fully understood. That is asking the Japanese to modify their Japaneseness, but no less will be required if they are to carry on making the pace. They have negotiated much greater changes before.

Poor Little Rich Country

When the black ships steamed into Japanese waters 140 years ago their initial purpose was to obtain port facilities for American whalers in the Western Pacific. The second and more vital purpose, pursued with especial intensity by the European powers who arrived shortly afterwards, was to demand trading rights. According to the thinking of the time, derived from the theories of the classical economists, a country which cut itself off from the comity of nations was acting immorally, since it was reducing the world's wealth-creating potential. The Japanese took the point, and soon enough trade was flourishing. Since then many ships have come and gone and the Japanese merchant marine has grown larger than any save the 'flags-of-convenience'. The foreigners have developed a new set of demands, somewhat different in tone but almost as insistent: Save less, invest less – Don't work so hard – Eat steak and oranges – Consume, and be merry – Stop chasing whales – Increase military spending and stand up to the Soviets – Be more like us – Join the gang – most important of all, Cut down those exports. So far, at least, the response has been less than overwhelming.

If there is one topic that instantly springs to mind on the rare occasions when the average Westerner thinks about Japan, it is trade friction, the seemingly interminable series of disputes that have soured relations with Europe and America for the best part of two decades. Almost every type of product traded, from baseball bats to machine tools, from peanuts to satellites, seems to generate its share of acrimony.

A special vocabulary has been created – of targeting, 'flat playing-fields', and NTBs (Non-Tariff Barriers). Politicians have fulminated. Lobbyists have haggled. Famous journalists have drawn comparisons with Pearl Harbor. Meanwhile, consumers have kept on buying.

Perhaps it is inevitable that a dramatic shift in the power balance of the sort now occurring should result in fraying tempers. After all, the traditional approach was war. In 1986 the Japanese clocked up an excess of exports over imports that amounted to 4 per cent of their GNP, an imbalance in the world trading system of an unprecedented scale. In the best of all possible worlds, as described in the economic textbooks, it could never have happened. The theory of comparative advantage holds that nations should concentrate on what they are best at doing, and trade the result. Under floating exchange rates the countries that produce the most of the best should see their currencies go stronger, thus pricing their exports more expensively and allowing them to buy more imports for the same money. The eventual result should be happy equilibrium, not $90 billion surpluses.

What went wrong? The standard Japanese view is simple. Foreign goods are not competitive, and foreign businessmen in Japan do not try hard enough. It is a view that cannot easily be discounted. European and American companies have not put much effort into the world's second largest market, believing it to be too exclusive or too complicated. Furthermore, if the citizens of their own countries display an overwhelming preference for Japanese goods, then it is hardly surprising that Japanese citizens do the same. However, several foreign companies have done extremely well in Japan. McDonald's is the largest restaurant company, Coca-Cola the largest soft-drinks company, IBM the second-largest computer company. Lipton's, Proctor & Gamble, and Kodak all have sizeable market shares, and since the appreciation of the yen in 1985 Porsche and BMW have started to do excellent business. Owning a sports car in Tokyo is akin to keeping a racehorse in the backyard, but foreign brand goods remain the accepted instruments for signalling financial and social achievement.

The view from the other side, often expressed with vehemence in Congress and the European Parliament, is that there is something uniquely underhand and unfair about Japanese business practices. The exact problem is rarely spelt out, but the inference is of subsidies, dumping and trade barriers. Actually Japan's tariff rates and import restrictions compare favourably with those in the West. In strictly legal terms the Japanese are justified in claiming their market to be the world's most open. None the less, for a variety of complex reasons, it is an extraordinarily difficult one to crack.

Japanese businessmen persist in speaking Japanese, a tongue in which the foreigners trying to sell to them usually have little facility. Japanese consumers are extremely demanding. Fierce competition between domestic producers has led them to expect the highest standards of design, reliability and service. Like the British and Americans in times gone by they naturally assume that home-made is best, and much time and effort is required to convince them otherwise. Even if successful, the process of getting goods to the final user is infernally convoluted. In most Western countries, the wholesale industry is usually double the size of the retail sector it serves, but Japan's is over five times as large. It is a sort of unofficial social-security system, providing jobs for hundreds of thousands of people who cannot be absorbed within the productive economy. The guiding principle is not profitability, but obligation bred of long personal association.

Cultural differences aside, Japan, like most other countries, deliberately protects sensitive areas of her economy, a strategy aided by the close connections between politicians, bureaucrats and businessmen. The Ministry of Health works hand in glove with the major pharmaceutical firms, the Ministry of Posts with the communications consortia, the Ministry of Agriculture with farming interests. When the authorities revealed their grandiose plan for an airport on an artificial island in Osaka Bay, the possibility of foreign participation simply never occurred to them. From the start the project had been developed in co-operation with the domestic construction industry, the country's largest employer and one of the most generous providers of political donations. Open bidding, which does not exist in Japan, would have defeated the whole object of the exercise.

All these factors have contributed to the poor results of Western companies in Japan, yet they explain nothing about the real cause of the imbalance – the overwhelming competitive power of Japan's exporters. The industries that have been leading the assault on Western markets do not receive any special favours or benefits. They compete on quality and price, and the results they achieve are not really surprising. In all probability, if both sides were to scrap their armouries of official and non-official restrictions, the result would be the annihilation of some small primary-sector and processing industries in Japan, and a massive increase in Japanese exports of cars, electronic goods and machinery.

Whatever may once have been the case, in the pot-and-kettle slanging match that is international trade politics Japan now has a reasonably defensible complexion. Western governments have placed an increasing proportion of her exports under quotas, special tariffs and 'voluntary restraints' in the name of protecting jobs. The process began long ago, in 1971, with the Japanese government's agreement to limit textile exports to the United States. Richard Nixon had been keen to garner the electoral support of southern textile workers, and in the reversion of Okinawa he held a powerful bargaining chip. Thus were created unfortunate linkages with geopolitical and electoral considerations that have yet to be broken. At the time Japan's markets were far from open, so there could be little complaint. In 1977, with the imposition of quotas on Japanese steel, matters were less clear cut. In 1981, when exports of passenger cars were limited, the Japanese had ample reason to feel aggrieved.

The auto restraints, negotiated by the strongest free-trade administration the United States has had or is likely to have, were a landmark in the slide to managed trade. The original justification was to give Detroit time to develop the 'X-car', a revolutionary small car that was going to conquer the world market. The X-car never really happened, but the quotas, supposed to last just three years, are still with us. Restricted in the number of units they could sell, Japanese companies began raising prices. Domestic makers followed suit, with the result that by 1984 American consumers were paying an extra $8.5 billion for their cars. Detroit recovered splendidly from the recession, clearing out of small-car manufacture in favour of import arrangements with Japanese companies. Great was the rejoicing, with special bonuses and share-option schemes all round. Meanwhile the Japanese were making fatter profits than ever before, and using them to develop up-range models that would be produced within the United States.

The next landmark was the limitation of Japan's exports of IC chips in 1986, agreed in return for the dropping of various dumping suits. Textiles, TVs, steel and cars were all mature products when the restraints were enacted, and some argument could be advanced for the stabilization of market share. ICs are still in the dynamic growth stage, and their pricing profoundly affects the future of the world electronics industry. Any slowing in the product-development cycle is bound to have an adverse impact on the pace of technological change. The obligations imposed by the pact were the most rigorous yet. Japanese makers had to surrender secret cost-accounting data to the American authorities so that 'fair market values' could be established, with price surveillance extending even to third-country markets. American companies are under no similar obligation, to their own or any other government. The Japanese government also undertook to 'encourage' domestic users to double their purchases of American chips, regardless of pricing or quality. Immediately after the agreement was signed prices of Japanese memory chips rocketed by 100 to 600 per cent to the government-mandated levels. That prompted howls of outrage from the American Electronics Association, some of whose members threatened to close down factories and move production offshore unless an adequate supply was resumed. When MITI proved incapable of preventing the spill of cheap chips from its domestic market, the US government imposed retaliatory tariffs on a whole range of unrelated products, a decision that was greeted with numbed shock in Tokyo.

One-third of all Japan's exports to the United States, by far her biggest market, is now subject to some sort of restriction. Machine tools were added to the list in 1987, the argument being that Japanese dominance of a product used in weapon manufacture was endangering national security. Still more strained was the use of the same principle to block Fujitsu's takeover of Fairchild, an American IC producer totally owned by a French multinational. Whatever the justification invoked, the negotiating technique is always the same – the offer that can't be refused. Since the Japanese are utterly reliant on the American market they have no alternative but to submit with whatever grace they can muster. In Europe the position is not much better. Germany is the only country with a domestic producer that does not impose limits on Japanese auto exports. Italy has maintained a quota of 2200 cars, or about 1 per cent of the market, since the 1930s. In 1982 France decided to route all Japanese VTRs through a customs post in the tiny town of Poitiers, where the worthy *douaniers* could subject the machines to a properly meticulous (and time-consuming) inspection. Since then the EEC has slapped restrictions on watches, machine tools, copy machines and audio and video goods, but the trade imbalance has shown little sign of shrinking.

Even in an ideal world of free trade and perfectly responsive exchange rates, Japan would still rack up large surpluses with the industrialized world. She is compelled to sell more manufactured goods than she buys in order to pay for her supplies of foodstuffs, fuel and raw materials. These she needs to import in greater quantities than any other country. For the West to demand absolute rectification of bilateral imbalances is equivalent to instructing the Japanese to shut up shop. For much of the post-war period Japan's current account was highly unstable, with large deficits alternating with even larger surpluses. In recent years the latter condition has been intensified by several factors specific to the economic climate of the eighties. Prices of the commodities which make up the bulk of the Japanese import bill have been in decline since the peaking of world-wide inflation. On the other hand, Japanese exports have a high degree of demand elasticity – meaning that the more money people have, the more of them they want to buy. Additionally, a large proportion – perhaps one-third – of all Japanese exports to the United States is composed of either goods that American companies do not make, such as videos, or components and peripheral devices that American companies incorporate into their own wares. The better the economic conditions, the greater the demand.

Japanese surpluses became structural and chronic with the 'strong dollar, strong America' policy that the Reagan administration followed until 1985. In the United States whole industries found themselves unable to compete with imports. They either bought in from low-cost Far Eastern producers, moved their own production offshore, or went out of business. High interest rates, imposed in order to squeeze inflation out of the system, attracted massive flows of Japanese and other foreign capital to U S treasury bonds, thus prolonging a valuation of the dollar that had no relation to comparative economic strengths. The result was a dangerous pattern of cross-dependence. Japan was relying on excessive American consumption to generate the growth that her domestic economy could not provide. Despite the animadversions of the various interest groups, American households and companies came to rely on Japanese goods. Most serious of all, the American government turned into a money junkie, relying on regular fixes of Japanese capital to fund its gargantuan internal deficit.

On the one hand, a country spending far more than it saves. On the other, a country saving far more than it spends. The two have clung together in a relationship of uneasy, often tempestuous intimacy. The Japanese have toiled diligently to provide American consumers with cheap, high-quality products that would otherwise be unavailable, and also lent the money needed to buy them. Americans have consumed with equal diligence, thus making the Japanese richer and richer. It's all fine while it lasts, but the strains on the world economy indicate that a change in habits would be healthier for all concerned.

So the Americans spend less, and the Japanese save less. Both propositions are more difficult of achievement than they sound, requiring the suppression of deeply ingrained cultural traits. The problem facing Japan is by far the more tractable and the more pleasant. Her citizens have yet to experience anything like the full benefits of the industrial success they have laboured so long and hard to achieve. Export markets may have been captured, huge portfolios of overseas assets may have been accumulated, but the domestic infrastructure remains in a miserably underdeveloped condition. Like everything else in Japan, the economic miracle has two sides.

Almost every Japanese one meets seems familiar with the phrase 'rabbit hutch', as applied to Japanese living conditions by a senior EEC official. That unkind description has achieved widespread currency not because it is resented but because it is recognized as apt. Japan is in the midst of a perpetual housing crisis. Although there are more than enough houses to go round, their quality and pricing is, by Western standards, absurd. 'Two-up two-down' prefabs in a dowdy suburb fetch more than well-appointed luxury homes in London's stockbroker belt. It is not unusual for middle-income families to live in ramshackle constructions of corrugated iron and plasterboard that would do tolerable service in a third-world shanty town. At the dormitories run by most reputable companies, young executives inhabit single rooms no larger than the cells of a maximum security prison. Altogether, the amount of residential floorspace per person in Japan's three major cities is less than in East Berlin. The main users of Japan's ubiquitous 'love hotels', candy-cake edifices that offer gadgety eroticism on a short-stay basis, are not bosses and secretaries, but married couples enjoying a few rare hours of intimacy away from the kids.

The reason for this sad state of affairs is not hard to identify – the price of land, which in Tokyo usually accounts for 80 per cent of the house price. The post-war concentration of one-third of Japan's population – equivalent to the entire population of Spain – into 1 per cent of her land area has created a severe shortage, exacerbated by a total absence of urban planning. During the seventies the situation was compounded by misguided tax policies and Byzantine zoning regulations which penalized anyone engaging in large-scale developments. The strange, jagged cityscapes, with their 'pencil buildings' and rhomboidal office blocks, result not from a quirk of taste but from strictly enforced plot ratios and rights to light. The laws of supply and demand have worked their usual magic. The average price of residential land in the six largest cities rose by 7800 per cent between 1955 and 1985, a period in which the consumer price index merely quintupled. One of the cramped apartments that the Japanese, with unconscious irony, call 'mansions' would, if within an hour's commute of Tokyo station, fetch around $300 million. The price of prime commercial land has reached the dizzy height of $60,000 per square metre. When Tokyo city government was considering a one-mile extension of loop road around the main business district, it calculated costs at $3 billion, or four times its entire road budget. Of that sum, 98 per cent would have gone in land acquisition. Japanese income differentials may be low, but there is a world of difference between those who hold property and those who do not. People who bought small plots in Tokyo in the early years of the economic miracle have seen their personal assets grow to a scale unattainable by a whole lifetime of loyal service to the company. Understandably, every Japanese wants to be a home-owner – it is the best investment in town.

Size and price are not all that is wrong with the housing stock. Only one-third of all Japanese homes are connected to the sewerage system, the remainder relying either on private cesspits or the vacuum trucks that patrol the residential districts. These are not the most efficient machines that Japan produces, and the odd token of their visit is sometimes left behind on the roadside. Even the sophisticated Ginza has spots where the stench of raw excrement sends the casual window-shopper scuttling for cover. In less salubrious quarters, house-holders still regularly burn their rubbish on the pavement. Much else could be improved as well. Tokyo has one-twentieth of the park space per resident of Washington, one-fifteenth that of London. Only 7 per cent of Japanese cities with populations of over 300,000 have ring roads, which compares with 90 per cent in Britian and the United States. In Tokyo only 20 per cent of communication cables run underground, against 70 per cent in Washington and 100 per cent in London.

Leisure facilities are insufficient in both quality and number, a fact which has made a major contribution to the diligence of the average worker. It has also kept personal consumption in the depressed condition which trading partners find so unsatisfactory. Once the Japanese salaryman has stocked his tiny house with electronic gadgets, there are simply not enough outlets left for discretionary spending. The presence of hordes of his fellow-citizens, all with similar tastes, information sources and income levels, can make a gruelling experience out of the most potentially pleasurable leisure-time activity. If, in midsummer, he decides to visit the municipal swimming-pool, he will know better than to attempt to swim. The water is so packed with bodies that locomotion of any sort is impossible, even in the vertical mode. If he plumps for the latest thriller film, he will have to resign himself to viewing the dénouement before the beginning: in order to ensure victory in the battle for seats, he will need to stand in the aisle for the last thirty minutes of the previous showing. If he fancies a game of tennis, he will have to book months in advance and then share the court with half a dozen other people, all volleying furiously over their two yards of net space.

Golf? Fine, if he can afford a membership fee high enough to fund the construction of an entire British course. A trip to the beach? Hundred-mile tailbacks and mud-coloured sands layered with trash. Goin' fishin'? With forty others alongside an 'angling trench' somewhere in the semi-industrialized wasteland of outer Tokyo. A weekend's skiing? All-night train journeys spent sprawled on the floor outside an ill-functioning toilet; two-hour waits at the ski lift; practice slopes cluttered with hundreds of colliding beginners. None of it is worth the candle. Japanese salarymen know that, for pure relaxation, nothing beats a good long day in the office.

The next target for the target-loving Japanese is to shift emphasis from export-led growth to the upgrading of the social stock, the one area in which they still badly lag behind the rich Western countries. Building regulations will have to be liberalized and more public and agricultural land made available for development. The private-sector resources now devoted to conquering overseas markets will have to be channelled into the creation of an environment in which it is enjoyable to live, work and relax. In the long term a more sensible geographical disposition of people and institutions will also be required. The trick will be to manage the operation without setting off another land-price spiral, without causing social dislocation, and without sending the United States into fiscal cold turkey. Much money will be required and much careful long-term planning, both of which the Japanese are exceptionally well equipped to supply.

4

The Social Mould

They are so crafty in their hearts that nobody can understand them. Whence it is said that they have three hearts: a false one in their mouths for all the world to see, another within their breasts only for their friends, and a third in the depths of their hearts, reserved for themselves alone and never manifested to anybody.

The Island of Japon, João Rodrigues'
account of sixteenth-century Japan

To be born a Japanese is to know that everything has a front and a back.

Takeo Doi, psychiatrist and social commentator

One of the many aspects of traditional Japanese life which delighted and shocked Western visitors of the mid nineteenth century was the custom of mixed bathing. Men, women and children performed their daily ablutions in the same public bath without inhibition or prurience. The rulers of Meiji Japan soon realized that this Eden-like condition of unselfconsciousness ran counter to the best principles of progress and enlightenment as expounded by the foreign savants and missionaries. In deference of the spirit of the times, remedial measures were taken. The bath-house owners built separate entrances for male and female customers, fitted with fine wooden signboards. Inside, the bathing facility itself was divided into two areas – by a piece of string hung through the middle. From the outside all appeared modern, well-ordered, entirely proper. Amidst the steam and the heat, people continued to follow the customs of association that suited them best.

It was a classic illustration of the difference between *omote* and *ura*. *Omote* is literally the surface or front of an object, *ura* its back or reverse side. Thus, *omote-ji* means the outer cloth of a kimono, and *ura-ji* the layer next to the skin. *Omote-dori* are large thoroughfares containing the smart offices and shops where people make and spend their money. *Ura-dori* are the cramped and cluttered backstreets where they have their homes. *Omote-Nippon* is Japan's eastern side, which bears the administrative and industrial apparatus of the modern nation. *Ura-Nippon*, the Japan Sea coast, supplies the votes that keep it going.

By extension the terms have come to describe a more abstract duality, and one of crucial importance in understanding how modern Japan functions. *Omote* is the official, public aspect of a person, event or institution, and *ura* its unofficial or private aspect. Thus, an *omote* signboard means a pretext or a figurehead, while 'to see the *ura* of a man's heart' is to understand his true feelings. Almost every sphere of Japanese society has its *omote* and its *ura*: as if by law of nature, phenomena divide into distinct but mutually-dependent realities. What may appear to the unfamiliar observer to be hypocritical or self-contradictory is often merely the result of this division. *Omote/ura* are two sides of the same coin, opposing and protecting each other.

Together they have played a distinguished part in Japanese history. For over a thousand years Japanese emperors reigned as living gods while a succession of warlords wielded actual power in the Imperial name. It was a useful pretence, conferring eternal security of tenure on the former and temporary legitimacy on the latter. The Tokugawa Shogunate developed a more sophisticated version of *omote* reality. According to the official ideology merchants were classed below samurai, farmers and craftsmen in the social hierarchy. In fact merchants supplied the nation's economic dynamism, and by the end of the period many of the samurai were sunk in debt to them. At that time the whole apparatus of admininstration had devolved into a complex set of interlocking illusions. The Shogun himself had become a puppet controlled by the regional lords, most of whom were completely under the sway of hereditary functionaries. They in turn were being manipulated by the lower-ranking samurai who carried out the day-to-day business of the domain.

In the modern political and business worlds there are many similar examples of the separation of authority and power. Generally, company presidents have nothing like the influence of their Western equivalents. Important decisions are made at middle-management level through a process of consensus-building. In extreme cases the president is little more than a corporate diplomat, of greatest use to his company when on the golf course with other presidents, clinching deals that were planned at lower levels. None the less he will still, by virtue of his position, command a degree of formal subservience unthinkable in a Western company.

The Japanese prime minister is not usually chosen for his leadership prowess but for his malleability in the hands of the various interest groups whose interaction decides the nation's destiny. Thus, being forced out of the premiership by a financial scandal proved only a minor obstacle to the political fortunes of Kakuei Tanaka. For the next ten years he sat in the Diet as an independent, and through the skilful deployment of his faction acquired a position of complete dominance over the Liberal Democratic Party, and thus national, affairs. His power to make and break prime ministers earned him the nickname of kingmaker.

What things are called is of crucial importance. Once Tanaka had designated himself as 'an independent', the whole context changed, and it was a simple matter for him to build up his influence within the LDP. A revealing instance of the same syndrome occurred when a pop group much featured on family TV shows and advertisements was accused of involvement in a sexual assault. The broadcasting companies moved quickly. The group was immediately purged from its usual programmes. Records were recalled from shops and melted down. All commercial activity ceased. Two years later the group reappeared in all its former glory, armed with a set of new contracts that kept its members on the screen every night of the week. They even used the same feeble gimmick as before, blacking up their faces and crinkling their hair. The secret of this sudden return to favour was simple: they had changed the group's name. Like Tanaka, they had been reborn with a new identity.

The Japanese military forces obtained their new name and identity shortly after the end of the war. Most countries have an army, a navy and an air force. Japan has a Ground Self-Defence Force, a Maritime Self-Defence Force and an Air Self-Defence Force. It was a necessary terminological adjustment, firstly because of the public odium in which the old military institutions were now held, and secondly because of the requirements of the post-war constitution. The supreme law of the nation is probably the supreme modern example of the *omote/ura* separation. Article Nine pledges the country to pacifism, but Japan now possesses the world's eighth-largest military force.

Countless other examples can be cited of rules and structures established, carefully maintained and systematically flouted. Everybody knows what is occurring, and understands its necessity. Public-works contracts are awarded according to competitive tender. In fact construction firms take turns in 'winning' with bids that have previously been agreed amongst themselves. Major companies have a gentleman's agreement not to begin recruiting graduates before the first of October. However, it is common knowledge that the best graduates are snapped up as early as May – a practice that is known as 'gathering the rice while it is green'. In sumo a wrestler in danger of losing his rank in the strict hierarchy of merit may visit his opponent of the next day and request his kind co-operation. The formal gift of an envelope of banknotes (known in the trade as 'an injection') will ensure that the bout has an outcome satisfactory to all who value the proper order of things. In each case the maximization of private advantage is skilfully reconciled with the decorous public arrangements.

The Japanese attitude to pornography is interesting for the insight it offers into the *omote/ura* process at work. In Japan pornography is not just a cultural excrescence, but one of the traditional game areas that society has marked out, vital to the set of economic and cultural conditions on which so much has been built. Without it the whole pattern of male and female relationships would crumble. Historically, pornography had a wide currency in the form of the highly explicit *shunga* prints which were turned out by some of Japan's greatest artists. Today Japan is probably the only country in the world where pornography is available from automatic vending machines sited at street corners. Even general-interest magazines carry photographic displays of naked women, often trussed up like hams and suspended from the ceiling, and most of the tabloid newspapers carry hard-core sado-masochist serials. Yet, despite the important function that is being fulfilled, strict regulations have been imposed. The full-frontal display of the human form is prohibited by law, and the government employs scores of housewives and students to ink out the relevant bits in imported copies of *Playboy* and *Penthouse*. World-famous paintings have been impounded at Narita Airport and dispatched back to their country of origin because they offered up a tuft of pubic hair to the gaze of the Japanese people.

Regulations exist not only to control behaviour but also to conceal it. In a highly pressured, overpopulated and combustible society such as Japan's, the preservation of stability and order is the overriding priority. Potentially anarchic appetites must be satisfied without disturbing the social fabric – a consideration which applies to the profit motive as much as to sexual desire. Japanese companies have shown themselves to be the most effective money-making organizations in the world, but they rarely present themselves as such in the 'aggressive' manner fashionable in the West. Instead they talk about their earnest desire to contribute to society as a whole, to mutual understanding between nations and the brotherhood of man. The typical Western reaction is likely to be incredulous. Do they really expect anyone to take them seriously? The answer is that they expect their *omote* to be accepted amongst all the other *omote* elements that make up Japanese group reality. The naked expression of capitalism red in tooth and claw would subvert the consensus-and-co-operation model which has enabled Japan to function so smoothly.

The gap between *tatemae* (face) and *honne* (real intention) is the same separation enacted at an individual level. Inevitably group reality and private reality have their own inner logics, and only a fool, or a foreigner, would expect them to match. Whether at home or at work, a Japanese is primarily a member of a group, and must present an aspect of himself that will enable group reality to succeed. Thus, all the elaborate forms of linguistic and behavioural etiquette that conventionalize Japanese human relationships. The expression of private emotion is frowned upon since it threatens the disruption of agreed communal reality by more powerful individual commitments. A well-bred young lady will smile politely as she explains how her brother died in a fire two nights ago. The parents of a student who has just passed into a good university will look despairing before the parents of one not so fortunate. For individuals to maintain their *omote* requires constant effort, constant strain. The cost of failure is immense.

It is an aesthetic experience just to behold a traditional *kaiseki* banquet, to savour how food and receptacle complement one another in shape and colour, and how both delicately allude to the passage of the seasons. To tuck in is almost a desecration. The Japanese, as they say themselves, 'eat with their eyes'. Similarly, the way a midsummer gift is wrapped is as important as the thing itself. The complex, tightly-layered assemblage of expensive papers communicates much about the desired relationship between giver and recipient. The Japanese set great store by surfaces, courtesies, the various wrappings of language. Appearances are to be valued and enjoyed, but not expected to correspond to realities. It is only necessary that both should have their uses.

Law and Orderliness

Picture a country where you never need to count your change; where the streets are free of litter, the walls free of graffiti; where no one feels compelled to vandalize public telephones; where people visit sports grounds not to engage in tribal warfare but to cheer good play; where there are no muggings, no skinheads, no hippie convoys, no recreational brawls on Saturday nights; where policemen are affable and courteous, and the pistols they carry are only fired a couple of times a year by the entire force.

That may seem like a flashback to a golden era of stability and calm. In fact it describes the present condition of the world's second largest economy. Despite dramatic transformations in the social environment, despite grave problems of overcrowding, Japan has maintained the highest standards of public order – a fact which must have a major influence on any assessment of relative qualities of life. Fewer robberies occur in Japan in a whole year than in two American days; fewer rapes than in one American week. Teenage girls can walk safely through red-light districts. Old ladies can sleep untroubled by worries of burglary and beatings. Cars can be left unlocked; large sums of cash carried on the person. It is possible to live in Japan for years without ever witnessing voices raised in anger, let alone fists flying.

The small civilities of life are still intact: the taxi driver's impeccable white gloves and cap; the mechanics saluting the plane as it takes off; the repair-man who refuses payment for such a small job. Japan is obviously a society that is working well, a perception confirmed by the relative absence of lawyers. Disputes between individuals and between companies are usually settled by negotiation and compromise. Only in the rare cases when such procedures break down is legal confrontation adopted as a last resort.

The obligation of the individual to the group is the primary fact of Japanese social life, inculcated at a very early age and confirmed at the various rites of passage. Individual rights and self-fulfilment may be enshrined in the constitution, but they have not made much headway against the long centuries of social training. In Tokugawa times, control in villages was upheld by the 'mutual responsibility unit' of five households which organized defence against marauders, resolved disputes, kept statistics on community life, and ensured that the detailed government regulations on dress, housing, food and most other areas of life were not being broken. Originally a system imposed from above, it gradually evolved into a local council which scrupulously enforced social norms consistent with official ideology. In modern Japan no such formal structure exists, but members of communities are constantly measuring their own conduct against what they see around them. The result is a high standard of conformity in dress, manner and outlook, and a society whose rules are enforced by strict internalized discipline.

Potential transgressors are no doubt deterred by the strong probability of retribution. Arrest rates are the highest in the world, and those brought to justice can expect little sympathy. Whatever the legal technicalities may suggest, the standard assumption is that arrest equals criminality. The press thinks so, and does not hesitate to condemn defendants long before guilt (or innocence) has been proven. The chief prosecutor of the Osaka High Court caused something of a stir when he complained publicly about the increasing number of not-guilty verdicts in his area. To his dismay, the rate had risen to 0.46 per cent, well above the national average of 0.21 per cent. The authoritarian instinct is no less evident in civil cases that involve the government as defendant – on average, plaintiffs are successful in just one instance in twenty. Pollution victims suing large corporations encounter similar difficulties, and, even if successful, they are often made to wait decades before their claims are upheld.

The character of the Japanese police force is an apt reflection of the society it protects. Every year one-quarter of its intake are university graduates, including a dozen from Tokyo University, Japan's Oxbridge. The National Police Agency has now overtaken the Ministry of Home Affairs to become the third most popular bureaucratic career amongst the nation's graduates, bested only by MITI and the mandarin Ministry of Finance. The responsibility and status of the job is confirmed by the five-point slogan in the policeman's notebook, which some forces chant at their morning meetings: 'Policemen devote themselves to the state and community with pride and sense of mission, Policemen lead pure and steady lives,' et cetera. It might not suit Dirty Harry, but it helps to keep morale high in the Japanese force.

The remarkable arrest rate achieved by the police testifies more to the quality of information possessed than to feats of Holmesian deduction. The network of 15,000 *koban* (police boxes), most of them manned twenty-four hours a day, enable policemen to merge into the life of the local community. In addition the *o-mawari-san* ('Honourable Mr Go-around', the local bobby) keeps discreet track of all the residents in his area, and often knows as much about their private lives as their next-door neighbours. He calls on each household once a year to ask a few innocuous questions and make sure that no irregularities are occurring. When laws are broken he has considerable discretion as to how to respond. In juvenile delinquency cases, for example, if the parents are sufficiently 'sincere' in their contrition, it is quite probable that no further action will be taken. If the policeman is less than satisfied he may decide to impose a small punishment of his own devising. Westerners might object to the intrusive and arbitrary powers of the police, but the Japanese consider it a small price to pay for the social stability which not only makes their country a pleasant place to live in, but contributes immeasurably to economic performance.

The Japanese are no angels. Certain activities classified as crimes are more or less sanctioned by custom. In the commuter crush, young ladies wearing short skirts are considered fair game for the groping hand. Tax evasion – through abuse of the savings system (*maru-yu*) – is rife, and in electoral fraud, industrial espionage and the bribery of public officials Japan can compete with the best. Diddling train fares has almost reached the level of a national pastime. One spot-check by Japan National Railways discovered 30 per cent of passengers underpaying their fares, including a gentleman who had travelled 600 miles for Y180 and another who, over the course of two years, managed to make economies of Y600,000 at the public expense. In most areas of behaviour,

Stability: the Social Comparison

	Japan	UK	US	WG
Murders per 100,000 people	1.5	2.8	8.3	4.5
Rapes per 100,000 people	1.7	8.8	33.7	11.0
Robberies per 100,000 people	1.9	44.6	213.8	48.1
Arrest rate (%)	60.0	37.0	20.0	46.0
Policemen per 100,000 persons	182.0	251.0	254.0	314.0
Lawyers per 100,000 persons	10.0	94.0	194.0	61.0
Divorce rate (%)	1.3	2.9	5.3	1.9
Illegitimate births (%)	0.5	19.0	17.0	23.0

Source: Keizai Koho Centre, PHP Kenkyujo, Bureau of Statistics

however, the sense of social responsibility is extremely strong. Pedestrians never cross the road against a red light, even if there are no vehicles for miles around. They fear that children might watch and imitate in more dangerous circumstances. Although the Japanese enjoy their alcohol as much as anyone, the injunction against drinking and driving is strictly observed.

In the jargon of the social anthropologists, Japan is a 'shame culture', not a 'guilt culture'. That is to say behaviour is regulated not by individual conscience but by public acceptance, and discrepancies between what is normal, what is customary and what is moral scarcely exist. As Arthur Koestler remarked, in Japan 'the urge to gain the approval of others is not considered as vanity, nor is anxiety to avoid disapproval considered a sign of weakness, as in the West, but as the very essence of ethical behaviour'. Individualistic crimes against property and the person present a direct threat to the cohesion of the group and must therefore be avoided at all cost. On the other hand crimes which nobody knows about – which stay *ura* – do not count as crimes at all. Tax evasion and ticket fraud and other 'victimless' crimes have the additional merit of spreading the loss equitably amongst a wide range of people, a notion which accords with the Japanese predilection for burden-sharing.

Another type of crime likely to escape censure is that committed in furtherance of the interests of a particular group – a company, political party or family – but against the interests of society as a whole. The Japanese find it hard to condemn a man for placing specific loyalties ahead of abstract principle. A government minister arranges a huge loan package for a prospectless shipping firm with which he is closely associated; a political secretary lies on oath to protect his boss – these are deeds which every Japanese can understand. Interestingly, when Hitachi executives were caught buying stolen computer data in an FBI sting operation, the prevalent reaction in Japan was outrage at the conduct of the American middleman. By secretly co-operating with the authorities he had shamelessly betrayed the trust reposed in him.

Japan, like any other country, contains groups who have excluded themselves from the social mainstream. In structure and behaviour they are unmistakably Japanese. Their members have received the same powerful cultural imprint as everyone else, and tend to reflect, rather than react against, the conventional values of discipline and homogeneity. Indeed some of the misfits, marginals and rebels of modern Japan have close similarities to the products of Japanese management training.

In Mitsuo Yanagimachi's *God Speed You, Black Emperor*, a documentary film about motorbike gangs, new members are shown introducing themselves to the club in a close copy of the formalized 'welcome parties' standard in Japanese companies. Each stands up in turn and gives a short speech of humorous self-deprecation which is warmly applauded. Afterwards, one member is fined for persistent lateness. Thus is established the important principle that, even for hell's angels, rules are there to be obeyed. The 'bamboo-shoot people', sometimes misleadingly referred to as Japanese punks, are just as highly integrated. Every weekend teenagers dressed in the most bizarre – but still clean and tidy – costumes dance to fifties rock 'n' roll in the streets of trendy Harajuku. They move not with the liberated dithyramb of jive, but in carefully-regulated group formations, each 'section' having a 'section leader' who directs activities by bursts on his whistle. It is probably the most conformist display of youthful rebellion in the world.

Japanese gangsters, the *yakuza*, have a profoundly ambivalent relationship with the society in which they operate. They are officially despised, unofficially tolerated, and hugely prosperous thanks to scrupulous attention to the laws of supply and demand. Their *métier* lies not in bullion heists or kidnappings, or any other activities which would bring them into conflict with ordinary citizens. Instead they concentrate on fulfilling society's unacknowledged *ura* needs – prostitution, pornography, loan sharking, debt recovery, and so on. In the early sixties there were some two hundred thousand *yakuza* in Japan, the product of a massive recruitment drive launched in advance of the Tokyo Olympics. Now the number has declined to under one hundred thousand, but the gangs have become much leaner, more efficient outfits. They generate an estimated Y1.5 trillion of revenues each year, giving turnover per head that ranks with the best companies in the country.

The *yakuza* have shown considerable ingenuity in fitting themselves into Japan's tightly ordered society. One sub-species, called a *sokaiya*, helps to organize the annual general meetings of listed companies. He skilfully exploits the fact that, although shareholders are nominally the owners of a company, Japanese business culture accords them no rights at all. The absence of a takeover mechanism means that their views are at best an irrelevance, at worst a nuisance. Using time-tested methods of persuasion, the *sokaiya* ensures that no awkward questions are asked at the meetings and that proceedings draw to a swift and harmonious conclusion. From time to time there are disputes with management over remuneration for this service, in which case the whole business will be much less agreeable for all concerned. When the *sokaiya* cut up rough the results can be spectacular, with insults and chairs flying. Sony's 1984 general meeting, called at a time when the company was undergoing internal upheavals, lasted a record thirteen hours, with some abuse-laden 'questions' taking more than twenty minutes. Fortunately ructions of that nature are few and far between. The average length of a Japanese annual general meeting is just sixteen minutes.

The *yakuza* provide other corporate services too. They have long enjoyed close relations with the construction industry, for which they act as a kind of temporary recruitment centre. Every morning unemployed slum-dwellers and deadbeats are rounded up and driven off in open trucks to building sites, to be remunerated, at rather less than union rates, on completion of the day's work. In the crazily spiralling property market, an equally valuable function is performed by the *jiage-ya*, a specialist in persuading recalcitrant landowners to do the decent thing and sell out. Japan lacks a compulsory purchase system, and developers planning the major projects that Tokyo so badly needs are often forced to negotiate separately with dozens of smallholders who bought for a song in the dim and distant past. Each knows that the longer he holds out, the higher the value of his plot, since the developer will pay dearly to finalize the acquisition. Enter the *jiage-ya*, corrector of the market mechanism and moulder of a better Tokyo, with his loudspeakers, and Molotov cocktails. Thanks to his efforts, the site can be swiftly wrapped up into one land-parcel and made over, at a respectable profit margin, to the most efficient user.

In structure Japan's *yakuza* syndicates closely resemble her *zaibatsu* industrial conglomerates. A few powerful, highly centralized organizations command allegiance from a collection of regional groups. The Yamaguchi-gumi, Japan's most prestigious gang, has nearly six hundred 'affiliates'. Competition between the different syndicates is extremely fierce, and nearly all the violence perpetrated by *yakuza* is visited on their own kind. Strict hierarchy prevails within each group, with titles, promotions, and badges similar to the emblems worn by Japanese salarymen. There are other similarities too. After the 'group-leader' of the Yamaguchi-gumi passed away, a special 'general meeting' was called to choose a successor 'through consensus'. Unfortunately *yakuza* respect for consensus has its limits, and after six months the new man was voted out in a hail of bullets.

The response was swift and well co-ordinated. The deceased's faction established a special 'revenge department', and one of the most promising young hoods was appointed 'department chief'. He explained his battle-plan at regular press conferences, from where they were relayed to the general public in much the same terms as the marketing strategies of blue-chip companies. The lengthy gang war that resulted was fierce and highly complicated, both sides using their network of affiliations to undermine the other. It ended only after the 'standing consultant' of the dissident faction was sent on a business trip to Saipan, where some important construction projects were being discussed. He was found floating in the lagoon, with a bullet in his forehead, ribs staved in, and tongue and ears missing. *Yakuza* tend to be very tough negotiators.

Japanese newspapers take a great interest in the doings of the *yakuza*, solemnly referring to the higher-ranking gangsters as *kanbu* (management), and the offices from where they conduct their affairs as 'branches'. Scores of these places exist quite openly in each of the major cities, and in fine weather junior *yakuza* can be seen strolling about the streets outside, sunning themselves during their lunch breaks. Another uneasy correspondence with the *omote* world is the growing appetite of the gangs for overseas expansion. The largest gangs have moved aggressively into South-East Asia, Hawaii, and the west coast of the United States, drawn by the massive potential of the drugs trade. By exploiting the familiar Japanese advantages of financial might, strategic skill, and absolute dedication to group goals, they could well win a sizeable market share.

The *yakuza* have their own peculiar rituals and protocol designed to reinforce group identity, mostly derived from the samurai ethos. The customs of lopping off fingers to atone for mistakes is a less comprehensive version of hara-kiri. Surprisingly, in view of the incompetence revealed, *yakuza* are extremely proud of their stumps, although the practice is growing less popular due to its disastrous effect on golf handicaps. General behaviour is supposedly governed by the moral code of *jingi*, originally the classic principle of 'justice and benevolence'. In theory *yakuza* are courteous characters, who use long elaborate greetings when encountering members of other gangs. In practice the exchanges tend to be rather more abrupt and to the point.

Despite their avowed adherence to the fine old ways the *yakuza* present themselves to the world in a manner which captures modern Japan at its most gloriously self-parodic. Sartorially they favour loud double-breasted suits and fat ties that would cause anguish to the sensibilities of the brashest mafioso. Sun-glasses are *de rigueur* at all times of night and day, and the standard *yakuzamobile* is a huge American gas-guzzler, totally unsuited to the job of cruising through the crowded alleys of Japan's entertainment districts. Altogether, it is an image of gangsterdom that owes more to Hollywood B-movies than to Confucianist ethics.

Ordinary Japanese have a complex attitude to the law-breakers in their midst. According to popular legend the *yakuza* were a force for stability in the chaotic years following the surrender. To the young salaryman they are comic-strip heroes who provide a welcome source of wish-fulfilment. Their real-life exploits can be followed in the tabloid press, appearing between the sex and the sport and chronicled in much the same sort of detail. Yet *yakuza* are deadly serious. They have access to some of Japan's most powerful politicians and industrialists. They control many areas of the sports and entertainment worlds, and performers who displease them do not stay performers for long. Except when gang wars are raging, their relationship with the police is, in the Japanese diplomat's favourite phrase, one of peaceful co-existence and mutual understanding. They know their business, and pursue it with ruthless diligence. Organized crime in Japan is, like almost everything else, organized superbly well.

The Educational Pressure Cooker

From the outside the Japanese educational system looks like one of the marvels of the modern world. Whereas Western education systems are bedevilled by falling standards, class-room violence and conflict between government, teachers and parents, Japanese schools are consistently turning out disciplined, well-informed citizens, fully equipped for the business of living in a modern industrialized state. Yet matters are more complex than they first appear. The consensus within Japan is that education is in crisis, and it is a consensus that, rarely enough, unites politicians of left and right, bureaucrats, unions and ordinary families. The interim report of the government's Council on Educational Reform makes blunt reference to 'a state of desolation'.

The extraordinary achievement of Japanese education speaks for itself. Despite the complexity of the written language, 99 per cent of the population is functionally literate, compared with under 80 per cent in the United States. High-school students are two years ahead of their Western coevals in mathematics and physics. Most Japanese young people can read music, know calculus, and have a fair grasp of basic statistical analysis. Over 90 per cent of Japanese children finish high school, and one half of those go on to some form of further education, one-third to university. There are more universities in Japan than in the whole of Western Europe, and they produce double the number of engineers per head of population than the United States. The system fails nobody. It produces no long lines of alienated, unemployable young-sters; no crack-snorting behind the bike sheds; no heated debates about whether education is about personal development or social engineering or the pursuit of knowledge. That question does not even arise. For Japanese society and for the individuals who compose it, education has always been about survival.

Schools are helped by the aptness of the raw material with which they are provided. Japanese children display what is to foreign eyes an astounding willingness to follow teacher's instructions, and a neatness of appearance that is almost eerie. Every morning the trains are full of serious-faced eight-year-old commuters, clutching expensive satchels of identical design and looking as well-groomed as the salarymen sitting next to them. In the evenings they return in exactly the same condition – no muddy knees, no torn trousers, no flapping shirts. Girls wear blue and white sailor suits. Older boys wear peaked caps and stiff serge jackets with brass buttons running up to the neckline, a rig-out copied from nineteenth-century Prussia. Behaviour in class is correspondingly obedient, which makes the process of instruction simpler for all concerned. Teachers do not have to waste their time and energy bellowing for quiet or sorting out who hit who first. A US government study of Japanese education noted that Japanese children spend one-third more of their class time than American children actually learning. Since the school year is fifteen days longer in Japan, and children study extensively over weekends and vacations, it is hardly surprising that the level of attainment is so much higher.

If IQ tests assess anything beyond the ability to do IQ tests, then Mr Nakasone may have had grounds for his belief in the supremacy of Japan's 'intellectual level'. Comparative studies show that Japanese schoolchildren now have the highest IQs in the world. Their average of 111 is 7 points above the level of the forties and 10 points above the US and Western European standard. Only 2 per cent of Americans and Europeans have IQs above 130, which compares with 10 per cent of the Japanese population. More than two-thirds of Japanese have a higher IQ than the average European or American. The main factor behind the rapid improvement in test results since the war is the change in dietary habits. Another may be the boost to conceptual skills that comes from intensive maths teaching.

Despite the high regard in which education is held, the resources committed are not exceptional. Japan spends a smaller proportion of her GDP on education than is usual in the West, and teacher–pupil ratios are high. In state schools a teacher may be confronted with a class of seventy pupils, some of whom have to use binoculars to read the blackboard. Particularly within the metropolitan areas, the quality of the facilities is poor: ferro-concrete blocks containing cramped, ill-heated classrooms and dingy play areas. At one not atypical private school the tennis club has neither rackets, balls nor nets, and its members spend their recreation periods endlessly practising their serve movements in the gym.

That Japanese education accomplishes such great things has little to do with the system itself, much to do with the assumptions and expectations that society holds towards it. Teachers are important figures in every community, addressed as status superiors by those of much greater age and economic power. They receive a higher starting salary than engineers, and there are five applicants per vacancy. Traditionally the Japanese have venerated the processes of learning and those associated with it. Examinations were first held in the eighth century in order to select officials for the Chinese-style bureaucracy. Sugawara no Michizane, a scholar-courtier of the ninth century, is worshipped as a god, and latter-day examination candidates regularly visit the shrines to him that exist in every sizeable city. According to the Confucianist ideology of the Shogunate the acquisition of knowledge is the path to wisdom, and the great samurai of the period were all men of letters. In Meiji Japan, learning was imbued with a new patriotic intensity, as the ability to soak up knowledge became the key determinant of security and wealth. Indeed the whole Japanese achievement of the past 120 years is an extraordinary feat of concentrated study performed on the national scale.

The Japanese are an extremely pragmatic people, and the value they place on education does not stem from an abstract love of knowledge. In the 'curriculum vitae society', as they call the world they have made, education holds the key to all that is most desirable in life – power, wealth, social respect, identity. The best universities lead on to the best companies, lifetime employment, fat bonuses and generous welfare arrangements. The most crucial moment in the life of a Japanese male comes when he takes his university entrance examination. It would not be surprising if, as he sat down to his papers, the whole of his future life flashed before him. A sufficiently strong result will take him to a prestigious university, and on to a career with Mitsui or Sumitomo. Since university final examinations are little more than formalities, he may never have to exert himself fully. The race for life's glittering prizes will be over, and the kind of person he will be at the age of forty – his salary, the number of his subordinates, the quality of his house, wife, and, of course, children's education – will be more or less determined.

Only a limited number of jobs are available at Japan's top companies, but every year there is massive demand from hundreds of thousands of graduates. In 1960 only 58 per cent of middle-school students went on to high school, and only 10 per cent progressed to university. Now the corresponding figures are 94 per cent and 36 per cent. The success of Japanese education in raising the average level of achievement has created intense strains within the system, with ferocious competition starting from the age of three. Attendance at an infant training course will increase the chances of winning a place at a good kindergarten which, in turn, will mean improved prospects of success in the commando course of elementary school, middle school and high school. Each stage in the progress of the future salaryman is marked by a fearsome array of tests, known collectively as 'the examination hell'. Only the toughest, clearest-headed and most dedicated can win through to the ultimate goal of a place in a top-class university.

One of the main purposes of the education system is to act as a giant sieve, separating out the particles of optimum shape from those which, though perfectly adequate in quality, fail to make the quantitative grade. Since the occupation-era reforms filleted the structure out of what had been a highly class-conscious society, there has been no other method of distributing life's uneven rewards. 'Education mamas', awe-inspiring figures akin to Jewish matriarchs, strive to ensure that their sons (daughters do not matter) are the ones to pass through the mesh. The key statistic, which they monitor with anxious vigilance, is the 'deviation from average', the amount by which young Taro either falls below or surpasses the norm set by his fellows. In order that the latter should be the more likely result, he is hectored and cajoled into hours of extra study.

Once safely ensconced in university, Taro takes a four-year holiday in which he clears his brain of the huge volume of information soaked up over the previous fifteen. The Japanese recognize university as a well-earned interlude between the rigours of the academic and the working life, and it is quite normal for students to attend only a handful of lectures and seminars over the entire period. The rest of their time is devoted to part-time jobs, parties, hiking, lying around watching television, and mastering the art of drinking in groups. According to market research by Nikka Whisky, the average student devotes one-fifth of his waking hours to this last activity, the only element of his university career that will prove its value in later life.

Universities are graded strictly, not subject by subject, but on an absolute basis. The quality of the tuition they offer is irrelevant. What matters is prestige, as measured by tradition and confirmed by the stringency of the acceptance criteria. Students with their sights on a job with a blue-chip firm compete for places in the six national universities and the eight most prestigious private universities. Sending a student to a private university in Tokyo will cost a family Y1.8 million per year in fees and living expenses, to a national university about Y1.3 million. Those are sizeable chunks of the parents' income, which averages Y7.8 million for the age group. They will, however, be comforted by the knowledge that the long hard slog is coming to an end. Soon the education loans can be paid back, and after that Taro will be out in the world, and the tables turned. At last, he will be responsible for them.

Curiously for a country which takes business in such deadly earnest, Japan lacks a developed system of post-graduate business studies. Companies recruit their staff on graduation, when they are considered most malleable, and train them in-house. Holders of post-graduate qualifications in non-scientific fields may well have difficulty finding suitable employment. However, most blue-chip companies do send several employees to American business schools every year. Some of the large banks and trading companies have several hundred

MBAs, which suggests that Japanese managers are not such devotees of Japanese management techniques as is sometimes supposed.

The kind of business school which does exist in Japan reveals much about the Japanese conception of both business and schooling. Every day the *Nikkei*, Japan's most prestigious economic journal, publishes advertisements offering fortnight-long courses of 'training in hell'. Apparently tens of thousands of salarymen have already profited from intensive study of such subjects as 'bellowing in groups', 'mountain crow practice', 'singing at the railway station', 'answering forty questions quickly', and 'the twenty-kilometre midnight walk'. The establishments concerned are boot camps, designed to inculcate salarymen with the qualities that they will need most of all in their careers – extroversion, obedience and bottomless stamina.

The official education system cannot cope with the demands imposed. Since it is part of Japanese orthodoxy that there be no streaming, fast-learning pupils are held back by the dead weight of the average. At public schools the smallest details of the syllabus and teaching technique are decided by Ministry of Education fiat. Large class sizes mean that attention to individual strengths and weaknesses is impossible. As a result most parents rely on the highly developed unofficial system, the part-time cramming schools known as *juku*. Forty per cent of Japanese children attend *juku* at some stage; 90 per cent of those who live in metropolitan Tokyo; 100 per cent of those who enter Japan's three most prestigious high schools.

Juku training is a necessary condition for future success, so it makes sense to begin as soon as possible – at the age of five or six. By the age of twelve young Taro is already spending his evenings swotting up algebraic formulae and English irregular verbs, a 'certain victory' headband tightly circling his fact-jammed brain. Five years later he is poring over his *juku* textbooks into the wee hours, perhaps even attending one of the all-night *juku* sessions on Saturdays. After he has failed to pass into the university of his choice, as he almost certainly will first time round, he will spend a whole year at a special kind of crammer's known as a preparatory school. In contemporary slang, he will be a 'masterless samurai'. Of the 3700 students who each year enter Tokyo University, the gateway to membership of Japan's power élite, over half have been crammed at one particular preparatory school. Not surprisingly, its proprietor is a multi-millionaire.

Juku schooling costs money – Y800,000 per year at the best establishments. In business circles it is recognized as one of the most promising new service industries. It generates annual revenues of Y900 billion and has 100,000 registered participants, ranging from neighbourhood English conversation classes to large enterprises, one of which is even quoted on the stock exchange. Another, the Yoyogi Seminar, has over a thousand teachers, twelve branches, several dormitories, and its own bookstores, doctors, opticians, psychiatrists and on-line computer system. Teachers use sophisticated methods and equipment, and students are carefully streamed according to ability in each subject. The reverent designation of *sensei* (teacher) sits somewhat uneasily on the *juku* entrepreneurs, sleek individuals who drive Porsches, drink in the Ginza, and talk animatedly about marginal profitability and market share. Yet their success is the inevitable product of an education system that is as overloaded as the Tokyo tube system. In the words of Mr Yamada of the Yamada Gijuku, conventional schools belong to the world of *tatemae*, *juku* to the world of *honne*.

The all-consuming purpose of Japanese education is the same in *juku*, state, and private schools – the passing of examinations. The type of instruction dispensed is determined absolutely by the format and content of examinations. Topics that will not be tested in examinations do not exist. Lessons are exercises in the absorption and retention of information that will be tested in the computer-marked multiple-choice papers. Pupils do not ask questions in class. They listen, write and remember. Not only science subjects, but literature, languages and history are taught according to the best utilitarian principles of Mr Gradgrind. Pupils can pass their entire scholastic careers without once attempting an essay, an omission which may explain the clumsiness with which even well-known journalists structure their discursive writings. The humanist tradition of teaching people how to think is completely alien to the Japanese. Whether intended or not, the effect of the system they have devised is the exact opposite: to programme people to distinguish and obey command signals.

The priorities of Japanese education help to explain why, despite the vast investment of time, money and suffering, proficiency in foreign languages is so pitifully inadequate. The 90 per cent of all Japanese who graduate from high school receive six years of tuition in English, and a good proportion of them take supplementary courses at *juku* as well. The result is a nation of people who have an intimate knowledge of the different usages of 'I will' and 'I shall', but cannot give a comprehensible set of directions. The standard of attainment is unsurprising, since many high-school teachers, and even college professors, are themselves extremely poor speakers. They teach the subject not as a means of communication but as a code to be cracked. That was fine for Japan the eager absorber of foreign knowledge. It is of little use in negotiating the modern world's complex patterns of interdependence.

Japanese schools have been suffering from a steady increase in disciplinary problems. They are of nothing like the extent or seriousness of the troubles afflicting many schools in the West, as is demonstrated by the fact that classroom violence still makes headline news. None the less the situation is extremely worrying to people not yet inured to public disorder. Intelligent adults also recognize the less healthy aspects of their own society in the strange pathology – so different from the Western version – of the 'incidents' that have been occurring with increasing frequency. The most publicized cases of recent years relate to the pressures and distortions of the 'deviation from average' mentality, and specifically to the phenomenon of *ijime*.

Ijime, usually translated as 'bullying' or 'teasing', is an elaborate method of mental torture which leads to several deaths every year. According to Ministry of Education figures, 155,000 instances took place between April and October 1985. The usual pattern of events is depressingly consistent. A child weaker, fatter, skinnier, more intelligent, less intelligent, newly arrived from another school – in some obvious way distinguishable from his fellows – is picked on, persecuted, and turned into a living wreck. Acts of petty cruelty come naturally to children everywhere, but *ijime* stands out for its relentless and systematic quality. The victim has no prospect of relief. His closest friends will desert him when they see the process starting. He will be lost, probably for several years. The power of the emotions unleashed can be gauged from one of the rare instances in which the victims fought back. Two boys of quiet disposition were arrested for murder. After being forced to commit an obscene act in front of their whole class, they lured their tormentor to a secluded spot where they set upon him, shattered his skull with a hammer, and gouged out his eyes.

Ijime is a product of Japanese group dynamics. For a Japanese child, to be excluded from the group is to lose all sense of meaning and to suffer hideous mental strain. On the other side, *ijime* seems to perform an important function in strengthening the collective reality of the group – which can only define itself through reference to non-group members. Japanese adults often assert that *ijime* is an inevitable part of growing up. If true, that gives a disturbing view of the society they inhabit.

Ijime, the examination hell, the *juku* boom, and similar phenomena have alerted the Japanese public to some of the excesses of the system. Parents are worried about the distorted development of children's personalities. Much more important in the Japanese context, industry is worried that the traditional ethos cannot answer the needs of an information economy. Learning by rote and deviation-from-average grading provided excellent material for the manufacturing bases of the catch-up economy. Now, however, Japan is in less urgent need of obedient factory hands and salarymen than of software engineers, biochemists and service-sector entrepreneurs of the *juku*-owner species. The next generation of correct answers will not be found in multiple-choice papers set by the US and Europe, but must be worked out by the Japanese themselves, with the appropriate blend of perspiration and inspiration.

The first politician to understand the scale of the problem was Yasuhiro Nakasone who, with typical brio, turned education into a major political issue. In his first term as prime minister he set up the Council on Educational Reform, and gave the world the benefit of his personal views in subsequent general-election campaigns. As so often with Nakasone, the primary impulse was ideological, grounded in his disapproval of 'a borrowed system that has no roots in Japanese society'. Mitsuo Setoyama, his first education minister, went further, claiming that the growth of juvenile delinquency was directly attributable to US occupation policies 'aimed at crushing Japan's pre-war morals, customs, and traditions'. Nakasone himself favours the teaching of 'Japanese ethics', a value system that has had mixed reviews so far this century.

The various reports issued by the Council on Educational Reform were an uneasy mixture of the ideological and pragmatic approaches. Individualism, always a boo-word to the Japanese, was condemned for 'spreading selfishness'. A revival of moral instruction and the fostering of a Japanese identity were recommended. On the other hand, education 'should train students so that they can voluntarily analyse situations, make their own decisions, and take responsibility for their own behaviour' – abilities suspiciously close to the dreaded individualism. The left, ever vigilant for signs of incipient ultra-nationalism, was loud in its condemnation, but only succeeded in identifying itself with an unpopular status quo. The bitterest protests came from the radical Teachers' Union, which was concerned about the effect of teacher-assessment programmes on job security.

No doubt the debate will continue for years to come, but it is not easy to see what substantive reforms can be made. The tremendous logistical problems of instructing and evaluating millions of children of similar aptitudes and aspirations will obstruct any radical departure from the present factory-farm system. As long as the Japanese retain their powerful appetite for excellence, the life of the average schoolchild will continue to be, in the words of Yoyogi Seminar's corporate motto, 'competition every day'. Neither parents nor children have yet evinced much enthusiasm for creativity or Japanese ethics; only for Japanese success.

The Confucianist Company and the New Humans

At six-thirty in the morning the unknown Japanese hero rises from his slumbers. His wife has already been up for twenty minutes preparing his breakfast of hot *miso* soup, fried egg and banana. 'Never let your husband see your sleeping face' – that was the traditional injunction. Young married couples pay little attention to the customs that governed their parents' lives, but it makes obvious sense for the hero's wife to send him off to work well nourished and at peace with the world. He will be strengthened, both mentally and physically, and thus better able to win commendation from his superiors.

Over breakfast she murmurs a few points about their children's education, to which the hero grunts his assent. Their eldest son has just started elementary school, and she is thinking of supplementing his education with English conversation classes at a *juku*. Other parents have started even earlier, she explains, so they must be careful that the boy is not disadvantaged. The hero leaves all matters concerning education to his wife's judgement, merely taking note of decisions, like this one, that are going to cost serious money. He has one eye on the TV business news. Nothing much of interest – no product announcements either from his own company or any of its rivals.

In his bachelor days the hero lived in a tiny 'three-and-a-half-mat' room in the company dormitory. Now he lives in the company accommodation for married couples, a grey ferro-concrete block containing identical three-room apartments. There are fellow workers above, below, and to either side. At seventy-five square metres the living space is not exactly capacious, but the subsidized rent is only one-fifth of the market rate. The hero is saving up for a house of their own. The place he has in mind, a two-storey prefab in a nearby suburb, will cost eight times his annual salary and take the next twenty years to pay off.

At seven-thirty he is bicycling towards the station. At seven-forty he is sitting on the train absorbed in the business pages of the *Yomiuri Shimbun*. The hero and his wife live near a terminus of the national railway line, a location which has both advantages and disadvantages. It takes an hour and a half to the office, but at least he is assured of a seat if he arrives five minutes before departure. If he has a hangover, which is quite often the case, he can use the wait to swig down one of the stamina drinks – concoctions of caffeine, nicotine and some mild stimulants – that are sold at the platform kiosk.

After scanning the paper the hero closes his eyes and drifts off into a light sleep. He is vaguely aware that the girl on his left is lolling against his shoulder, which he doesn't mind, and that the middle-aged man standing in front has been jammed forward so that his groin is no more than four inches from the hero's face. That is less agreeable, and a further reason for catching up on his sleep. At the penultimate stop, instinct jolts him awake. He jumps out of the train, runs along the platform, and shoves himself into the first compartment, taking a position near the door. This compartment is much more crowded, suffocatingly so, but at the terminal its doors hiss open right in front of the escalator. Wriggling free of the press of bodies, he is first out of the train, then bounding up the steel stairs, marching crisply through the morning crowd, and into the concrete castle where he feels more at home than anywhere else on earth. At last, he escapes from the anonymity and formlessness of the crowd. At last, he begins to exist.

'Good morning, section leader,' chant the girls at the front desk. They bow, not as deeply as they would to a department leader, but still with a deference that no 'flat' (untitled) worker could command. He gives them his most authoritative grunt, and steps into the office.

The hero is section leader in the personnel department of Mitsutomo Electric Industries, proud possessor of top market share in microwave ovens, VTRs, photocopiers and numerous other useful devices for home and office. It is also one of the largest and most profitable companies in the Mitsutomo group, a mighty industrial empire comprehending everything from shipbuilding to the fast-food business. Wearing the Mitsutomo badge on the lapel of his blue Terylene suit gives him a special kind of pride. It lets the world know that he works for one of the most prestigious groups in Japan.

The hero joined Mitsutomo after graduating from one of the Big Six private universities. His degree was in economics, but actually he spent little time on academic work, attending only five lectures in his first year and none in his second. Most of his energy was devoted to arranging and enjoying parties and outings with friends from the hiking club, the volleyball club and the English-speaking club. It was excellent training for his career with Mitsutomo, since it taught him the complex art of Japanese social relations, mastery of which is essential for smooth progress through the corporate hierarchy. At the time he had no special interest in either electronics or Mitsutomo – in fact he tried the examination for Sumikawa Plastics as well. However, one of his seniors from the university hiking club had joined Mitsutomo two years before and strongly urged him to follow suit. He accepted, thus creating a subtle bond of obligation between them that has been useful to both their careers. His senior is now section leader in the Number Two Sales Department and a strong candidate for deputy chief. The hero always assigns the brightest new graduates to that section, and in return he gets full enrolment for the time-consuming optional training programmes he has developed.

The hero has been working in personnel for two years already and should be rotated into a new job next year. He doesn't want to be transferred to a distant branch office or, worse still, overseas. That would mean living apart from his wife and children for several years, an extremely inconvenient arrangement. Of course, if asked, he would accept with pleasure. To decline would be to join the ranks of the 'window tribe', lost souls who have been condemned by illness, incompetence or some other flaw to a life of dishonourable idleness. Therefore, he would prefer not to be asked. Much better if one of his superiors recognized his suitability for a post in the accounting department or (his secret ambition) the president's office.

In outline one day at Mitsutomo is much like any other. In detail every day has its own incidents and fascinations. Meetings, telexes, memos, accounts paid, budgets approved – all contribute to the grand metabolic process through which the corporate organism thrives and grows. The people with whom the hero works are family. The department chief is a father figure, gruff and omniscient. The girls who sit at his section desk are daughters. He keeps a discreet eye on their behaviour. Last week Sonoko wore the same outfit to the office two days in a row, a worrying sign. He would feel happier if she showed more interest in Nakamura, the young Kyoto University graduate who joined the section last year. He is a quiet, diligent fellow with excellent prospects in the company. After a few drinks he does an impersonation of Sammy Davis Junior that is truly impressive.

There is a break for calisthenics at half past ten. In every room in the building, loudspeakers blare out the 'Love is Blue' melody and a dulcet female voice instructs everyone to stop what they are doing. Even people using the telephone join in, bending knees, one, two, three, yes, now elbows. At twelve sharp, Mitsutomo employees surge into the streets in search of lunch. The restaurant is already jam packed, so the hero takes a counter seat away from his companions. Since his meal of rice and curry sauce, the only dish on the menu, is ordered, delivered, and consumed in five minutes flat, that is no special hardship. Anyway, a curry rice restaurant is no place for conversation. All that can be heard are the noises of eating and the squeak of chairs as customers give up their places to those waiting behind them.

Back at the office, time passes quickly. The hero prepares next year's recruiting schedule. He arranges a hot-spring holiday for the Number 5 Production Team at the Nagoya factory. He checks how many workers have undergone the annual health examination at the company clinic. In spare moments he studies a new psychological grading technique developed in the United States. Apparently all workers are either triangles, squares or circles, and it is important to group them carefully in order to achieve optimum efficiency. The department chief must be square. He has a square head. Nakamura, with his long bony arms, is probably triangular. Sonoko, on the other hand, is obviously round . . .

He finishes work at seven-thirty. The department chief has invited all members of the section out for the evening. That means that the hero will not have to pay for everyone else, as he would if he were the most senior man present. On the minus side, he will not be able to grumble and make jokes about his superiors, as he would if he were with fellow section leaders. Still, the department chief will not keep them late. He has recently started to sponsor a hostess from one of the plusher night-clubs, and must be on hand to take her back to the apartment he has provided.

At the first place they all drink saké. At the second they all drink beer. Their complexions get redder, the jokes funnier. Everyone knows that the department chief is itching to sing his favourite song to the backing of the 'empty orchestra' cassette-player. As the second in seniority, the hero has the job of preparing the ground. First, he takes the microphone himself, and gives a spirited rendition of 'I Left My Heart in San Francisco', taking care to miss all the top notes. Then, he entreats the department chief to efface the memory of his own humble performance. With great reluctance the department chief rises to his feet, loosens his tie, and croons the sentimental lyrics of 'North Country Spring'. When he has finished everyone in the bar applauds. The hostesses throw streamers. 'Bravo, departmental chief,' they all cry.

At nine o'clock Sonoko and the two other girls go home, or so they say. They are replaced by a couple of hostesses who pour drinks, brush thighs with fingertips, and make giggling noises at the appropriate moments. The men drink whisky and water, then brandy. The room gets hotter, the conversation bluer. '*Sukebe*,' the hero hisses to Nakamura, investing the word with a whole alphabet of sibilants. Everyone laughs. *Sukebe* means incorrigibly lewd in thought and deed. It is a compliment of the highest order.

When the time comes to leave they clatter unsteadily into the elevator, somehow remembering the correct order of precedence. The *mama-san* and the hostesses trill out elaborate farewells, as if parting with their dearest friends. The bill will be delivered to the company at the end of next month. It shouldn't be for more than £1000. In the cool mauve of the Tokyo night they go their separate ways, the department chief to his assignation and the hero and his subordinates to the last train home. An hour's snooze to the rhythm of the rails, then taxi from station back to home. 'Never go to sleep before your husband' – that was the traditional rule. The hero and his wife have no time for the old feudal ways, but it makes obvious sense for her to wait up in order to prepare his late-night bowl of noodles. It will help him to sleep easy, so that he rises fully refreshed, ready to face the challenge of another day.

There is an interesting story, possibly apocryphal, about the Bureau for the Promotion of the Forty Hour Week, a semi-governmental organization dedicated to the noble purpose of persuading Japanese companies to change their working habits. So zealous were the committee members in their appointed task, and so formidable was the challenge it posed, that they felt obliged to put in long stretches of overtime and extra hours on Saturdays and Sundays. The remarkable productivity with which guidelines, exhortations and blueprints were churned out soon came to the attention of high-ups in the bureaucracy, and all concerned received plaudits for their selfless devotion to the national good.

Despite all the committee's efforts, there has yet to be much change in the Japanese work ethic. Japan still works much longer hours than any other advanced economy. In large companies it is normal for male staff to remain at their labours until eight or later, night after night. If you wander through the streets of the Marunouchi business district at any time before midnight, you will notice lights blazing in the strategy departments of banks, insurance companies and trading houses. Given that the average commuting time in Tokyo is about eighty minutes, it is hardly surprising that half of all salarymen claim to suffer from chronic shortage of sleep.

Less than 30 per cent of Japanese companies operate five-day weeks. Civil servants, bankers and teachers are amongst the various professions who report for duty on at least two Saturdays in the month. The official minimum paid vacation is six days per year, and reputable companies offer at least a dozen. However, no salaryman worth his salt takes anything like a full allowance, most contenting themselves with a couple of days each at New Year and the summer Festival of the Dead. It is not uncommon for the most committed workers to surrender their holidays altogether.

As anyone who has worked in a Japanese office can testify, by no means all the long hours of service are usefully employed. Much time is devoted to meetings, the outcome of which has been decided in advance, routine document shuffling, and strengthening human relations – i.e., chatting. Senior executives spend considerable portions of their mornings browsing through the newspapers and arranging their golf schedules. Even the impressive amount of overtime is not quite what it seems. If a salaryman has to work through the evening his colleagues will feel duty bound to keep him company, perhaps opening a bottle of saké to help boost morale. It is doubtful whether 'workaholic' is the correct term for the Japanese. A more accurate designation would be 'kaishaholic'.

Kaisha is the Japanese word for company. If the two characters with which it is written are reversed, they read *shakai*, which means society. The salaryman's company is his society, providing the network of relationships that gives meaning to his whole existence. In comparison all other human activities are unfocused, lacking in reality. Private life, as Westerners know it, is merely a basic support system which enables the proper business of life to be carried out with the minimum of difficulty. Foreigners wonder if the Japanese work such long hours out of compulsion or out of genuine devotion to the job. The answer is neither. The Japanese worker defines himself in terms of his company, just as an Englishman would in terms of home and family. Surveys have shown that Japanese workers claim less 'pride in their job' than Europeans and Americans. That is because the concept itself is foreign. Tending machines or adding up rows of figures are activities worthless in themselves. What gives them meaning is the context in which they are performed.

The samurai salaryman has not always existed, nor is he to be found in all sectors of the economy. In the early years of Japan's industrialization skilled workers moved from company to company, selling their labour to the highest bidder. In order to secure a stable supply of this valuable commodity, powerful companies established the system of lifetime employment, with its concomitant welfare schemes and payment by seniority. Thus the two areas of a worker's life normally looked after by his union – job security and wage increases – were already covered. By deliberately recalling the social patterns of the feudal era, when swapping allegiances for a higher stipend would have been considered the basest form of treachery, companies were able to secure a loyal, well-motivated work-force prepared to forgo the maximization of current earnings for the promise of future benefits. The highly conformist and nationalistic atmosphere of pre-war Japan aided the process, as did the formation during the war of the inter-company Patriotic Associations. In the years of reconstruction, employers were again successful in cementing the ties between worker and enterprise. Company uniforms, oaths and anthems were introduced in order to promote company spirit.

The full Japanese employment system, with guaranteed tenure, company housing and payment by seniority, has only ever covered a minority of the work-force, probably under 30 per cent. In the small-company sector, patterns of job mobility are not very different from those in the West. None the less the systems and practices developed by the large companies, which are also by far the most profitable and efficient companies, have had an enormous impact on the psychology of work throughout the economy. They have created the idealized version of the Confucianist company, where everything and everybody remains in their proper place, and loyalty, self-sacrifice and harmony are the governing principles.

To the Japanese salaryman employment is not a necessary evil, Adam's curse, or a way of paying his way in the world. It is the provider of the individual's identity. The standard answer to the question 'What do you do?' is 'I work for X'. Whether as lathe operator, software engineer or accountant is a minor detail. Since triennial job rotation is the rule, the salaryman has very little attachment to the particular job he happens to be performing at a given time. What matters above all else is the company's prestige, which is his prestige. Indeed, strangers will often refer to him personally by the company name – as, for example, Toyota-san, or Mr Toyota.

In Japan's large-company sector the identification is extraordinarily intimate. Male employees spend their careers amongst the same set of colleagues. As bachelors, then as husbands, they live in company accommodation. They may well marry one of the soft-smiling girls who make their tea, clean their ashtrays and photocopy their documents. If they cannot manage it under their own steam, their department chief will probably be willing to set up an arranged-marriage meeting with a suitably qualified candidate of his own acquaintance. Once married, the average employee spends his evenings drinking and playing mah-jong with his colleagues, not returning home till the train schedules insist. He will take weekend holidays with them at hot-spring resorts, leaving his wife behind to take care of the children. Sometimes he will go to the company recreation centre. If he doesn't play himself, he can support one of the company's sports teams, often composed of specially recruited athletes who spend the entire working day at practice.

Altogether, the average employee will spend a greater

proportion of his life with company colleagues than with any other human being, including parents, wife and children. In most companies family members are expected to support, even participate in, the QC (Quality Control) movements which help to boost efficiency on the factory floor. Matsushita Electric has a model worker of Stakhanovite proportions who, in the course of his career, has submitted 20,000 suggestions for productivity improvements. He claims that the happiest time in his life is when he and his wife prepare new proposals together. Even in the public sector, where labour relations are more confrontational, high standards of loyalty and homogeneity are expected and enforced. Two employees of the national railway company who decided to grow moustaches found themselves transferred to careers in the toilet-cleaning division. Japan's largest ceramics company has taken its relationship with its staff one step beyond lifetime employment. In the cool, wavy bamboo groves between Kyoto and Osaka, Kyocera has established a corporate tomb. 'We have no religious troubles,' the managing director states serenely, 'since all our employees are of the Kyocera sect above all else.'

The restriction of the labour market has had obvious benefits for the Japanese economy as a whole. The motivation and adaptability of the work-force have reached remarkable levels. Companies have invested heavily in training programmes, secure in the knowledge that they are not financing competitors' future assaults on their market share. They have been able to get away with paying top technologists what are, by Western standards, measly salaries. Yet there are disadvantages as well. The labour market, like any other market, contributes to the efficient allocation of resources within the economy, passing on valuable information about the changing patterns of business activity. So far, the high degree of uniformity and flexibility amongst Japanese workers has compensated for the absence of such a mechanism, but the cultivation of knowledge-intensive and service industries will require greater fluidity and a stronger relationship between output and remuneration. Paying workers according to their needs, not according to their abilities, only makes sense when expectations, skills and the requirements of the employer all show little variation.

While foreign interest in the Japanese employment system has steadily grown, the Japanese themselves are becoming increasingly sceptical of its durability. A more mature economy offers slower promotion prospects for bright graduates. Today the average age of a section leader is thirty-eight, which compares with thirty-two in 1975. Longer life spans mean that enforced retirement at fifty-five, necessary to sustain lifetime employment, is growing less acceptable. Meanwhile rapid economic change is necessitating more flexible corporate structures. Hit by stagnant domestic demand and strong foreign competition, the Japanese steel industry has decided to lay off one-third of its entire workforce, making a nonsense of the guarantee on which corporate loyalty is based. The city banks, the most conservative companies in Japan, have started mid-career recruitment schemes in order to acquire communications and computer expertise. Japan's largest securities house has a man in his forties on its main board. In high-demand areas such as foreign-currency trading and software development, job-hopping has already become an accepted way of life. Even in ordinary manufacturing companies, personnel policy is shifting from the cultivation of loyal generalists to the training of specialists. Everywhere merit payments are occupying an increasing proportion of overall remuneration.

A succession of surveys carried out by government agencies and the mass media has registered a major change in the work attitudes of young salarymen. Unlike their elders they are primarily motivated by financial rewards. They believe they have little chance of reaching the top of the corporate hierarchy, and are keen to develop friendships and interests in the outside world. They find more satisfaction in mastering areas of specialist knowledge than in following orders. They are impatient about deferring to possibly less creative older men. They see nothing wrong in taking up their holiday entitlement. They are even willing to contemplate moving companies in order to improve their lot.

These developments, so far gradual and marginal, are more than just alterations in working conditions. They have profound implications for the whole of Japanese society and culture. The terms of the basic trade-off between the individual and the economic unit are starting to shift towards the Western model. Inevitably, attitudes are moving in the same direction.

Is the Japanese work ethic innate, or a conditioned response to special circumstances? It will take the rest of the century to find out, but the evidence points tentatively towards the latter conclusion. When carousing under the cherry blossom or staggering home arm in arm from 'forget-the-year' parties, Japanese salarymen lose all resemblance to the diligent constructors of the economic miracle. Throughout Japanese history there has been a strong tendency for the victors in the competition for wealth and power to lapse, often with remarkable speed, into idleness, ease and impotence. There have also been whole periods, such as late Taisho (1912–25) and Genroku (1688–1704), when the ethos of the city-dwellers turned from the accumulation of wealth to its ostentatious enjoyment. Perhaps it is not surprising that the Japanese who experienced the last war and its aftermath are looking with some alarm at the young people just coming to maturity.

These are the first generation of Japanese never to have known any condition but prosperity and the immediate satisfaction of their desires. As children they were weaned on television. They slept not with their brothers and sisters but in their own individual rooms. Their favourite food was cheeseburgers, their favourite hobby playing video games on the 'Family Computer'. They were fact-crammed at *juku*. Before going on to university they faced the Unified Entrance Examination, which requires students only to make blotches on multiple choice answer sheets and is 'marked' by a computerized scanning device. Their values are so different from those of their parents, indeed from those of their elder brothers, that they have been dubbed 'the new humans'.

What does it actually mean to be a new human? It means

to follow the mercurial shifts of the fashion world with rapt attention. Young males read glossy style magazines and use facial packs, lipsticks and eyebrow liners – not to shock, but with the same discreet skill as their girlfriends. It means to do your drinking in bars that look like film sets; to spend Saturday nights in mirror-plated discos, gyrating with your reflections; to enjoy scuba-diving, Hobson's ice-cream, and splatter videos. It means to use the telephone like an audio product and the Walkman like a neural implant. It means to measure behaviour not against broad social conventions but against the ever-fluctuating standards of a small, self-selected peer group. It means to take the serious things in life lightly, and the trivial things very, very seriously. A research group established by Hakuhodo, Japan's second-largest advertising agency, characterizes the breed as follows:

They do not want to make deep commitments because they do not want to accept the responsibilities that commitments require . . . They do not have a historical perspective. They know nothing of World War Two, post-war recovery, 'oil shocks', et cetera . . . The thought of not having enough money to spend bothers them. Unlike their elders, who equated not having money with having to struggle to survive, Japanese young people today often equate it with the possible loss of friendships . . . Without friends, they feel they would have no signposts in life to indicate the appropriateness of their attitudes . . . They worry that other people might consider them 'strange' or possessing some defect in character. Above all, they fear that not having friends means not having anyone to acknowledge their existence. Life without friends is tantamount to no life at all.

Contemporary Japan has certain features in common with the America of the late fifties and early sixties: a comfortable build-up of overseas assets; vistas of prosperity stretching out to the horizon; a growing challenge to rigid social conventions. The 'new humans'/'old humans' confrontation is strongly reminiscent of the generation gap of a bygone era. Naturally there are important differences as well. The new humans are notable not for their rebelliousness but for their meek conformism; not for their political radicalism but for their yawning apathy; not for their rejection of materialism but for their obsession with designer-brand clothes. To the Westerner the new humans are probably more comprehensible than the average salaryman. In Japanese eyes their values are deeply subversive of the most cherished national self-image. Loyalty, self-sacrifice, perseverance — to the new humans these concepts make no more sense than the tenets of State Shinto.

Yasuo Tanaka's *Nantonaku Crystal*, a novel which won the prestigious Bungei prize in 1981, gives a revealing if deeply depressing account of the new-human consciousness. A female student at a good university leads a life of listless, introspective hedonism. As deadened and alienated as the protagonist in an existential drama, she shops, telephones friends, stares out of the window, has perfunctory sex, drifts from day to day in a cloud of *katakana* brand names. In the book's last paragraph she gazes into the future and articulates her most powerful aspiration: 'When I'm in my thirties, I want to be the sort of woman who looks good in a Chanel suit.'

The new humans have received a fair drubbing from public opinion and the mass media. The main complaints are of selfishness, thoughtlessness and a general lack of moral fibre. Two young air force pilots, finding their fuel gauges flicking on empty, press their eject buttons, and ten billion yen of machinery goes screaming into a nearby hillside, narrowly missing a cluster of farmhouses. New humans in action, the press announces smugly. A promising sumo wrestler is granted the exalted status of Grand Champion, but then proceeds to lose the first three fights of the next tournament. He withdraws, claiming injury. No spirit of endurance, comes the derisive comment, typical new human. According to Akiyuki Nosaka, one of Japan's most respected modern novelists, new humans can be characterized as 'apolitical, egotistical, inarticulate, blindly conformist, lacking in enterprise, perseverance, consideration, imagination, and common sense, illiterate, cowardly, bigoted, clumsy and stupid'.

These are pretty serious charges, though not unfamiliar.

Ever since Plato's time people have been bemused and disturbed by the upcoming generation. Yet Japan's new humans really are different. The attitudes of the young are the most sensitive indicators of the changes their parents have wrought, and post-war Japan has experienced change on a momentous scale. Throughout, the guiding light has been a special kind of mass pragmatism which has required the sacrifice of individual satisfactions for the economic good of the group. When that is no longer necessary, what is supposed to replace it? No one knows, least of all the new humans, but it is they who must find the answer.

Trading partners hoping that more Western attitudes will result in a slackening of economic performance are likely to be disappointed. The new humans are certainly not lazy. Unlike their parents, they may not submerge their personalities in the corporate culture, but they direct the same obsessive energy into performance of the job itself. In their own way, they are just as perfectionist, just as hungry for information and novelty. In addition, they have some valuable qualities previously in short supply. From their unpredictability, fascination with games, and highly attuned sense of design, Japan may derive just what is needed to push her industrial development one stage further.

Women at Work

The first words that Natsume Soseki, one of Japan's greatest modern novelists, addressed to his prospective bride were brief and unsentimental: 'I am an intellectual and have no time to trouble myself with you. Please understand that.' To someone of Soseki's generation, born in the dying years of the Shogunate, there would have been little remarkable in the attitude revealed. *Bushido* – the way of the warrior – entirely lacked the female-venerating traditions of European chivalry. Polygamy had been common amongst the rich and powerful. Men of all stations had been permitted to divorce their wives for such trivial offences as talking too much, but women could not initiate separations of any sort unless their husbands had committed serious crimes. The basic legal unit of Japanese society was the *ie* – the house. Upon marriage a woman entered her husband's *ie*, thus abandoning her own identity. Young brides were treated as servants, to be bullied mercilessly by mothers-in-law if their performance of menial tasks was unsatisfactory. They endured, fortified by the knowledge that in thirty years their turn to vent a lifetime of frustration would come.

The occupation authorities abolished the *ie* as a legal concept, established female suffrage, and gave Japanese women stronger constitutional protection than exists in the United States, but they could not legislate away deeply-entrenched habits of thought. The participation of women in Japanese society is much less advanced than in other rich countries. Japan has no feminist movement worth the name. The standard assumption, held by both sexes, is that the primary purpose of a woman's life is to take care of her man and rear his sons.

Japanese women no longer walk ten paces behind their men, but they are still far from catching up. Sex-role differentiation is encoded in the language. The ideograph for man depicts 'power in the field', for woman 'womb'. The familiar word for wife means 'inside-the-house'. From an early age Japanese women are taught to defer to the men in their family, to cover up their mouths when they laugh, to cultivate a cutely submissive personality that will give subtle boosts to the male ego. The language they learn differs from male Japanese not just in tone and register, but in grammar and lexis as well. It is softer, more self-effacing. The concomitant attitudes – that ambitious women will not find partners, that sexual fidelity is only required from women – are just as deeply inculcated. In behaviour, speech and outlook, Japanese men and women are so far apart that they seem to belong to different races.

Today about one-quarter of marriages are 'arranged' – not blind like Soseki's, but suggested and prepared by a go-between. Almost all Japanese people experience at least one *o-miai* (honourable meeting, i.e., formal introduction to a marriage candidate) during their years of eligibility. These affairs are managed like job interviews, with detailed CVs being exchanged beforehand and personal characteristics woodenly enumerated before an audience of expectant relatives. The go-between, usually a person of considerable marketing prowess, supplies the build-up: 'Yasuko here is an extremely kind girl. Last month she helped her sick brother with his studies.' On Sunday afternoons in the coffee lounges of luxury hotels, the late luncher can hear couples being matched up all around him. Much more than the joining of kindred spirits is being discussed. Whether arranged or not, most Japanese marriages involve a complex adjustment of interests between two families, which must satisfy themselves of their broad similarity in status, outlook and income. Private detectives are widely employed to ensure that nothing is amiss. A grandmother with mental illness, a younger brother in trouble with the law – these are facts which would necessitate an abrupt termination of the whole process.

Social pressure explains why the vast majority of Japanese get married at or close to the 'ideal' age – twenty-five for a woman, twenty-seven for a man. If everything goes according to schedule, their second child will leave university just before the husband's retirement. Single people are not considered proper adults, since they are free of the network of obligation that defines adult life. Those who remain single into their thirties are known as 'left-over goods', the subject of whispered warnings and snide remarks. That is a particularly unfortunate condition for a woman, since the path to economic advancement is long and arduous. Japan's low divorce rate may be more the result of fatalism than marital bliss. In a survey of silver-marriage couples made by Taisho Insurance, only one husband in four and one wife in five said they would marry the same partner if they had their lives over again. Today's young people have higher expectations and much better chances to acquaint themselves with the opposite sex, but pressure to make the right sort of marriage, and quickly, is still intense.

Japanese weddings reflect the social importance attached to

marriage. They are secular, highly stylized events, attended not just by relatives and friends but also by ranking officials of the bridegroom's company, teachers and local worthies. The actual ceremony is conducted in private by a priest, often in a shrine or chapel within the hotel that hosts the reception. The priest may even be a hotel employee. The main point, however, is the reception itself – the interminable succession of speeches, the elaborate protocol and, most of all, the display of wealth. Some $14,000 is expended in the two-hour duration of the average wedding, and it is not unusual for ordinary middle-class weddings to cost as much as $50,000. Brides change their costumes several times, from kimono to white wedding dress to evening frock. Grooms may also switch from traditional garb to tails to white suit. Expensive seafood dishes are laid out before the guests, and on departure they are often handed gifts of a value above that of their own contributions. In recent years various histrionic details have been added to the basic routine – candle-light parades, dry ice billowing up from the floor, the happy couple descending from the ceiling in a gondola. It is pure *Kabuki*, designed to dramatize their induction into the adult world of money-making and money-spending.

After marriage, male and female territories are clearly separated. Within the home, Japanese women have complete authority, managing the household accounts and supervising the children's education. Husbands hand over their monthly pay packets and are given a regular allowance in return. They are not expected to cook or help with the housework, indeed any inclination to do so is considered a sign of insufficient virility. Japanese children are accustomed to never seeing their fathers on weekdays, and only for short periods at weekends. A husband's proper field of endeavour is the company, where he must labour to secure the best housing and education in his powers. His wife will forgive him the all-night mah-jong sessions, dalliances with hostesses and sex tours to South-East Asia just so long as that basic bargain is kept.

Women belong at home – that is still Japanese orthodoxy,

but no longer Japanese actuality. Between 1967 and 1984 the number of working women grew from ten million to fifteen million. Now more than one-third of the work-force is female, and one half of all married women are at work – rates equivalent to the European and American levels. Where the difference shows is in the type of job being performed. Only a tiny proportion of working women are in positions of responsibility. The overwhelming majority are stuck in repetitious clerical jobs that offer no prospects of advancement. The average Japanese woman earns only 52 per cent of the salary of the average Japanese man. That is a differential far wider than exists in any other rich country, and wider than in many developing countries as well.

Women take home so much less than men because they are dealt out of the system through which the greatest rewards are secured. Lifetime employment, with its steadily rising seniority payments and bonuses, is a male preserve. Most large companies encourage female employees to 'retire' on marriage, which usually means at the age of twenty-five. A single woman in her late twenties becomes an 'Old Miss', a source of embarrassment to everyone around her. She will probably know more about her department's work than her male colleagues, who are shifted to new postings after three years, but no Japanese man will take advice, let alone orders, from a woman. Younger women will resent her. Managers may feel guilty about failing to fulfil her parents' expectations. All will be discomfited by the ever-increasing gap between her status and experience.

When recruiting women many companies give preference to high-school graduates, who have seven years of work before marriage, over university graduates, who have only three or four. From the day that they join, female employees are separated from their male colleagues and given special training in bowing, answering the telephone politely, and offering tea to visitors. They are usually equipped with rather staid uniforms that must be worn inside company premises. Unlike single men, they are not provided with company accommodation, but are expected to live with their parents.

They receive none of the on-the-job training that turns fresh-faced students into loyal company men, nor are they acquainted with the invisible map of personal connections by which the world of work is navigated.

In the Japanese business world a good supply of winsome O Ls (Office Ladies) is a corporate status symbol, rather like thick-pile carpets or company helicopters in the West. Their function lies not in the series of simple errands they perform – photocopying, filing, coffee-making – but in the tone and atmosphere that they provide, and the sense of comfort they inspire in guests. Essentially they are decoration, like the various elevator and escalator girls in the department stores. They also represent a valuable fringe benefit for male employees too busy to go far afield in search of prospective mates. 'Internal procurement' is especially common at the large trading houses, and recruitment policies place due emphasis on looks and elegance.

There are compensations. Women are remunerated almost as well as men in the early stage of their careers, before the seniority payments start to count. They do not have to work long hours of overtime, take exhausting, inadequately funded business trips or invest large amounts of time and energy ingratiating themselves with superiors. They will not be obliged to move their abode to the other end of the country at the drop of a hat. They are not expected to exhibit the same degree of zealous company spirit. If Japanese women miss out on the rewards of the system, they also miss out on some of the heavy sacrifices it demands – which may explain why they have been less aggressive than their Western counterparts in forcing entry.

The 50 per cent of married women who return to work are overwhelmingly concentrated in the small-company sector, where they perform book-keeping and general office tasks of higher importance than routine O L duties, but are kept away from management positions. Many work on a part-time basis, which disqualifies them from union membership, bonuses and severance payments. Without doubt the sharp increase in their participation in the work-force has had a generally depressive effect on wage rates. Women also feature prominently in the retail and service industries. In the rural areas they are still to be seen working on construction sites and navvying on the roads. Female representation in politics and professions other than teaching is still at an extremely low level. Any successful woman immediately becomes an object of intense public interest, rather like the koala bears and other exotic animals which set off periodic booms in the mass media.

Change is coming, not due to any increase in female political consciousness – of which there is no sign whatsoever – but as a natural consequence of profound economic and social movements. Single women are now the most important group of consumers. With food and board provided by parents and no mortgages or education expenses to worry about, they have the highest ratio of disposable income in the population. They are superbly skilled at spending it – on clothes, cosmetics, foreign travel, hobbies and sports. Their contribution to domestic consumption, otherwise chronically sluggish, has been of vital significance, and shows the way to new patterns of economic growth. Japanese industry has quickly recognized the potential of the new market and, in order to exploit it to the full, has been forced to turn to the experts – the young women within its midst. Companies like Mitsubishi Electric and Suntory have set up all-female design and marketing teams charged with developing products for the female consumer. Female entrepreneurs have scored notable successes in the fashion, media and new service businesses. According to the Teikoku Data Bank there are now over 28,000 female company presidents. They are concentrated in small entrepreneurial companies in the service sector, now the most dynamic part of the economy.

In all sectors of industry slower growth is forcing Japanese companies to optimize the use of the assets under their control. Japanese women are highly educated, often more proficient in languages than their male colleagues, often less bound by convention and group-think. To consign them to lives of trivial, routine work represents, for both individual companies and the economy as a whole, an immense waste of human resources. Competitive forces will not allow it to continue for long. Japanese women are already making inroads into such vital new areas as biotechnology, now one of the most popular subjects for female undergraduates. Out of the 320 biotechnology researchers at Mitsubishi Chemical's central laboratory, 122 are female. The attributes of precision, flexibility and intuition, traditionally identified with Japan's women, lend themselves to the information industries on which the country's future prosperity depends. The success of the high growth era could not have been accomplished without a flow of disciplined, well-educated workers from the farms to the factories. The degree of success Japan achieves in the next stage of her development may well depend on the ability of companies to generate a new flow of talent from the women workers they already possess.

For all the repression of the Tokugawa era, women have made substantial contributions to Japanese history and culture. The native religion, Shinto, is one of the few to accord its central position to a female deity – Amaterasu Omikami, the reclusive partygoer and sun goddess. Early Japanese society was matriarchal, with female shamans holding sway. The Chinese *Wei Chronicle*, which gives the only contemporary account of third-century Japan, describes the unification of warring tribes by a ruler noted for her specialist skills in 'the Way of the Demons'. Empress Himiko is supposed to have had a thousand female slaves on her books, and permitted only one male – a provider of food and messages – to enter her headquarters. When she died a hundred young men and women went with her.

The balance of power shifted with the development of agriculture and the importation of Confucianism and Buddhism, both of which have strong misogynist currents. Although gradually stripped of political and property rights, women retained some of their influence in cultural life. The greatest work of Japanese literature, *The Tale of Genji*, was written by a woman. Hiragana, the basic Japanese script, was developed by women for private correspondence and poetry. Even kabuki theatre, in which the female roles are now taken by men, is reputed to have been started by an itinerant actress. The connection between the female and the divine, originating in the native religion, has not lost its power. Japanese ghosts are mostly the spirits of wronged women. Shrine attendants are exclusively female, as are the blind mediums still found in remote northern districts.

In modern Japan women have shown what they can do, given the chance, as diplomats, entrepreneurs, professional golfers, gangland bosses and, most recently, political leaders. They have also supplied the motive force in the conservation, civil rights and consumer movements. In literature and traditional arts, such as tea ceremony and calligraphy, they continue to transmit the finest elements of Japanese culture. Greater participation by women in matters of moment is sound economic sense. It may also put the Japanese back in touch with an aspect of their culture that has been comprehensively suppressed.

The Senile Citizens' Society

Things to do with a Gran.

In the case of a Gran with a sweet tooth. Spread honey or syrup (either will do) all over your crockery. When she has finished licking it off, the crockery will sparkle like new.

In the case of a Gran whose face is covered in wrinkles. How about using it as a puzzle? Pretend it's a maze and trace the lines with a toothpick. Alternatively, put an ant into one of the wrinkles and try to guess where it will come out.

In the case of a Gran who is no good for anything. Use her as bait when you go fishing for piranha or sharks.

The above are selections from a long series of Gran jokes created by Beat Takeshi, favourite comedian of the new humans. Somewhere between Lenny Bruce and Benny Hill, Takeshi has made his name by exploiting society's most sensitive taboos. In contemporary Japan, ageing, and the attendant prospect of ending up helpless, useless and unwanted, is one of the most sensitive subjects of all.

The life expectancy of the Japanese people is the highest in the world, exceeding even that of the long-lived Icelanders. For a man the average lifespan is now 74.8 years, for a woman 80.4 years. In 1947 the comparable figures were 50.1 and 54. In forty years the Japanese life span has increased by one half. The effects of this extraordinary transformation have yet to be fully assimilated.

In 1960, at the beginning of the economic miracle, only 5.7 per cent of the Japanese population was over the age of sixty-five, an extremely low percentage by the standards of developed countries. Although the average life span has since risen so dramatically, the depredations of the last war, in which two million Japanese died, have meant that the over-sixty-fives continue to form a relatively low proportion of the total population. However, the proportion is now accelerating at a rate which no other country has ever experienced. By the year 2000, over-sixty-fives will make up 15.6 per cent of the Japanese population, and by the year 2020, 21.8 per cent. This will be far in excess of all other countries except Sweden. It is the demographic equivalent of what happened to Ursula Andress at the end of *She*.

Competitiveness is certain to suffer. Throughout her rise to prosperity, Japan has had the great advantage of the industrialized world's most favourable balance of productive to non-productive population. As this alters, economic dynamism will diminish. Whether through public or private funding, the Japanese economy will have to devote fewer resources to capital investment and more to current expenditure. Increasing strains will be placed on the comparatively undeveloped social welfare systems. Today the public pension scheme has ten working members per retiree. Early next century there will be just three. The national health insurance scheme is likely to face similar difficulties. Already suffering from endemic over-prescription by GPs, it can hardly sustain a heavier burden. The Japanese government has not been blind to the problem and now makes patients foot 10 per cent of their medical insurance bills, but costs are bound to soar with the increase in expensive medication that old people require. The lifetime employment system will also come under pressure. Retirement at the age of fifty-five is acceptable if the average life span ends ten years later, less so if there are another twenty years – equivalent to two-thirds of a man's working life – still left to run.

Perhaps the most profound effect will be on social structures and attitudes. Confucianism, the dominant ideology of Tokugawa and Meiji Japan, considered filial piety to be the primary virtue. Children were taught exemplary stories about heroic sons who sacrificed all for the sake of their aged parents. In contemporary Japan this aspect of Confucianist thought, like many others, retains a powerful influence. 'Respect for the Aged Day' is a public holiday, and the Japanese political and business world is controlled by men in their seventies and eighties. It is not unusual to hear of young men giving up promising careers in order to return to their native villages to support aged parents. However, there is another tradition in Japan, older and darker. This is the tradition of *ubasuteyama*, literally 'the mountain for throwing away old women'. Into the last century this form of forcible euthanasia was practised in the impoverished mountain districts of central and northern Japan.

Can Japan's aged expect reverence from the generation they brought into the world, or will they be consigned to the modern equivalent of *ubasuteyama*? The dislocations caused by rapid economic growth have played havoc with Japan's extended family system. The proportion of nuclear families has risen from 44 per cent in 1960 to over 60 per cent today, and the average family size has declined from 4.8 persons to 3.3 over the same period. While some recent opinion polls reveal a strong yearning for the good old days of the three-generation family, there is little prospect of much change in the established trend. The economic context favours greater mobility, and family-centred relationships have been replaced by the dominant structure of the Japanese company. That values are changing is obvious from the popularity of Takeshi and his jagged humour. A generation ago no one would have found him funny.

In comparison with Europe and America, Japan provides little in the way of special amenities for the aged. Government-run old people's homes are non-existent, and the small number of private institutions are exclusive and exorbitant. The only recent development has been the proliferation of gateball, a sport which can best be characterized as croquet without the excitement. It says much for the obsessionalism and competitiveness of the Japanese that this gentle pastime has already been invested with the full paraphernalia of league tables, gruelling practice sessions and expensive uniforms and equipment. There have even been suicides by players ashamed by their poor scores.

Predictably, Japan's omniscient bureaucracy has taken an active interest in the coming of the ageing society, with institutions ranging from the Ministry of Construction to the Police Agency churning out detailed reports on the topic. The boldest and most controversial is the Ministry of International Trade and Industry's Silver Columbia Programme, which, in all seriousness, has been timed and named to echo the five hundredth anniversary of the discovery of America. MITI's plan is to encourage Japan's grey army to emigrate to climes where the cost of living is more reasonable, such as Australia, Brazil or southern Europe. The government and the private sector will combine to establish mini-colonies, with exclusively Japanese populations, Japanese property rights, Japanese food and television and, of course, Japanese as the lingua franca. Indeed, apart from the weather and the prices, there will be no evidence that the happy retirees are not living out their lives in a tranquil, well-equipped Japanese town.

Ironic that Japan, herself so negative to immigrants except as breeding-stock in depopulated areas, should now be promoting population transfers. Still it is an interesting idea, which should settle complaints from foreign businessmen about lack of market access. The market would be right there in their midst. Whether the project will ever come to fruition depends on the attitudes of those for whom it is designed. In MITI's survey on the subject 6 per cent of the sample expressed a desire to live abroad and 47 per cent said they would consider it 'if recommended to do so by their companies or the government'. Thus, on the face of it, half of the one million Japanese workers who stop working every year are potential émigrés. However, the response as gauged in private conversation is much less favourable. Comparisons with *ubasuteyama* and Chairman Mao's 'useless mouths' policy are frequently drawn. More profound criticisms focus on the irony of the situation. MITI, the grand architect of Japan's export-oriented industrial structure, is now advising those whose herculean labours built it up that they would be better off following the stream of manufactures overseas. The result of all the years of unstinting sacrifice has been the creation of a super-competitive economy with poor social amenities and the highest cost of living in the world. As for the benefits of the super-powerful yen, they can only be experienced elsewhere.

Whatever the surveys might suggest, it would be right out of character for Japan's elderly to board MITI's *Santa Maria* and sail off to peaceful decrepitude in distant parts. Reversing the trend in other countries, Japanese workers and unions are keen to raise the retirement age, and it is not unusual for ex-salarymen to take up second careers as caretakers or car-park attendants. That is partly due to necessity: most small and medium-sized companies release their employees at the age of fifty-five with a lump-sum payment, but no pension. It is also due to a strong desire to remain within the productive economy. Workers are so unaccustomed to leisure and private time that they cannot cope with the long blank waiting for them outside the controlled environment of the company. Retiring from being Japanese is not so easy.

5

Media: Directing the Deluge

Youthfully stride through the early morning breeze, newsboys!

Official slogan for Newsboys' Day

All human affairs are rooted in greed and lust.

Motto of the *Shukan Shincho* magazine

As one might expect of a people so literate and so hungry for
information, the Japanese are avid consumers of printed
matter. Salarymen spend their train-time reading. In lunch
breaks they fill the large city bookstores, packing the lanes
between displays almost to rush-hour density. Even the tramps
slumped in the underground corridors squint rheumily at
papers they have filched from trash bins. The bare statistics
are impressive enough. Newspaper circulation per head in
Japan is the highest in the world. The *Yomiuri Shimbun*, the
largest daily in the non-communist world, publishes nine
million copies of its morning edition and five million of its
evening edition. There is a plethora of general-interest magazines, many of which count their circulations in the hundred
thousands. In order to cope with the scale of consumption an
efficient recycling system has been devised through which
households can exchange the mounds of newsprint they ex-
trude for rolls of toilet paper.

More important than the volume is the content of what is
being so voraciously devoured. Although the *Yomiuri* has a
circulation greater than those of the *Sun, Mirror* and *Star*

combined, it is a serious newspaper. Japan's quality press is one of her greatest national assets, making a major contribution to the spread of shared values and objectives. Three-quarters of all Japanese households take a quality national paper, which provides a comprehensive analysis of domestic and world affairs. As a result the average Japanese is highly informed about the economic and technological forces that act upon his life, far more so than the average European or American. It is a rare London cabbie who has a sound grasp of events in the world currency markets or upcoming shifts in his country's population structure. For his Tokyo equivalent it would merely be par for the course.

Japan's quality press takes very seriously its mission to inform. The scrupulous presentation of facts always comes before opinion and comment, a priority that is probably encouraged by the absence of signed articles. There are no star reporters, no centre-page polemics, no Japanese Bernard Levins or George Wills. Indeed the most famous column in the whole Japanese press, the 'Voice of the People' in the *Asahi Shimbun*, is anonymous. If a Japanese reader wants controversy, there is plenty of it in the weekly and monthly magazines. The most important demand he makes of his newspaper is that it communicate necessary information as clearly and rapidly as possible. The four major newspapers are far from neutral in their political outlook, but their prejudices rarely spill over into the news coverage. Articles on the semiconductor trade dispute or the New Kansai Airport or developments in French politics will look much the same in all the four papers. Even within one paper the treatment of different topics shows hardly any variation. The same painstaking assembly of precedents and comparative statistics can be found on both the economics and sports pages. The consequence is a certain flat uniformity which most Western readers would find unacceptably dull. However, when it comes to the absorption of potentially useful facts the Japanese have an extremely high boredom threshold.

The companies behind the quality newspapers are huge information-gathering conglomerates which, in typical Japanese style, engage in ferocious oligopolistic competition. The *Yomiuri Shimbun*, for example, has over 400 bureaus within Japan, an editorial staff of 3000, and uses communication satellites to print same-day editions in Europe and America. Its other interests include Japan's most famous professional baseball team, a nationwide television channel, a 150-acre amusement park, a travel agency and a symphony orchestra that has featured performances by Rubinstein and Ashkenazy and been conducted by Mstislav Rostropovich. The Japanese press has played an invaluable role in the collection, sifting and presentation in digestible form of information from foreign countries. Thanks to its endeavours people who have never travelled abroad and have little knowledge of other languages can familiarize themselves with the latest technological breakthroughs, economic heresies or new-wave rock bands. Several provincial newspapers have over a dozen overseas bureaus, and the *Asahi Shimbun* has more than three times as many foreign correspondents as *The Times*. The Japanese believe that information is power, and they intend to secure as much of it as possible.

The quality papers publish seven days a week, with thinner evening editions appearing every day except Sunday. The printing process is carried out in several regional centres simultaneously, and the largest papers now transmit by satellite to the US and Europe for same-day publication. Thanks to modern communications technology, introduced by the Japanese in the mid seventies, colour photographs can be reproduced to decent resolution, and typographical errors are almost unknown. In format there is little difference between the three largest dailies. The morning *Yomiuri* has twenty-four pages, about eight of which are given over to hard news. The rest contains features, readers' letters and financial information. By the standards of the Western press the proportion of advertising space is extremely low. Like the other papers the *Yomiuri* always carries a serialized novel, often by one of Japan's leading authors. On Sundays it publishes a high-quality colour reproduction of a famous painting. The comment that accompanies it carefully explains the salient points of the painter's life, the school to which he belonged, and the accepted critical opinion of the work in question. The Monday evening paper contains a couple of pages of readers' *haiku* verses, together with comments by various famous practitioners of the art. The total *Yomiuri* package is comprehensive, well written and presented, intensively civilized. The *Asahi* and the *Mainichi* offer similar packages, albeit with slightly different political emphases.

The journalist working in the quality press may never become a household name, but he will share in the social prestige of his institution. The figure he cuts is far from the standard image of the Western journalist. He is a superior sort of salaryman, committed to the same company for his entire working life. Even junior reporters travel around Tokyo in company limousines adorned with little red flags. For longer trips they use the company helicopter. The respect that the Japanese have for their press manifests itself clearly in Gallup's International Value Survey. Significantly *fewer* Japanese than Europeans and Americans claimed confidence in the armed forces, parliament, major companies, civil service and education systems of their respective countries. The only institution in which a greater proportion of Japanese had confidence was the press. The result is not as surprising as at first it may appear. The Japanese have well-placed confidence in the quality of products marketed by their major companies, but equally they do not expect those companies to act in any other than their own corporate interests. The same goes for politicians and civil servants. The quality press, on the other hand, is expected to maintain a disinterested sense of social responsibility.

Not all Japanese newspapers enjoy the same standing as the four great dailies. The difference between the quality papers and the tabloids is a typically Japanese phenomenon, a classic of *omote* and *ura*. A foreigner who formed his impressions only from the quality press would be driven to the conclusion that Japan is a nation of earnest, nature-loving, moderately left-wing *haiku* enthusiasts whose major interest is cross-cultural understanding. Anyone who relied solely on the tabloids for his information would assume that the Japanese are obsessed with perverse sex, plane crashes and the doings of gangsters. In itself that is hardly unusual – the press in most Western countries displays similar extremes. What is surprising and of huge significance is that exactly the same people read both sorts of newspaper. Few Britons read both the *Sun* and *The Times*. They are directed at entirely different markets. In Japan a similar cultural gulf is effortlessly bridged. Straphanging to work on the morning train, you soak your sleep-fugged mind in the conventional wisdom of the *Asahi* or the *Yomiuri*. Sixteen hours later you need the sensationalism of the tabloid press to keep your encephalic circuits a-buzz.

In scurrilous, scabrous attention to the lowest common denominator Japanese tabloids admit no superior. They pander, quite literally, to the Mr Hyde in every loyal, work-worn salaryman. The *Nikkan Gendai*, which sells one million copies a day, regularly carries three hard-core pornographic serials and a cartoon strip featuring the somewhat predictable adventures of a sexual organ. In every issue it reviews a couple of the city's multitudinous houses of prostitution with the fine discrimination that other papers might reserve for restaurant or theatre criticism. In another column a face-reader makes use of his mysterious skills to divine the sexual characteristics of well-known singers and actresses. Like many *Gendai* writers he gives the impression of being a gynaecologist *manqué*. The front page of the paper usually contains violent abuse of the Liberal Democratic Party (LDP), the back page violent abuse of the Yomiuri Giants baseball team. In comparison the stupid-and-proud-of-it heartiness of the British tabloids seems positively refreshing.

The history of the Japanese press is quite short. The Tokugawa regime provided a far from hospitable atmosphere for the free dissemination of news, the only unofficial media being the *kawaraban* handbills posted up on walls and street corners. These were filled with lurid accounts of murders, scandals and disasters, much the same stuff as is peddled by the *Gendai* and its ilk. The first modern newspaper published in Japan was produced by an Englishman in Nagasaki in 1861. In the 1870s the *Mainichi, Yomiuri* and *Asahi* were founded, and later developed into mass-circulation dailies. The rapid growth of the national press coincided with Japan's great surge of modernization. Newspapers introduced and explained the rush of strange new ideas that were creating such huge transformations in Japanese society and which it was essential to understand in order to prosper.

The *kawaraban* had been downright subversive. Japan's national press began its life as a vehicle for the political parties striving against the Meiji autocracy. It soon developed a more mature and objective attitude to news reportage, but through the early part of the twentieth century regular confrontations occurred between the press and civil authorities over imagined slights to the Emperor, insufficient patriotism, et cetera. A free press inevitably meant less control of government over people, an eventuality that the militarists of the thirties were no more prepared to countenance than the Shogunate had been. As far as the ultra-nationalists were concerned, publication of the wrong sort of comment was ample pretext for assassination. Eventually the military took direct control of the press and turned it into a propaganda machine dedicated to glorifying the just war. Newspapers were compulsorily merged, and journalists were forced to print what they knew were false accounts of heroic naval victories and 'tactical re-dispositions'.

The occupation authorities clearly understood the power of the Japanese press. In contrast to the policy in Germany, existing newspapers were allowed to continue in business, although several staff members had been named as war criminals. Pre-publication censorship was imposed, first to prevent a resurgence of nationalism, then to stifle leftist opposition to GHQ policy. Again, newspapers were being deliberately used to shape public opinion. When the occupation ended, the triple alliance of bureaucrats, businessmen and conservative politicians became the new establishment with a new set of priorities to be promoted.

History has moulded the Japanese press and helps to explain

its uneasy, ambivalent relationship with authority. In Japan there is no tradition of objective inquiry, just the simple alternative of subservience or animosity to the controlling interests of the day. Journalists found little difficulty in switching from support of a *zaibatsu* industrial group in the twenties, to bellicose nationalism in the war years, to high-minded leftism in the fifties. In contemporary Japan the quality press usually adopts an adversarial attitude to the government party, but it can always be relied on to place the national interest ahead of an abstract public right to know. The men who sit on the editorial boards of the great newspapers believe that information, like liberty in Lenin's dictum, is precious enough to need strict rationing.

The rationing function is performed with great efficiency and discretion by the highly Japanese institution of the press club. A Japanese press club is not a place where hard-drinking journalists relax and swap stories. It is a news factory, where information is assembled and wrapped for consumption. All ministries, government agencies and political parties maintain, and usually fund, press clubs on their own premises. Every day unattributable announcements, interviews and briefings are made at regular club meetings attended by the same group of accredited reporters. Since Japanese media organizations have huge numbers of staff at their command, they can detail different specialist reporters to, for example, MITI and the Ministry of Finance, or to the Abe and Miyazawa factions. Inevitably the result is a close community of interests between the originators of news and its disseminators. No important institution would think of announcing a newsworthy development outside the familiar atmosphere of its own press club. No journalist would think of ignoring what he has been told. Consequently many newspaper stories are little more than reprints of press releases, usually introduced by some vague and pompous phrase such as 'It was recently made clear that a plan has been established to . . .' It is the unmistakable voice of power, booming down from the mountainside.

The closest equivalent of the Japanese press club in the non-communist world is the British parliamentary lobby, a docile, politically reliable in-group charged with conveying signals from 'informed sources'. Membership of a press club is a privilege. Reporters from weekly magazines and commercial TV channels are excluded, and the foreign press in Japan has been waging a long and valiant struggle to secure limited rights of attendance. Existing members are naturally anxious to guard their information monopoly. More important, foreigners do not understand, and magazine writers will not heed, the complex unwritten code which establishes the extent of the news that is fit to print. Expulsion is a sanction rarely employed, but all reporters know that such an eventuality would immediately cut their access to the most important news of all – what the authorities are planning to do next. That is a competitive disadvantage which no newspaper could tolerate for long.

Police bungles, boardroom squabbles, the problems of the outcast and minority groups, the political manoeuvring of shady tycoons, the execution of criminals – these are just some of the stories that will never see the light of day in the straight press. Investigative journalism, as it is understood in the West, is used only against victims who are powerless or those who have been marked for a fall. An instructive example of how the press reacts when the *ura* side is suddenly flipped over was provided by the Lockheed affair. Every reporter working on LDP affairs must have long been aware of the extent of political corruption, but only after the story had been broken in a non-club magazine, and then taken up in the foreign press, did Japan's quality newspapers feel ready to enlighten their readership. From then on, of course, they pursued the story with unrelenting zeal, detailing battalions of reporters to the task.

Despite their incorporation into the power structure, Japan's great newspapers have traditionally taken a leftist line, especially on military and diplomatic issues. That most British newspapers hold conservative political attitudes is not really surprising. They are usually owned by rich entrepreneurs, and their survival depends on their ability to respond to market forces. In Japan the natural pose of a newspaper is high-mindedly critical of government policy. Until the early eighties the Big Three were all leftist, pacifist and critical of the LDP. It was often said, with much justification, that Japan had only one newspaper, for there was hardly any distinction between them either in reportage or in editorial policy. However, a strong personal connection between Yasuhiro Nakasone and top management at the *Yomiuri Shimbun* swung the free world's largest paper firmly behind the LDP, thus breaking the rather sanctimonious homogeneity of the press as an institution.

The *Asahi Shimbun* is Japan's self-appointed conscience and guardian against militarist revival. It still provides far more credible opposition to the LDP than any of the political parties, regularly thundering out its displeasure with Mr Nakasone and Mr Takeshita and the rest. No matter that the electorate has chosen to vote the LDP into office on every one of the last twelve general elections. The *Asahi*'s editorialists continue to display absolute confidence in their knowledge of 'the national consensus' and what 'the voice of the people is demanding'. Despite the vehemence of its attacks on the LDP, the *Asahi*'s posture is neither socialist nor at all radical. It would not dream of disturbing the complex set of economic trade-offs and accommodations on which Japan's prosperity is based. Instead, *Asahi* journalists concentrate on highly abstract issues, such as the breaching of the 1 per cent limit on defence expenditure, official visits to Yasukuni Shrine, and the enactment of anti-spy legislation. The most serious issue of all is the war experience. The *Asahi* regularly serves its readers up with graphic descriptions of the suffering that their countrymen underwent. To ram the point home, editorials stress the merits of 'peace diplomacy' and make strident criticism of politicians who favour a stronger military presence.

The *Asahi*'s pacifism has become an intellectual reflex, an assumption from which other arguments flow. Because war is horrible and because there are American bases in Japan, the *Asahi* is anti-American. Similarly, because it opposes increases in defence spending, it must take a relaxed view of Soviet activity in the Far East, which in turn leads to a touching faith in the good intentions of Soviet leaders. When that faith is betrayed, the *Asahi* reacts more in sorrow than anger, as was demonstrated by its editorial on the shooting down of the Korean airliner in 1983: 'What we should do now is not to let the Soviet shooting fuel tensions between East and West, but to request that the Moscow Government show its sincerity by identifying the cause of the mishap quickly . . .'

If all the world were as sincere as the *Asahi*, there would be fewer of these unfortunate mishaps to worry about. Tension is always the enemy, and tension is, almost by definition, caused by two sides to an argument failing to achieve sufficient 'mutual understanding'. On the Korean peninsula the position is the same. The North is presented as a land of smiling workers and traditional folk-dances, and its every declaration of peaceful intent is warmly applauded. The occasional relapse, which may include the assassination by claymore mine of half the South Korean cabinet, must never be allowed to fuel those distressing tensions.

Outside the press clubs, far from any considerations of historical role or social responsibility, stand Japan's weekly magazines. Salacious, libellous, utterly unreliable, they are the most vital of all information sources for anyone who wants to know what the Japanese are really thinking. Between the sadistic cartoons and the brothel reviews, they feature material that the conventional press cannot print, concerning the endless struggles for power in the LDP factions and the boardrooms. Most of the important scandals of recent years have been broken in either the weekly or monthly magazines. If they did not exist it would be impossible to make head or tail of political developments and many corrupt businessmen would still be prospering. Altogether there are several dozen weeklies, all competing strenuously to deliver new tales of greed and lust. They provide the stimulus that keeps the quality press from deteriorating totally into a complacent and compliant adjunct of the power structure. In fact the three great dailies have affiliated weekly magazines which pump out journalism of the yellowest hue. The Japanese have access both to officially processed 'club' reality and to the murky rumour-world of the weeklies. Neither is adequate on its own, but in combination they enable the discriminating reader to form a reasonable picture of what is actually going on.

The women's weeklies are interesting mainly for the insight they offer into the psychology of the modern young lady. Predictably, acres of space are devoted to the quotidian activities of pop stars and actresses. Equally predictably there are countless articles on how to marry rich doctors, how to force your boyfriend to propose, how to hide your extra-marital affairs, how to catch out your husband in his, and so on. More startling is the obsession with deformed babies, amply catered for by regular photographic supplements. The new humans are now looking beyond movies for their jolts of modern horror. In the letters columns bizarre sexual experiences are described in the sort of detail that would pass muster in the tabloid press. Indeed, one of the men's magazines has taken to reproducing a weekly choice of the most lubricious, evidently recognizing that its own writers would be hard pressed to dream up anything more titillating. At one stage there were even complaints in the Diet about the kind of material being set before the young flowers of Japan. The politicians did not seem to realize that it was the flowers themselves who were doing most of the writing.

No overview of the weeklies would be complete without mention of the phenomenal success of two particular magazines, slightly different in character from the conventional salaryman-oriented product. Both *Focus* and its imitator *Friday* have circulations of over one and a half million copies per week, making them easily the largest-selling general-interest magazines in Japan. Such is their popularity that they are usually unobtainable three days after publication. Launched in the early eighties, they have both reflected and helped to establish the mood of the decade. Everyone reads them – schoolboys, secretaries, Buddhist priests, company presidents, *sushi*-shop proprietors. The appeal they make is to a very simple and very common human impulse – voyeurism. For the reasonable price of Y150, you get a Japanese version of the *News of the World* with the production values of *Life*: thirty pages of large, high-quality photographs and gleefully facetious text, each topic headed by a fashionable Janglish expression: 'event', 'street', 'out of bounds', 'café', 'catch'. Altogether, they provide enough evidence of other people's suffering to get you through another week.

The features that most entertain the schoolboys, priests and secretaries are sex, death and fame, preferably in some sort of combination. The naked body of a dead actress is the perfect picture, and one that can be rustled up with surprising frequency. Other well-remembered achievements of the 'two Fs' have included glossy photographic essays on the headless body of Yukio Mishima, the bodyless head of a railway suicide, the death agonies of a poisoned Korean schoolgirl, sado-masochist perverts giving each other enemas, an Arab being torn apart between two Jeeps, and a Filipina AIDS victim (nude, of course). The regular fare includes stills from the latest pornographic videos, colour close-ups of mangled car crash or plane crash victims, and sneak shots of actresses and sportsmen emerging from love hotels with the wrong person. The purveyors of this fare are far from being back-street smut specialists. On the contrary, they are amongst Japan's largest publishing houses, companies with long and distinguished traditions of educational work.

Perhaps it's the strain of working too hard. Perhaps it's a reaction against the official posture of humble pacifism. Perhaps it's the chemical cocktail in the water supply. The fact remains that there is a huge market in Japan for images of human damage and defilement. There is even a ghoulish genre of popular movie which specializes in the compilation of documentary footage of executions, torture and air crashes. The movies are shown on unrestricted general release, and extracts of the delights they contain are broadcast quite openly on prime-time television commercials. The appetite is not entirely new. In the Edo era, wood-block artists like Yoshitoshi catered for it in blood-drenched renderings of famous murders and suicides. When stripped of all fancy and art, all that remains is the beady-eyed craving to know the very worst.

The opposing influences, for escapism and wish-fulfilment, are catered for equally well. One of the most remarkable features of Japanese reading habits is the tremendous popularity of *manga*, the comic magazines, often as thick as telephone directories, which are avidly consumed by Japanese of all ages and all walks of life. There are different *manga* for different sorts of people – romantic *manga, ero-guro* (erotic and grotesque) *manga*, baseball *manga*, mah-jong *manga*, gourmet *manga*, even 'information *manga*' which weave dramatic stories out of such unpromising material as *Trade Friction* and *The Budget Deficit*. The Socialist Party issued a *manga* version of its unarmed neutrality thesis, an excellent match of medium and message. The LDP countered with a sententious effort in which two judoists discuss Japan's proper role in the world. However, not all politicians are so stuffy in their tastes. One was recently photographed whiling away a dull debate with a lurid fantasy comic on his knee. His excuse, unlikely to pass muster in any primary school, was that he had been passed the offending object by someone from a rival faction.

Manga is huge business. Over five hundred different titles are published every week, the most successful of which has a circulation of three million. Annual production is one and a quarter billion – equivalent to ten magazines for every man, woman and child in the country. Some indication of the genre's status within Japanese society is given by the fact that six *manga* artists feature among the nation's 500 top payers of income tax.

At the start of the *manga* boom, in the early sixties, the readership was mostly under fifteen years old. That generation, like those that followed, never managed to put away the things of childhood. Today, forty-year-old executives who make investment decisions that affect livelihoods all over the world can be seen poring over comic books, wearing the same earnest expressions as when scrutinizing balance sheets. The peculiar process of retardation reveals itself in the following pattern. Surveys reveal that the favourite publication of nine-year-old boys is a *manga* called *Shonen Jump*. It is also the favourite of every age between ten and eighteen. Statistics are

not available for school-leavers, but the same *Shonen Jump* is
frequently read by men well into middle age. The phenomenon is best explained in psychological terms – the subconsci-
ous desire of the Japanese adult to return to the one period of
his life when he was free from the tensions of duty and
obligation. For similar reasons, women nearing the optimum
age for arranged marriage (twenty-five) still collect teddy
bears and wear Snoopy-emblazoned socks.

Most of the *manga* read by adults are less innocent in tone
than the simple-minded, exaggerated gags of *Shonen Jump*.
Manga intended for the male audience contain heavy doses of
violence and sexual sadism, often involving pneumatic
blondes. The heroes are hired assassins or racing drivers or
'the Son of Hitler'. They do not commute to work every
morning and bow respectfully to the various grades of boss.
They wear sharp New York fashions; they gamble, rape and
blow people's heads off with proper panache. *Manga* for the
female audience feature the romantic exploits of glamorous
foreign-looking ladies and the handsome millionaires who
pursue them. It is a common and rather depressing sight to
see dating couples in coffee bars immersed in their *manga*
reading; he deep in male fantasy, she in female.

Manga artwork is variable in quality, ranging from childish
line drawings to highly wrought exercises in sexual symbol-
ism. As in traditional woodblock prints, scale is inconsistent,
with mighty warriors towering over their enemies. The artist
may even change styles from frame to frame in order to suit
the mood. When the hero seduces a night-club singer, he is
tall, sharp-featured and masterfully handsome, every detail of
his person closely delineated. When thrown over by his
childhood sweetheart, he suddenly becomes a lightly-sketched
caricature, button-nosed and small of stature. Such sudden
shifts do not worry the *manga* reader, who is interested only
in certain key images, not in flow or development. In *manga*
there is no history, no future, no need to refer to anything
outside the current frame.

Annihilating reality requires ever greater efforts. In recent
years, in keeping with trends in other media, the *manga* have

become more violent and obscene, more bizarre in their storylines. Yet, however startling to the eye, once read, they are instantly forgotten. *Manga* readers are the perfect consumers. They require more and more of the same product, the same images and stories, until, after a while, consumption becomes an end in itself. At that stage, the ultimate *manga*-reading fantasy is laid bare – to carry on reading *manga* for ever.

The Electronic Villagers

Kazuyoshi Miura is no woebegone strap-hanging salaryman, but a sophisticated modern-minded Japanese. He runs an import and export business specializing in fashion goods. He speaks English, makes frequent trips abroad, dresses casually and expensively, is tall and handsome in a reptilian sort of way. He looks and acts as if he is in a television commercial for some new kind of Italian aftershave that costs seven times as much in Japan as in Italy.

He is, however, not immune from misfortune. On one of his periodic business trips to Los Angeles he and his wife are attacked by a group of men, shot down in broad daylight. Miura's thigh wound soon heals, but his wife, who has been shot in the head, lapses into a terminal coma. He takes her back to Japan and makes a tearful appearance on television which, naturally enough, attracts widespread public sympathy. America is a violent country, where murders of Japanese visitors occur every year. Miura's experience seems to confirm what many Japanese have long suspected – that home sweet home is the safest place to be. Additionally, his obvious devotion to the welfare of his dying wife strikes a chord. Everybody would like to appear as noble as Miura in such distressing circumstances.

Not long after the death of Mrs Miura, the *Bungei Shunju* magazine begins to unearth some inconvenient facts, most notably the huge life insurance policy her husband has taken out on her before they made their trip. Details of the shooting itself are obscure. There were no witnesses, and nothing was taken. Miura's personal life doesn't bear much scrutiny either. It transpires that he has a record of petty convictions stretching back to adolescence, when he took an indecent photograph of a member of the Imperial family and tried to use it for blackmail. He inhabits a twilight world of wife-swapping clubs and marijuana parties and has some heavy connections in the gangster syndicates. Acquaintances claim that he has long been obsessed with the idea of the perfect murder.

The plot thickens. One of Miura's many lovers has been missing ever since she made a trip to Los Angeles two years previously. Dental records sent from Japan reveal that selected bits of her anatomy are stowed in a 'persons unknown' locker in the L A city morgue. Things go from bad to worse when a pornographic video star claims to have been paid by Miura to kill his wife on a previous overseas trip. She explains to a weekly magazine how she struck Mrs Miura with a hammer, but did not have the nerve to finish the job. Miura's denial of involvement contains several inconsistencies and coincidences that he cannot explain.

The Japanese police are dilatory, the American police not very interested. Eighteen months elapse between the start of suspicions and the arrest. During that period something very strange happens. The Miura case is transformed from the sort of incident that might be worth two or three columns in the weekend press into a national obsession. In order to feed it, whole forests are chopped down, weeks and weeks of television time expanded. Japan's gigantic media consortia set up special 'Miura departments' and detail squadrons of reporters to the story. Every week at least thirty articles are published on the 'L A suspicion', covering not just the immediate context of the case, to which there are obvious limits, but all aspects of Miura's personality and lifestyle. Nude photographs of him are published. Ex-lovers are paid to describe his sexual habits; ex-employees to describe his business methods. Travel agents even run special 'Miura package tours' to Los Angeles, featuring bed and board at the hotel where the couple stayed and guided trips to the murder site. The craving to know more about the man is almost insatiable. Miura has to build a barricade around his house to ward off the packs of reporters who follow him everywhere. He goes into hiding in London, but is soon tracked down by the intrepid media men. His return to Tokyo several months later causes pandemonium at Narita Airport on the scale usually reserved for foreign rock stars.

At times media activity was so frenetic that it almost achieved the impossible and inspired sympathy for the creepy Miura, hounded from pillar to post, libelled every day of the week. However, the relationship gradually took on a symbiotic character. He received large fees to appear on television and defend himself from the reporters' charges. The book he wrote about his experiences became an instant best-seller, and he was even offered the part of a detective in a television drama. The end finally came when he was arrested in an underground car park packed with hundreds of expectant reporters. There were even two men from Asahi TV in the car with him at the time, a scoop which infuriated their rivals who were left to bang on the windows in frustration. As the police took him away for questioning they were accompanied by a phalanx of press cars and helicopters, which retailed back his every gesture and facial expression. All scheduled television programmes were halted in order to broadcast the scene live, and special panel discussions were hastily convened.

The initial breaking of the Miura suspicions coincided with the death of a genuine Japanese hero. Naomi Uemura, the first man to make a solo crossing of the arctic circle, was lost in a blizzard on Mount McKinley. All eyes were concentrated on Miura, and the fruitless search for Uemura passed by almost without comment. What, apart from novelty, did the Miura story have that gave it such overwhelming appeal? There was sex and violence, of course, and there was wish-fulfilment. Miura was a new type of Japanese, suave, self-confident, at ease in foreign countries – an 'internationalist', in crime as in business. Almost as much as Uemura, Miura was a loner, depending for his survival on an accommodation with overwhelmingly powerful hostile forces – not snow and ice, in his case, but the mass media. Furthermore, his story, unlike Uemura's, had an outside and an inside, a duality of the sort the Japanese recognize and enjoy. Uemura's bravery was simple and unambitious. Miura's villainy was complex, more in accordance with the modern Japanese experience. Most Japanese have to learn how to move between different realms of experience – Western and traditional, public and private, *omote* and *ura*. Miura's case was extreme, the differences polarized into good and evil.

It was a story introduced, developed and concluded by the mass media, an eighteen-month serialization in real time. After the arrest, control over events was taken over by the police, and the national fascination with Miura suddenly abated. At times it had run close to hysteria. Without a doubt Miura had become the most famous person in Japan – combining the roles of Dr Crippen, Sid Vicious and Goldstein, subject of the five-minute hate in *1984*. For the sake of consistency he should have been tried and executed on television as well.

Shortly after the Miura story broke, a less glamorous villain was dispatched before the gaze of the viewing public. In characteristic fashion the Japanese media had set off on a concerted hue and cry after a suspected confidence trickster. For days on end several dozen reporters camped in the corridor outside his dingy apartment, bellowing requests for interviews and filming his every move. The hubbub caught the attention of two self-styled 'philosophers' who, impatient with the lackadaisical attitude of the authorities, decided to mete out some do-it-yourself justice. They strode through the journalistic throng and, while the cameras fizzed, flashed and whirred, prised away the bars that protected the apartment window, forced their way inside, and proceeded to hack the occupant to pieces. This having been duly accomplished, they clambered back out and gave an instant blood-bespattered press conference. So excited were the assembled reporters that it was left to one of the murderers to demand that the police be called. That night the whole gruesome episode was broadcast to the nation on specially extended news programmes, complete with slow-motion replays – which is how one bedridden old lady was apprised of her son's decease.

★

Welcome to 'the advanced information society'. That is the slogan the Ministry of International Trade and Industry has invented to describe modern Japan. It is a reasonable-enough designation, since the social influence of television is probably greater in Japan than in any other developed country. The diffusion rate of colour TV sets is the highest in the world; 99 per cent of all households own one, against 88 per cent in the US, and 83 per cent in the UK. TVs are suspended from the walls in snack bars and *sushi* shops, fitted into the backs of taxi cabs, set up in banks to entertain the ever-patient customers. Middle-aged men at the beach watch the baseball on pocket-size liquid crystal TVs. Giant screens gaze down at the crowds of teenagers waiting for their dates at Shinjuku Station. The quantity of the output is almost as remarkable. Some channels broadcast from five-thirty in the morning to three o'clock the subsequent morning. In Tokyo the seven available broadcast channels together pump out 140 hours of programming every day. At average viewing rates, that would take two months to consume.

Japanese people spend triple the amount of time watching television as on any other leisure-time activity. On Sundays jaded salarymen often spend the entire day sprawled in front of the endless cycle of quiz programmes and slice-'em-up samurai dramas. Because Japanese houses are small, usually with one cramped living-room, the TV is always physically close at hand, occupying a central position, much like the hearth in a Western home. Families settle down to their breakfast, lunch and dinner before the flickering tube. Even if a guest is present it is not considered discourteous to keep one eye on the screen all through the meal. Although there may be no interest in the programmes being broadcast, the set is rarely switched off. It acts as a kind of visual muzak. As the guest tucks into his *suki-yaki* he is but dimly aware of the rape of the doctor's assistant; the comedian waddling around with his trousers around his ankles; the Giants' *sayonara* home run; the screeching of tyres and the swishing of swords.

Middle-class Japanese lack the sense of uneasiness about television felt by most educated Westerners. They regard it not as a source of entertainment but as a utility, like the gas or the water supply: a constant flow of sound and image always ready to be accessed. There is no guilt involved in watching television or, for that matter, in appearing on it. Taro Okamoto, Japan's best-known sculptor, regularly guests on slapstick variety shows, where he nonchalantly capers around with comedians and pop singers. Nagisa Oshima, the doyen of new-wave cinema, is to be seen on *How Much?* quiz programmes, guessing the price of a barrel of Tibetan yak cheese. Nobody seems to think any the worse of them – it merely demonstrates what good fellows they are. Similarly, serious artists can endorse products in commercials without any apparent damage to their credibility. Shusaku Endo, one of Japan's most distinguished modern novelists, advertises instant coffee: 'For the man who knows the difference . . .' Almost as surprising to the Westerner is the assumption that a writer of his calibre can influence the choices of ordinary consumers.

Two television channels are operated by NHK, a public broadcasting corporation modelled on the BBC. It is funded by licence fees and takes no commercials. NHK Educational is, rather as BBC2 was intended to be, a serious channel exclusively devoted to art and instruction. It broadcasts useful courses in modern languages and science, as well as performances of Shakespeare, *Noh, Kabuki*, et cetera. Education is of vital importance in Japanese society, and the channel adopts a suitably grave, almost funereal approach to its appointed task. The budgets are modest, but the quality of the programming uniformly high.

NHK General takes a similarly stern attitude to its task of entertaining the nation. It is as far removed from the lame-brained slapstick of the commercial channels as the *Asahi Shimbun* is from the *Gendai*. Its drama serials are finely acted and soberly directed, its documentaries highly informative without being tendentious. Although, as one would expect, NHK follows the establishment line in its news coverage, it manages to preserve an intelligently balanced attitude to the political controversies of the day. The NHK viewer is put in possession of all the facts he needs – and usually a great many more – in order to make up his own mind. The usual NHK tone is patriotic, paternalistic, relentlessly optimistic, rather like the Reith BBC's. It presents the Japanese people with the image of themselves which gives them most comfort – that of a united, hard-working nation of happy families. The worst that can be said about the channel is that its constant worthiness can sometimes fade into dullness.

NHK was responsible for the *Oshin* drama serial, one of the great popular successes of modern times. It captured a national obsession just as surely as *Dallas* did in the United States – the Japanese obsession being not with money and power, but with suffering. Broadcast in fifteen-minute instalments at eight in the morning, the programme achieved a Nielson rating of 30 per cent, unprecedented for the time of day. Indeed, the word *oshin* passed into the language, meaning 'to endure silently'. The story concerned the trials and tribulations of a peasant girl growing up in northern Japan before the war. Toiling in the fields as a child, sent out to work as a servant, tormented by an overbearing mother-in-law – through all, Oshin endures uncomplainingly, holding fast to the values of diligence and devotion to those around her. At the conclusion of the serial this JR antithesis has become a wealthy supermarket owner, free of travail for the first time in her life. As was obvious to everyone who watched, the programme was a retelling of the modern Japanese experience. By dint of hard work and spiritual toughness, Oshin triumphs over terrible adversity, exchanging rural poverty for well-earned urban comfort. Significantly, as the serial reached the final stages, its popularity began to wane. Oshin contented with her lot seemed almost a contradiction in terms, her existence lacking in force and meaning.

Commercial television is everything which NHK is not – sensational, lewd, repetitive, dishonest and stupefyingly banal. Naturally, people love to watch it. During 'golden hour' (eight to nine in the evening), the ratings for the least popular commercial channel are usually treble NHK's. Ratings are, of course, the name of the game. Most of Japan's commercial TV companies are financially strong, being members of large multi-media conglomerates, but they cannot afford to relax. Since 1980 the growth in TV advertising revenues has consistently underperformed the growth levels achieved by other media. The companies are competing furiously in a stagnant market.

The viewer is left in little doubt that advertisements are the main point of commercial TV and that the programmes have been devised merely to fill the gaps in between. The rigidities caused by the sponsorship system mean that baseball transmissions can come to an abrupt end in the ninth inning with the scores level and the bases loaded. Similarly, a commercial can break into a suspense movie just as the dying man is croaking out the murderer's name. However, it is not just the timing or numbing frequency of commercials that establishes their importance. In terms of money and talent invested they far outclass the programmes that surround them.

The best Japanese commercials form a genre of their own, close in style and spirit to pop videos. Their objective is to create a memorable series of images that consumers will associate with a particular brand name. The product itself may only be cursorily mentioned at the conclusion. To describe its supposed merits or pricing would be entirely self-defeating. The Japanese public is fully aware that there is not much difference between Suzukis and Yamahas, and any attempt to convince it otherwise would only evoke suspicion. Denigration of competitive products would be considered an insult to the intelligence.

To a Japanese audience the most effective images are those that exploit the taste for the exotic and the bizarre. A juggler, a dwarf, a fire-eater and a large lizard wander through a desert landscape. The voice-over makes some vague reference to Rimbaud, the symbolist poet – 'Merchant of the desert, poet of eternity . . .' It wouldn't sell much Haig or Jack Daniels, but it hits the right note with drinkers of Japan's most successful whisky. Japanese advertisements can sum up national moods, perhaps even create them. A lovely woman gazes wistfully at a large and elaborate sand-castle being destroyed by the waves. A dynamited skyscraper collapses in slow motion. The motif is fashionable ennui – the weariness, perhaps, that comes with over-achievement. A cartoon penguin gazes at the late summer sunset, and a large tear plops out of its eye – that is a beer company appealing cleverly to the infantalism of the new humans. An old man, wrinkled as a dried fish, but with longish hair and trendy clothes, frolics about in front of a 28-inch T V screen. This is how an electronics manufacturer targets the fast-growing 'silver' market. It is also a vision of how the new 'high-touch' super-long life is likely to end up – wisdomless and alone, with just the cathode-ray spirits for company.

The programmes themselves are no better or worse than their equivalents elsewhere. Although many of the concepts are taken from the American networks, the actual quantity of bought-in programmes is extremely small. *Dallas* flopped. *Dynasty* never happened and foreign sitcoms and cop operas are thin on the ground. When it comes to producing high-grade garbage for the small screen, the Japanese have stuck to their usual policy of import substitution. Since the Japanese spend such a large amount of time watching the programmes, their presentation and content deserves some examination. They hold up a distorting mirror to popular taste and what is revealed is often characteristic, if unflattering.

There is, for example, the obsession with foreigners. Only the Japanese would devise a quiz series in which contestants have to guess which example of their national cuisine foreigners find the least appetizing. Gales of laughter are occasioned by the sight of some benighted New York shop assistant grimacing over a dollop of fermented bean paste. Probably, the all-time low in this kind of entertainment was reached when a Japanese T V station shipped a family of Bushmen over to Tokyo. Japanese audiences had been greatly amused by a South African movie about a tribe of these primitive people who worship a Pepsi bottle. They were still more amused by the Bushman's confused reaction to chopsticks and pickles. Years after the event, Japanese comedians can still win easy laughs with their Bushman imitations.

Amongst all the mindless frivolity some deep-seated

changes in social values can be glimpsed. Just as Yasuhiro Nakasone challenges taboos on defence spending and visits to Yasukuni Shrine, so Japan's comedians challenge the established bounds of good taste with jokes about deformity, excretion and senility. A drama series about the extra-marital affairs of a group of bored and wealthy women attracts an enormous audience, wakening the fantasies of restless housewives and the fears of workaholic husbands. Late-night television becomes increasingly salacious, prompting questions to be raised in the Diet. On one chat show the female interviewees remove their underwear and hand it to the host, who sniffs the garment and then tosses it in a frying-pan like a pancake. On another, female university students strip off for prizes and engage in erotic banana-eating contests. Since the abolition of the licensed quarters in 1961, commerce in sexuality has spread through the whole of society. Prostitution was once considered an honourable way for a peasant girl to alleviate the poverty of her family. It is now a fashionable sideline for well-off college girls planning overseas trips. With nothing to suffer for, Oshin's granddaughters are adrift.

Children's programmes have their own distinguishing features. The best-loved characters are huge robots who stride over the city landscape, battering various monsters with death rays and karate chops. The human heroes are insignificant figures, all identically uniformed, who inhabit control rooms in the robots' chests. Occasionally they venture outside to skirmish with opposing teams of evildoers, but always retreat to the safety of the control room from where the real battle is conducted. The unspoken moral is clear: the power of high technology and the danger of being without it.

Perhaps the most striking aspect of Japanese TV is that the same personalities appear night after night, sometimes several times on the same night. These are the denizens of what the Japanese misleadingly call the *Geinokai*, the 'world of art and talent'. What art and talent they have at their command is spread desperately thin. Their job is to provide familiarity, a constant point of reference. The most popular stars may appear on twenty TV shows a week, most of them broadcast live, as well as six or seven commercials. It is overwork on a scale that even the most conscientious salaryman would think twice about, and the rewards are far from princely. Most of Japan's TV personalities are employees of large enterprises called 'productions', which pay them a fixed salary amounting to under 1 per cent of the massive sums their appearances generate. Not surprisingly, their life cycles are as short as those of the products they advertise. The pubescent female singers known as *onapets* (*ona* from onanism, *pet* as in pet of the month) are an extreme example, making their debuts at fifteen and 'retiring' to an ordinary existence at eighteen. They are not supposed to be able to sing or dance, still less play any musical instruments or compose songs. They don't even have to be especially good-looking. Outstanding qualities of any sort would prevent the perfect identification with their fans that is the secret of their success: the more ordinary, the greater the adulation.

Just how intense the identification can be was demonstrated in April 1986 when one of the most popular *onapet* singers took a step into space from a high window. She had been as effortlessly ordinary as her role required, better at mathematics and English than she ever was at singing. After her suicide, a mini-cult sprang up almost over-night. Busloads of youngsters travelled up to Tokyo to gaze upon the spot where she had fallen. A minor sensation was caused when a group of school-girls claimed to have seen her bloodied ghost standing in the background during a pop music TV show. By the end of the same month twenty-eight teenagers had committed suicide, more than half by jumping to their deaths. The average for the previous year had been four per month. The victims of the 'Yukiko syndrome', so named after the unfortunate idol, seemed normal well-balanced youngsters, with no apparent problems at home or at school. Notes left behind gave either trivial reasons ('School is boring now my teacher has changed') or mentioned Yukiko directly ('I want to follow where she has gone . . .'). In death the uncharismatic, untalented sixteen-year-old had achieved a communion with her fans more powerful than that of the greatest Hollywood stars.

The ordinary-ordinary and the famous-ordinary interact directly in the many audience-participation programmes on Japanese television. At peak viewing times about one-third of the output is devoted to quiz, game and amateur talent shows, many of them of a vulgarity unparalleled anywhere in the world. In *The Endurance*, groups of students compete in the performance of such tasks as crawling through tubes filled with snakes and lizards. In the various *Love Clinic* programmes newly-wed couples are interrogated by smarmy comedians on the details of their sex life. For both viewers and participants the attraction lies not in the prizes on offer, indeed there are often no prizes at all. The point is in the participation itself, the intimate relation between the watchers and the watched. In *Cheerful TV* dozens of ordinary people – doctors, bus drivers and secretaries – clown around with Japan's most famous 'talents', performing elaborate mass charades in the streets of Tokyo.

According to the late Andy Warhol, in the future everyone will be Elvis Presley for fifteen minutes. Science-fiction writer Yasutaka Tsutsui has an amusing story which sets the idea in a Japanese context. Suddenly, for no apparent reason, an ordinary salaryman is catapulted to nationwide fame. The most banal details of his daily life are reported in the newspapers. His emotional problems are solemnly discussed on television panels, and his route to work is tracked by press helicopters. His desultory efforts to win the favours of a female colleague become a topic of national importance. When, flattered by the attentions of a celebrity, she succumbs, his fame suddenly evaporates. The story is a fantastic version of a process that takes place quite regularly in the Japanese media – the apotheosis of the mundane. Miura became a sacrificial god, Yukiko a virgin goddess demanding sacrifices. The wedding of the most famous *onapet* singer was treated in exactly the terms which other nations reserve for royalty, with twelve hours of live coverage and reverent commentary.

The Japanese inhabit a scaled-down version of McLuhan's global village, their sense of group values being reinforced by the vast quantity of vicarious experience they have consumed together, more powerful than anything the individual encounters in his everyday life. Small wonder that cable TV has never caught on: what is being sought is not choice but mass intimacy. The cathode-ray spirits which visit Japanese homes every night have assumed the function that the pre-war symbol of national identity has vacated. The programmes themselves may not be much good as entertainment, but they have succeeded in meeting social needs far more profound.

6

The Imperial Institution:
At the Still Centre

His Majesty's reign shall endure a thousand ages
Until pebbles have grown to mossy rocks

Japanese national anthem

To lose face in Japan is to lose everything. But to lose
everything is not necessarily to lose face.

Leonard Mosley, *Hirohito, Emperor of Japan*

The time of the breaking of nations, most recent version, has
faded into the the history books. Hitler, Stalin, Churchill, de
Gaulle, Mao, Montgomery, MacArthur – the leaders and
their generals have long passed into that realm from whence
they may return only under the control of biographers and
movie directors. Just one of the main figures lingered right
through the post-war period, long enough to glimpse the
waning of the two superpowers that brought about his
country's first defeat. Japan's Emperor Hirohito opened his
eyes to a world of pomp and empire, of Franz Josef, the
Manchus, the Ottomans, the Tsar, the Kaiser, and the British
Empress of India – when being an emperor carried some
weight. When he closed them for the last time, he was the
only Emperor left outside Africa, and the few European
monarchies that remained had degenerated into fodder for the
gossip columns.

The Japanese respect continuance, the proof of adaptation
to flux. Emperor Hirohito represents continuance on the
grand scale – the longest-reigning emperor in the world's

longest-reigning dynasty. His was a reign containing flux also on the grand scale, which has made the continuance all the more notable. He saw his people emerging out of feudalism, charging headlong into militarism, bombed flat, conquered for the first time in history, occupied, struggling for recovery, then more prosperous than ever before. He was a god and nearly a war criminal and then hardly thought about at all. His face appeared on neither stamps nor currency. In no Japanese living-room was his photograph propped up on the sideboard. He rarely gave speeches or interviews, rarely left the Imperial palace. You could stay in Japan a long time without being aware that an emperor existed.

The Western envoys who arrived in Japan 130 years ago did know of the Emperor's existence, but were understandably confused as to his exact function. As the Shogun seemed to be the man in charge in Tokyo, which seemed to be the centre of power, they concluded their treaties with him, and even referred to him as the 'temporal emperor', in contrast to the 'spiritual emperor' languishing in Kyoto. The British quickly realized that the political momentum was with the forces favouring imperial 'restoration' and began intriguing accordingly. Algernon Mitford, legation attaché and grandfather of the famous sisters, was among the first Britons to set eyes on a Japanese emperor:

As we entered the room the Son of Heaven rose and acknowledged our bows. He was at that time a tall youth with a bright eye and clear complexion: his demeanour was very dignified, well becoming the heir of a dynasty older than any other sovereignty on the face of the globe. He was dressed in a white coat with long padded trousers of crimson silk trailing like a lady's court-train. His eyebrows were shaved off and painted in high up on the forehead; his cheeks were rouged and his lips painted with red and gold. His teeth were blackened. It was no small feat to look dignified under such a travesty of nature.

Ten years later Emperor Meiji was a constitutional monarch on the European model, complete with a military uniform and a smart moustache. When Mitford first saw him, he was performing the same function that his ancestors had for over a thousand years. The emperors had always been shamans, conductors of the magical rites that safeguarded the nation's prosperity. Their prayers to the gods were efficacious because they went through the ancestral hot-line. Presumably the emperor once exercised civil and military power as well, but, if so, that function was divested before historical records began. Already by the sixth century, the pattern had become established whereby the actual government of the country was carried out by the dominant court family of the time.

The most powerful of these families, the Fujiwara, took an iron hold on the institution, filling all the major offices of state and supplying the imperial consorts. Eventually all imperial mothers and grandmothers and present and prospective empresses were Fujiwara women, and the succession was decided by Fujiwara policy. The Emperor himself was often an infant, who was then encouraged to retire to the priesthood as he neared adulthood. Having grafted themselves on to the imperial organism the Fujiwaras soon began to suffer from the same syndrome. They became absorbed in the enervating ceremony and intrigue of court life, and power devolved to those more interested in its exercise. Striking up a recurrent theme in Japanese history, the Fujiwaras gradually degenerated into puppet figures, but those who replaced them were careful not to disturb their titular function. As a judoist makes use of his opponent's strength, so the various usurpers made use of the strength of tradition.

The next 600 years is the story of the rise and fall of regionally based warrior clans who chose to establish their legitimacy through imperially conferred titles, such as Shogun. Occasional attempts to reverse the flow of events ended in miserable failure. When the retired Emperor Go-Toba launched an ill-advised military expedition against the Shogunate established in the eastern city of Kamakura, the outcome was humiliating defeat, his own exile, and the confiscation of large tracts of court land. The reigning emperor of the time, a child of two, was deposed after only three months on the throne. After that salutary lesson, the court settled into impecunious decline with better grace, and left the roughnecks in the east to carry on with what they were good at – fighting each other. Imperial turnover was rapid, the fourteenth century containing thirteen different reigns, and the role of the emperor remained uncertain until Ieyasu Tokugawa grabbed the reins of power in 1595.

Like the Fujiwara before them, the Tokugawa Shoguns sought to safeguard their ascendancy by institutionalizing their relationship with the Imperial family. In the long centuries of civil war which preceded the unification of the country under Ieyasu, the court had fallen on hard times. Lack of funds had delayed the burial of one emperor for six weeks and the enthronement of another for twenty years, and courtiers had been reduced to selling calligraphy to make ends meet. Ieyasu put an end to this Micawberesque existence by granting the court a generous stipend from the national treasury. At the same time he drew up a set of edicts which restricted its proper function to the promotion of scholarship and explicitly assigned control over all matters of state to his own government in Tokyo. The Imperial family was thus assured of a life of comfortable and cultured impotence – which probably matched its tastes exactly. The literary disposition of the Imperial family goes back to the early contacts with T'ang China, when the ability to write Chinese poetry marked familiarity with the imported culture. In modern times the Imperial family is still its own laureate, producing a crop of *haiku* verses every New Year. Scholarship – not, of course, the army – is the natural calling for princes and heirs. Emperor Hirohito himself was a distinguished marine biologist with full membership of the British Royal Society and a dozen learned publications to his name.

The Tokugawa Shogunate, despite its sound foundation, eventually suffered the fate of most Japanese regimes. It allowed itself to be absorbed in the formalities of power while political and economic change gradually undermined the foundation. When Lord Elgin's trade mission arrived on the scene in 1859 the Shogunate was already in a state of advanced decay. After a yacht was presented to the Shogun as a mark of Queen Victoria's esteem, Elgin's secretary wrote:

He, too, has been exalted to so high a pitch of temporal dignity that his lofty station has been robbed of all its substantial advantages, and he passes the life of a state prisoner, shut up in his magnificent citadel, except when he pays a state visit to Miako [Kyoto]. It was a cruel satire upon this unhappy potentate to present him with a yacht; one might as well request the Pope's acceptance of a wife.

Not long afterwards the last of the Shoguns was cast out of the magnificent citadel and an imperial restoration declared. What this would entail few could have had any idea beforehand, least of all the Emperor himself.

In the 130 years between the Meiji restoration and the end of the Showa era, only three emperors reigned: Meiji himself, his son and his grandson. Emperor Hirohito, the 124th in the official chronology, was born in the opening year of the twentieth century. Like his father, he was educated at Gakushuin school, the Japanese Eton, where he studied Western subjects as well as the Chinese classics. At the time the headmaster was General Nogi, hero of the victory over the Russians at Port Arthur and a notable proponent of the set of values known as *Bushido* – 'the Way of the Warrior'. While Hirohito was at Gakushuin, Nogi and his wife committed *seppuku* – suicide – on the eve of the funeral of Emperor Meiji, Hirohito's grandfather. This sensational act was partly an atonement for the shame of losing the imperial standard in battle nearly forty years before, partly an assertion of traditional values over the forces of modernization and Westernization. The young Crown Prince is said to have disapproved, but the conflict that Nogi's suicide expressed was to provide the leitmotif of his entire reign.

In 1921 Hirohito became the first Crown Prince to travel abroad, an event which excited violent opposition amongst the ultra-nationalists. On his trip to England, which he later referred to as the happiest time of his life, he had his portrait painted by Augustus John, met Lloyd George, and played golf with the future Edward VIII, who became his ideal of the modern prince. In Paris he travelled incognito on the metro and apparently long afterwards treasured the ticket he bought there. Given that from 1632 to 1865 no reigning emperor had even ventured outside the palace in Kyoto, it must have been an exhilarating experience, all the more so since there was no possibility of it ever being repeated in Japan. The *arahitogami* (living god) does not do the Charleston.

Hirohito became Prince Regent in 1921, taking over the formal duties of state from his father. As a small boy the Emperor Taisho had suffered from meningitis, which to treat properly would have involved unthinkable acts of lesemajesty. Therefore nothing was done, with the result that he suffered from increasingly serious bouts of derangement all through his life. In these he would often give vent to an unhappy predilection for using his whip on people, animals and objects that got in his way. At his last state opening of parliament, instead of reading out his speech he rolled it up into a tube through which he squinted quizzically at the astonished parliamentarians. In pre-Meiji Japan it would not have mattered, indeed several of the early emperors were celebrated for their psychotic behaviour. In Taisho Japan, it was clear that Taisho had to go.

Hirohito was brought up by his tutors, notably the liberal statesman Prince Saionji, to fulfil the role of constitutional monarch. He was to be the focus and symbol of Japanese patriotism, but not to exercise any power of his own, merely ratifying the decisions of his ministers. However, while the substance did not differ much from the European model, the presentation was of an entirely different order. When the Meiji oligarchs 'restored' the emperor in 1872 they had been confronted with a blank sheet of paper. They wanted a stronger Japan, economically and militarily, and they knew that they were the men for the job. They also knew that their only claim to legitimacy lay with the imperial institution that they had been responsible for dusting off and thrusting into the centre of the national consciousness. The greater the authority they could invest in it, the greater the acceptance of the immense changes they were planning to work. Hence, the establishment of state Shinto, a centralized and highly chauvinistic form of the native ancestor cult. Its fundamental tenets were the sacred nature of the Japanese nation (*kokutai*) and the divinity of the emperor. These had been implicit in traditional belief, but were now inflated into an official ideology, backed by all the organs of a modern state.

The Meiji Constitution, in force from 1889 until the end of the Second World War, gave expression to the twin purposes of the Meiji leaders. The very idea of a constitution was Western, and one of the main reasons for its adoption was the need to impress the foreign powers with the progress Japan had made, thus preparing the way for the abolition of the 'unequal treaties'. However, it was also a useful vehicle for reinforcing the link between the *kokutai* ideology and the new dispensation. The first article set the tone: 'the empire of Japan shall be reigned over and governed by a line of emperors unbroken for ages eternal'. No emperor had governed anything outside his palace for hundreds of years, but those claiming to rule in the imperial name had their justification for overriding the institutions of government. The emperor was 'sacred and inviolable', whereas the role of parliament was restricted to providing an ill-defined 'consent' to the actions of ministers. Naturally not everyone believed in the living-god theory, and not everyone believed in it in the same way. None the less almost everyone believed that it would be advantageous to believe it. Even men like Prince Saionji considered it a necessary instrument in promoting national unity. The ultra-nationalists and later the militarists saw it as a justification for imposing their own will on government policy. The common people, who had just emerged from 200 years of doing exactly what they were told, provided ideal material to work on.

Shinto fundamentalists, like fundamentalists everywhere, insisted on the absolute historicity of myth and symbol. According to their analysis the imperial lineage extends back through the ages to the first emperor, Jimmu, who took the throne on 11 February 660 BC. He had all the right qualifications for the job, his father being the great-grandson of the sun goddess and his mother the daughter of a giant alligator. The early sections of the *Kojiki* and the *Nihon Shoki*, the two ancient books on which the *kokutai* ideology was based, are fantastic concoctions more reminiscent of Freudian nightmare than historical chronicle. A cast of thousands of indistinguishable gods, all with long similar-sounding names, jostle for attention in the primeval murk. As depicted, they are hardly ancestors to be proud of. Even by the standards of other primitive deities they are a pretty appalling lot, sadistic and sex-crazed, spending most of their time exposing their genitals, defecating at banquets and wreaking random violence on more or less anyone they encounter. None the less, in the bowdlerized and structured form in which the tales were presented, they managed to fulfil their purpose – the inculcation of awe and submission.

Throughout the Meiji and Taisho eras the *kokutai* ideology grew increasingly powerful. The Imperial Rescript on Education, contrived by conservative bureaucrats and scholars in order to quash agitation for political rights, affirmed that devotion to the emperor and obedience to the decisions of the authorities were one and the same thing. In accordance with the fiat of the Ministry of Education, it was read out aloud at every school in the land. Imperial portraits, which had to be bowed before, were displayed on all ceremonial occasions. Headmasters of schools where damage was done to the portrait – by fire, for example – atoned with their lives.

While popular reverence for the imperial institution was assiduously cranked up, there was no question of Emperor Meiji actually having any influence over the decisions that mattered. Although punctilious in performance of his military and ceremonial duties, he had no enthusiasm for the expansionist wars that Japan waged against China and then Russia. Shortly before the start of the latter, he composed the famous poem that his grandson was to recite on the eve of Pearl Harbor:

> On all four corners of the earth
> I thought that men were brothers
> Why in this world
> Must the wind and the waves
> Rise up and contend?

What he thought was irrelevant. The 'restored' imperial institution was lapsing back into the figurehead role it had been occupying less ostentatiously for centuries. When Hirohito ascended the chrysanthemum throne in 1925 the process was well advanced. For a public figure to criticize the *kokutai* propaganda was to risk death. Failure to gaze earthwards when the imperial carriage passed invited the attentions of the *kempeitai* secret police. At the same time ultra-nationalists felt no compunction in assassinating those of the retinue they deemed to be obstructing the Imperial Way – something which the sincere of heart felt better able to comprehend than any scheming courtier. Serving military officers occupied the Ministries of the Army and Navy, purportedly exercising the imperial prerogative, and bureaucrats and elder statesmen continued to regard parliament as a rubber stamp for policies of their own devising.

Hirohito decided to name the new era 'Showa', meaning 'enlightened harmony'. That is the name by which he became known after his death, thus creating, according to the Japanese tradition, a perfect unity between the person of the Emperor and the period of his reign. Hirohito was personally well-equipped to preside over the admixture of values his era name suggested. He was highly educated, sane and conversant with all the major problems of state. He was the first monogamous emperor, the system of concubinage having been abolished in 1922, and the first to have direct knowledge of foreign countries. However, his reign was hardly to live up to the billing he had assigned it. The great earthquake of 1923 had marked the end of an era of good fortune and economic progress just as clearly as the outbreak of the Great War had in Europe. Japanese territorial ambitions were creating strains with the older colonial powers, exacerbated by the discriminatory immigration policies followed in the United

States and British dominions. After the Anglo-Japanese Alliance was dissolved in 1923 Japan remained without allies until she joined the Axis seventeen years later. Economically, despite rapid industrialization, she was vulnerable as a marginal supplier to increasingly volatile world markets. The period of vigorous party politics known as Taisho Democracy proved to be a false dawn, and the Mitsui and Mitsubishi industrial groupings gradually tightened their hold over parliamentary affairs. Depression brought social and political unrest; then, as the march of events quickened, came the rise of the militarists, conquest in Asia, and world war. 'Harmony' degenerated into totalitarianism. The model for 'enlightenment' became the new political system developed in Italy and Germany.

Historians will debate for ever the exact role Hirohito played in Japan's slide to disaster. On the few occasions when he did make his opinions felt, the effect was immediate and dramatic. His angry response to the 1936 coup ('I will command the Imperial Guard Division to control them. Get me my horse') was instrumental in averting an armed conflict. Seven years earlier, an imperial reprimand to Prime Minister Tanaka was enough to bring his immediate resignation. Tanaka had promised to deal severely with whoever was behind the assassination of Chang Tso-lin, a Chinese warlord favourable to Japanese interests in Manchuria. In fact, the deed had been planned and executed by Japanese army officers who were 'punished' by mild administrative measures imposed locally. Tanaka, who had no control over the deeds of the Japanese Manchurian Army, had unintentionally misled his Emperor. The third and last time that Hirohito intervened in matters of state was to take the most momentous decision that had ever confronted a member of the Imperial dynasty – acceptance of the terms of the Potsdam Declaration.

If the Emperor could end the war, why couldn't he prevent its beginning? Probably, clear public opposition to the policy of the militarists would have acted as a brake on their activities. However, for the Emperor to impose his personal opinions on political developments would have been to contradict the idea of constitutional monarchy not just as it was understood in Japan, but as it is still understood in Britain and elsewhere. The occasions on which he did intervene were strictly defined by circumstance. In August 1945 the cabinet was deadlocked and took the unprecedented step of requesting an imperial decison. At the time of the 1936 coup the prime minister was presumed assassinated and the forms of constitutional government in abeyance. The Tanaka case, though less clear, could be justified by the failure of the executive to carry out an agreed decision. Paradoxically, it was the Emperor's steadfast adherence to the constitutional forms – while the actions of others were turning them into a mockery – that kept him from using his influence with greater vigour.

Apart from the challenge to his constitutional role, for the Emperor to have spoken out against the policy of military aggression would have been to defy the national consensus. Especially after the 1936 coup attempt, the drive to war was popular in nearly all sections of society. It resolved serious tensions between the bureaucracy, the military establishment and the industrialists. As in Germany's case it offered a way out of economic recession and the promise of raw-material bases. Additionally, by the light of previous experience, there could be little objection to a spot of military adventure: in her wars against China and Russia, Japan's resounding victories had brought her useful overseas possessions and considerably enhanced prestige. Indeed, it was only after she had demonstrated her capacity for military conquest that she had been admitted to the club of serious nations. Those easy successes also had the unfortunate effect of spawning the myth of invincibility, thus subverting the soundest argument of all against warmongering – that it might end in defeat and self-destruction.

As the course of the war turned against Japan, the Emperor's mystique became an even more important tool in boosting national morale. Imperial saké was distributed to kamikaze pilots, chrysanthemum-print cigarettes to soldiers at the front. The Emperor himself inspected the bomb damage and conducted reviews of the home-front troops; but for the mystical authority of his role to be exploited to the full it was necessary that he be kept as remote as possible. At the end of the war the process of abstraction had advanced so far that fanatical die-hards ransacked the imperial guest house in search of the surrender recording, which they planned to destroy. By that time it had become possible for loyalty to the imperial institution to comprehend the thwarting of the Emperor's clearly expressed will.

The broadcast of that recording on 15 August was the first occasion on which the Japanese people heard their Emperor speak. Many were unable to comprehend the quavering, static-shot voice that intoned, in a classical form of language obsolete outside the Imperial palace, one of the greatest understatements in history – that 'the war situation has developed not necessarily to our advantage'. The people, assembled in village squares and factories all over the country, knelt for the speech and heard it in silence. Afterwards, some wandered around for hours in a daze – not so much because the war was lost, which had been patently obvious for some time, but because the Emperor had spoken to them. It was a moment of intensity never to be repeated, for what the Emperor had said meant the end of the *kokutai* ideology.

After the surrender, Hirohito narrowly avoided being tried as a war criminal – which, given the context in which the Far East Tribunal was operating, might well have meant execution. Proposals to scrap the imperial institution or to force an abdication were resisted by the occupation authorities, who saw how vital the Emperor would be for Japan's regeneration. Instead, he volunteered a 'denial of divinity' or, as the Americans put it, 'degodded himself', on New Year's Day 1946. The Imperial Rescript ran as follows:

The ties between us and our people have always stood upon mutual trust and affection. They do not depend upon mere myths and legends. They are not predicated on the false assumption that the Emperor is divine and that the Japanese people are superior to other races and fated to rule the world.

It went down well internationally, but at home the message had already been fully absorbed. The Japanese, always well attuned to symbols, had understood the significance of the newspaper photograph of the Emperor's first meeting with General MacArthur, Supreme Commander of the Allied Forces and shogun of the new dipensation. In a test of wills, MacArthur had waited for the Emperor to call on him, and the Emperor had come. The photograph, whose publication the Japanese authorities attempted to suppress, showed MacArthur in open-necked shirt, arms akimbo, towering over the diminutive and formally dressed Emperor. It was a brutally clear demonstration of who was boss.

'In that instant I knew I faced the First Gentleman of Japan in his own right' – that was how MacArthur later described the meeting. But what does a First Gentleman do, and what is he for? In the years of reconstruction the Emperor set about democratizing the job, donning a baggy suit and Homburg, inspecting factories, going down coal-mines, offering words of encouragement to hard-pressed workers and farmers. It was not a role to which he was suited by nature – his speeches were stilted and characterless – but he still commanded reverence. Amongst the major political parties only the communists were in favour of scrapping the imperial institution. The occupation authorities had changed everything. They had brought in a new constitution, a new industrial structure, a new agricultural system, a new educational system, a new and more plausible set of verities. They had abolished the aristocracy, purged the militarists, given the vote to women, and generally turned the world upside down. But the Emperor remained, the most visible link with native Japanese tradition.

Since then even greater changes have taken place in Japanese society. Post-war chaos and inflation were followed by painful recovery, then breakneck economic growth, industrial success, and then unparalleled prosperity. Families shrank, cities burgeoned, values were transformed out of all recognition. For the pre-war generations the existence of the Emperor became one of the few signs that they were still living in the same country. As national confidence improved, the Emperor became more self-effacing, confining himself to the ceremonial duties laid down in the new constitution. The success of the Tokyo Olympics, which he opened in 1964, marked Japan's return to international respectability. In 1971 he revisited Europe, where he paraded through the streets of London and renewed his acquaintance with the Duke of Windsor. In 1977 he travelled to the United States for the first time, pausing at Disneyland to review Mickey and Donald's procession. A second Disneyland has subsequently been built outside Tokyo. There one can watch the microprocessor-controlled puppet of a famous Meiji statesman repeating a speech on liberal education.

The Emperor was left with ample time to pursue his hobby of marine biology, originally recommended to him as a less dangerous course of study than history. He spent much of his time in the Imperial palace, which occupies a large green space in the centre of Tokyo. On maps, it looks like the hole in a doughnut, suggesting an odd sort of correspondence with the void left in the national psyche. The grounds, 200 acres in all, have no tube lines running under them and, until recently, no adjacent buildings could be built high enough to peer over. Amid the oppressive density and hurly-burly of the metropolis they are an island of calm, protected from time and reality by moats, walls and Japan's finest electronic surveillance gear. Inside, there exists a surprising profusion of flora, fauna and landscape styles, ranging from the classical Japanese garden to large patches of wilderness. Hirohito, in keeping with his training as a natural scientist, favoured the latter. The only wild plants which he disliked were those of foreign origin, which he extirpated as soon as he saw. Twice a year, on New Year's Day and his official birthday, he appeared on the balcony of the palace to accept the *banzai* of the assembled crowds. Hirohito was also seen in public at sumo tournaments, which he enjoyed, at receptions for foreign dignitaries, and at garden parties.

It was a long way from an open monarchy on the Scandinavian model, far even from the British example. Hirohito rarely spoke in public except from a prepared text, which he read in a halting monotone. His remarks to the ordinary people he met were bland and formulaic: 'Thank you very much for your efforts', 'Please continue to do your best for Japan'. He took no part in any public discussion, even on such subjects as conservation where his opinions would have carried weight. In other words he performed his role to perfection. The Japanese, who are suspicious of individualism in any context, expect their emperors not to do, but to be. The appearance of an 'involved' or, still worse, a 'committed' emperor would threaten the dynasty's very existence. The last example – the fourteenth-century Emperor Godaigo – brought about a schism in the Imperial family and the downfall of his own line. Hirohito's achievement has been to convey absolute dedication to his people's welfare while rigorously subsuming his personality to the set forms.

The Japanese refer to their Emperor as the *tenno* – the heavenly king. Other nations have their sovereigns, but only the Emperor of Japan is *tenno*. Since there is no need to distinguish him further, his personal name is rarely used. Instead, after their deaths, all emperors take on the names of their eras. In Japan, 1985 was not 1985, but the sixtieth year of Showa. The late Emperor is Showa. He chose the name, and it is the name he is now known by. The Japanese experience time through the medium of the imperial system, which applies only within the confines of the Japanese islands. Of course they are also aware of world time – indeed, 'preparing for the twenty-first century' is a popular slogan for businessmen and politicians. But it is a remote and vague concept, entirely lacking in the immediacy of the traditional counting method. Just by surviving, the imperial system manages to reinforce Japan's tendency to solipsism. Perhaps the practice of going back to year one at the start of every reign also contributes to the Japanese ability to negotiate 180-degree changes in direction with such nonchalance.

Divinity is like virginity – gone once, gone for ever. Only the lunatic fringe still sticks to the old belief. None the less, many respectable nationalists believe that the Emperor's role should be given more prominence. It is a sign both of their influence and the growing robustness of public opinion that Hirohito's sixtieth year on the throne was celebrated with rather more pomp than his fiftieth had been. Yasuhiro Nakasone was so enthusiastic about the event that he had it moved up from December, the natural anniversary, to May. In June he called a general election. Hirohito became more directly involved in politics during the official visit of South Korea's President Chun in 1984. His oblique apology for Japan's forty years of colonial rule had a clear political context, following on from Nakasone's skilful solution of a troublesome trade dispute. Unlike Chun, the Emperor was not head of state, but he gave the impression of speaking on behalf of the Japanese people – a constitutionally dubious notion. Given the long history of unhappy relations between the two countries it was a constructive move, and one which went down well in Korea. However, to the left any hint of a greater role for the Imperial family is the thin end of the militarist wedge. Even such a minor patriotic gesture as singing the national anthem at graduation ceremonies is fiercely resisted by the radical teaching union, as is display of the Rising-Sun flag.

Amongst the general public, attitudes to the Imperial family are changing rapidly with the population structure. Only one-third of today's Japanese were alive at the war's end, and only one-quarter are old enough to remember the years of the living god. Most of those identified powerfully with Hirohito as bearer of the national experience. It was an identification with the person more than the institution, with the man who experienced the defeat most intensely of all, yet never lost his dignity. The post-war generations see just the institutional side of the dignity, which is not all that compelling. According to a poll taken by Kyodo News in 1984, only 34 per cent of the public felt well disposed towards the Emperor, down from 50 per cent in 1975. The proportion feeling indifference rose from 25 per cent to 46 per cent over the same period. This tendency is likely to accelerate, since over 70 per cent of those in their twenties were indifferent. Personal observation confirms that most young Japanese are better acquainted with the doings of the heir to the British throne and his princess than with those of the self-effacing Akihito.

The modern Imperial family is compact, comprising only six full-time members. Empress Michiko, daughter-in-law of Hirohito, was the first commoner to marry a Japanese crown prince, having met her future husband on a tennis court. The wedding, in 1958, was hailed as opening up a new era of closeness between the Imperial family and the people, a promise which was never really fulfilled. Her son, Crown Prince Hironomiya, is probably better known to Japanese people than any member of the Imperial family has ever been. He spent two years at Merton studying medieval canal systems, during which time his darts play in Oxford pubs and valiant but vain efforts in local discos were set before the nation in solemn detail.

For several years the women's weeklies have been running breathless articles on the Crown Prince's marital prospects. Now that he has passed the average age for marriage – twenty-seven for a male – the magazines are getting increasingly excited. In marriage, as in most other aspects of Japanese life, an average is not just a mean. It is the target, even for royalty. Although another love story would please everybody, the bride will probably be chosen by a committee which includes officials of the Imperial Household and an ex-member of the Police Agency. According to the conditions leaked to the press, the successful candidate must be a virgin intacta of pure Japanese blood who speaks two foreign languages and does not wear spectacles. She will have neither attended a coeducational school nor worked in a job that gave her status superiors, and she must be shorter than the Crown Prince, who stands five foot four in his socks. If these specifications were not demanding enough, it is also laid down that she must never have featured in the gossip magazines, and they have already covered nearly every Japanese woman who fits the bill. One can only wish good luck to all concerned.

The media approach to Crown Prince Hiro, as to the rest of the Imperial family, is cautious, gingerly even. Japanese magazines are quite happy to print embarrassing photographs of foreign royalty – bald patches and wind-hoisted skirts being the favourite themes – but with their own they are less sure of their ground. Jokes, of course, are out of the question. The relationship is nothing like secure enough to permit them. No doubt the media attention will continue until the marriage question has been satisfactorily resolved, but close public scrutiny does not really suit the Imperial family, not even Crown Prince Hiro. Their tradition dictates passivity, whereas the media, as always, wants action. It is difficult to imagine the Crown Prince and his future bride playing a role of the sort performed by the British royal family. There is simply not enough going on to sustain the same level of interest. No interviews, no speeches, no overseas tours, no Koo Starks, not even any hunting and shooting. Just the imperial presence.

With the succession of a new Emperor the meaning of that presence is bound to change. However well-respected, Akihito will never achieve Emperor Hirohito's symbolic importance. The sense of shared experience will be gone. Instead, he will continue going about his formal duties and performing the secret rites, and the imperial institution will gradually fade into the background – which is the ideal place for surviving the next few millennia.

7

Politics: The Democratic Ceremony

Politics is reality. Politics is motion.

Kakuei Tanaka

Demanding classical morality from modern-day politicians is like asking for fish in a greengrocer's.

Keichi Hatano, Minister of Justice, 1983

If politicians are to be evaluated on the results of their policies, then the rulers of post-war Japan must be judged men of remarkable wisdom and far-sightedness. They have withstood a buffeting succession of crises in domestic and world affairs, leading their nation on from strength to strength. At international summit conferences they are regularly berated by their foreign equivalents for being too successful, and implored to be less so. After all, no one likes a swot.

Even in purely political terms the progress made has been astonishing. Only fifty years ago Japan's immature democracy was assailed by the swords of ultra-nationalist officers. On 26 February 1936 three senior political figures were assassinated in their homes and central Tokyo was sealed off by rebel tanks. Prime Minister Okada took refuge from the marauding rightists in a maidservant's airing-cupboard, and sensibly stayed out of sight for the next three days. Eventually, the coup was broken, but it spelt the end of the party system. The subsequent takeover of the organs of government by the military had little popular backing, but met equally little resistance. Japanese fascism, if such it can be called, was not a popular revolutionary movement, but a set of concepts imposed from above on a people conditioned by centuries to obey with absolute docility. The institutions of parliamentary democracy had been similarly imposed and lacked any sort of organic tradition to sustain them.

Today Japan is politically one of the most stable countries in the world. Japanese intellectuals can even afford the luxury of complaining of excessive stability. National elections are held with great frequency and usually attract high turn-outs. There is a noisy diversity of opinion, comprehending both the self-styled heirs of February 1936 and one of the strongest communist parties in the free world, which, however, rarely threatens to spill over into serious conflict. All statements about contemporary Japanese politics must be viewed in the context of this extraordinary transformation. Yet it would be still more extraordinary if Japanese democracy were just a carbon copy of Western political processes and nothing of the old habits of thought remained. In fact, despite the formal similarities, the functional differences are very great indeed.

First impressions of the practitioners of Japanese politics are bewildering. Aged men in swallow-tailed jackets mill around in huge fund-raising parties. They travel in black limousines to secret meetings at expensive restaurants. They give *banzais* at village festivals. They appear at weddings to beam beneficently on the happy couple. They look doleful when junior associates are hauled away to the public prosecutors. They nurture obscure rivalries. They prosper in mysterious ways. They speak in hints and allusions: 'Perhaps, a strong wind will blow this autumn . . .' At interviews they appear practically inarticulate, wheezing out ambiguous, long-winded answers to even the most straightforward questions.

There is an opposition which opposes and a government party which governs. Both know the roles they are expected to play and remain comfortably within them. That the Liberal Democratic Party (LDP) should hold power is not written into the constitution, but it is a greater certainty than many things that are. When one discusses the future course of Japanese politics, one is effectively discussing the LDP's internal developments, the interaction of its leading personalities, their alliances and subterfuges. When Susumu Nikaido, Kakuei Tanaka's right-hand man, linked up with the opposition parties to stand against Yasuhiro Nakasone for the premiership in 1983, was he really breaking faith with his boss, as everyone thought at the time? Afterwards, the weekly magazines reported that the two men had been sighted laughing together over the fuss they had created. Or was that report itself a phony, planted by one of the three masters of dissemblance? The job of a political commentator in Japan is not to examine the burning moral issues of the day, but to pick through these tangles of motivation and explain who is doing what to whom, how, and why.

The terminology alone is complex enough. To understand LDP politics clearly, it is important to bear in mind the difference between the mainstream, which is in charge, and the anti-mainstream, which wants to be in charge. More politicians belong to the mainstream than to the anti-mainstream, which is why it is called the mainstream. Sometimes, however, part of the anti-mainstream takes power, in which case part of the mainstream will join the remainder of the anti-mainstream. There is also the non-mainstream, sometimes called the sidestream, which may join either the mainstream or the anti-mainstream, depending on the strength of the current. Mr Nakasone belongs to the sidestream, used to be anti-mainstream, but now occupies the centre of the mainstream. Mr Miki, meanwhile, has stuck to the anti-mainstream sidestream. That is how the LDP river keeps on rolling along.

The proceedings of all these gentlemen are viewed with complete indifference by most of the people they represent. The subject is not discussed in the office, in the family, or even over a drink. To bring it up, even in a non-controversial manner, would be considered boorish or perverse. Partly, this is a vestige of times long gone when politics was a dangerous business that no sensible man would have anything to do with. Partly, it derives from the basic Japanese urge to avoid all subjects which could prove contentious. Most of all, it is a function of the fact that today's Japanese are well content with their lot.

According to the regular *Yomiuri Shimbun* survey, the percentage of people claiming no party affiliation rose from 6 per cent in 1966 to 27 per cent in 1986, giving them a larger share of the sample than all five opposition parties put together. Over the same period, support for the Japan Socialist Party has shrunk from 28 per cent to 10 per cent. The trend is even more striking in what were once the most radical sections of the population. A poll conducted by the Federation of Iron and Steel Unions, supposedly the vanguard of the labour movement, revealed that 55 per cent of its members support no political party, 16 per cent support the Liberal Democratic Party, 11 per cent the minor Democratic Socialist Party, and only 10 per cent the Japan Socialist Party, to which the organization is formally pledged.

The other half of the Marxist alliance displays an even lower level of political consciousness. The university magazine *Mahoroba* polled students at ten of Japan's most prestigious institutions of female learning. In addition to uncovering such statistical gems as that the average time devoted to study was one hour per day, the survey gave a fascinating account of the thinking of contemporary bluestockings. Few of them had even heard of the Star Wars scheme. When asked what should be done about a celebrated Death Row inmate, the most common answer was 'It doesn't bother me either way.' The politician most favoured was Yasuhiro Nakasone, the reasons being 'he's nice-looking', 'he's important', and 'he reminds me of my father'.

Political consciousness has responded to the shift in Japan's economic circumstances, the current state of happy apathy being a relatively recent development. Contrary to what many Japanese believe, there is nothing in the Japanese national character or social structure that makes it inevitable. Left-wing activists look back nostalgically to the Security Treaty riots of 1959, a cathartic surge of anti-Americanism which almost destroyed Japan's new democratic structures. The campus unrest of the late sixties caused Tokyo University, one of the subjects of *Mahoroba*'s survey, to close down for a year. In ferocity of purpose and idealistic incoherence, Japan's student radicals were more than a match for any. Their successors in the terrorist groups of the extreme left are still waging war on society and each other, conducting their dialectic with steel pipes.

In normal circumstances the Japanese find it hard to conceive of the political process as a forum for the clash of ideas or the discussion of moral issues. Traditionally, politics has meant the struggles for dominance between different clans. No great principle such as parliamentarianism or freedom of religion can be invoked to describe the course that the struggles took. It was all too inchoate for that. In modern Japan the warlords have been replaced by interest groups. The system that has grown up to balance their requirements is referred to by the political scientists as 'distributionism'. It is perhaps a purer form of politics than is practised in the West, since the competition for power and wealth is recognized for what it is, without any distracting references to moral concepts. However, the spectacle of other people adjusting their interests is not an especially fascinating one, and the general public should be excused their inattention to its mechanics.

The electoral system itself encourages the depoliticizing of Japanese politics. Japan's multi-seat constituencies elect from three to five members to the House of Representatives, and in many districts the hardest-fought contests are not between right and left, but between the various conservative candidates belonging to different factions of the ruling party. In extreme cases seven or eight LDP members, as well as several opposition choices, might compete for the five seats available. The outcome will depend not on what an individual candidate's views might be on the proliferation of nuclear weapons or interest rates, but purely on the extent of his influence in high places. Local politics is even less political. Usually, about 30 per cent of mayoral elections are uncontested. Powerful candidates can be backed by combinations of parties which are supposed to be in bitter dispute at the national level. In certain cases the same candidate has been supported by the LDP, the socialists and the communists together.

Editorial writers and others who are paid to pontificate have been quick to censure what they see as the voters' dereliction of duty. They were especially aggrieved by the failure of the electorate to turn out the LDP in the late seventies. Perhaps they should be more grateful for the mild circumstances in which they find themselves. Throughout Japan's modern history the national mood has veered between fanatical idealism and solipsistic content with the status quo, or to put it differently, between the code of the samurai, ever seeking to justify his existence, and the wiles of the merchant. Experience suggests that the latter is the happier alternative for all concerned. It lacks nobility, perhaps, but Japanese history provides excellent proof of Dr Johnson's dictum that a man is never so innocently occupied as in the making of money.

There is certainly no compelling reason for change. The Japanese are now richer than they have ever been. They have not been involved in an international conflict for forty years. Events are going Japan's way without any obvious need to worry about them. In that sense the lack of interest shown in the doings of politicians is the best of all tributes to their accomplishment. Countries where politics is taken seriously are not usually happy places. In Japan, politics is only taken seriously by the politicians themselves.

The Diet, as the Japanese refer to their national parliament, is housed in an imposing granite edifice near the Imperial Palace. It has a classical frontage, a squat, heavy tower, and a pyramidical roof topped off with a nipple-like protuberance. Even for Tokyo it is a queer *mélange* of styles, but none the less appropriate for that. Inside are contained the two components of Japan's bi-cameral system, the House of Councillors and the House of Representatives.

The House of Councillors, or Upper House, is roughly equivalent in function to Britain's House of Lords, possessing certain restricted powers of obstruction and delay. That the Japanese themselves do not take the House of Councillors all that seriously is demonstrated by the kind of representatives they dispatch there. The Liberal Democratic Party has long been active in recruiting stand-up comedians and other television personalities, people with names like Knock Yokoyama and Columbia Top. Japanese celebrities fit the bill admirably, since they are, according to the adage, famous for being well known, rather than for any skill or accomplishment they might offer. Ironically, once in the Diet they are expected to give up their television performances and thus cut themselves off from the source of their popularity, making re-election for a second term a difficult proposition. Further proof of the relaxed attitude which the Japanese have towards their Upper House is supplied by the relatively large proportion of women representatives — 8 per cent against just 1 per cent in the Lower House. In the 1986 campaign the LDP, which has no female Lower House members, fielded several 'Madonna candidates' in the Upper House constituencies. The most successful was Mrs Kiyoko Ono, a former Olympic gymnast who campaigned under the slogan, 'healthy, fresh, and mother of five'.

The House of Representatives, equivalent to the Commons in Britain, is where all legislation is initiated and where the prime minister is appointed. Given the peculiarities of Japan's factional system, the latter procedure can be more than a formality. After the 1979 general election, for example, the LDP was unable to agree on a nominee for prime minister and two names were put before the House. This had the strange consequence of giving the opposition parties power of decision over who was to lead an LDP administration.

In the Lower House, as in the Upper House, bills are debated and amended through the committee system before being presented to a plenary session for final approval. If the LDP has an absolute majority, it can stack the committees in a way that ensures that legislation will never be voted out. Since it is almost unheard of for members to vote against their party affiliation, this means that the executive has an iron grip on the legislature. Sometimes, when particularly incensed by a proposed bill, the opposition parties resort to the highly Japanese device of boycotting the Diet. For the

LDP to muster a quorum on its own and force the bill through would be thought extremely bad form. The only course of action is to wait until some sort of compromise inveigles them back again.

In the fifties, debates tended to be somewhat boisterous affairs, with much bad-tempered shoving and elbowing of the sort one never sees at subway stations. The police twice had to be called into the chamber to sort out the scrummaging parliamentarians. Today proceedings are usually managed in a calmer spirit, but there are still members whose area of speciality is not telecommunications or tariff law, but judicious use of the elbow and fist. One particular LDP representative, a man who once had the misfortune to be convicted of manslaughter, is renowned for his handiness when tempers are boiling over. In controversial debates it is one of the opposition's recognized ploys to obstruct access to the ballot boxes and the microphones. The LDP members, by dint of superior numbers, will eventually manage to force their motion through, but not without a physical demonstration of democracy in action.

The road to success for an LDP politician is through mastery of the Lower House committee system. If he learns how to utilize its workings he can rise through the various stages of power like a judoist through the *dan* gradings. 'Freshmen' representatives are appointed as ordinary members to one of the several committees – the Transportation Committee, the Defence Committee, the Education Committee. There they take part in drafting and debating legislation, developing close contacts with the relevant ministry officials and industry groups. Second-time victors became parliamentary vice-ministers, a post which carries great influence over the timing and drafting of legislation. A third electoral success will mean assignment as a vice-minister of a different ministry, offering the opportunity to establish another network of contacts. A fourth will bring a position on one of the party's own policy affairs committees, where the ideas behind legislation are originated. After his fifth victory, the now highly experienced political operator can expect to return to one of the standing committees as chairman, or perhaps even to enter the cabinet.

Some committees are more important than others in the quality of influence they command and, therefore, the amount of political donations they generate. From the point of view of the members, the ideal committee should handle non-controversial legislation containing a plethora of complex specifications and affecting rich and powerful interest groups. It must be possible, of course, to produce an outcome favourable to these groups' wishes. The Agricultural and Fishery Committees were once highly sought-after postings due to the significance of the farmers' vote, but the increasing difficulty of satisfying farmers' demands has reduced their attraction. Today it is in technology and trade areas that the most far-reaching decisions are being taken. Whether to approve a certain aircraft type or to allow foreign bidding for a public-sector telecommunications system could affect the future development of whole industries. However, even more modest areas of authority have their potential. Apparently, LDP dietmen responsible for the educational sector have managed to establish, in the favourite Japanese phrase, a 'mutually beneficial relationship' with private-sector suppliers of school lunches.

Japan's bureaucracy plays a major role in planning and drafting legislation. Indeed, no bill can even reach committee stage without the backing of one of the relevant ministries. The three groups working in combination – bureaucrats, politicians and extra-parliamentary pressure groups – constitute a formidable power bloc. Ties between them are strengthened by the fact that many LDP politicians are ex-bureaucrats who, on entering the Diet, work on the committees that they formerly dealt with as ministry officials. The legislation that results is intelligently framed and responsive to the needs of those who sponsored it, but not necessarily in the public interest. In 1986 a scandal broke concerning the misdeeds of the marvellously named Japan Yarn Twisters Association, which, in order to obtain tax concessions for its members, spent much money and energy wining and dining MITI officials. The association also made cash payments to an LDP dietman known as the Don of Textiles and even went to the length of bribing an opposition member to ask awkward questions in the House. Given the comprehensiveness of the operation, it is unsurprising to learn that the government has been highly sympathetic about 'structural changes' in the textile industry.

The Permanent Government

The only time that Japan has ever experienced a left or socialist government was in the turbulent period between March 1947 and October 1948. Subsequently she has been ruled by the conservatives: at first by successive Liberal Party and Democratic Party administrations, then, since 1955, by the merged Liberal Democratic Party. This unbroken tenure of power has no equal in any modern democracy. There is no evidence to suggest that it will not continue well into the next century. Even the oil crises and recession of the seventies, which put paid to governments all over the globe, could not disturb the pattern of LDP dominance, nor could a massive political scandal which resulted in the highest office-holder in the land being convicted of a criminal offence.

The party's success is hardly based on the rigorous application of conservative principle. Nothing has been conserved. Instead, the processes of change have been managed by whatever means seemed best at the time. Complete volte-faces of the sort which would attract hoots of derision in other countries have been accomplished without an eyebrow being raised. Since the LDP is a highly eclectic organization, comprehending the entire range of non-left opinion from ultra-nationalism to free-market liberalism to bureaucratic centralism, it always has a wide variety of policy choices available. The replacement of one alternative by another may indicate the rise of a certain intra-party group, but constitutes no threat to the overall dominance of the party itself. Thanks to this structural flexibility, on the rare occasions when the opposition parties have developed ideas with strong public appeal, the LDP has been able to appropriate them, put them into law, and take all the credit. In the early seventies, pollution control and greater social security were powerful reformist issues which directly challenged the way the economy was being run. However, it was the LDP which brought in the far-reaching legislative programmes required. In the eighties, education is similarly a key issue but, again, the debate is being conducted solely on LDP terms. As before, the strongest potential to change the LDP-created status quo lies within the LDP.

Cynics have remarked that the LDP is no more of a party than it is liberal or democratic. The reference is to the factional system, not peculiar to the LDP, but found there in its most highly developed form. A faction, the basic unit of Japanese political activity, is a clique centring around an elder statesman of acknowledged fund-raising and power-broking prowess, usually a former prime minister. Nearly all LDP parliamentarians, and certainly all with any serious ambitions, belong to one of its five main factions. The key determinant of the Japanese political scene is the balance of power between these units, which are engaged in a constant process of machination and manoeuvre, carve-up, trade-off and sell-out. The prize at stake is control of the nation's high offices, particularly the important economic ministries. To command them is to be able to attract large contributions to the war-chest, thus ensuring the further health and growth of the factional organism.

The balance of power between the factions after the 1986 election was as follows: Tanaka 142 members, Miyazawa 88, Abe 83, Nakasone 84, Komoto 34. Thus there are three medium-size groupings, one large, and one small. The largest faction is numerically and financially stronger than the largest opposition party, but it is still not powerful enough to accomplish its ends without recourse to alliances. The law of dynamic equilibrium has so far ensured that if one faction threatens to take absolute control, the others combine against it and cut it down to size again. Over the years the tendency towards larger and more powerful factions has been steadily gaining strength. At the formation of the LDP in 1955 there were eight factions and nearly one hundred 'neutral' members of the Lower House. Today, there are five factions, and only twenty of the LDP's Lower House representatives are unaffiliated to any of them. The Tanaka faction's strength means that it can dictate political developments.

A powerful faction leader can exert more influence than a prime minister. Indeed, through astute deployment of his factional resources, he can make and break prime ministers – by shifting alliances or encouraging splits in opposing blocs. In his heyday Kakuei Tanaka, although officially not even an LDP member, nominated three prime ministers in a row – Ohira, Suzuki and Nakasone. His view, stated in characteristically robust terms, was that the prime minister was merely 'a hat' worn by the governing party – capable, presumably, of being removed when no longer fashionable.

Elections for the LDP presidency, which automatically brings the premiership, are held every two years. In the bad old days these were decided by negotiations in smoke-filled rooms and the distribution of large sums of money amongst LDP dietmen. The richest faction, Tanaka's, usually got its way. In 1978 the system was modernized. A preliminary election was established in which all one million LDP members could vote – 'You too can choose the prime minister' was the slogan adopted. The natural consequence was the spread of the factions throughout the nation and the distribution of smaller sums of money on an absolutely massive scale. Only the Tanaka faction can afford to campaign properly.

The qualities required in a faction leader are many and various. Obviously, recourse to large sums of money is vital. More than that, the leader needs to have an instinctive grasp of the personalities and motivations both of those under his sway and of his potential enemies. 'Fast Ears' Eisaku Sato, who served four successive terms as prime minister between 1966 and 1972, was famed for his detailed knowledge of other people's problems. Information gleaned from a masseuse about a lump in the abdomen of his chief rival is supposed to have contributed to his ascent to the premiership.

Inter-factional loyalties and rivalries are fierce and often life-long, but have little discernible ideological content. One of the main features of recent political history was the 'Kaku–Fuku ten-year war', an acrimonious feud between ex-prime ministers Kakuei Tanaka and Takeo Fukuda. It would be a hard matter to identify any ideological difference between these two men, or indeed to distinguish what either of them stood for in the first place, other than the aggrandizement of his own interests. Usually what appear to be differences of opinion about policy questions are no more than surface ripples caused by the much larger conflicts going on underneath. If, for example, an elder statesman urges the prime minister to show greater sincerity in his handling of the defence problem, it will be appreciated by all concerned that defence is the last thing on his mind. Probably he has got wind of an impending cabinet reshuffle in which his faction's representation is to be reduced drastically. Once his worries have been appeased he will feel free to commend the same defence policy as being entirely in the best interests of Japanese national security. Through careful analysis of these ripple patterns, observers of Japanese politics can infer how the power struggle is developing, just as, in the Maoist period, skilled China watchers could trace what was happening from official pronouncements on classical literature.

Between 1972 and 1985 Japanese politicians were so intently occupied in factional intrigue that they had no spare time to devote to the government of the country. That was left in the capable hands of the bureaucratic élite, the best-educated and best-informed component of the Japanese power structure. The overall policy, long established by national consensus, has been beautifully simple – to pursue the course of maximum economic advantage. It was left to the ministries to identify the most suitable means available. Meanwhile the factional struggles raged with an intensity that sometimes reached the verge of self-destruction. In May 1980, for example, the Miki and Fukuda factions abstained in a no-confidence vote sponsored by the socialists, thereby provoking a general election. That was sweet revenge for the untimely removals from the premiership of Takeo Miki in 1976 and then Takeo Fukuda in 1978, both engineered by Kakuei Tanaka in revenge for his own ouster in 1974.

Newspaper editorials and members of the weaker factions occasionally call for the break-up of the factional system and the abolition of 'money politics'. Indeed, in the wake of the Lockheed scandal the factions did officially disband themselves, only to reappear immediately in the guise of 'study groups', a fine instance of the Japanese talent for changing the form while preserving the substance. The factional tendency was embedded in Japanese politics long before the concept of representative democracy arrived. In feudal Japan a samurai owed absolute loyalty to his clan: its alliances and enmities, which could date back generations and yet be reversed overnight, were automatically his. In return the clan provided him with security and advancement. By contrast, the samurai's loyalty to the national government – the Shogunate – was secondary and conditional. If ordered by his clan leader to assist in its overthrow, he would do so without hesitation. In modern Japan, factions exist in all walks of life, from the playground to the boardroom. In tea ceremony, flower arrangement, karate, indeed nearly all traditional arts and sports, different sects compete for supremacy just as bitterly as large corporations do for market share. The urge to seek security in powerful groupings, which maintain their identity by fiercely opposing other similarly constituted groupings, is a fundamental characteristic of the Japanese psyche.

Politically, the existence of the factional system has enabled fluidity and stability to co-exist, has helped to stave off boredom, and has averted a long-term concentration of power in one man's hands. Because the ultimate power to propose and dispose rests with the factional leaders, on whose sufferance the prime minister continues in office, few have seen the job as an ultimate goal. Once a prime minister has overstayed his welcome, either through trying to accumulate too much power or by becoming too unpopular in the country, the other factions have ganged up and disposed of him. Paradoxically it was because Yasuhiro Nakasone's faction was so numerically inferior that he was able to maintain his grip on power. Of the seven prime ministers since 1972, all but one have continued to exert influence after leaving office,

Inside Japan

in most cases stronger influence than they ever had while occupying it. Nobosuke Kishi, who resigned the premiership in 1960, is still a powerful background figure in party affairs, being father-in-law of 'New Leader' Abe and a member of the group of elders (*juro*) who are called on to make important party decisions. While the leadership of the country has changed hands fairly smoothly, senior Japanese politicians have proved considerably more reluctant to pass on factional control. Yasuhiro Nakasone has retained the leadership of his faction since 1966. The political world, like the business world, is a gerontocracy, and those who rule it seldom retire to a life of gardening and afternoon strolls.

Over the years circumstances have favoured the continuance of conservative rule. The LDP has been fortunate in its opposition, which has never looked capable of managing so much as a celebration in a saké factory. Whenever the LDP's various misdeeds have threatened to stir up lasting public odium, the opposition parties have failed to produce a comprehensive – or even comprehensible – alternative. In Diet management or electioneering the difference between the LDP and the other parties is the difference between professionals and amateurs.

The longer the LDP stays in charge, the less convincing the opposition seems by contrast. The object of all political parties is the attainment of power, and parties which have never looked like attaining it and whose leaders have never held office are bound to lack credibility. More important, the LDP has been left in exclusive command of the pork barrel for so long that it has built a formidable network of the strongest support of all – that based on direct self-interest. To disturb the status quo would be to invalidate too many relationships which have already proved their use. Voters know that only LDP men have the power and connections to bring government subsidies or private-sector capital to their constituency. A vote for the opposition might be a nice idea, but it would contribute nothing to the parsnip-buttering process. In recruitment the case is the same. Budding politicians know that there is only one party which can give them the opportunity to make things happen.

In psephological terms, change is difficult to envisage. At the 1986 general election the LDP was the only party which ran enough candidates to capture a majority of the 512 Lower House seats. It put up 353, whereas the Japan Socialist Party, the largest opposition party, put up only 138. Here the multi-member constituency system exerts a decisive influence, serving to entrench the current balance of power. If, for example, the JSP were to run two candidates instead of one in a four-seat constituency, it would risk splitting its vote and ending up with no seats at all. It would have to be very sure that its base of natural support had expanded before mounting a stronger numerical challenge.

LDP dominance has built up its own psychological momentum as well. Even in periods of dynamic change, perhaps then most so, the Japanese feel comfortable with the familiar and the long-lasting. There are twelve professional baseball teams in Japan, but over half of the population supports the same one, the Yomiuri Giants. It is not necessarily the best team, but it contains all the star players. They are stars by virtue of the fact that they play for the Yomiuri Giants. Other teams may take the trophies, but they can never hope to attract the same gates. In the summer months, Giants games are broadcast live six nights a week. The romantic exploits of Giants players are pored over in the women's magazines. Whatever the quality of its current team, the popularity of the Giants is self-perpetuating, self-aggrandizing. For the Giants is not just a baseball club, it is an institution through which Japanese people can reassure themselves of their essential fellowship. Voting for the LDP, like supporting the Giants, is a method of registering your acceptance of the status quo that everyone has constructed together.

In fairness, it should be added that another important reason for the LDP's long stint in power has been that it has done a remarkably good job. It has presided over a massive increase in living standards: the economic miracle of the sixties and its consolidation in the seventies. If Japanese voters measure their current prosperity against the sum of previous experience, they will feel better off than the citizens of any other rich country. The LDP's role has been not as a leader of events but as a consensus-smoother, mediating the tensions between different interest groups. Since these tensions have never grown serious enough to disturb the pursuit of economic advantage, its performance of this valuable task must be judged successful.

The ultimate secret of the LDP's success lies not in what it does but in what it is. The LDP is quite simply the most Japanese of Japan's political parties. All the epithets, both complimentary and derogatory, that have been applied to the Japanese people can be applied with even greater force to their Liberal Democratic Party. It is cliquish, inward-looking, devious, pragmatic, quick to respond, quick to synthesize, supremely competent. Its workings and its appeal are based on *giri* (obligation) and *ninjo* (debt), *chu* (loyalty), *mentsu* (face), and *oyabun/kobun* (mentor/pupil) link, and other traditional concepts by which the Japanese still like to define their social behaviour. In fact the only organizations in Japan which are more scrupulously traditional in this respect are the gangster syndicates. By contrast, the opposition parties, try as they might, are forever lumbered with imported and highly abstract ideas which have never had any relevance to Japanese life.

Compared to the LDP the opposition parties even sound un-Japanese; strident, always full of complaints, wanting to change what does not need to be changed and to preserve what does not need to be preserved. They seize on human failings. They get excited. Their language is abusive and bombastic – insults like 'liar', 'crook' and 'fascist' are everyday currency – but everyone knows that the difference between them and the LDP is not one of morality, but one of scale. In contrast, LDP men who nurture lifelong hatreds of each other appear in newspaper photographs stepping out of expensive restaurants arm in arm. That is the Japanese way to quarrel. Even in election campaigns they rarely resort to verbal attacks on opposition figures or even policies. After scoring his spectacular election victory in 1986 Yasuhiro Nakasone promised that he would listen with the utmost humility to the proposals of the opposition parties. Since opposition proposals are, almost by definition, the mirror image of LDP intentions, there could be little point in paying them any attention at all. None the less, Nakasone's statement was widely appreciated. It helped the opposition parties to preserve face at their moment of deepest shame.

LDP men are rarely angry because they are not idealists: they do not expect human nature to be other than flawed, indeed their monopoly of power depends on it remaining so. Yet they can be sentimental as well as brutally cynical. Shortly after Kakuei Tanaka had been found guilty of accepting a bribe from Lockheed, he held an emergency meeting with Yasuhiro Nakasone in a plush suite of the Okura Hotel. When Nakasone emerged he was questioned by his senior colleagues as to what matters of moment had been discussed. Tanaka, replied Nakasone, had explained how his granddaughter was being teased at school and then had burst into tears. He, Nakasone, had wept as well. Upon hearing this, several of the LDP elders began to blubber in sympathy. The opposition parties have nothing that can compete with that.

If the opposition were to form a government in Japan it would mark not just a realignment in the power structure but a fundamental change in the way the Japanese think. That is not to say it could never happen, but it would require exceptional circumstances. Only a drastic deterioration in the economic climate would suffice to invalidate the LDP's whole approach to government: a trade war much more serious than anything experienced in recent memory, or a massive miscalculation of policy. Social and economic strains in Japan will increase greatly between now and the end of the century. The population is ageing rapidly, unemployment will increase to levels unknown in the years of rapid growth, the patterns of mass obedience will gradually lose their hold. Of themselves, these are not enough to constitute a drastic change, but they will make the business of government considerably more difficult. Japanese voters will continue to leave it to the experts.

Party Pieces

In the best of circumstances, the Japanese left would be faced with an uphill struggle. Ninety per cent of Japanese people profess to consider themselves middle class. Income differentials are amongst the lowest in the world. Life under the capitalist system may not be perfect, but it has created a dramatic rise in living standards within the memories of most voters. Persuading them of the benefits of socialism was never going to be easy. Failure to move away from Marxist theorizing has made it impossible. By refusing to adapt to new circumstances, the left has turned its back on the dominant characteristic of modern Japan. As reminders of a simpler world, now for ever gone, the parties of the left command a special kind of nostalgic respect. They do not, however, command many votes.

The history of the Japanese left since the war has been a succession of missed opportunities. The Japan Socialist Party (JSP) started out in life with a massive store of electoral goodwill, its antecedents being the pre-war proletarian parties who had offered the strongest opposition to the militarists. In the late fifties it was supported by 30 per cent of the electorate and held one-third of the seats in the Lower House. It was the natural vehicle for the millions of workers who flooded into the cities from the agricultural districts. It was during this period that the party began its long and fatal obsession with the defence issue. In 1960 it supported a series of mass demonstrations against the Security Treaty that culminated in the most serious outbreak of public disorder in Japan since the coup attempt of 1936. The precious consensus on which the nation's hopes of recovery rested had almost been shattered, a state of affairs which few Japanese were prepared to tolerate. One side of the confrontation, the Kishi government, was sacrificed immediately. The sacrifice of the JSP took longer. Over the next decade the newly formed centrist parties gradually drew off JSP votes and funds. The JSP, meanwhile, remained aloof from the transformation in values being wrought by the 'income-doubling'. Equally, it failed to profit from the social libertarianism which broadened the appeal of European socialist parties.

The JSP managed to hold its position throughout the seventies, usually enjoying double the Lower House representation of the third-largest party, the Komeito. For much of this period the balance of forces between the parties was roughly even. In only three of the fourteen years between 1972 and 1986 was the LDP's majority sufficient to give it control over all Diet committees. As the largest opposition party the JSP could exert considerable influence over the framing of legislation. Its members led the barrage of criticism of Tanaka plutocracy and LDP corruption, an approach which attracted many non-socialist members of the public. At the time it seemed that the Tanaka issue was the best thing that could have happened to the Japanese left. In retrospect it seems like the worst. By concentrating its energies on a narrowly defined 'political' issue, the JSP lost all touch with the far-reaching social and economic developments that were occurring at the time. When Tanaka was forced out of active politics by illness in 1985, the JSP was left high and dry.

The JSP never really discovered how to deal with Yasuhiro Nakasone, the first prime minister in a decade to enjoy personal popularity amongst the electorate. In the 1986 election the party made an astonishing tactical error in waging a campaign of *ad hominem* abuse. Economic conditions were deteriorating rapidly and LDP policy was failing to respond, thus calling into question its entire *raison d'être*, but the JSP chose to concentrate on Nakasone's 'dishonesty' in concealing the timing of the election. The results were disastrous. The party won only eighty-six seats, a loss of twenty-five and the lowest total since its foundation. Suddenly it was no longer the 'Number One opposition party', but merely one amongst several small mutually reliant groupings. The LDP's comfortable overall majority meant that the JSP's capacity to influence events had declined to zero, and the prospect loomed of another collapse in support to match that of the early sixties. Chairman Ishibashi, hailed just two years previously as 'the JSP's last trump', resigned his post to take responsibility for the electoral defeat, the fourth successive JSP leader forced to that humiliating necessity.

It was emblematic of the party's dismal condition that at first nobody could be found to take over the job – a pointed contrast with the LDP's overabundance of prospective leaders. The original deadline for nominations passed without a single candidate coming forward, suggesting that not only did the JSP lack appetite for power as a party, but that it contained no individuals with any personal ambitions either. Finally Takako Doi, the vice-chair, was drafted into the post at the insistence of the top party executives. She is not just Japan's first female party leader, but the only woman to have made any progress at all in Japan's male-dominated political world. Of the Lower House's 512 members only 7 are women – 2 socialists and 5 communists. If Doi is able to make a success of the demanding task ahead of her, it will augur well not just for the JSP but for the greater participation of Japanese women in professional life.

The JSP has a close and long-standing relationship with the labour movement, both the party's greatest sustenance and its fatal weakness. Compared to their European equivalents, Japanese unions are simply not powerful enough to form a national party around. The unionization rate in Japan is low and falling, now barely half its post-war peak. The enterprise union system acts against the formation of class consciousness, and most private-sector unions tend to favour the moderate Democratic Socialist Party. In the public sector the LDP's administrative reform policies have cut into the membership of the Prefectural and Municipal Workers Union, the largest of the unions pledged to the JSP. The break-up of Japan National Railways has done irreparable damage to Kokuro, the largest railway union. Even those unions that have maintained their strength are likely to grow less enthusiastic about their relations with a party now so remote from power.

Japanese public-sector unions do not provoke the same degree of hostility as their British equivalents traditionally have. The absence of the right to strike has prevented them from engaging in the most debilitating forms of industrial action. None the less they are far from popular, even amongst their fellow unionists – the militant steelworkers' union has denounced them as 'tax-eaters'. The general public considers their membership to be overpaid, underworked and boorish of manner, and Nakasone's administrative reform programme as just come-uppance. The irony of the JSP's position is that it remains dependent on the public-sector unions for funds, campaign workers and votes. The party itself is weak, attracting only one-quarter of the contributions of the much smaller Communist Party. In the 1986 election 46 per cent of all JSP candidates were ex-union leaders, as are nearly all the top party officials. They can still summon up the organizational votes that are vital in Japanese politics. For the JSP to reduce its links with the union movement would be to take a bold gamble with its future. Yet, if the party is to develop a series of policies that can arrest the decline in its support, it has little alternative.

Policies have never been the JSP's strong point. For most of its history it has relied on a collection of attitudes that distinguished it from the LDP as much as possible. It has consistently been much further to the left than European socialist parties, espousing a Marxist-Leninist theory of class struggle that has little relevance to the conditions of modern Japan. On specific issues, such as administrative and educational reforms and privatization of the national railways, it slavishly follows the vested interest of the unions involved. It insists that all Japan's nuclear power-stations, which supply 20 per cent of the country's electricity requirements, should be shut down. In foreign affairs it has favoured the abrogation of the US–Japan Security Treaty, the disbandment of the Self-Defence Forces, and 'unarmed neutrality', a policy that no major country has ever contemplated. It refuses to recognize South Korea, Japan's sixth most important trading partner, preferring the credentials of Kim Il Sung's 1984-style regime in the north.

Historically the JSP has been plagued with inter-party factional disputes almost as much as the LDP has. LDP quarrelling is comprehensible in form, if not in substance – it arises out of competition over the distribution of power. That also means that it always stops short of self-destruction. In contrast, JSP disputes are based on obscure points of ideological principle and have frequently done the party irreparable damage. The brief administration the JSP formed in 1948 was brought down by its own left wing. The fifties were punctuated by a series of splits, secessions and purgings which served to stimulate the growth of the centrist parties that ate into JSP support over the next decade. Even in its newly reduced circumstances the party still houses seven factions, each one bitterly critical of the others. The most extreme is the Socialist Association, a group of Marxist academics which takes a perverse pride in rejecting all tendencies to pragmatism. On one occasion it sabotaged an attempt to divert some of the defence budget to welfare spending on the ground that such an act would betray the JSP's stand on the absolute unconstitutionality of the self-defence forces.

Until Masashi Ishibashi took over the party chairmanship in 1983 the outcome of the various factional showdowns had always been the same – victory for the ideologues of the Socialist Association and exit from the party of any members in favour of more realistic and electorally attractive policies. Ishibashi himself was a man of the left, author of a best-selling book called *Unarmed Neutrality* and one of the leaders of the ouster of the moderate Eda group in 1977. He had learnt both his socialism and his anti-Americanism as a leader of manual workers on the Sasebo air base. Ishibashi was well aware of the need to move away from East-European-style socialism if there was to be any hope of ending the LDP's hold on power. Against noisy criticism from the Socialist Association and the other leftist factions, which was only pacified after a three-week adjournment of the 1985 party convention, he succeeded in forcing through the adoption of the 'New Declaration', a policy document to replace the Marxist 'Road to Socialism' which had defined JSP objectives since 1964.

Ishibashi did his best to promote an image appropriate to the 'New Socialist Party' phrase which he had coined. Previous JSP leaders had opposed the visits to Japan of US presidents on the ground that they affirmed the hated Security Pact. Ishibashi welcomed Ronald Reagan's visit in 1984 and made his own trip to Washington in 1985. On the Self-Defence Forces, he came up with the classic formulation that they were 'unconstitutional but lawful', and tried to muddy the waters on Korea and nuclear power in similar fashion. Circumstances did not shine kindly on his efforts, although they were highly rated by most political commentators. In 1986 he attempted to visit South Korea to hold discussions with the opposition to General Chun, but was denied an entry visa – at LDP insistence, according to the rumour. The Chernobyl disaster undermined the New JSP's softer stance on nuclear power generation, and shortly afterwards the party voted against Sino-Japanese nuclear co-operation.

Part of the problem lay in Ishibashi's presentation. Although a man of integrity and determination, as well as an accomplished party tactician, he lacked the flair to put the new image across to the public. Particularly in comparison with the photogenic Nakasone, there was something irredeemably dreary and old-fashioned about his manner. Short in stature and owlishly bespectacled, he delivered his speeches in an earnest monotone. Like most of his colleagues, he seemed locked in a fifties time warp. It was no coincidence that JSP members in the Lower House have the highest average age of all the parties.

Whether the party can convince the electorate that it has something better to offer will depend greatly on the skill and popular appeal of its leader. Takako Doi is not exactly a new face in Japanese politics, having won election to the Diet seven times, but her promotion to the chairmanship does indicate the party's readiness to take risks. Female politicians in the West have risen to power in step with similar moves in business and the professions. Doi's success is still an isolated example, and it is not clear that the Japanese electorate is ready to endorse it. On the other hand, half of all voters are female – slightly more, in fact, if turn-out ratios are taken into consideration. There should be a large latent supply of support for Japan's only important female politician.

In background, as well as sex, Doi stands apart from the usual run of JSP leaders, having neither factional affiliation nor links with any labour union. Formerly an academic specializing in constitutional law, she was recruited into the party in 1969 as a 'name' candidate. While she lacks Ishibashi's expertise in the mechanics of party business, she has a more general appeal in the country and a non-doctrinaire feel for diplomatic and women's issues. Her hobbies – *karaoke* singing and pinball – are appropriately demotic and, most unusually for a Japanese socialist, she has a sense of humour. Her high recognition factor amongst the general public was demonstrated by the impressive sales of a telephone card which bore her photograph. More than public relations successes will be required to halt the long slide in the JSP's fortunes. Doi will have to confront the basic questions about the nature of Japanese socialism which have defeated her predecessors.

The Japan Communist Party is probably the best-organized party in Japan. It has 400,000 members, more than five times the strength of the JSP, and usually rakes in a larger annual income than the LDP. Unlike the two largest parties it has no institutional backing, nearly all its funds being derived from membership dues and sales of *Akahata*, the party newspaper. The JCP claims a circulation of 3.5 million for *Akahata* which, if correct, would rank it with the British tabloids. Usually, the JCP has been the fourth-largest parliamentary party, with strength enough to influence events in periods of stalemate between LDP and opposition forces. However, in the last two elections, although the number of seats gained remained stable, there was a noticeable slump in the party's share of the vote. Added to the slow but steady decline in the circulation of *Akahata*, it could prefigure a gradual unwinding of the gains made in the sixties.

Founded in 1922 under the direction of the Comintern, the JCP began its existence as an underground organization, subject to stiff repression by the government. Since early Meiji times Japan's leaders had recognized that a thriving proletarian movement was incompatible with the quasi-mystical authoritarianism they were assiduously promoting. In the pre-war years developments in China made them even warier of dangerous Western ideas. By the mid thirties all the main JCP activists were in prison or exile or had been forced to recant their beliefs. As a result, right up until the early eighties, the party was controlled by a generation of politicians whose knowledge of the revolutionary struggle was rather more than theoretical. For example Kenji Miyamoto, the overlord of Japanese communism from 1958 until his death in 1982, spent twelve years in prison before and during the war.

The communists originally hailed the occupation forces as an army of liberation, but soon, as the cold war intensified, shifted back to the advocacy of violent revolution. The authorities responded with the Red Purge of 1950, in which thousands of suspected communists were barred from political activity and dismissed from their jobs. On the outbreak of the Korean War the JCP took its militancy one stage further and embarked on a terrorist campaign that, far from stimulating a popular uprising, alienated great numbers of the party's remaining sympathizers. As a result, in the 1952 general election, the communists lost all thirty-five of their Lower House seats. From that nadir the JCP gradually recovered its momentum, with Miyamato promoting the image of a 'self-reliant and independent party' dedicated to a 'democratic revolution'. By 1972 it had achieved greater electoral success than ever before, with some anti-LDP voters preferring its clear-cut style of opposition to the fuzzy attitudinizing of the JCP. In 1976 the phrase 'dictatorship of the proletariat' was dropped from the party's platform document, and 'scientific socialism' was substituted for 'Marxist Leninism'. However, the party's support had reached a plateau, and Miyamoto's dreams of a Euro-communist-style breakthrough remained unfulfilled.

The relationship with the JCP has always been a vexed one. Contention between the two parties stretches back to the purge of communists from the unions and the establishment of Sohyo (the General Council of Labour) as an anti-communist labour federation. One of the reasons why Japan's anti-nuclear movement is so weak, despite the fact that eighty million people are said to have signed an anti-nuclear petition in 1982, is the interminable feuding between rival JCP- and JSP-backed groups. Gensuiko and Gensuikin are Tweedledum and Tweedledee organizations in agreement about the iniquity of American nukes, but in bitter disagreement about the merits of the Soviet and Chinese versions, as well as a host of extraneous ideological issues.

Both parties recognize the need for a coalition if the LDP's dominance of the Diet is ever to be challenged. Since the mid seventies the JCP has been assiduously courting the JSP as its partner in a prospective alliance of the left. Recently, however, the JSP has been making suggestive noises to the Komeito, which itself has an intimate relationship with the Democratic Socialist Party (DSP). To confuse the issue further, the DSP has shown a frank interest in the virile attractions of the LDP. Amongst all the potential entanglements, the JCP is the suitor whose ardour is least likely to be requited, since it still suffers from the ideological halitosis of the Moscow connection. The JSP is carefully distancing itself, since it knows that no coalition can ever include both the JCP and the DSP. In any regrouping of the opposition forces the JCP is almost certain to remain out in the cold. Its one consolation is the chance of luring away radical JSP voters disillusioned with the move to moderation.

In the eyes of the Japanese electorate the LDP is government, is the pragmatic exercise of power. Similarly, the parties of the left are the real opposition, because they live by ideology, whereas the LDP has none, and because they have never held power and are never likely to. Thus the choice that voters are familiar with is a sharply delineated one between LDP and 'non-LDP'. Exactly what policies the non-LDP forces favour is not particularly relevant as long as they are fiercely opposed to the LDP. They are its mirror image. Japan's centrist parties suffer from a lack of definition. They want power, indeed often cook up elaborate schemes in attempts to secure it. They claim to be pragmatic, and yet oppose the very institutionalization of pragmatism, the LDP. If they were truly opposed to the LDP they would be ideologues, like the socialists and the communists. If they were truly pragmatic, they would join the LDP – in which case, of course, there would be no need to vote for them.

In fact, joining the LDP is a course of action that the Democratic Socialists have been hinting at for several years. The DSP itself was formed in 1960 by defectors from the JSP, and is funded by Domei, the umbrella organization of private-sector unions. As the enterprise unions are merely different avatars of the corporations that fund the LDP, the relationship would be quite logical. For most of its life the DSP has espoused an amorphous 'social democracy', better understood as opposition to the JSP's Marxism than as a coherent body of policies. Originally the party advocated revision – but not abrogation – of the Security Treaty and the expansion of the welfare state. Today the DSP is more hawkish than some sections of the LDP. The welfare state has not been a popular issue since the rapid growth of pensions and medical insurance payments in the seventies began to threaten government finances. Accordingly, the DSP has become an enthusiastic proponent of 'administrative reform'. From time to time party members have suggested removing the word 'socialist' from its name, since the party no longer promotes socialist policies. Instead, it has campaigned with some success amongst small business associations hurt by structural changes in the economy.

The DSP has, at various times, suggested alliances with the Komeito, the JSP, and the anti-mainstream LDP factions, in all the various combinations. In its unabashed yearning for power the DSP has been following the pragmatic principles of its founder, Suehiro Nishio: 'A cat that does not catch mice is no cat.' Unfortunately all available mice have been pounced on by the LDP, and it is not clear that another mouser is required. The only contribution that the DSP could make to an administration would be to perform the purely mechanical function of stabilizing it if the parliamentary majority were not secure. Since the 1986 election the LDP's majority has been more secure than ever before and, after twenty-five years, the DSP still lacks a convincing *raison d'être*.

★

The Komeito, the third-largest party, is in its way a political phenomenon as Japanese as the LDP. After all, many countries have communists and socialists and democratic socialists, but none other than Japan has a political party formed by a Buddhist sect that teaches its adherents to chant for whatever they require from life. The Soka Gakkai (Society for the Creation of Value) has been easily the most successful of Japan's 'new religions', attracting eight million members in Japan, and an estimated nine million worldwide. Its teachings, which derive from the Nichiren school of Buddhism, stress the necessity of changing one's karma by spiritual effort, symbolized by the repeated invocation of the Lotus Sutra.

Nichiren, one of the great figures in Japanese Buddhism, lived in the fourteenth century, a time of social and political confusion that he identified with *mappo*, the last degenerate stage of human history. In contrast to the arcane doctrines of the traditional sects, he propounded a simple relationship between faith and salvation that anyone could grasp. Soka Gakkai offers its believers a modern-day version of the same consolation, plus a tight communal structure, including schools and neighbourhood study groups, which replicates the social involvement of village life. Its appeal is to those disoriented by the upheavals of our own times, and often to those with physical, mental or financial problems. Undoubtedly many unfortunate individuals have attained a remarkable inner balance and cheerfulness through their practices. The self-help philosophy can, however, be taken in an alarmingly literal way. The following 'testimony' is taken from *UK Express*, the monthly bulletin of the organization's British division:

I started chanting about a car that in fact I had up for sale for about seven months and which nobody had any desire to buy. So I thought, right – if this Buddhism is that great, I want to sell my car today. When they heard me chanting, my mother was quite frightened . . . In fact that day, of course, I sold my car. Both my parents chanted the same day and also my grandfather, who for 18 months had been looking for accommodation to suit him because he was 82. That day he also found a flat which he now lives in.

Not even Japan's best-connected pork-barrel politicians could ever compete with that.

Komeito (Clean Government Party) began life in 1964 as the Soka Gakkai's political arm. Its stated purpose was the promotion of Buddhism in national politics, a dubious notion given the strict division of religion and government mandated by the constitution. The only clearly political idea it embraced was world disarmament, pacifism always having been a major theme in Soka Gakkai teachings. In the late sixties Komeito's close relationship with the religious organization began to generate bad publicity, especially after the party, with the help of Kakuei Tanaka, attempted to suppress the publication of a polemic called *I Denounce Soka Gakkai*. Tanaka's ministrations were of no avail, and the book, replete with allegations of brainwashing and electoral manipulation, eventually became a million-seller.

In 1970 the Komeito was re-established as an independent political party, dedicated to the furtherment of 'humanitarian socialism', a concept so diffuse as to be meaningless. Initially the party flirted with radical leftism, but then, after a murky episode in which Soka Gakkai signed a 'ten-year non-aggression pact' with the JCP, began its gradual shift to the right. A key turning-point was the 1978 decision to recognize the Self-Defence Forces and the Security Treaty, thus preparing the way for a coalition with moderate and conservative forces. None the less the Komeito has kept up its contacts with the JSP, leaving open the possibility of a left-centre alliance. Despite its support for a realistic defence policy the party retains strong pacifist leanings, and has none of the enthusiasm for higher military spending of the DSP. The symbolic issue of the annual visit by cabinet ministers to Yasukuni Shrine rankles especially, since it evokes memories of the suppression of Buddhist organizations by militant Shintoists before and during the war. The founder of Soka Gakkai, Tsunesaburo Makiguchi, died in prison in 1944 after being found guilty of undermining State Shinto.

In electoral terms the Komeito has been easily the most successful opposition party of the eighties, consistently attracting between 9 per cent and 10 per cent of the popular vote. In parliamentary strength it is now larger than the DSP and JCP put together and is moving up fast on the JSP. Its performance in the 1986 contest was a convincing demonstration of the party's organizational strength – only one seat was lost in the face of the LDP landslide. As a result the Komeito has acquired decisive influence over the nature of any possible realignment of opposition forces. Without the intervention of Komeito the only alternative strategy for the DSP is engulfment by the LDP, and for the JSP isolation on the left. If the new opposition grouping that is sometimes discussed ever came into being, it would almost certainly be based on Komeito, with support from the DSP and the JSP right.

Although Komeito has come a long way from the rather glutinous religiosity of its early years, doubts remain about its suitability to lead the opposition camp. It is still overwhelmingly dependent on the Soka Gakkai for funds, organizational skills and votes. Certainly many Japanese retain an understandable suspicion of the party and its motives, especially since a spectacular outbreak of scandals and feuding has revealed the Soka Gakkai to be subject to the same strains that afflict all Japanese power groups. That a party of inherently limited appeal has come to occupy such a key position speaks volumes about the poor quality of the other opposition parties.

The Favour Market

One day in the spring of 1980 a van driver going about his business in the Ginza came upon a paper bag sitting on top of a fence. He picked it up and opened it and found that it contained Y100 million in fresh notes. Being a public-spirited fellow, he did the decent thing and handed the money over to the police. Despite considerable publicity in the media, nobody came forward to collect it and, in a fitting end to a moral tale, the van driver became a rich man overnight.

'Political money' was the rumour, never substantiated. Still, it was an understandable-enough supposition, since at that time the Lockheed trial was revealing how similarly large sums of money had changed hands at assorted drop-off points around the city. The heyday of 'money politics', as it is popularly known, had occurred in the early seventies. Under the stewardship of Kakuei Tanaka the LDP is supposed to have expended Y100 billion in the 1974 Upper House election. 'Five to win, three to lose' was the unofficial party slogan – meaning Y500 million would ensure a candidate's election, whereas only Y300 million would mean his defeat. Party officials staggered to secret meetings hauling plastic shopping bags stuffed with cash. Since the largest denomination of Japanese note is only Y10,000, successful political management required a sturdy pair of shoulders. Where this money came from and where it eventually ended up are mysteries.

The LDP fared badly in that contest – the Japanese public does not like to see misbehaviour so utterly lacking in refinement. Yet little of substance has changed. Financial flows still determine numerical support, which determines power, which in turn determines the ability to generate further financial flows. Including both official and unofficial contributions, Japanese politics is a one-trillion-yen industry – one-third of the size of the defence budget – and it is growing at 20 per cent per year, even at times of economic slow-down. That the most successful politicians are the richest, not just personally, but in their access to other people's money, goes without saying. A Japanese politician with no money is like a car without petrol. However impressive the appearance, there can be no question of a performance to match.

Japanese politicians are paid extremely well by most standards. In a country where the average salary is Y4 million, an ordinary dietman is given Y15 million, plus Y7 million in expenses, plus free housing, two secretaries and a rail-pass. The top LDP leaders are rich men in their own right, possessing large holdings of land and securities and, usually, several golf-club memberships. They deal actively and profitably on the stock exchange, making excellent use of their range of business contacts. This is not held against them. Rather, astute management of personal finances is regarded as an essential qualification for the job of running the national economy. Yet, whatever the scale of their officially declared assets and income, it is nothing like enough to satisfy the financial demands to which they are subject. As a party the LDP is not particularly well off. Year after year it takes in less contributions than the Japan Communist Party, which has only one-tenth the number of dietmen. It is left to the individual LDP politicians to generate the necessary income however best they can.

Money is required for a multitude of purposes. Funds have to be distributed amongst faction members in order to keep them faction members. Loyalty may be the central Japanese virtue, but it is always contingent on a firmly understood quid pro quo. Twice a year, in the summer and winter gift-giving seasons, the faction leader hands out what are picturesquely known as 'cannon-balls' – contributions to operating expenses of several million yen. Funds are also needed to smooth relations with important bureaucrats, to obtain the support of opposition parties in difficult votes and, above all, to fight elections, both national and intra-party.

At the constituency level, sitting dietmen are faced with a similar set of demands. LDP representatives in particular have to keep their supporters sweet in case other factions decide to run candidates against them in the next election. Their constituency office, like their support organization, is paid for not by the party but from their personal and factional resources. The loyalty of the voters has to be cultivated by organizing, and funding, banquets, sports contests, resort holidays complete with Filipino entertainers, and visits to the Diet followed by nights out on the town. Important local-interest groups – temples, farmers' groups, senior citizens' clubs – need periodic donations to top up their sense of obligation. Staying popular is an expensive business.

The Japanese expect politicians to represent their interests in a much more direct way than is the case in the West. Politicians are known as *sensei*, a term with a wider reference than 'teacher', the standard translation. Doctors, writers, lawyers, university professors and many other wielders of expertise and authority are *sensei*. The politician is a *sensei* not because of any wisdom he might dispense, but because of the good works he performs. He is at the centre of the complex interchange of favour and obligation through which most important transactions are settled. He is expected to help to resolve land disputes, find respectable jobs for untalented sons, and husbands for unlovely daughters. He is responsible for the economic health of his constituency, for promoting local redevelopment plans, building new factories and preserving unprofitable railway lines. He is at the centre of the network of *kone* (Janglish for personal connections) through which most things in Japan are proposed and disposed. Tickets to sumo or baseball, jobs in blue-chip companies, places in medical school – only connect, and they are yours.

When favours are asked and obligations assumed, cash often changes hands: not used notes in a brown paper bag, but crisp new yen of the sort the delivery man found in the Ginza. Because the Japanese are very particular about appearances it is usually enclosed in a special white envelope emblazoned with propitious Chinese characters. Japan is a gift-giving society, and special exchanges have been devised to clarify and strengthen social relationships – mid-year gifts, year-end gifts, wedding gifts, funeral gifts, promotion gifts, graduation gifts, housewarming gifts, parting gifts, holiday gifts. In July, the peak month, sales of special gift packs make up over 20 per cent of the total business of the major department stores. The complex interrelation of *on* (favour) and *giri* (duty) signalled by these exchanges is powerful enough to settle a marriage, or an election, or a multi-billion-yen construction project.

With the birth of modern Japan, the Meiji-era statesmen were faced with an immense problem in trying to forge national unity out of a loose collection of feudal kingdoms. Their solution, emperor worship, is no longer valid, but the problem remains. Although the Japanese sense of racial identity is remarkably strong, that by no means implies a willingness to sacrifice local interests for the benefit of Japan as a whole. Particularly in the rural and semi-rural areas, which supply 70 per cent of total LDP support, the national interest is but dimly perceived as an extension of what is good for the region. Japanese dietmen usually represent the same constituency throughout their political lives. If they lose one election they rarely move on to contest a safe seat elsewhere, but dedicate themselves to improving their local connections in readiness for the next time. An 'outside' candidate would have little chance of understanding the interplay of economic and personal interests that characterizes each district.

The acknowledged master of pork-barrel politics is Kakuei Tanaka. The residents of the Niigata No. 3 constituency have good reason to be grateful to their parliamentary representative. Thanks to him, the once-underdeveloped patch of snow country has a new bullet-trainline which enables them to make the 200-mile trip to Tokyo in under two hours. Niigata Prefecture as a whole now has the highest ratio of public investment per head in the whole country: if the national average is indexed at 100, Niigata registers 255, Tokyo less than 40. One famous example of Tanaka's largesse is the Shiodani tunnel, which cuts through the mountains to a tiny village of sixty households. It was built at a cost of Y1 billion – in other words about Y17 million per household. No wonder that one Niigata town is reputed to maintain a special Tanaka shrine in the basement of the local government hall.

Where does all the money come from? Ultimately, from the industrial and other interest groups desirous of influencing policy decisions. After the Lockheed scandal broke, a political-contributions law was enacted which is supposed to restrict and clarify the flow of funds, but it is, to say the least, imperfect. Although political parties must disclose the source of all donations above Y10,000, for the support groups of individual politicians the limit is Y1 million. Since most politicians have three or four support groups, usually masquerading as research organizations, and since large companies have a number of subsidiaries and industry associations through which they can operate, it is an easy matter to split up quite substantial contributions into non-disclosable chunks. Furthermore, while all contributions to an individual politician (as opposed to support groups) must be declared, if he passes the money on to his support group, he can subsequently withdraw it without any obligation to disclose the use. Transactions between the various support groups are entirely unregulated, which enables money to be switched back and forth until any attempt to track it is rendered useless.

It has been suggested, from time to time, that Japanese politics is in an exceptionally corrupt state. The mass-circulation dailies certainly thought so in the late seventies, when they pursued Kakuei Tanaka like hounds after a wounded stag. Citizens' movements sprang up demanding an end to money politics, and it seemed to many observers as if change was in the air. The results of the following general elections refuted that expectation comprehensively. Japanese voters showed that they were quite satisfied with the status quo, or at least that they favoured it over the alternatives presented. Political scandals have been occurring in Japan ever since rules to prevent them were first dreamed up. 'Black mist', as the Japanese call the controversy generated, is as prevalent as the more ethereal kind celebrated by the *haiku* poets. That the Lockheed affair concerned a foreign company, a fact which incensed many patriotic Japanese, is hardly unique either. In 1914 a mighty row was caused by revelations that Vickers of Britain and Siemens of Germany had been paying large kickbacks to naval officials, both companies for what they supposed were exclusive rights of supply. In every decade of the twentieth century except, significantly, the militarist thirties, there has been at least one spectacular scandal. Of Japan's sixteen post-war premiers, nine have been subject to official investigation for graft at some stage in their careers. If corruption is taken to mean degeneration from a once-pure condition, then it is doubtful whether Japan's case fits the bill.

The electorate knows what kinds of politician it wants, and it knows what it wants them for. Receiving and dispensing bribes are criminal offences, yet those implicated rarely incur electoral unpopularity. In 1983 Tanaka recorded the highest vote in his career just three months after being sentenced to a term of imprisonment. Another Lockheed bribee achieved a resounding victory in the 1986 general election weeks after having his appeal rejected. As far as the voters were concerned, the specific benefits they had received from these men far outweighed any abstract breach of political ethics. Interestingly, in the same election an opposition dietman suspected of having accepted a pitifully small bribe was soundly defeated. The voters knew that, lacking sufficient power to ride out the storm, his usefulness had come to an end.

In few countries do law and custom make perfect matches, but in Japan they frequently seem to belong to different worlds. In one, the judges, the newspapers and the intellectuals, all subscribing to abstract codes of behaviour; in the other, voters and their representatives still interacting in the time-honoured way. The latter world is usually identified with the rural areas, where traditional thought patterns remain powerful, and the former with modern-minded city-dwellers. In purely electoral terms that is accurate enough, but in a wider sense the distinction is a false one. In most business and social relationships the interchange of favour and obligation, stretching far into the past and expected to continue far into the future, still dictates the response to ethical choices. That is as true inside large companies, including media concerns, as in Tohoku farming communities, though, of course, the intervention of a politician is not equally necessary. The conflict of values can even exist inside one individual – who may be bitterly critical of political fixing, but quite prepared to use the *kone* network in his personal life. For a Japanese, no matter how 'progressive' his views, to deny himself access to that network would be to take a serious risk with his future.

The Japanese attitude to money itself is complex and liable to wild fluctuations. Traditionally the samurai disdained it, as did the ultra-nationalists of the thirties. Even today Japanese people are quite gingerly in their handling of cash, the sight of which is considered vulgar. Counting one's change or divvying up a Dutch treat are simply not done. Instead, money passes from wallet to hand with lightning speed. In more important transactions the magic white envelope is employed, once inside which money is transformed into a token of sincerity which is suitable, for example, as a wedding gift. Yet money is also greatly respected as a transmitter and repository of value. It is always kept clean, never creased, never scrawled on. Like *o-kome* (rice) and *o-sake* (rice wine), *o-kane* (money) is one of those fundamental nouns which automatically take the honorific prefix *o* no matter what the relative status of the speakers. It is the god within the thing itself which is being honoured.

Money is precious, not just for what it can buy, but for the social and economic relationships that it signifies. Traditionally, honesty and dishonesty have been defined through those relations – how one keeps a trust or returns a favour, not by mechanical rules. It is no accident that the Japanese who are most conservative about the uses of money have least resistance to the signals it carries. In rural districts, shopping on credit may be frowned on, but vote-buying is a fact of life. The politicians understand the paradox and make it work for them.

Vote Games

Japanese elections mean noise, unbearable noise. Politicians wearing white gloves – to signify purity – stand in front of railway stations and bellow speeches at the rush-hour crowds. The less interest the crowds display, the louder they bellow. Megaphone vans patrol the streets, booming out their supplications: 'We humbly beg your honourable support, we humbly beg your honourable support . . .' When two opposing vans close in on each other, the result is a bawling cacophony of ingratiation which tests the *shirankao* (face of indifference) of even the most blasé passers-by. On polling day itself, low-flying aircraft buzz over the suburbs, exhorting the people to their citizenly duty. The same refrain is given out hourly through the ubiquitous loudspeakers by which district governments communicate their various warnings and instructions to local residents. For those who are hard of hearing there are sternly-phrased slogans ('One vote can make the difference') on the front pages of the newspapers, on street-corner hoardings, even flashed up on the scoreboard at baseball games. There is good reason for the decibels – the physical distance between candidate and elector prescribed by law. House-to-house canvassing is strictly forbidden, since it would provide too obvious an opportunity for favour-benefit exchanges. Those exchanges are still made, but not in such quantity and with such directness as they used to be. If candidates have any envelopes to deliver, they must do it outside.

In a Japanese election the level of support obtained is just one variable. Just as important is the number and positioning of the candidates. Mastery of the multi-seat constituency system requires a fine strategic sense and painstaking calculation, nowadays performed by computer. A candidate who runs and is defeated may be a valiant loser, but he may also have caused a serious drain on his party's support. A landslide victory can have the same effect. Matching supply to potential demand is as difficult a task for politicians as it is for businessmen. The acknowledged master of the art is Komeito, whose links with the well-disciplined Soka Gakkai organization enable it to quantify support far more accurately than the other parties. If necessary it can optimize resources by shifting members' official residences from one constituency to another. In the 1983 general election the Komeito brought off the feat of improving its parliamentary strength from 34 to 58 seats while its share of votes cast increased only from 9 per cent to 10.1 per cent. Remarkably, all but one of its candidates were victorious.

The LDP's internal power structure means that there is always a potential excess of candidates to votes. Each faction tries to obtain official nominations for as many of its own pet candidates as possible, even if this damages the party's overall prospects. Further complications are caused by the profusion of unofficial candidates, most of them conservatives who failed to make the party slate. There are usually about one-third as many of them as official LDP nominees, the successful ones being anointed with party approval immediately after the event. If in a small constituency there is not enough room for all LDP factions to run official candidates, one or more may well back 'independents', thus drawing away support from their own party's agreed choice. Some 'independents' are as well funded and connected as their officially backed rivals, enabling them to make equally valid contributions to the Japanese political process.

The opposition parties have problems of a different sort. Their only hope of ever wielding power, and a pretty dim hope at that, is through the formation of a coalition. However, the Japanese electoral system does not facilitate the co-operation that should be the first element in an alliance of forces. Since voters support personalities, not ideas, tactical voting is a risky strategy to apply, particularly in multi-seat constituencies where the range of choices is so wide. The LDP has cleverly exploited the opposition's disarray. Both the 1980 and 1985 general elections were 'double elections', in which the dissolution of the Lower House was timed to coincide with the end of the Upper House term. The huge sums of money and sophisticated organization needed placed a heavy strain on the opposition's resources.

The multi-seat system throws up some interesting contests, such as that between Yasuhiro Nakasone and Takeo Fukuda in the Gumma No. 3 district. Fukuda has beaten Nakasone into second place on six successive occasions, including two when the latter was serving as premier, the only instances of such an indignity ever occurring. The good people of Gumma have not forgotten Nakasone's abrupt 'betrayal' of Fukuda in the 1972 leadership contest. However, in the same district's Upper House constituency, Nakasone's son has managed to turn the tables. In 1986 he came top of the poll at his first attempt, narrowly ahead of Fukuda's seventy-five-year-old younger brother.

This sort of dynasty-making is common enough in the LDP. The Japanese see nothing wrong in a politician who has made good providing for those close to him, indeed it is viewed as evidence of his essential decency and sense of family values. Naturally there are few better forms of provision than a seat in parliament. Yukichi Fukuzawa, the great Meiji-era educator, is supposed to have been highly impressed that nobody he met in the United States could inform him what had become of George Washington's descendants. In modern Japan such questions would not require much thought. Ichiro Hatoyama, son of Japan's fourth post-war premier, is top choice on the LDP's Upper House slate and has two sons of his own sitting in the Lower House, as are the sons-in-law of ex-prime ministers Suzuki and Fukuda. 'New leader' Shintaro Abe is the son-in-law of ex-Prime Minister Kishi, who is the brother of Eisako Sato, Prime Minister from 1966 to 1972. Sato's own son is a long-serving member of the Tanaka faction. Strangely enough, the Japanese like to describe their society as a perfectly egalitarian one, the contrast being with class-ridden Europe. True, there is no longer any system of titles to mark the transmission of hereditary power, but the phenomenon exists just as surely. Altogether, 25 per cent of the LDP's Lower House members were 'bequeathed' their seats through family connections, a proportion that has been rising as the LDP's position of dominance has become increasingly entrenched.

At election time the 'triple alliance' between businessmen, bureaucrats and politicians shows its true worth. The large companies bankroll the LDP's campaign, and even detail groups of staff to work at the headquarters of favoured candidates. Whether they are conservative supporters is, of course, beside the point. The role of the bureaucracy is almost as important. Reportedly, top LDP officials keep a list which ranks the various ministries A to E according to the co-operation they show in elections. The specific points under consideration are, apparently, (1) whether they set quotas of votes and funds for the organizations and companies under their jurisdiction, (2) whether they set up secret campaign headquarters of their own, and (3) to what extent they mobilize former and incumbent bureaucrats to help the campaign. The Construction, Agriculture, and Communications ministries usually achieve straight As, MITI and the Ministry of Finance Bs. The fact that so many LDP candidates are ex-bureaucrats (about 25 per cent of the total) means that co-operation is easily arranged.

Japanese campaigns are also renowned for the less subtle forms of persuasion employed. In the rural districts the envelope-passing custom is still widely practised. Campaign workers take busloads of voters to the polls, then, on the way home, stop off at a restaurant for an early celebration of the *sensei*'s victory. A box of seaweed or a fancy cigarette-lighter may be presented to commemorate the happy occasion. In local elections, where a small number of votes can separate success from failure, the mischief-making is on a different scale. On the island of Shikoku personation is something of a regional speciality. The *senkyoya-san* (professional election-fixer) will buy up voting vouchers beforehand, then distribute them to teams of substitutes who probably each vote half a dozen times altogether. It is a skilled job, since each substitute must be close to the original in age, sex, and, if possible, appearance. Some of the candidates are just as unusual as the methods of selection. In the 1983 unified local elections a candidate with ten criminal convictions, including a sentence for armed robbery, succeeded in winning a seat on a town council. As the newspaper account indicated, he is a man with strong roots in the area:

The head of a gang of about sixty members was elected to the Odate City Assembly arousing criticisms from local citizens. But the gang boss, Tsuyoshi Yagami, who is head of the Yagami Gang, said in an interview after being questioned by police on suspicion of bribery that he believed he could contribute to the development of the city as an assemblyman. The Yagami Gang was established in 1938 by Yagami's father, the late Kinzo Yagami, who served four terms as an Odate City assemblyman from 1951 to 1967, including one term as speaker of the assembly.

How widely the electoral malarkey extends is difficult to judge. It is not restricted to remote and backward country areas. One of the most notoriously corrupt constituencies – Chiba No. 2 – is within commuting distance of central Tokyo. In the 1979 election it yielded 300 arrests, believed to be a modern-day record. Nor are LDP and conservative forces the only culprits. It came as no surprise when immediately after the 1983 mayoral election in Fukuoka, the wife of the successful 'reformist' candidate was arrested for distributing bribes to powerful local temples. Her husband's campaign pledge had been to remedy the graft of his conservative predecessor and inaugurate an era of clean government. But then again, as the Japanese proverb states, if water is too clean, no fish can live in it.

Healthy muddiness was plentiful in the 1986 general election, when 10,500 people were questioned by police on suspicion of vote-buying and 990 arrested. Since many experienced *senkyoya-san* will have absented themselves immediately after the polls closed, and since only a fraction of their activities will have resulted in complaints to the police, the true number of electoral violations is probably several factors higher. The National Police Academy, with its usual attention to detail, reported that the average price of a vote bought was Y7167, more than double the going price in the previous election. That these offences are considered no more than venial was clearly demonstrated immediately after the election. Yasuhiro Nakasone appointed as his Minister of Justice a man who had once been convicted of bribing local assembly members in the course of an election campaign.

It should be emphasized that Japanese elections are, apart from the noise, peaceful events. Strong-arm tactics are entirely absent. The atmosphere is festive: much saké is consumed, many mutually beneficial relationships established. The methods that politicians use to win power would probably not satisfy a Jefferson or a Washington but, given the roles they are expected to perform once in office, that is hardly surprising. Japanese intellectuals are given to shaking their heads in despair and complaining that their country is not a real democracy. That is rubbish. The electorate is regularly presented with a choice similar to that which exists in most Western countries – between being governed by conservatives, or socialists, or in-betweens. The result that emerges with such consistency may not be pleasing to the intellectuals, but there are no grounds for supposing that it is not a fair reflection of public opinion. All in all, the Japanese electoral system does the job which is asked of it, and provides considerable entertainment into the bargain.

8

Japanese Leaders:
The Consensus Merchants

The qualification of the leader rests primarily on his locus within the group, rather than his personal merit. If his mind is too sharp and he is excessively capable in his work, the men below him lose part of their essential function and may become alienated. The leader is expected to be thoroughly involved in the group, to the point where he has almost no personal identity.

Chie Nakane, anthropologist

'Pop stars last one year, prime ministers two' – such for many years was the conventional wisdom in Japanese politics. To most voters the name of the Japanese prime minister has usually been an irrelevancy. Issues of policy have been decided not by direction from the top but by the balance of power between the various competing interest groups and factions. In the seventies the job was occupied by a bewildering succession of ideologically indistinguishable senior politicians who mumbled emollient words in public and worked Byzantine intrigues against each other in private. They came and went, and few lamented their passing.

The archetype of the prime ministerial cipher was Zenko Suzuki, who held the post from 1980 to 1982. A graduate of the Tokyo University of Fisheries, Suzuki had clambered up the LDP hierarchy with the assistance of the various fishermen's organizations whose interests he represented. Until his unexpected propulsion to the premiership by the hand of Kakuei Tanaka, he was unknown to the general public. To this day it is difficult to decide whether he is a politician of great wisdom or great ineptitude. As prime minister he rarely ventured opinions, and when he did they were so garbled and ambiguous as to be incomprehensible. In fact he rarely initiated any activity at all, preferring to let events fall into their natural patterns and then to adjust his position accordingly. He emptied his administration of policy rather as Zen priests are supposed to empty their minds of thought. In his sublimely placid features, Suzuki has a striking resemblance to a Japanese Buddha, though his earlobes are not quite long enough to denote true holiness.

In ironic tribute to his passivity, the vogue-word *zenkoru*, meaning 'to do nothing', was coined from his given name. Pressure groups grumbled and foreign governments seethed with frustration, but Suzuki remained serene, which was his victory. When he finally did do something, it was completely unexpected. In the autumn of 1982 Suzuki suddenly resigned, not, like most of his predecessors, elbowed out by rival factions, but of his own accord. In a resolution worthy of a Zen parable he expressed himself for the first time through an act of self-abnegation and managed to confuse everyone in the process.

Suzuki was a product of a political system which accords the highest value to the building of consensus. Every action creates an equivalent reaction, so shifts in policy must be undertaken with the utmost caution, having obtained the understanding of all those directly affected. Once consensus has been achieved, far-reaching decisions can be implemented smoothly and efficiently. The expert politician does not force them through. He waits until the time is right. The problem with that kind of approach is that not all political conflicts will yield a consensual solution. Waiting for the left and the right to agree, for example, on a proper defence policy would be like waiting for Godot. On what were once more tractable issues, the growing interrelation between domestic and foreign affairs means that the interests of those who do not understand the consensus mechanism have to be accommodated as well. A Japanese prime minister now has to address himself to European industrialists and U S congressmen as well as Tohoku agricultural associations.

Most modern-day Japanese prime ministers have been in the Suzuki mould. However, the political world has also occasionally spawned a different species of leader, the dominant larger-than-life figures who have imposed their personalities on the flow of events. The great historical examples are the leaders of the Meiji Revolution, little-known samurai from the remote Kyushu fiefdoms who, without the benefit of experience or precedent, guided Japan through a traumatic era of change. In contemporary Japan the only politicians to transcend the ordinary consensus-forming process have been Kakuei Tanaka and Yasuhiro Nakasone, two men who have come to symbolize the eras in which they held power, and even enduring traits in the national character. It is meaningless to talk of 'Suzuki politics' or 'Fukuda politics', but everyone understands what is implied by 'Tanaka politics' and 'Nakasone politics', including those most vigorously opposed to them. Although referring to style as much as content, the terms are as clear as Thatcherism or Reaganomics. Unusually for Japanese politicians, both Tanaka and Nakasone are popular with the public. Equally, they have generated controversy and media criticism of rare intensity – a tribute that most Western leaders would understand.

The Bulldozer

Tanaka's life story has acquired the status of a legend, partly because of his own repeated reference to it in speeches and books. No doubt many elements have been given that apocryphal touching up which is essential to all good legends, but it is undoubtedly a remarkable story, and one which could never occur in contemporary Japan.

An indispensable part of the American dream is supposed to be the presidential potential of any child, no matter how humble its background. Tanaka's success represents the Japanese dream. Modern Japan is a 'curriculum vitae' society run by ex-bureaucrats and graduates of Tokyo University Law School. Tanaka came from nowhere, with only an elementary-school education to guide him on his way. Many supporters believe that his downfall was the establishment's revenge – the press, the courts and the politicians ganging up against the unrefined upstart who had the temerity to break into their charmed circle. Be that as it may, his rise to power took place in one of those rare periods of creative turmoil in Japanese history when the whole world is temporarily turned upside down and men of ambition and talent can attain the highest goals. In the immediate post-war years all social and economic definitions temporarily lost their relevance, clearing the way for the political entrepreneurship of Tanaka and the business entrepreneurship of Honda and Sony's Morita.

Tanaka was born in a poverty-ridden farming village, no more than a cluster of 150 roofs between the mountains and the Japan Sea. The nearest town was Nagaoka, a remote and backward place at the time, but now a prosperous well-developed city which boasts a station for the bullet-train. It has good cause to be grateful to its favourite son. Tanaka's home prefecture is Niigata, in the heart of snow country. Its people are as tough as they need to be in the face of the icy winds that blow across from Manchuria and Mongolia. Traditionally they have had a reputation for surly independence, and a distinct animus against the central government. In the Meiji Revolution the region remained fiercely loyal to the Shogun and, in the eyes of its inhabitants, was victimized for its allegiance by Japan's new regime. The chip is still on the shoulder today, and helps to explain the obsessive adulation of Tanaka. The more he is vilified in Tokyo, the more votes he gets in Niigata.

For generations the Tanaka family had suffered high infant mortality on the male side. Kakuei's elder brother died in the cradle, and he himself caught diphtheria at the age of two. According to village superstition his providential return from death's door was an omen of future greatness. Tanaka's mother worked in the fields. His father was a horse-dealer whose chronic insolvency meant that young Kakuei frequently had to do the rounds of neighbours and relatives asking for financial help. The practical experience he gained of the traditional Japanese ethic of duty and obligation must have been a tremendous asset in his political career. After completing elementary school Tanaka began work as a ditch-digger in the local paddies. At the age of sixteen he left home to seek fame and fortune in Tokyo. His mother sent him on his way with some useful precepts, such as 'Even if you forget who you lend money to, never forget who you borrowed from'. She also left him with 'three prohibitions': don't drink, don't make promises that you can't fulfil, and stay away from horses.

Working from five in the morning until midnight, Tanaka soon made his mark in the Tokyo construction industry. By the age of nineteen he was *sha-cho* (president) of his own construction company. After brief war service as a private in Manchuria, terminated by illness, he built his company up to sizeable proportions, and by 1943 it was ranked amongst the nation's top fifty construction firms. Over the next few years there was to be plenty of work for the Japanese construction industry. By the end of the war Tanaka was rich enough to finance his ascent into the political world. According to one version of events, his first attempt on the citadel of power failed when an employee used the electoral funds with which he had been entrusted to procure his own election. In the 1946 general election Tanaka stood unsuccessfully as a Progressive Party candidate. His maiden electoral address gave a foretaste of the pork-barrel rhapsodies with which he was later to entrance the entire nation:

What we'll do is demolish the mountain range between Niigata and Gumma prefectures. Then, the winter winds from the Japan Sea will pass straight over to the Pacific and we'll be able to avoid the heavy snows ... The earth? We'll use it to fill in part of the Japan Sea and make a land bridge to Sado Island!

The following year Tanaka tried his luck on the Democratic Party platform, and was elected. Within a year of entering parliament he crossed over to the Liberal Party, the conservative mainstream; and at the age of thirty he was appointed Vice-Minister of Justice in the second Yoshida cabinet. Shortly afterwards occurred his first contretemps with the law, when he was arrested in connection with shady dealings in the coal industry. He announced his candidacy for the next election from prison, and was duly re-elected to the Niigata No. 3 constituency. Eventually his conviction and six months' suspended sentence were quashed on appeal.

On the merger of the Liberal and Democratic parties in 1955 Tanaka became one of the protégés of Shigeru Yoshida, the father figure of modern Japanese conservatism. His progress up the party hierarchy was swift and sure, taking in two of the posts considered essential for a future prime minister, those of the cabinet secretary and chairman of the policy affairs committee. He was Minister of Posts at the age of thirty-nine (1957), making him the youngest minister since the Meiji Era; Minister of Finance at the age of forty-four (1962); Minister of International Trade and Industry at the age of fifty-three (1971); and finally Japan's youngest post-war prime minister at the age of fifty-four (1972). In gerontocratic Japan, where men well into their eighties still wield considerable political and economic power, it was an extraordinary achievement. In the first Nakasone cabinet, for example, only six of the twenty-one appointees were under sixty, and not one was under fifty.

All the while, Tanaka was carrying on his complex business activities. Several commentators have pointed to the curious fact that while none of the many companies that Tanaka was associated with prospered at all – most, indeed, going into rapid decline – his own personal finances went from strength to strength. His forte was real-estate dealing, in which he often displayed an uncanny foresight into government-initiated redevelopment schemes. His skill at making money and, more important, his skill at spending it made him the most influential politician in Japan. In all his ministerial posts he dispensed midsummer and winter presents to the bureaucrats under his control, and kept them sweet even after moving to his next appointment. He dished out cannon-balls (working funds) to dietmen from opposing factions, creating strata of secret Tanaka sympathizers within the camps of his closest rivals.

Eisaku Sato, the prime minister of the day and head of the faction to which Tanaka belonged, plumped for Takeo Fukuda as his successor. Both as a personality and as a political animal, Fukuda was the antithesis of Tanaka – reserved and patrician in style, very much the product of his élite training at Tokyo University Law School and the Ministry of Finance. In ambition and command of political intrigue, he was simply no match. Tanaka had already formed his own group of supporters within the Sato faction, and in the 1972 leadership election he stood against Fukuda and defeated him. In the thunderous exchange of cannon-balls, Tanaka's firepower was overwhelmingly superior.

In the country, Tanaka was a popular choice as prime minister. In his public appearances he cultivated a demotic charisma that set him apart from the usual run of stuffy conservatives. He wore *geta* (wooden sandals) with his business suit and flapped a large white fan to cool his permanently sweaty face. When Minister of Posts, he had appeared in a nationally broadcast song festival and performed a swaggering ballad of gangland revenge. His speeches, delivered in a gravelly rasp, were full of salty aphorisms and anecdotes about his early life. As a mark of intimacy, rarely bestowed on a politician, Tanaka was known to the public as Kaku-san, an abbreviation of his given name. Other nicknames included 'the computerized bulldozer', 'the builder', 'the kingmaker' and, most famously, 'the shadow shogun' – in all, a collection far surpassing any other politician's in both number and vividness. The mass media was rapturous in its welcome for the new star in the political firmament, who was, if nothing else, a journalist's dream. For the next twelve years Tanaka was to remain the best news story in Japan. The *Asahi Shimbun*, later to become his most relentless foe, commented on his nomination:

For a long period, we have sensed the futility of the Japanese people's expectations of political change. However, with the appearance of Prime Minister Tanaka, hopes of political change have been brought back to life. The new prime minister's youthful sensitivity to changes at home and abroad, his lack of connection with school and family cliques, and his unpretentious individuality lead us to hope for not just a change in the holder of power, but for the germination of a political revival.

As premier, Tanaka identified himself with two main policies, both of which were greeted with enthusiasm. Restoration of diplomatic relations with China was favoured by the electorate for sentimental reasons and by the business community for pragmatic ones. All Japanese had been seriously discomfited by the implications of Richard Nixon's surprise visit to Peking. If Japan did not move fast enough she might find herself in diplomatic isolation. A dynamic leader was required to coax the necessary consensus into place. Tanaka fulfilled his self-appointed task perfectly. Using his connections with the opposition parties – he had remained friendly with Komeito since the *I Denounce Soka Gakkai* affair – he arranged a trip to Peking within three months of taking office. After his meeting with Mao a statement was issued in which the restoration of diplomatic and trade relations was agreed. During the course of negotiations Tanaka even composed an extemporaneous poem in the traditional Sino-Japanese style.

His second major policy fared less well. Throughout his career Tanaka had been intrigued by grandiose construction projects – out of which he had personally made vast profits. As prime minister he intended to reconstruct the whole of Japan. His book *Remodelling the Japanese Archipelago*, published in 1972, sold over one million copies. Its theme, highly relevant as the Japanese became increasingly dissatisfied with the pollution and congestion of their cities, was the need to break the concentration of population in the industrial belt. The Tanaka solution, which required a massive commitment of public funds, was to rebuild the decaying regional cities, drawing people and businesses into a network of secondary centres. It was a bold, imaginative concept, way ahead of its time in many provisions. Development of Shikoku, the neglected fourth island; establishment of 'industrial parks'; expansion of the bullet-train and highway network; the potential of new electronic media to link physically distinct work places;

the need to build upwards, not outwards – in the eighties these have become the common currency of discussion. It will probably be several decades before Tanaka's vision can be enacted, but Japan requires some such master plan if her limited natural resources are to be exploited in a balanced way.

Unfortunately the early seventies was exactly the wrong time to embark on futuristic redevelopment schemes. As in Britain, the government's easy money policies stimulated a wave of speculation in land and stocks, and the oil shock of 1973 decisively brought to an end the high economic growth on whose continuance the remodelling had been premised. In 1974 consumer price inflation in Japan was higher than in any other industrialized country. Inflationary bottlenecks were creating shortages of key goods, as was graphically demonstrated by the 'toilet-paper panics' which afflicted urban housewives. The popularity rating of the Tanaka cabinet suddenly plummeted. Simultaneously, revelations about Tanaka's creative business activities began to appear in the press. The respected *Bungei Shunju* monthly had been searching for a political-corruption scoop to match the Watergate affair. It was not disappointed. A young free-lance journalist called Takashi Tachibana, backed by a corps of researchers, performed the herculean task of unravelling the tangled web of Tanaka's financial dealings. The story was publicized by *Newsweek* and the foreign press, and then pounced on by the domestic media. Tanaka decided that resignation would be the surest method of stemming the growing tide of public criticism.

That was only the beginning. In 1976 Tanaka's name was mentioned in a senate hearing into the bribing of foreign officials by US multinational corporations. In testimony later given to Japanese prosecutors in exchange for legal immunity, representatives of Lockheed Corporation claimed to have paid Tanaka Y500 million in order to convince him of the merits of Tri-Stars over DC 10s – part of the successful marketing strategy the company had been pursuing all over the world. Tanaka was arrested and charged accordingly, together with a selection of top business executives who had been involved in the flow of money. Japanese justice proceeds at a leisurely pace, and it was not until October 1983 that the verdict was handed down. The judge accepted almost all details of the prosecution argument, and sentenced Tanaka to four years' imprisonment, the heaviest punishment exacted for bribe-taking in Japanese legal history. He was immediately freed on bail pending appeal, the technical condition in which he remains. The case could, if necessary, be dragged out until the end of the century.

Richard Nixon was forced to resign at roughly the same time as Tanaka. The comparison between the fates of the two men is instructive. Although never charged with a criminal offence, Nixon was spurned by his own party and withdrew completely from public life, his influence over political events reduced to zero. Tanaka was forced out of the premiership, and then left the LDP, choosing to sit in the House as an independent. Like Nixon he was transformed into a political ogre, the target of sustained assault from the mass media and the opposition parties. Citizens' movements sprang up to demand his ouster; the public-sector unions led snake-dancing street demonstrations past his office; his life was threatened by radicals of both left and right. There the similarities end. Despite the charges against him, Tanaka's political influence continued to grow by leaps and bounds. From being the strongest of Japan's senior politicians, Tanaka came to wield almost unrestricted power over LDP and national affairs. He contrived the falls from the premiership of first Takeo Miki, then Takeo Fukuda. The next three prime ministers – Ohira, Suzuki and Nakasone – were effectively all Tanaka appointees. Throughout Japanese history power had been exercised behind the scenes by various regents, retired emperors and shoguns who used the authority of the figurehead ruler to their own advantage. Tanaka's ascendancy was in the grand tradition.

Tanaka appreciated more clearly than his rivals that strength lay in numbers, and invested massively in new faction members. The amount of money he was prepared to disburse at elections and the benefits available through his network of bureaucratic and business connections made his faction first choice for any aspiring dietman. Within the political world it became obvious that cabinet jobs and other privileges could best be secured through membership of the Tanaka faction. In 1976 his faction had only forty-four members in the Lower House, nine less than that of Fukuda, his chief rival. After the 1983 'Tanaka-verdict election', it was sixty-three strong, while the Fukuda grouping had declined to forty members, making it only the fourth-largest of the five LDP factions. After the 1986 landslide the Tanaka faction, now minus the leader's guiding influence, had eighty-seven members in the Lower House, more than the largest opposition party. Its size and coherence made it by far the most important single power bloc in Japanese politics.

Factions had always existed in the LDP, but until Tanaka's time senior politicians had not bothered to expand their groupings aggressively, preferring to rely on informal alliances. With a Lenin-like grasp of the dynamics of power, Tanaka set about fulfilling the political potential of the factional unit. In the land of factions the Tanaka faction came to acquire the status of a Mount Fuji, both dominating and symbolizing the rest of the terrain. The fascination it exerted spread far beyond the narrow world of political manoeuvring, as was indicated by a poll of top executives taken by *Diamond* business magazine. Over half of the sample expressed approval of the Tanaka faction, and the most common views were 'it is the natural result of people gathering together' and 'its organizational strength is impressive'. Clearly, the men who drive the Japanese economy found something to admire in Tanaka's supremely efficient power-dispensing machine.

Takashi Tachibana, who had kept up a barrage of ferocious and entertaining criticism, took a rather more severe line:

The Tanaka faction is a gang of thugs and criminals . . . If it were an ideological group that had hijacked a political party in order to realize ideological aims, everyone would immediately be aware of the danger and abnormality of the situation. However, the Tanaka faction has nothing so elevated as an ideology. As Tanaka himself is reported to have told a Nakasone faction member, 'ultimately, all our guys want is cash and positions'.

The trouble with Tachibana's argument was that it ignored the Tanaka faction's repeated electoral successes. The conspiracy stretched much wider than the membership of the faction, wide enough to encompass the whole nation at times. Amongst the general public the disapprovers tended to be the more Westernized type of Japanese, those who believed in the overriding validity of abstract principles. Traditionally Japanese businessmen and private individuals in dispute avoid invoking legal remedies wherever possible, preferring to rely on the services of an intermediary, often a politican. The common assumption is that social relationships are too subtle and multifarious to be governed by the reductive logic of the law.

In the eyes of admirers, the Lockheed scandal was an unfortunate accident which could have befallen any important politician. As faction spokesman Kozo Watanabe put it, 'There are few politicians who have never violated the Public Office Election Law. Although it may seem to laymen that the Lockheed case is a serious blow, politicians do not think that way. Most politicians sympathize with him. There are very few politicians who have not accepted political funds . . .'

A branch chief in the Tanaka back-up organization took an even more benign view of the issue: 'Politics is a dirty business. The *sensei* [Tanaka] works in that dirty business for the good of his home town. He took money from Lockheed, but he used that money to do politics with. Taking five hundred million from the Americans – that shows what an important man the *sensei* is.'

Naoki Komuro, political commentator and holder of a law doctorate from Tokyo University, likened Tanaka's acceptance of Lockheed's Y500 million to the shoplifting of tissue paper from a supermarket. In his view all charges against Tanaka should have been dropped in recognition of his services to the country. A precedent for that sort of extra-legal procedure had occurred in 1954 when Eisaku Sato had been saved from arrest by the intervention of Prime Minister Yoshida. Komuro's argument was interesting, because it confronted what many critics chose to ignore – the profound nature of the Tanaka appeal: 'Every Japanese has a Kakuei Tanaka in himself or herself. No one in this country can blame Tanaka for his avariciousness. Those who dislike Kakuei are those who must resemble Kakuei. No doubt, Kakuei Tanaka is the embodiment of today's Japan.'

Tanaka understood the Japanese political mentality perfectly. There was nothing new about his methods – they had always been at the heart of the system. Tanaka differed only in the scale on which he operated, and in the effectiveness of his power. The most complimentary word the Japanese have for a politician is *jitsuryoku-sha* (man of practical strength). Tanaka was the ultimate *jitsuryoku-sha*, the hub around which the wheel of interests whirled. Through his intervention all problems could be solved, all conflicts smoothed away. He was the perfect example of what the Japanese expect a politician to be, and the language he spoke was the language everyone understood – money. Yet financial power alone could not explain Tanaka's dominance. Many of his rivals were almost as wealthy, but none could match Tanaka's strategic skills and instinctive understanding of how Japanese political and social relations work. Hideyoshi Toyotomi, the warlord who unified Japan in the sixteenth century, is described by Lafcadio Hearn as follows: 'a son of peasants, an untrained genius who had won his way to high command by shrewdness and courage, natural skill of arms, and an immense inborn capacity for the chess-play of war'. To his faction members, Tanaka was a second Hideyoshi. Here is Watanabe again: 'All politicians want to be a Tanaka, but none of them can be as successful as Tanaka. Mr Tanaka is a genius born once in several hundred years . . .'

Few outsiders agreed with that assessment. To most commentators in the media, Tanaka symbolized the corruption of Japanese politics and his continued popularity the immaturity of Japanese democracy. In the opinion of JSP Chairman

Asukata, 'We cannot blame delinquent boys and girls when a prime minister is committing crimes.' According to Seiichi Tagawa of the New Liberal Club, Tanaka was 'the root of all evil'. The Big Three newspapers published long investigations into his alleged misdeeds, often referring to him as Criminal Defendant Tanaka. The Japanese media has scant regard for the formalities of the legal process, and articles were published with titles like 'The Prime Minister's Crime'. Small-circulation newspapers, such as *Weekly Peanuts*, named after the codeword for the Lockheed payoffs, sprang up to attack Tanaka's 'money politics'.

There was a strange fervour behind the street demonstrations, the sponsored marathons, the hunger fasts and the indignant editorials which suggested that, as in Richard Nixon's case, something other than the downfall of an individual politician was being sought. The strains of the double life, the everyday conjunction of Western and traditional values, were somehow being exorcized, and in the process Tanaka had been transformed into a Japanese Everyman, vicariously living out the private experiences of the masses. In terms of media reaction the only possible comparison is with the Miura affair, which related to the double life in a different way, Miura being a more sinister version of the Everyman figure. The Japanese people were consumed by an intense craving to absorb as much knowledge about Tanaka as possible. Bookstores were filled with racks of Tanaka books, some critical, some laudatory, many of them of the how-to type – *Let's Steal Kakuei Tanaka's Knowledge*; *Could You Become a Kakuei Tanaka?*; *Kakuei Tanaka – The Novel*; *How to Read Kakuei Tanaka*; *Kakuei Tanaka and the Japanese*; *The Secret of Kakuei Tanaka the Human Being*; *Latest Data on Kakuei Tanaka*. All sectors of society seemed to share the fascination. In 1978 the Association of Student Newspapers asked 10,000 students in twenty-seven public universities which contemporary or historical figure they admired the most. Easily leading the field was Tanaka, followed by Roma Sakamoto, a hero of the Meiji Restoration, and then Ieyasu Tokugawa, founder of the dynasty that ruled Japan for 250 years.

Opinion surveys taken before the guilty verdict suggested that over 80 per cent of the population wanted Tanaka to resign from politics. Yet, in Niigata he was still the object of veneration. Women cried in the streets when the news of his conviction was announced. In the subsequent general election, Tanaka polled 220,000 votes, by far the highest total in the country, and 20 per cent above the personal record he had set when prime minister. In the 1986 contest Tanaka was unable to campaign at all, having been crippled eighteen months previously by a stroke. But in Japanese politics a *jitsuryoku-sha* of sufficient renown is assured of election even if he is bed-ridden, speechless, and half dead. Again, Tanaka topped the poll in his five-seat constituency, collecting the third-highest number of votes in the nation. Voters must have known that they could expect little from his influence in future, but obligations previously incurred still had to be worked out.

After the 1983 guilty-verdict, Tanaka continued to sit as an independent in the Diet. Essentially nothing had changed. A mechanism existed for demanding the resignation of a member convicted of a criminal offence – ironically, Tanaka himself had created it fifteen years previously in order to force out a scandal-tainted colleague. However, despite their vocal criticisms, neither the opposition parties nor the non-mainstream factions had the stomach for a protracted battle. Tanaka loyalists, knowing that their leader would be triumphantly returned in his home constituency, forced Prime Minister Nakasone to call a general election in December 1983. The LDP suffered a humiliating reverse, but Tanaka was able to point to his own result as an answer to opposition calls for his resignation. Which was worthy of more attention, he could ask: the opinion of a judge or the democratic choice of the people? Within the LDP the numerical supremacy of his faction protected him from the anti-mainstream leaders. Gradually the assaults of the opposition parties began to lose energy, and the public grew tired of the sanctimonious moralizing about money politics.

Although Tanaka appeared to have seen off the worst of what Fate had in store, the effort had cost him greatly.

Always a heavy drinker, he was reported to have substantially increased his alcohol consumption, a reckless move for a man with an uncertain heart condition. Furthermore, his faction had grown so large that unity was becoming difficult to preserve – there were simply not enough posts and other benefits to distribute amongst the qualified members. Much to Tanaka's chagrin, the prime minister he had created was showing increasing signs of independence, and seemed bent on building up a public persona to rival Tanaka's own.

The first indication that Tanaka's grip was weakening came in the autumn of 1984 when his trusted lieutenant, Susumu ('My hobby is Kakuei Tanaka') Nikaido, allied himself with the opposition parties and mounted a challenge to Nakasone's re-election as party chief. That failed, but worse was to follow. The following spring another protégé, Noboru Takeshita, suddenly announced that he was setting up an intra-faction 'study group' called 'Soseikai', 'the creative politics association'. More than half the members of the Tanaka faction expressed their intention of attending the inaugural meeting. Tanaka was incensed, perhaps remembering how he himself had wrested control of the Sato faction twelve years before. Shortly afterwards he was felled by the stroke that ended his active career in politics. At the age of sixty-seven, still young for a Japanese politician, the ultimate 'man of practical strength' was reduced to an invalid slumped in a wheelchair. The unmistakable voice which had rasped out speeches and jokes and commands that powerful politicians had scuttled to obey was now no more than an incoherent mutter.

Without the master's guiding hand the Tanaka edifice began to crumble. The faction was split between Takeshita's Soseikai and the anti-Soseikai members, led by Nikaido. Tanaka's daughter quarrelled with the executives of Etsuzan-kai, the 90,000-strong support group that had supplied the hard work behind Tanaka's electoral successes. All restraining influence on Prime Minister Nakasone disappeared and, with consummate skill, he began to expand his own power base, playing off all the factions and splinter groups against each other. Media interest in Tanaka petered out; the editorialists ceased their fulminations, or rather redirected them towards Nakasone: the works of Kakuei-ology disappeared from the bookshelves. Apart from the occasional photographs of a slack-faced old man in a wheelchair, there was no indication of Tanaka's continued existence.

Tanaka's removal from the political scene has left much unresolved. Without his presence the debate about what the Japanese require from their political system lacks all focus. Apart from the restoration of diplomatic relations with China, Tanaka accomplished little of lasting value during his brief tenure of the premiership. Yet what he was, rather than what he did, remains of greater significance than the careers of men who stayed for far longer. The Tanaka story is another side of the *Oshin* story, which is also the story of post-war Japan. Tanaka came to Tokyo to escape the grinding poverty of his rural background. Not just perseverance but ambition and native guile lay behind his rise to power and riches. Throughout, he never lost his essential Japaneseness – the command of the rules of behaviour he first learned in his snow-stifled Niigata village. His greatness lay in his understanding that Japan is just a larger version of that village, and that exactly the same rules apply. One of the neatest summations of the whole Tanaka phenomenon is made by traditional folksinger Haruo Minami:

> Oh, let's all go to Rice Mountain
> A pleasant mountain at cherry blossom time
> I'm a Tanaka
> You're a Tanaka
> We understand each other so happily
> Let's sing out the festival song

The Weathervane

Yasuhiro Nakasone was the first Japanese prime minister to achieve international recognition. Even the soldier–politicians who took Japan into the Second World War were no more than names to the rest of the world and, indeed, to most Japanese as well. Nakasone's premiership coincided with the belated appreciation of Japan's status as an economic super-power both domestically and abroad. The massive trade surpluses that she was generating provided the unmistakable evidence. New strains were created, new responsibilities had to be assumed, and a new mood needed to be expressed. Nakasone fitted the bill superbly.

General de Gaulle had once referred to a Japanese prime minister on a state visit as 'a transistor salesman'. Better, perhaps, than a perfume or handbag salesman, the Japanese might consider in retrospect. Still, it was a remark that hit home at the time. Japanese politicians seemed unable to rise above the economic interests they were representing. They had no sense of the big picture, the balance of world power, the historical tide, and all the other grand matters with which statesmen are supposed to be occupied. They didn't even look convincing. They shuffled around apologetically at summit meetings, unable to communicate without their interpreters. They were short of stature, and, as all Japanese were quick to notice, were unfailingly positioned at the end of the line in photo calls.

Nakasone was different. He looked smooth and confident, appropriately 'international' in mien. He was physically an impressive figure: tall, with strong features, and always smartly attired. His English was of the lockjaw grind-it-out type that the Japanese call 'guts English', but, unlike some of his linguistically better qualified predecessors, he appeared at ease with foreigners, quite comfortable with his Japanese identity. Unusually for a Japanese politician, he looked people in the eye when he spoke, and his words were measured and logical. Even more unusually, he sounded as if he meant what he said, and said what he meant. In photo calls he stood next to President Reagan.

Nakasone stood out from the run of Japanese politicians in many other ways. Since his power base within the LDP was weak, he had concentrated on winning popularity, not with the bureaucrats or fellow LDP men, but with the general public – a wholly new idea in Japanese politics. Much as Western politicians do, he had skilfully used the mass media to market his image to the voters. He was rewarded with three terms in office, the longest premiership since the retirement of Eisaku Sato in 1972, and the largest landslide victory in the history of the LDP. After fourteen years of political confusion and unedifying personality conflicts – in which he had played a significant part – Nakasone led the party to its greatest-ever election success. Never one to hide his light under a bushel, he claimed to have established a new political dispensation, a '1985 structure' in place of the '1955 structure' created by the merger of the Liberal and Democratic parties. Certainly the LDP had never before held such a position of dominance over the opposition parties.

Nakasone entirely lacked the understanding of group relationships that had made Tanaka the classic *oyabun* (mentor-figure), and was considered too cold-blooded to make a good factional leader. Instead he offered a different kind of appeal that lay beyond the domain of factionalism. It was an appeal to national pride, to faith in Japan's potential, to the desire to confront difficult issues that had previously been ignored, and to a certain restlessness with the status quo. Whatever doubts one might have about the Nakasone premiership, it was hardly going to be boring. Different voters had different ideas of what a proper 'settlement of the post-war accounts' should include, but evidently most agreed with Nakasone that circumstances were changing fast and that Japan should have the confidence to jettison whatever structures and systems were no longer of use. No other politician, conservative or left-wing, demonstrated an equivalent appetite for change.

Most important of all, Nakasone had ideas of his own, which he never ceased to articulate. He had little time for consensus-building, or for bureaucratic centralism, or for the other traditional aspects of Japanese government. Having only a small faction at his command, he was in no position to participate in the 'distributionist' style of politics epitomized by Kakuei Tanaka. By presenting the electorate with ideas he forced his rivals to counter with ideas of their own. Men like

New Leader Kiichi Miyazawa defended Japan's post-war achievements and the structure which had supported them. The debate that resulted was intelligent and useful.

In the early sixties Nakasone came up with the suggestion that the Japanese premier should be chosen by direct vote, like the American president. The idea fell on stony ground, but he continued to promote it at later stages in his career. In 1985 he told a classmates' reunion that he wanted to become 'a presidential prime minister, like Mrs Thatcher or Mr Hawke'. Not only on his self-projection to the electorate, but also in the close relationship between personality and policy, Nakasone succeeded in exerting a quasi-presidential influence over the national mood.

There was more legerdemain than legend involved in Nakasone's ascent to the premiership. Although atypical in so many ways, he came from a background highly conventional for Japanese politicians. After a full education in the mountainous area of central Japan that he now represents in parliament, Nakasone went on to Tokyo Imperial University, the traditional breeding ground for Japan's governing élite. He took a degree in political science and, in 1941, passed near the top of his year in the entrance examination for the Ministry of Home Affairs. The pre-war Home Ministry was a much more formidable institution than the modern version, exercising total authority over all non-military aspects of Japanese life. In recognition of its almost mystical powers of control it was known as 'the bureaucracy of all bureaucracy'.

One week after taking up his post Nakasone volunteered for duty in the Imperial Navy. He was given a short commission as a lieutenant paymaster and took part in an amphibious assault in the Philippines. Nakasone is the only one of Japan's post-war prime ministers to have seen action, and also the only one to have headed the Defence Agency, a combination which helps to explain his predilection for extravagant and sometimes pretentious military metaphors. In a 1985 television interview he described the profound psychological impact of the war experience: 'We were forged in the war. It was an extremely shocking experience to spend one's early twenties in the midst of that huge tragedy. One feels one has grabbed on to life and held it close. From that point of view I feel sorry for today's young people who have never had that kind of experience.'

For a crusty British conservative of Nakasone's generation to keep up a military manner and hark back to the war years with some nostalgia would be nothing out of the ordinary. In the climate of opinion that prevails in modern Japan it re-quires considerable courage in the face of enemy fire. Nostal-gia for battle is a sign of the samurai ethic, an element in the national character which the Japanese have learnt to suppress and sublimate. Few of Nakasone's contemporaries are willing to offer any personal reflections on what must have been the most powerful experience of their lives.

On demobilization Nakasone returned briefly to the Home Ministry, where he worked as a supervisor in the police affairs department. In 1946, at the age of twenty-eight, he left the civil service to run for parliament as a Democratic Party candidate in his home town. Like future prime ministers Suzuki and Tanaka, he won his seat in the 1947 general election, the last held under the old constitution. Nakasone soon acquired the reputation of being a fervent nationalist with a taste for publicity. In his first election campaign he rode around on a white bicycle, apparently a reference to the Emperor's white stallion. Shortly afterwards he formed the Blue Clouds School, an association of young worthies dedi-cated to saving Gumma Prefecture from communism, and used it to help break an electric-power strike. Throughout the occupation period he favoured black ties – to symbolize mourning for Japan's independence. In 1951 he delivered a 'Petition to General MacArthur' to GHQ, making some rather abstract criticism of the political structure that the occupation forces were attempting to establish. When John Foster Dulles visited Japan, Nakasone, who held no official post at the time, sent him a 'Demand' concerning the necessity for Japan to embark on a nuclear power programme.

Nakasone was clearly a young man in a hurry, but his political affiliation stood in the way of a speedy rise to power.

The Democratic Party to which he belonged lacked the Liberal Party's close association with business and the bureaucracy. On the merger of the two parties the ex-Democrats became the sidestream part of the LDP. The conservative mainstream, centring on the imposing figure of Shigeru Yoshida, had developed highly pragmatic policies which placed economic reconstruction above all else. These were popular and, of course, extremely successful. The sidestream contained the pre-war party politicians and their heirs, united by little except an antipathy to the 'GNP-ism' of the dominant mainstreamers, most of whom were ex-bureaucrats. Like many Japanese rivalries, the mainstream/sidestream conflict was more a product of loyalty and tradition than ideology. Even now the Nakasone faction contains some of the most liberal and the most right-wing members of the LDP. Of the main figures in recent Japanese politics, Nakasone and Miki have belonged to the sidestream; Tanaka, Ohira and Suzuki to the mainstream. Mainstream factions have long held the majority within the LDP, and have usually controlled events regardless of the prime minister's affiliation.

As a group, the sidestreamers were particularly concerned with tricky problems of national identity and foreign relations, themes that have remained important to Nakasone throughout his career. On the restoration of diplomatic relations with the Soviet Union in 1956 his emotional speech of consent ('While drinking tears, I am forced to express consent . . . The atrocities carried out by the Soviet army in Manchuria will never be erased from the memory of the people . . .') was struck from the Diet record. Like many of the non-mainstreamers he was sceptical of the value of the alliance with the US, believing that the ability of Japan to defend herself unaided was a vital expression of national independence: 'In this fluid international situation we should manage the Security Treaty flexibly, and think about abolishing it in the future. We should maintain national security through our own power, withut depending on America.'

From this period dates the long Nakasone obsession with constitutional revision, the most powerful of the many symbolic issues by which ideologues of left and right still conduct their struggle for the nation's soul. Since the L D P has never come close to the two-thirds majority required before any tampering can be attempted, the debate has remained theoretical, but none the less bitter for that. For many years the mere mention of the subject was sufficient to provoke resignation demands and indignant newspaper editorials.

Nakasone and other nationalistic politicians have several objections to the 'new' constitution. They do not like the non-aggression clause which restricts Japan's defence policies, nor the enforced separation of government and religion which prevents politicians from honouring the war dead. They do not like the fact that the Emperor has been demoted from head of state to nebulous 'symbol of the state and of the people's unity'. However, more important than the individual provisions is what they represent in sum. In the view of Japanese rightists the meaning of the constitution cannot be separated from the circumstances of its adoption.

After the surrender the occupation authorities decided that a new constitution would be necessary to effect the drastic restructuring of Japanese society which they were planning. Since Russian interference was expected, time was of the essence. The Japanese government was asked to produce a draft of its own, but the results were not nearly radical enough. In response, the mostly young and liberal advisers to the Supreme Commander wrote their own version, which was put before the Japanese cabinet on the understanding that failure to adopt it could result in the Emperor's prosecution as a war criminal. The document betrays its origins. As the nationalists complain, its language of individual rights and liberties and the 'pursuit of happiness' has no relationship with Japanese tradition, and not much with contemporary Japanese reality. Unfortunately they have nothing credible with which to replace it.

One of Nakasone's earliest contributions to the debate was his 'Song of Constitutional Revision', performed in a Tokyo theatre to the tune of a popular war ballad called 'Daddy, You were Strong'. The opening verse ran:

As long as this constitution endures
So will unconditional surrender.
To preserve the Mac constitution
Is to stay a slave of General M.
Oh, those who would develop the motherland's destiny
Are filled with the spirit of national revival.

Not exactly Bob Dylan, perhaps, but the message is clear enough. The constitution is a symbol of Japan's spiritual defeat which must be exorcized from the body politic. It is a belief that Nakasone has never relinquished. In 1983 he was to tell the *Washington Post*: 'Revision is a delicate problem – I have a long-term plan in my heart, but I can't say anything about it in the Diet.' Indeed, he cannot, for the issue still stirs up violent opposition.

Critics have always had two great complaints about Nakasone, which at first seem to go rather uneasily together – he is both a dangerous rightist ideologue and an unscrupulous opportunist. Certainly, while deviating little from the nationalism of his early years, Nakasone has shown remarkable facility in switching personal loyalties and shifting position on specific policies. Inflexibility is a charge which even his worst enemies have never made. On the death of Ichiro Kono in 1965, Nakasone took over the leadership of a small faction of twenty-six members and kept up a barrage of criticism against Prime Minister Sato, who had been Kono's victorious rival in the battle for power. However, in 1967 Nakasone accepted an invitation to enter Sato's next cabinet as Minister of Transport, making the following classic comment: 'Politics can't be changed by a dog howling in the distance. Politics means getting within a sword's reach.' Nakasone's non-mainstream background made cabinet positions doubly important, for without them it would have been difficult to raise the contributions necessary to keep his faction together.

In 1969, with emotions running high about the extension of the Japan–US Security Treaty, Nakasone returned to his pet theme of an independent defence capability: 'We should abrogate the treaty around 1975.' Following the general election at the end of that year, he was offered another cabinet post, this time the Defence Agency. Suddenly his opinion changed – the treaty was 'semi-eternal'. After the resignation of Sato in 1972 Nakasone was expected to run for the party leadership or, if not, to support Miki or Fukuda. However, Nakasone came out in favour of 'structural revival and the overthrow of convention' – in other words, Kakuei Tanaka. He was rewarded with the Ministry of International Trade and Industry. When Tanaka was forced out of office the next prime minister, Takeo Miki, gave Nakasone the post of L D P Secretary-General, the most important in the party. Under Miki's successor, Fukuda, he served as Chairman of the Policy Affairs Committee, another key job for an aspirant to the premiership. In whatever configuration power was disposed, Nakasone was able to secure himself a useful piece of the action. In the musical-chairs game of modern Japanese politics, the Nakasone posterior was always fastest to the cushion.

It was not all plain sailing. Nakasone had his share of the scrapes that few of Japan's senior politicians seem able to avoid during the course of their careers. There was a stock market 'incident', a dam construction 'incident', and a curious affair in which he revealed secret party information in a recorded message to constituents. While he was in charge of the Defence Agency, Yukio Mishima was given high-level approval to drill his private army at facilities belonging to the Ground Self-Defence Forces. After Mishima's suicide Nakasone showed extraordinary alacrity in issuing a statement of condemnation, a deed which alienated some of his support on the extreme right. In the public mind he was still identified with the ultra-nationalist old boys' network. During the Lockheed investigation Nakasone was closely questioned in the Diet about his relationship with the shady Yoshio Kodama, reputed to be one of his most important backers.

Kodama, who died while on trial for bribery in 1984, is one of those extraordinary figures from the unwritten (*ura*) history of modern Japan whose lives could have been designed to gladden the hearts of conspiracy theorists. Never referred to in the conventional media, they inhabit a twilight world where politicians, businessmen and gangsters freely interact for their own and Japan's benefit. Kodama began his career as a right-wing terrorist leader in the twenties, being imprisoned for a total of nine years for threats against moderate politicians. After the militarists took power he was rewarded by being posted to China as a secret agent, with special responsibility for procuring war supplies. His procurement policy seems to have been highly successful, for he returned to Japan fantastically rich.

After the surrender he spent another three years in prison as a Class-A war criminal. This was an invaluable experience, allowing him to make contact with other powerful Class As, such as future Prime Minister Kishi, who were to dominate Japan's post-war politics. On his release Kodama contributed a massive sum to the establishment of the Liberal Party, and set himself up as a 'business consultant'. As proof of his success his name was mentioned in half a dozen of Japan's biggest post-war corruption scandals. In 1958 Kodama began his secret consultancy work for Lockheed, the only one of his deals that led to the pressing of criminal charges. On his deathbed twenty-five years later, he stated: 'I always thought I would be punished for the Lockheed business. I made the mistake of my life in acting as agent for a corporation from the enemy country that killed our soldiers in the Great East Asian War.'

In his heyday Kodama's network of influence stretched everywhere, from the police force to the mass media. He was himself the owner of *Tokyo Sports*, probably the most insalubrious of Japan's many insalubrious newspapers. He kept a private army which he trained in South Korea and which, during the Security Treaty disturbances of 1970, he armed and readied for action. According to his own testimony he was requested by a senior police officer to 'join the fight, if we can't hold the line'. Luckily, the help of his patriotic force of two thousand was not required. Kodama also had strong connections in the criminal underworld, having sworn blood oaths with the bosses of Japan's main gangster syndicates.

'Gang leader Taoka [head of the Yamaguchi-gumi gang] and myself are like brothers,' he told a *Newsweek* journalist in 1974. 'We are united in our opposition to communism.'

In the political world Kodama associated himself with the Kono faction, and had a particular liking for its charismatic young lieutenant. Exactly how the connection developed will probably never be known, but Nakasone was Minister of International Trade and Industry at the time of the Lockheed affair. According to the affidavit sworn by the Lockheed representative, Kodama phoned Nakasone and asked him to use his influence with All Nippon Airways on the company's behalf. Nakasone was summoned before the Diet's Special Investigation Committee, where he denied all involvement and claimed that his relationship with Kodama extended no further than accidental meetings in a Ginza massage parlour. The matter was eventually dropped, without any satisfactory explanation being found for the apparent conflict in evidence.

Throughout the period of political turbulence Nakasone used his factional leverage to maximum effect. Lacking numerical strength, he was forced to rely on sheer unpredictability in order to make his presence felt. His strategy of switching alliances at crucial moments earned him the nickname of 'the weathervane', bestowed half in contempt and half in wonder. It was a designation that disturbed him not in the least, as is demonstrated by his repeated references to Takamori Saigo, a hero of the Meiji Revolution: 'All great statesmen are weathervanes. The greatest weathervane of them all was Saigo. With a keen eye on the changes of the times, Saigo contributed to the progress of history. You can find many weathervanes amongst people like Saigo who create new eras.'

In the end Saigo quarrelled with the new Meiji government and led a force of samurai against its overwhelmingly superior conscript army. He demanded a return to traditional values, was defeated completely, and committed *seppuku*, thus fulfilling all the main qualifications for national heroism. Nakasone's survival instincts have been much stronger, yet the self-identification is interesting. As with Saigo, Nakasone has the impulses of a nationalist reactionary, but the policies he favours are opening up Japan to the world and breaking the simple loyalties that he admires most. Unlike his chosen hero, he understands the paradox and has adapted himself accordingly.

Under the Suzuki administration Nakasone was made Director-General of the Administrative Management Agency, tasked with implementing a programme of budget cuts and privatization. It was an extremely difficult and unpopular job, but one for which Nakasone's background suited him perfectly. He was an ex-ministry man himself and so could be expected to understand the bureaucratic mentality, but his political affiliation was with the party men of the 'sidestream' factions. Cutting the bureaucrats down to size would mean carrying on his political heritage. Nakasone took to what was, in the eyes of the public, a rather dull job in characteristically flamboyant style – pronouncing that 'the great administrative war is one of the most important since the Russo–Japanese war'.

Administrative reform, like market liberalization, was to become a major theme of the Nakasone premiership. From the first he saw it as something more than a method of improving the efficiency of government. 'Administrative reform is a great house-cleaning. First, we clean out the rooms then we put in place a splendid constitution. That is what I believe our course should be.' Nakasone wielded the broom with some success, earning good reviews from the business world, with which he had had little previous contact. His reputation as an ideologue began to soften as his involvement grew with specific details of economic management.

On the resignation of Suzuki in 1982, Nakasone ran for the party leadership. His previous attempt, in 1980, had ended in defeat by a substantial margin, but this time he had the all-important support of the Tanaka faction behind him and came in well ahead of the field. His first administration was criticized, with some justification, for the heavy Tanaka influence. Sympathizers of the Shadow Shogun took key positions in the 'Tanakasone' cabinet, including those of Chief Cabinet Secretary and Minister of Justice. Of course Nakasone had no choice but to accommodate them, his own faction being still too small to provide him with an adequate power base. Tanaka had only to give the word, and Nakasone would have been out in the cold again.

Although Nakasone had finally achieved the nation's highest office, initial prospects were not all that encouraging. Most political commentators were forecasting that the life of his administration would be even shorter than that of its predecessor. The Tanaka connection was simultaneously his only sustenance and the bane of his existence. With the Lockheed verdict one year away, criticism of political corruption was bound to intensify, and much of the blame would rub off on the leader of the government. If he attempted to distance himself from a still powerful Tanaka he would pay the penalty. On the other hand, if Tanaka suffered heavy political damage they would go down together. Whichever way events went, the result could only be more instability.

Nakasone compounded his difficulties by beginning as if he meant to pack all his 'settlement of the post-war account' into his first six months in office. In his first press conference as prime minister he alluded to the taboo subject of constitutional revision. Soon afterwards he made a series of imprudent remarks in an interview given to the *Washington Post*. It was his wish, he explained, to turn Japan into 'an unsinkable aircraft carrier', words that immediately evoked memories of the *Yamato* (meaning, coincidentally, 'Japan'). The vessel, the largest battleship ever built, has the same symbolic import for the Japanese as the *Titanic* for the British. Hailed as unsinkable in 1944, she was sent to meet the American fleet with a one-way fuel supply, and now has brightly coloured fishes wafting in and out of her portholes.

Nakasone went on to explain how Japan should have the capacity to blockade the four straits around the islands, thus preventing the passage of Soviet submarines, and to 'secure the sea lanes' within a radius of 100 miles. No other Japanese leader had dared to broach such subjects – indeed, Zenko Suzuki's Foreign Minister had been forced to resign in 1981 for having the temerity to suggest that Japan and the United States had a military alliance. To the great consternation of colleagues and the delight of the opposition, Nakasone went straight to specifics. There was an obvious relish about the manner in which he discussed the incursion of Backfire bombers, national emergencies, control of the straits and other shudder-provoking eventualities that the Japanese people felt much happier not hearing about.

According to the famous proverb, the nail that juts out gets hammered down. By all rights, Nakasone was due for a severe pounding. Indeed, within three months the support rate for his cabinet had plunged from 40 per cent to 34 per cent, while the non-support figure rose from 37 per cent to 45 per cent – the worst performance for a new cabinet in over a decade. The mass media gave him a roasting of the sort usually reserved for Kakuei Tanaka. Yet Nakasone survived relatively unscathed. Even a serious electoral setback in December 1983 failed to disturb his hold on power. Nakasone had been aggressively insistent on Takeo Fukuda's resignation after the collapse in the LDP vote at the 1978 election. When his own number came up he managed to fend off the criticism with a display of contrition: 'Having lost our majority in the House, I am keenly aware that my responsibility requires my resignation as prime minister. I offer my heartfelt apologies to all party members.'

In 1986, when the next election was called – this time at the discretion of the prime minister rather than the Tanaka faction – Nakasone was enjoying higher approval ratings than any of his predecessors. To the evident distaste of the opposition, the media, and most of his LDP colleagues, Nakasone had become by far the most popular politician in Japan. The dynamics of the LDP power struggle, a shift in the national mood, his own record of achievement – all made indispensable contributions to the success of the Nakasone premiership.

The considerable expertise that Nakasone had accumulated in manoeuvring between larger power blocs was taxed to the full during his turbulent first two years in office. After the Tanaka verdict he maintained a neutral public attitude, claiming that any comment on the subject would offend against the constitutionally guaranteed separation of powers. Tanaka was enraged at his appointee's high and mighty airs, and gave his feelings strong expression at a factional meeting: 'There's a fellow who thinks he's the only person fit to be prime minister. Idiot! He should stop being so impudent.' However, with the other factions keeping their distance, he was no longer strong enough to bring Nakasone to heel. In particular, he was relying on the prime minister to call a general election that would enable him to 'purify' himself before the voters. When the LDP went down to defeat, Nakasone took the anti-Tanaka New Liberal Club into coalition in order to secure an absolute majority, and pledged to rid the political world of Tanaka's influence. He gave Tanaka-faction members exactly the same number of cabinet positions as before, in keeping with their numerical strength. But the key posts of LDP Secretary-General and Chief Cabinet Secretary went elsewhere. It was a delicate balancing act, but one that worked. In the next leadership contest Tanaka had little alternative but to support an extension of Nakasone's term.

The stroke that Tanaka suffered in 1985 offered Nakasone a golden opportunity, suddenly removing the focus of all the trouble from the political scene. No longer would he be expected to tailor his administration to suit the whim of the convicted former prime minister and suffer public odium for his pains. The opposition parties and the various LDP factions had for years been disposing their forces in reference to Tanaka. Without his dominating presence, political alignments quickly began to lose their definition. The Tanaka faction itself lost the coherence that had always been one of its main weapons. The Soseikai group needed Nakasone's co-operation in order to wrest control from Nikaido, who was nominally the head of the faction. Elsewhere, the long-awaited 'change of generation' was taking place, and the 'new leaders' were jockeying for position in the next leadership contest. It was in Nakasone's interests to promote this process, since the 'new leaders' lacked the credibility and experience of the men they were replacing. At the time of the 1986 general election

Takeo Fukuda handed over the leadership of his faction to heir apparent Shintaro Abe, and Zenko Suzuki handed over his to Kiichi Miyazawa. Meanwhile Noboru Takeshita had won effective control of the Tanaka faction. Each of the three men campaigned furiously in order to establish himself as Nakasone's natural successor. The result of all their endeavour was the LDP landslide that handed Nakasone his unexpected third term.

Nakasone's skilful exploitation of political instability enabled him to hold on to office despite the numerical inferiority of his own faction. At the same time he used the prime-ministerial influence to build up his own power base. At the start of his first term the Nakasone faction had been a relatively minor grouping, well behind the Big Three factions in scale. After the 1986 election it had grown into the third-largest overall, only slightly smaller than the Suzuki/Miyazawa grouping. Thanks to the 'change of generations', Nakasone was now the longest-serving factional leader by more than a decade. Since the master of the largest faction was no longer active, Nakasone could justly claim to be in the forefront of the LDP's *jitsuryoku-sha*. When he finally gave up the premiership his position of authority in the party's inner councils would be assured.

Even before the Lockheed verdict, public approval of Nakasone's performance began to increase. The major cause was the talent and enthusiasm he displayed for diplomacy, traditionally the weak point of Japanese politicians. One of the first acts of his premiership was an official visit to South Korea which resolved a nagging trade dispute. That was quickly followed by the American trip during which he gave the controversial *Washington Post* interview. Dismay at the hawkish rhetoric he spouted with such equanimity was tempered by appreciation of the good reviews he had received from American newspapers and politicians.

It wasn't just a question of style, although that had its importance. The Japanese are acutely aware that not just their national security but their whole economic well-being is

dependent on good relations with the United States, the
home of their swelling portfolio of overseas assets, their
largest export market, and their main supplier of foodstuffs.
Japan and the US may not have quite the 'most important
bilateral relationship in the world', to quote the American
ambassador's astute piece of flattery, but certainly from the
Japanese point of view there is none of comparable value.
Especially since the early eighties, many Japanese had become
extremely worried about the consequences of the long-term
shift in economic strength away from the United States. The
intensifying trade frictions had reached a pathological condition, and some hair-raising remedies were being proposed.
For a US President to be popular in Japan would be a
dubious accolade. For the Japanese Prime Minister to be
popular in the United States was now a strong point in his
favour.

It is hard to imagine any other Japanese politician striking
up a relationship with an American leader similar to the
much publicized 'Ron–Yasu' relationship. The Japanese had
grown accustomed to seeing their prime ministers smiling
and nodding in the face of ever more strident American
demands. American frustration, Japanese impotence, mutual
misunderstanding. It was an unhappy synthesis to be classed
with that large body of phenomena – political, environmental
and meteorological – that can only be answered with a shrug
and *shikata ga nai* – 'it can't be helped'. Nakasone could not
stem the tide of demands merely by getting on first-name
terms with the President, but he could communicate the
Japanese point of view without being suspected of deceit.
Almost incredibly, the Americans seemed to trust this man
whose twists and tergiversations had made him a byword for
political opportunism at home. Being trusted, even if vicariously, was a radically new concept to the Japanese, who had
considered misinterpretation by foreigners to be part of the
national destiny. It made trade frictions seem no more than
what they were, the strains of competition between two
powerful economies, and not the latest manifestation of some
elemental racial and cultural conflict.

President Reagan is the pitcher and I'm the catcher. When the pitcher gives the signs, I'll co-operate unsparingly, but if he doesn't sometimes follow the catcher's signs, the game can't be won.

This also was radically new – previous Japanese prime ministers had been closer to the position of hot-dog vendors. Nakasone was proposing, and acting out, a relationship of equals in which Japanese sensibilities and priorities would have to be respected. The Americans had provided a structure for modern Japan – educational, legal, political – and defended her with the same military power that had previously destroyed her. They had laid on the Korean War and the Vietnam War and offered up the largest market in the world. They had set the circumstances in which modern Japan had happened. Those were the facts which had informed the old political relationship. The new facts included the inability of the American automobile and electronic industries to compete with the Japanese and the funding of American consumption by Japanese savings. Perhaps, only a politician from outside the accommodationist mainstream could develop the next stage in the relationship.

In fact the catcher made very few signs to the pitcher, and the pitcher mostly kept on with his natural game. Still, Nakasone was given credit abroad for his market-opening measures and his increases in the defence budget. Other premiers had abolished more tariff barriers and raised defence spending by roughly the same percentages, but Nakasone deserved the credit because the initiative was his. The others had moved under pressure and reluctantly. Nakasone appeared to understand where Japanese interests and those of foreign countries might coincide. On defence, the continual American demands for more spending were the perfect match for his own natural hawkishness. With Nakasone in charge, Japanese participation in the Strategic Defence Initiative was never in doubt. The campaign he launched to encourage every Japanese family to buy $100 of imported goods had little immediate effect, but it helped to establish the important principle that buying foreign could be patriotic. Nakasone took a personal interest in the details of the various market-opening programmes assembled during his premiership, ensuring that the political initiative was not swallowed up in a morass of bureaucratic inertia. It can be safely assumed that if Zenko Suzuki had stayed in power the American administration would have had a great deal more difficulty in keeping the lid on protectionism in Congress.

Western leaders generally approved of Nakasone not only because his views on defence, market liberalization and small government chimed with the prevailing international consensus, but also because they saw in him a politician of their own kind. Rather than bleating on about mutual understanding and peaceful co-existence, he made no bones about the fact that he was representing national interests. He presented himself as if he were in charge, as if he could make things happen. In fact he didn't have anything like the power he claimed, but that again was a condition with which many Western leaders could sympathize. At least there was little doubt about what he wanted to do if given the opportunity. Unlike any of his predecessors, Nakasone stood for something.

All of these attributes were viewed with ambivalence at home. Many Japanese were unsettled by the abrupt departure from convention that Nakasone represented. He was articulate, eloquent even – qualities that the Japanese identify with insincerity. He showed little hesitation in disturbing the long-established consensus on such matters as the annual visit to Yasukuni Shrine. He was ambitious, and appeared actually to be enjoying the premiership in a quite unseemly way. Then, there was the popularity with foreigners. That was un- doubtedly of benefit to Japan but it indicated a certain failure of Japaneseness – a good understanding with those outside the group means a weaker relationship with those inside it. Tall, with a prominent nose, he even shared some of the foreigners' physical characteristics. A *Mainichi Shimbun* journalist expressed his disquiet in a magazine article: 'Nakasone-san is in many ways unlike a Japanese. Japanese people brought up in the usual way have some sense of shame. However, in Nakasone-san's case, it is extremely weak.'

Ironically, the fervent patriot is accused of being insuffic-iently endowed with the requisite national characteristics. The same article went on to attack Nakasone's 'narcissism', a word that crops up repeatedly in the comments of his oppo-nents, and to liken his use of the media to Hitler's. Ever since his white-bicycle days, Nakasone had shown himself adept in building up a public image, and as prime minister he made good use of the larger opportunities that were presented. In the West it is standard practice for politicians to communicate their ideas and personalities through the media. In Japan, as the criticisms quoted above indicate, people are far from ac-customed to that sort of self-projection. Traditionally Japanese politicians have secured their positions through inter-factional manoeuvring, not through direct appeal to the electorate. The very idea of courting popularity is still a strange and dubious one, not just to left-wing journalists but to most of Nakasone's LDP colleagues as well.

The image that Nakasone presented to the world was interesting in its own right. It was the image of a man with wide-ranging cultural tastes and accomplishments – with 'eight faces and six elbows', as the Japanese say. He was an active sportsman, enjoying not only golf, the politician's favourite context for relaxation and intrigue in the open air, but swimming and tennis as well. He was noted as one of the best painters in the Diet, his landscapes being acclaimed for their vigour and dynamism. Usually the only people in Japan who make a fuss of their Zen experiences are foreign students, but Nakasone frequently referred to the benefits he derived from his regular meditation. An enthusiastic singer of Japanese ballads and French chansons, he once held a *karaoke* singalong contest with South Korea's President Chun. No record was ever released.

In 1985 Nakasone did publish a collection of his *haiku*. It sold 30,000 copies, a considerable number for a book of poetry. Predictably, critics in the media gave Nakasone's maiden work a frosty welcome, but it was clearly the product of a genuine poetic inspiration. Not many politicians, Japanese or Western, could lay claim to as much. It was also a shrewd political move, since there are ten million practitioners of the art in Japan, rather greater than the number of trade unionists. The publication of the book probably enabled Nakasone to sew up the *haiku* vote. Appropriately for a convention-breaking conservative, Nakasone's *haiku* were unorthodox in style, some making symbolic allusion to political events, some omitting the 'season-word' insisted on by traditionalists. The following, written to mark the funeral of Soviet leader Chernenko, is a fairly typical effort:

> farewell
> under frozen clouds
> draped in a red flag

Several poems were given in foreign translation as well – English, French and Chinese. Publication was timed to co-incide with an official trip to Europe, during which Nakasone dished out copies of his book to French intellectuals and politicians. He gave a speech at the Sorbonne in which he described *haiku* as 'the essence of Japanese culture', capable of 'summoning up passion in a few words and symbolizing nature and space'. Perhaps he remembered the jibe about the transistor salesman.

Nakasone's public image was *nauii* (trendy), far from that of the usual dull L D P politico. He pursued both Western and Japanese pastimes without any sense of strain. Perhaps not coincidentally, the traditional hobbies he favoured, Zen and *haiku*, were those most accessible to Westerners. Noh-chanting or incense-smelling would not have served nearly as well. The whole exercise also tied in with Nakasone's extension of the scope of politics beyond the economic management which had preoccupied leaders from the mainstream tradition. Naka-sone entertaining Ronald Reagan in the traditional surround-ings of his private villa – it was an image that captured the 'settlement of the post-war account' as neatly as Reagan-back-at-the-ranch did 'pride in American values'. According to the whisper, many of the elegant tea-ceremony implements that gave the scene its tone were theatrical props borrowed from a friendly producer. If so, it was an appropriate setting for the meeting between two consummately skilful political actors.

What exactly was the 'settlement of the post-war account' that Nakasone was so keen to promulgate? Like many important ideas, it was much greater than the sum of its components. It began as a rejection of the structures introduced during the occupation – not so much because they were flawed, but because they had been imposed on a conquered nation. Reform was to be more than just mechanistic improvement. It was an abstract assertion of sovereignty, a remaking of Japan in the Japanese image. The main substantive issues were increased defence spending and constitutional reform. The symbolic issues, which received almost as much attention, included visiting Yasukuni Shrine, and greater use of the national flag and anthem. As a political philosophy it was negative and backward-looking, little more than the mirror image of leftish orthodoxy. Nakasone's great achievement, perhaps not entirely deliberate, was to transform the standard appeal to national pride into a method of adapting to Japan's new role in the world.

The account could be settled most easily in foreign relations. Nakasone's high-visibility diplomacy, the greater assertiveness in international councils, the more mature approach to the security issue – these were clear demonstrations of the curing of the various post-war phobias. In the long run, however, Nakasone is likely to be remembered more for the domestic reforms he promoted, particularly those relating to economic management. Taken in combination with the revaluation of the yen and the constant pressure from trading partners, they have the potential to work profound transformations in Japanese society. Ironically, most of the new economic policies, such as privatization, deregulation and tax reform, originated in the United States and Britain, and the direction in which they will take Japan is away from the values and structures that most people think of as typically Japanese.

Administrative reform was a broad policy outlook that covered a number of different heads. Its immediate goals were closing the government deficit without tax increases, lowering the number of civil servants, and cutting through the huge mass of subsidies and grants that had been institutionalized during the period of high growth. Limited success was achieved on all three counts, but the important principle was established that government interference in the market mechanism should be kept to a minimum. As prime minister, Nakasone directly challenged the authority of the bureaucrats by convoking special blue-ribbon committees of his own appointment to make recommendations on the great issues of the day.

Nakasone's various market-opening programmes were initially developed in response to the insistence of trading partners. Their cumulative effect, like that of the privatization policy, will be to reduce the control of bureaucrats over the economy and to disturb the unwritten social compact by which efficient, internationally competitive industries subsidize the low-productivity domestic sectors. The surge in the value of the yen will hasten the process, as companies increasingly favour low-cost foreign suppliers and move their own production offshore. The financial deregulation that moved into gear under the Nakasone administration will also loosen the bonds between companies – as competition, rather than group loyalty, comes to decide the choice of bank. The setting up of an offshore banking market will enable borrowers and lenders to interact free of ministry supervision.

The Nakasone enthusiasm for tax reform, like his enthusiasm for changes in the educational system, was primarily ideological in origin. Japan's complex tax system is the slightly modified handiwork of Charles Schoop, a financial expert commissioned by the occupation authorities. The reforms suggested by Nakasone's tax panel include easing of the steeply progressive income tax, abolition of the *maru-yu* tax-free savings system, lowering of the high corporate rate, and introduction of a value added tax. Again, in the guise of undoing occupation reforms, Nakasone was bringing the Japanese system closer to the Western model. Lowering of income-tax rates should promote entrepreneurship and payment by merit. Abolition of *maru-yu* would mean the end of the policy, established in the Meiji era, of officially encouraging savings in order to channel low-cost capital to industry. The value added tax would break the system of latent subsidization by which large companies and salarymen pay taxes on behalf of millions of farmers and inefficient small businesses who do not.

These reforms are absolutely necessary, but the first attempt to introduce them ended in disaster. An unholy alliance between the left and the distribution industry, which feared having to disgorge the massive profits it was hiding, succeeded in stalling debate on the value added tax. The Japanese are extremely sensitive about tax issues, and Nakasone failed to persuade the public of the fairness of his proposals. It was his only real defeat, but one which damaged his credibility beyond repair. In the local elections of April 1987, all the LDP-backed candidates declared against VAT, and, humiliatingly, not one invited Nakasone to help the campaign. However, broadening the tax base remains a national priority, and it is hard to see what measures other than those Nakasone suggested can accomplish the task.

The main Nakasone privatizations were NTT (the national telecommunications company), the Japan Tobacco and Salt Corporation, and Japan National Railways. In telecommunications Japan followed the British, rather than the more radical American example, preserving the old monopoly intact. However, three credible long-distance communications companies soon set themselves up in business, offering rates significantly below NTT's. The privatization of the railways was a much more drastic exercise, probably the boldest privatization carried out anywhere. It required the splitting up of a mammoth public enterprise and the shedding of 80,000 excess workers. Early on in the proceedings Nakasone showed that he would brook no institutional obstructionism. The top management of JNR was adamantly opposed to privatization. Instead of going the usual route of trade-off and compromise, Nakasone took a hard line, forcing the chairman's resignation and installing his own man. In the West such a move would be considered standard practice, but in the context of Japan's stable, tightly knit business world, it was quite startling. It was also highly effective, and the massive task of turning the world's least profitable company into six going concerns was accomplished without any serious hitches.

One of the main factors behind JNR's chronic indebtedness had been the overmanning resulting from the need, in the early post-war years, to soak up unemployment. It had always been run as a social amenity, with conservative politicians promoting the construction of local lines as part of the trade-off for votes. By insisting that the railways be run as a business Nakasone was not just promoting economic efficiency, but altering the nature of the relationship between the LDP and its support base. Equally radical was his proposal to reform the previously sacrosanct 'food-management system' – the mechanism for transferring wealth from city-dwellers to farming households. No doubt Nakasone's analysis of the 1986 LDP landslide demonstrated to him the value of cultivating the allegiance of the city-dwelling floating voter. 'Our victory was connected to the creation of a new market in the cities,' he told a factional seminar, for once abandoning the language of the samurai for that of the merchant.

In 1985 Nakasone charged the Maekawa Commission, headed by a former governor of the Bank of Japan, with investigating the necessity for changes in Japan's economic structure. Its conclusion was that the economy should be steered away from export-led to domestic growth, with the emphasis on consumer demand and the accumulation of social capital. This marked a drastic change in the macro-economic policy that has governed post-war Japan, and will no doubt take years to realize. None the less the commission's argument was irrefutable. Leaving aside the trade frictions that resulted, it was simply not in Japan's long-term interest to continue to depend on foreign countries for her economic growth. Nakasone's critics complained that the commission's report was little more than a propaganda exercise, designed to appease frustrated trading partners. In fact its main themes fitted well with the strategy that the Nakasone administration had been pursuing – the replacement of the consensus-building and burden-sharing of Japan Inc. with a more open and mature economic order. From saving to consumption, from exports to imports, from catching up to learning how to relax – if fully realized that would bring to a conclusion, not just the post-war account, but the whole century-long forced march to modernization.

It is doubtful whether Nakasone himself understood the scale of the task ahead. Indeed, he often confessed himself to be 'economically tone-deaf', a dangerous attribute in a period of financial turmoil. The defeat on value added tax was partly due to his failure to propose a balancing stimulus to consumption. Like most of the Japanese establishment, his instinctive approach to fiscal policy was so niggardly as to be almost anal-retentive. Repeatedly he blamed the soaring of the yen – the inevitable result of the policies his administration had been pursuing – on 'speculators'. Amongst the general public, a bizarre theory gained currency that the radical economic restructuring that Japan was experiencing was the result of a plot hatched by International Jewry. Masami Uno, the theory's main proponent, became an over-night superstar, selling one million copies of his effusions and being taken quite seriously in top business circles.

Nakasone, the ardent nationalist and would-be overturner of the occupation reforms, had apparently succeeded in transforming himself into a smooth internationalist, striding about the world stage in imposing style and aggressively promoting his country's image. It was a phenomenon that fitted well with the dramatic expansion in Japan's political and economic importance – from exporter of interesting electronic devices to the world's primary supplier of capital and second-largest national market. Yet inside the new Nakasone, usually so plausible and pragmatic, the rash-tongued chauvinist of the fifties and sixties could sometimes be discerned struggling to get out. He had never given up his desire to scrap the 'Mac' constitution, nor his urge to wring some emotional justification from the wartime experience. In speeches he often referred to the advantages of Japan's mono-ethnic identity, sometimes straying well beyond the limits of legitimate Gaullist pride. At the fortieth anniversary of the destruction of Hiroshima, he waxed eloquent on the subject before an audience that included Korean bomb victims. In 1986, three weeks after firing his education minister for making controversial remarks about Korea, Nakasone delivered his infamous comment about the 'knowledge level' of American minority groups.

Nakasone is the most fascinating of Japanese politicians precisely because of his ability, even in his blunders, to epitomize Japanese moods and conflicts. He demands internationalization, but remains obsessed with his own national identity. He is both reactionary and forward-looking, both ideologue and pragmatist. He is popular, but not liked; respected, but not trusted. He is a highly ambiguous figure, whose contribution to Japanese politics will be the subject of endless arguments. There is nobody, inside or outside politics, who so neatly symbolizes what Japan has become.

Back To Consensus

Nakasone's replacement was Noboru Takeshita, one of the three so-called 'new leaders', men in their mid sixties who have been patiently waiting on the doorstep of power for the best part of a decade. When he took office in October 1987, Takeshita was already older than Mrs Thatcher, then striding through her record ninth consecutive year as prime minister. The contest for the succession had all the classic features of Japanese political theatre – rumoured alliances and treacheries, secret meetings in restaurants, much bowing, smiling, and soothing chin music. No ideas or policies were outlined, let alone debated. Instead, the three competed in expressing their admiration for Nakasone's achievements, his support being the crucial factor in the result. It surprised no one familiar with how Japanese politics works that Takeshita, consistently rated the least popular of the three in opinion polls, took the prize. The troublesome and divisive business of voting was omitted, and, after several rounds of intensive haggling, Nakasone appointed as his successor the leader of the largest faction. In Japanese terms it all made perfect sense.

Takeshita is the polar opposite of his ally in character, political behaviour, even in physique. Only 156 centimetres tall, baby-faced, and with a large head bobbing on narrow shoulders, he is reminiscent of the wise, koala-like creatures in *Star Wars*. Although Takeshita's first job after graduation was as a reserve English teacher at a country high school, he speaks no foreign languages, and at summits reverts to the traditional expedient of smiling and nodding. In comments to his domestic audience, he favours a rambling, elliptical style that carefully steers away from judgements and commitments, and sometimes from any meaning at all. He admits, with typically cheerful self-deprecation, that his manner of expression is often confusing, not mentioning that this is a political technique of proven value. Takeshita is a man who has risen to the very top by deliberately allowing people to underestimate him.

Home territory is Shimane Prefecture, not as snowy as Tanaka's Niigata but even more remote. The Takeshita family have been saké-brewers for several generations, and the future prime minister grew up in a prosperous and progressive atmosphere, his parents having abolished the harsh apprentice system traditional in the industry. At school, Noboru was a skilled judoist, rising to black belt, fifth dan. According to classmates, nearly all his bouts ended in draws, indicating that even then the compromise and consensus instinct was well developed. Not outstanding in personality or academic work, he was none the less bright enough to pass into Waseda, a more liberal school than the 'élite' Tokyo University, and therefore less well represented in the Japanese establishment. Characteristically, Takeshita has capitalized on what might have been a disadvantage, winning support from Alma-Mater-boosting Waseda graduates in business and the media, and even in the opposition parties. After returning to take up a teaching job, he went into local politics. Later, one disgruntled cabinet colleague would claim that Takeshita had never risen above the level of a local assemblyman. Perhaps, but if so then Japanese politics as a whole has never risen above the level of a local assembly.

Takeshita is the first Japanese prime minister to have won his seat after the merger of the Liberal and Democratic parties in 1955. He did not experience the chaotic post-war period in which splits, secessions, and constant political upheaval reflected the disorienting energy of industrial recovery. Unlike his predecessors, he was not a political entrepreneur, but a political salaryman, who joined the largest faction of what was then by far the most powerful party, rather as an ambitious graduate might join a blue-chip company. He worked his way up the LDP hierarchy with diligence and skill, cultivating bureaucrats in the most important ministries. He became particularly close to the farm and construction lobbies, amongst the most generous suppliers of political funds, and married his daughter into the founding family of one of Japan's largest building companies. As a rising member of the Tanaka faction, he had a plum franchise on the most dynamic operation in the whole great industry of Japanese politics. Takeshita's mastery of the art of fund-raising proved invaluable in the contest to succeed Nakasone. In 1987, he pocketed a record Y2 billion from a single fund-raising party, selling 70,000 invitations at Y30,000 each. It was fortunate that only one-fifth of the tickets were actually used, for the congestion in the hall was close to Shinjuku-station levels.

Kakuei Tanaka did not care for his young lieutenant, perhaps sensing the ruthlessness beneath the rustic modesty. Takeshita watched and waited, taking note of his chief's famous motto: 'Politics is power, and power is in numbers.' Finally, he made his move, setting up a 'study group' that was in effect a faction within a faction. Tanaka roared with rage when he heard about the project, but was powerless to prevent the majority of his faction members joining. Shortly afterwards, he suffered the stroke that took him out of politics, and suddenly the way was clear. Takeshita moved with caution, using his relationship with Nakasone to neutralize the rump of Tanaka supporters who opposed him. His chief bugbear was Susumu Nikaido, the cigar-chomping, hasty-tempered factional chairman. Nikaido was outspoken in his contempt for Takeshita, and, at the age of seventy-seven, 'staked his political life' on standing against him for the premiership. This was one match that didn't end in a draw, for Nikaido had to pull out in humiliation having failed to gather enough support to legitimize his candidacy.

Takeshita himself had some pride-bruising setbacks, notably when he was refused entry to a New Year's party at Tanaka's residence. It was a *manga*-like depiction of the feudal structure of Japanese politics. At the festival of renewal, when the clan gathers to celebrate its togetherness, the main gates were slammed shut in the face of the disloyal retainer. Being a modern politician, Takeshita turned away not to roam the frozen, wind-blasted streets in search of lodgings, but to fund-raising parties and secret meetings in restaurants. With time and, more important, money on his side, he could afford to take the insult philosophically. His 'ripe-persimmon strategy' of waiting for power to fall into his hands was already close to ultimate success.

As prime minister, Takeshita has performed as expected, making few blunders and offering few initiatives. Despite the bad omen of a world-wide stock-market collapse on his first day in office, circumstances have been kinder to him than to Nakasone. The Japanese economy has emerged from the strong yen recession more powerful than ever before. The crazy land-price spiral has come to a halt, not through any government measures, but merely because the market was already too high to bring in new buyers. Trade frictions nag on, but 'Black Monday' has made American politicians painfully aware of their reliance on Japanese money flows. The only new idea which Takeshita has promoted is 'the home town concept', meaning increased investment in the regions, such as Shimane, and dispersion of government functions out of Tokyo. More of a slogan than a policy, it contrasts sharply with Nakasone's 'internationalization'. Its slightly atavistic appeal to the sense of origin and territory suggests a Japan more interested in consolidating her massive gains than in opening up to the rest of the world.

Like Suzuki, Takeshita is a facilitator, a smoother-over-of-differences, not an originator. His definition of successful politics is getting things done without anyone noticing what has happened. He has no ideological principles, only a desire to respond to circumstances in a way that will minimize the strains. He does not have Nakasone's great fault of promising abroad what he could never deliver at home, nor is he chauvinistic by instinct. His strength within the LDP and his range of contacts in the bureaucracy should enable him to create a consensus on controversial issues like tax reform that defeated his predecessor. Since the basic agenda was already set in the Nakasone years, qualities of pragmatism and competence are now more valuable than flair. Just as it took an anti-communist like Richard Nixon to develop détente and relations with China, so an interest-group politician like Takeshita may have the best chance of 'selling' reform to the interest groups. Certainly, his close connections with the construction industry helped him to defuse the long-running dispute over bidding on Japanese projects. If he can bring the agricultural dispute to a conclusion as well, his performance will be rated highly.

The Takeshita administration is reasonably popular with the general public, though most of those polled are unable to identify in what respects they approve of it. The diplomatic initiative has been retaken by the Foreign Ministry, and economic growth has been buoyant. There have been a couple of squabbles at home which revealed Takeshita's weaknesses as well as his conflict-resolving skills. In the interests of factional balance, a noted brawler was appointed chief of the Diet committee, and had to be removed after using his position to insult members of the opposition. Then, like Nakasone, Takeshita had to purge a reactionary cabinet member who had annoyed the Chinese and Koreans with his musings on the rights and wrongs of the Second World War. In both cases, events seemed to be running out of control, much to the satisfaction of the opposition. Takeshita said nothing, but pressure was brought to bear, and the two individuals tendered their resignations.

From the comments of the media and fellow politicians, Takeshita is still being underestimated, which is probably just what he wants. Still, doubts remain. Can the traditional system, of which he is the epitome, cope with the huge power now under its control, with the insistent demands of foreigners to be let into the game, and with the sheer pace of economic and financial change? Eventually, some sort of vision will be required, and not just of the home town.

9

Power Players

To work to your utmost, make money, win fame, beat the opposition – I have realised just how great these things are.

Yoshihisa Tabuchi, President of Nomura Securities

The driving force behind the growth of Japanese industry has been motivation and the eagerness of industry itself. Whether or not a country can pull together and wield its collective strength, at least as far as I can ascertain from Japan's case, depends more upon the initiative and fire of the people themselves than on the government.

Dr Makoto Kikuchi, Director of the Sony Research Centre

'The land of harmony' was one of the early names the Japanese used to describe their country. Glossed both positively and negatively, it has become the dominant image in the minds of foreign businessmen, pundits and politicians. To the outsider the Japanese seem like a well-drilled army, moving with relentless purpose towards an agreed goal. The impression is not entirely groundless. Assessments of national priorities are fairly well standardized, and in disputes confrontation is adopted only as a last resort. None the less it is important to recognize that Japan is a complex society, fast growing more complex, in which tensions and conflicts are never far below the surface. Even the best-run companies have different factions jostling for dominance, often espousing radically divergent strategies. Inside the bureaucracy the various ministries compete for territory with the same fierceness with which the consumer electronics companies battle for market share. Farmers, labour unions and small companies stand outside the power structure, but their interests must also be accommodated. Consensus on major policies results not from some mystical bonding of perception but from a dynamic process of trade-off and compromise.

Life is getting more difficult. In the multi-polar world of interdependent economies, where a decision on monetary or tax policy taken by one powerful country instantly reverberates through the international financial system, the consensus mechanism is bound to come under increasing strain. Urban consumers may find that their interests are closer to those of American than Japanese farmers. Exporters of electronic components may find that their views on government policy match those of foreign telecommunications companies, but differ substantially from those of the chemical manufacturers within their own industrial groups. The power players whose interaction has set the course for modern Japan will find that new circumstances require entirely new responses. Harmony will be harder to come by, though even more valuable than before.

The Rice Growers

When Japanese farmers come to Tokyo to demonstrate – as they frequently do – against the government or the Americans, it seems like the invasion of another race. They are much darker of skin than the standard salaryman, stockier and sharper of eye. They wear straw hats or towels on their heads and walk with an agricultural roll, as if bearing a large sack of mountain potatoes on their backs. They swap remarks with passers-by, even foreigners, and look as if they are enjoying themselves.

They come from distant climes, where livelihoods are still determined by the struggle against snow and wind. There, the festivals which mark the phases of the agricultural year are performed with a vigour and seriousness never seen in the showy processions of the large cities. Even today, in the more isolated districts women can be seen doing their wash in the river. Rural Japan, like everything else, is not what it used to be. Modern agricultural methods and communications have seen to that. None the less its values are still those by which great corporations and institutions function. The co-operative endeavour that put irrigation channels through the paddies is the same instinct that has enabled managements, unions and suppliers to overcome common difficulties together.

City-dwellers have a deeply ambivalent attitude towards their country cousins. They are simpletons, of course, who cannot be expected to know anything of the latest fashions and gadgets. Inevitably they are the butt of thousands of feeble jests made by television comedians. In a famous personnel directive, Tokyo's largest bookstore forbade the employment of ladies who were 'ugly, midgets or bumpkins'. Accent is the give-away, especially the clamped vowels of the northern prefectures where, according to popular belief, it is too cold to open your mouth properly.

Farmers inhabit *inaka*, rendered in most dictionaries as 'countryside'. In casual usage the word also signifies any place considered inconveniently remote from the centre of things. Someone who admits shamefacedly to living 'in a very countryside area' probably inhabits a district where people, cars and buildings are to be found in even greater concentration than in central Tokyo. Countryside = distance from new developments = unsophistication = the condition which Japan has expended so much energy leaving behind.

The *inaka* is still psychologically close. Many Japanese have two distinct ways of speaking, standard Japanese for normal everyday affairs and their local dialect for use when they return to their home town. For the home town, the subject of many a lugubrious ballad, is an important point of emotional reference. During the August Festival of the Dead, it is Tokyo which is the ghost town, most of its inhabitants having returned to their places of birth to greet the spirits of their ancestors. All the year round, Japan still works to the farmers' clock. In midsummer the sun rises at four in the morning and has already set by seven in the evening, which may be convenient for those tending crops and animals, but makes little sense for consumers of electricity.

A few generations ago nearly all Japanese were farmers. Indeed, under the Tokugawa regime the rank of the farmer was above that of artisan and merchant, for he was the primary producer on whose efforts the country's survival depended. The radical young officers of the thirties took the same physiocratic line, and occasionally assassinated a merchant or two to get their point across. Further back in the mists of time, sumo wrestling and the Shinto religion had their origins in fertility rituals devised to safeguard the rice crop. The Imperial family itself was probably the most successful set of farmers, and thus the quickest to move out of production and into administration.

Japanese farmers do not see themselves as agro-businessmen. They consider the cultivation of the nation's staple food to be a patriotic duty, contributing to the nation's capacity for survival. One-third of the population can remember a time when respect for agricultural producers was something more than a verbal reflex. In the years immediately following the war, mass starvation in the cities was narrowly averted by emergency shipments of US grain and rice. All who could went to live with relatives in the countryside, where food was still comparatively plentiful. Those who had no such connections were left to survive on the official ration of two cups of rice a day, supplemented with whatever could be obtained from the black market. It was an experience that has left a profound impression on Japanese public attitudes and agricultural politics.

Politicians are more aware than most of the importance of rural Japan. Because constituency boundaries have not been redrawn to reflect demographic change, votes there can be worth four or five times as much as in newly urbanized areas. Only 190, or 37 per cent, of the seats in the House of Representatives are assigned to constituencies in the industrial belt, the remainder being distributed amongst the agricultural and semi-agricultural areas. Farmers are natural conservative supporters, and the LDP knows how to take care of its friends. All of Japan's last nine prime ministers have represented rural constituencies throughout their political lives.

Inevitably the rapid economic growth of recent years has created increasing tension between the interests of agricultural producers and the rest of the nation. Japanese housewives are paying six times the world market price for their rice. Fruit and vegetables are highly protected by a complex array of tariffs, subsidies and support prices. Imports of beef, sugar, soy bean and several other products pass through special public corporations which buy cheap on the international market and sell on to wholesalers at the high domestic price, pocketing the difference. Foreign wheat, for example, accounts for 90 per cent of Japanese consumption. In order to keep the producers of the remaining 10 per cent happy, its price doubles as it passes through government hands. In the rice market, where no imports are allowed, the reverse occurs. The government buys from producers at a high price, then sells on to consumers at a price 20 per cent lower, thus incurring a huge deficit year after year. Although it is true that all the advanced economies protect their farm sectors to some extent, it is also true that the Japanese level of protection is by far the highest – almost double the E E C's, according to the Policy Conception Forum, a well-respected think tank. A continuous government-directed transfer of wealth is taking place, from the city consumer to the farmer.

The agricultural sector absorbs 9 per cent of all workers and 10 per cent of the budget, roughly the same as defence, but contributes only 3 per cent to gross national product. To add insult to injury, Japanese farming households are extremely wealthy, with average annual income one-third higher than that of ordinary families. In an all-too-familiar pattern, generous price guarantees have stimulated chronic overproduction of crops which are then left to moulder in government warehouses. That too costs money. The complicated range of tax incentives available to farmers has given rise to the 9/6/4 motto – ordinary salarymen pay 90 per cent of their taxes, doctors 60 per cent and farmers 40 per cent. Furthermore, the skyrocketing of property values over the past twenty years has automatically benefited all who hold land at the expense of those who do not. Rateable values are correspondingly high, but taxes on land shown to be 'under cultivation' are negligible. As a result, even within urban Tokyo, where the shortage of land for development has driven prices up to absurd levels, there are more than 90,000 acres of legally defined farmland, many plots bearing no more than a couple of peach trees. That is enough space for half a million new homes. Altogether, the economic power of the farmers now closely matches their political influence. Their co-operative union is one of Japan's most formidable business organizations, generating an annual turnover greater than Toyota's. It controls distribution of the nation's staple food, is a major trader of fertilizer and machinery, and has interests in retailing, travel and financial services. The farmers' bank, the Norinchukin, is the ninth largest in the world and a major player in the international financial markets.

Japan's farmers produce a wide variety of crops – more species of vegetable, for example, than are cultivated in the United States. Fruit is abundant: excellent mandarin oranges, large tasteless apples, grapes, plums, persimmon, and a host of other native and imported species. Apart from turkey, whose smell they abhor, the Japanese raise most known types of livestock and fowl. Their beer-fed, carefully massaged cows produce Kobe beef, justly renowned for its marbled texture and exorbitant price. However, animal husbandry, which has a history of only 120 years in Japan, suffers from the lack of good grazing. The main point of Japanese agriculture is still the production of rice. It occupies 55 per cent of all agricultural land and causes most of the political ructions.

For the Japanese, rice still retains its semi-mystical associations as the sponsor of life and nourishment. It is served unmixed with other food, pristine white. Tradition-minded mothers insist that their children scrape every last grain from the bowl. None the less, thanks to the high retail price and the changing tastes of young Japanese, demand is in a secular downtrend which government advertising campaigns have had no effect in remedying. Per capita consumption has fallen continuously, from 118 kilos in 1962 to 75 kilos in 1986.

Meanwhile, in defiance of economic logic but in perfect accord with political logic, the retail price has steadily increased.

In terms of productivity per acre, Japan's rice farmers are amongst the most efficient in the world. However, geographical constraints ensure that, despite their good yields, they are never going to be competitive with producers in better-favoured countries. The average size of a Japanese farm is 1.2 hectares, one-fiftieth the size of the average British farm and under one-hundredth the size of the average American farm. Furthermore, over 80 per cent of all Japanese farms are tiny one-family businesses under one hectare in size. Small-scale, inaccessible lots mean labour-intensive production which in turn means high costs.

Every summer the government negotiates changes in the intervention price, based on compensation for costs incurred, and then adjusts the retail price accordingly. It is a well-established ritual in the agricultural calendar, bringing coach-loads of nut-brown farmers down to Tokyo to make their noisy case. Regardless of the state of demand, lowering the standard of living of agricultural households is politically impossible. Even when declines in interest rates and fertilizer prices substantially lower the cost of production, the producer price is usually kept flat, thus providing the horny-handed sons of toil with a welcome gain in real income.

The artificial price structure, apart from piling up excess production, has seriously distorted the allocation of resources within the agricultural sector itself. As a result Japan is already the world's largest net importer of foodstuffs, and dangerously dependent on foreign producers. She satisfies only 54 per cent of her people's total calorific intake from domestic production, down from 80 per cent in 1960. The farmers and their friends in high places have been skilful in playing on the Japanese fear of impending disaster in order to prevent further import liberalization. However, the policies which have been pursued so far have had the effect of restraining the production of food that people want to eat and thereby actually deepening Japan's reliance on foreign sources. The higher the intervention price, the more rice is produced in preference to other crops, and the less consumers are willing to buy.

Self-sufficiency in Food

	Japan	US	UK	WG
Total calorific value	54%	150%	70%	75%
Wheat	12%	320%	110%	105%
Meats	80%	100%	68%	90%
Pulses	10%	150%	50%	20%

Source: Economic Information Centre

The Japanese are understandably concerned about their lack of self-sufficiency in food, now at a level where even the most sanguine of countries would begin to worry. Actually Japan is rather more vulnerable than the figures suggest. Although her farmers are producing a decent supply of meat, over 70 per cent of the foodstuff they use is imported. Furthermore Japan is overwhelmingly dependent on geographically remote supply sources – 40 per cent of her food imports come from North America. It makes no sense for Japan to boost her defences, as her allies are urging, unless she can provide her people with much more food than she can now. If they are to improve self-sufficiency, the Japanese will first of all have to improve the efficiency of agriculture. That will inevitably mean disturbing the cosy relationship between farmers and politicians that has built up in the decades since the war.

As is the case with all special-interest groups and their issues, the farmers feel much more strongly about farm support than anyone else does. However, even Japan's long-suffering consumers are wearying of the special treatment being accorded to the agricultural sector. Despite the farmers' political muscle the consensus is gradually moving against them. Criticism from foreign governments is increasing year by year, with American rice farmers leading the way. The Keidanren (Federation of Economic Organizations), worried that retaliatory measures will be taken against exports of manufactured goods, is strongly in favour of the dismantlement of agricultural protection. Food manufacturers are concerned about the import of cheap ready-processed products. Amongst the general public there is enthusiastic support for tax reforms which would remove some of the present inequities. Most important of all there has been a perceptible shift in the balance of electoral advantage. In the 1986 general election, for the first time, the LDP gained a similar proportion of votes in the urban as in the rural districts. In order to hold its absolute majority into the next decade the party will have to ensure that urban floating voters are kept happy.

The government's policy has been to promote the cultivation of non-rice crops and encourage a gradual reduction in the agricultural population. The number of farms has already declined from 6 million in 1960 to the current 4.5 million. Over the same period the number of full-time farms has fallen from 2 million to 600,000. About 70 per cent of all farming households now derive more of their income from non-farming sources than they do from their traditional livelihood. Schoolteachers and railwaymen are particularly enthusiastic weekend peasants. On average, Japan's rice farmers derive only 15 per cent of their income from rice-farming. The direction of the producer price remains of great financial interest to them, but it hardly constitutes a matter of life and death. It should be possible to persuade more of the part-timers, nearly all of whom are owners of small paddies, to move into alternative employment.

Japanese agricultural policies have inevitably become part of the never-ending trade frictions which have been part of the news for over a decade. The United States, which operates a 'voluntary' quota on Australian beef and permits imports of Japan's mandarin oranges in only five of its fifty states, has been particularly vociferous in demanding further liberalization of the Japanese foodstuff markets. In response the Japanese have pushed the national security argument too far. In case of the putative international crisis, Japan could probably survive without any domestic supply of peanuts and tomato ketchup, two products which she has exempted from GATT.

As for beef, probably the most controversial item, it was not eaten at all in Japan until the first American consul had a cow slaughtered in 1873. From the official adoption of Buddhism in the seventh century right through to the Meiji period, the Japanese stuck to a vegetarian diet supplemented with fish and eggs. In a typically effortless transformation, they have now become great carnivores, devouring, amongst other delights, raw horse and chicken liver, pig intestines, and, as a sign outside one Tokyo restaurant explains, 'womb meat'. Domestic livestock farmers are no more efficient than the crop cultivators, and consumers have to pay through the nose for the privilege of keeping them in business. Beef imports are subject to quota agreements and intervention buying that keeps prices at four times the American standard. As a result Japanese tourists clutching slabs of frozen meat have become a familiar sight at the Narita Airport arrivals lounge. Farmers argue that protection is necessary since their Friesian herds are also supplying Japan's milk requirements. The counter-argument that they should concentrate on the efficient production of dairy products has not met with much favour. Even in pork, where there is no volume restriction on imports, the domestic producer is insulated from competition by an equalization tax that ensures that his prices are never undercut. All in all, the Japanese livestock farmer is as mollycoddled as his famous Kobe steers.

The future of Japanese agriculture is primarily a Japanese domestic issue to be settled through the domestic political process. From the point of view of trading partners, the sums of money involved do not justify the heat generated. Even if Japan's rice market was liberalized completely, her $100 billion trade surplus would be reduced by only $3–5 billion, equivalent to less than a week's export production by the Japanese auto industry. Furthermore foreign countries should ask themselves whether they really want to see a more efficient Japanese economy, with all the financial and labour resources now expended on the primary sector being diverted into new growth industries. The Japanese would have to export greater quantities of high-value-added goods in order to pay for their increased food imports. Foreign farmers would benefit at the expense of their industrial sectors, and the unbalanced trading pattern, by which Japan exchanges manufactured goods for foodstuffs and raw materials, would be further strengthened.

There are also delicate problems of political stability involved. The LDP power base has broadened over the years, but agricultural organizations still provide one of the few absolutely dependable sources of support. With 70 per cent of its seats in rural and semi-rural constituencies, the LDP might not survive a sudden alienation of the farming vote. Animal slaughter and meat-processing, like leather-work, another industry under foreign pressure, have tradi-tionally been the preserve of the *burakumin* outcasts. A sudden liberalization of imports without any easing of the age-old patterns of social discrimination could have disastrous results on their livelihood. Any balancing of the interests of con-sumers and producers will have to be undertaken gradually and carefully.

The wider and more intriguing question revolves around the Japanese sense of identity. Now that the Japanese are so rich, farmers and city-dwellers alike, will they stick to the hardship-bred habits of co-operation and equalization, or will they follow the path of efficiency and economic logic? A similar conflict, between the instincts of the farmer and those of the merchant, is taking place within many Japanese organiza-tions, groups and even individuals.

The Business Cabinet

The Keidanren (Federation of Economic Organizations) is an important wielder of the toasting fork in the demonology of Japan Inc. Together with MITI and the great *zaibatsu* (indus-trial conglomerates), it supposedly dictates long-term strategy, targets weak foreign industries for doom, and generally works its surreptitious wiles to the benefit of Japan and the detriment of everyone else. Perhaps the Keidanren leaders covet the power that is ascribed to them; no doubt they would dearly like to be able to claim the foresight. In fact, however, their competence is considerably more modest – to adjust the balance of advantage between sectors of the economy. It is essentially a passive role, analysing events and trends and judging the correct response. Like many other institutions the Keidanren is finding that its job is being made increasingly difficult by the growing scale and dynamism of Japanese industry.

It is certainly true that the Keidanren has a mystique and authority which big business organizations in other countries cannot match. That is partly because business itself is taken more seriously in Japan than elsewhere, partly because of the highly integrated industrial structure. When top Keidanren executives meet Ministry of Finance officials to discuss economic matters, as they periodically do, the conclusions reached have an import greater than that possessed by LDP policy group or, sometimes, cabinet decisions. They set the terms by which the balance of advantage between industries is decided. On specific issues the government would be unlikely to ignore its policy recommendations. In keeping with the Japanese pattern of negotiation, its own members will always back consensus decisions, even if they appear to damage specific interests. Next time round, those interests will be properly compensated.

In years gone by the organization exercised an overtly political function. Keidanren public statements are believed to have played a crucial role in promoting the 1955 merger of the Liberal and Democratic parties into the LDP, and then, five years later, in bringing down the right-wing Kishi administration which had become identified with a dangerous polarization of public attitudes on national security. It was appropriate that the representative business organization should steer Japan away from the aftershock of war and back to the traditional arts of money-making. Today the Keidanren still finances the LDP, but it no longer leads policy debate, let alone takes sides in the fractious power struggles. Indeed, on the major economic question of the decade, the need for Japan to reorient its economy away from export dependency, the Keidanren's suggestions have been remarkably unhelpful. Like all organizations the Keidanren is a product of the interests of its members, and those are no longer so well defined or so easily managed as they once were. Still less do they automatically redound to the greater good of the national economy.

There are four major economic organizations in Japan, often sharing members and attitudes, but with fundamentally different purposes in life. By no means do their interests always converge. The Japan Chamber of Commerce represents small and medium-sized businesses. The Nikkeiren (Japan Federation of Employers Association) bargains with labour. The Keizai Doyukai (Japan Committee of Economic Development) is a forum for discussion of more abstract and long-term policy questions. It demonstrates its progressive credentials by including five ladies amongst its 1200 members – which is a larger gesture than it seems, given the pitifully low proportion of female executives in Japan.

The Keidanren itself is the organ of big business, being composed of representatives of 100 industry groups and 800 of Japan's largest companies. There are over 1.5 million companies in Japan altogether, and those with corporate membership of Keidanren account for only about 8 per cent of the workforce and 15 per cent of private-sector revenues. Furthermore the companies most strongly represented are of a particular sort – key elements in the heavy industrial structure which Japan built up in the sixties. The Keidanren chairman is traditionally from the shipbuilding, steel or heavy electrical industries. Of the thirteen men elected to the board in 1986 only three came from companies which participated fully in the latest and most impressive stage of the Japanese miracle. The others have their backgrounds in troubled or less efficient sectors of the economy, some of which are in serious structural decline. Industries not represented on the Keidanren board include pharmaceuticals, retailing, apparel, advertising, transportation, construction, food and beverages, ceramics, computers and communications – in other words, most of those sectors which will benefit from the next major shift in the Japanese economy.

The chairman of Keidanren, appointed by a mysterious process of consensus-building, has one of the most powerful posts in Japan. Each of the last three incumbents has managed to impress his personality on economic events. Toshio Doko, who led the organization from 1974 to 1980, is one of the most remarkable businessmen that Japan has ever produced, setting an inspirational model both through his business successes and, more important to the Japanese, through his moral attributes. Shortly after he took over the chairmanship at the age of seventy-eight, a television programme acquainted the public with Doko's personal frugality. Coming in the midst of the revelations of Tanaka plutocracy, the account of his lifestyle seemed like an exemplum from a Confucianist primer:

Every morning Doko rises at four, in good time to perform his fencing exercises and clear his lungs out with some Suntra-chanting. He shaves using a brush that he has owned for fifty years, then breakfasts on home-made vegetable juice and yoghurt. In the evening he dines on a single sardine, fried cabbage and a bowl of rice, before retiring at nine. Unless receiving guests he never uses a heater or cooler, whatever the temperature. He contributes most of his salary to charitable causes and avoids luxury and ostentation like the plague. Of all things in the world, he considers work the most enjoyable: 'Working is my hobby' is his motto. Once in the early postwar years there was an unfounded suspicion that he was implicated in a bribery scandal. When the investigators called at his home, Doko's wife explained that he had just left to catch the bus to work. On hearing that, and on viewing the humble circumstances in which he lived, the investigators immediately realized that they had been after the wrong man.

Perhaps there was some exaggeration. Still, Doko's career record attests to the thoroughgoing nature of his austere philosophy. Time and again he obtained results. His success in turning round faltering companies such as Ishikawajima, the shipbuilders, then Toshiba, which in the sixties was plagued by bad labour relations and low productivity, earned him the nickname of 'the god of reconstruction'. His strategy involved drastic cost-cutting, with strong leadership from management, and rationalization of unprofitable business areas. On assuming office as Keidanren leader, Doko was confronted by a macro-economic crisis to match anything he had faced as a company president. In early 1975 wholesale price inflation was running at 37 per cent, the worst rate of any of the developed economies. Industry had lost control of its costs, and the government's loose monetary policies had badly misfired.

Doko was suited by temperament to the fight against inflation, and continually stressed the importance of tight money, lower wage settlements, and more efficient administration. At the same time the government was able to follow a fiscally expansive policy, since, unlike other governments facing similar problems, it could launch a new round of deficit spending funded by the high savings of its citizens. The recipe was an unqualified success, and Doko's leadership took much of the credit for the resulting quantum leap in Japan's international competitiveness. When his term ended in 1980 he was appointed head of the First Committee on Administrative Reform, then, in 1982, head of the Extraordinary Commission on Administrative Reform. When he handed in the committee's recommendations he was eighty-nine years old. Their substance − smaller government, deregulation, privatization, less subsidies, less mollycoddling of interest groups, fiscal reconstruction without tax increases − has set Japan's political programme for the rest of the century. Most of the policy initiatives which earned Yasuhiro Nakasone his reputation for bold innovation were no more than enactments of the Doko Committee's precepts.

Doko's successors at Keidanren have not been as well matched to the economic circumstances they have faced. The most serious problem of the eighties is how to deal with the strains caused by Japan's huge trade surpluses. Yoshihiro Inayama, ex-President of Nippon Steel, came out in favour of managed trade, with import and export quotas for all categories of product traded between Japan and the US. This unfortunate idea has been echoed by his successor, Eishiro Saito, another Nippon Steel man. In fact Inayama had long been a proponent of cartels in the steel industry, arguing that price stability was vital for orderly industrial planning. His own career in a strategic heavy industry provided him with little experience of the creative potential of the market mechanism. Managed trade would undoubtedly please many sections of the Keidanren membership, allowing them to lock in market share and raise prices. The only people to suffer in the short term would be consumers, smaller exporters and competitors from third countries, none of which has much lobbying power in government circles. In the long term, by resisting the flow of economic events, managed trade would contradict the very impulse that makes Japan outstanding amongst modern industrial nations.

Inayama's economic philosophy was a passive version of Doko's more creative austerity. The word he used to encapsulate it was *gaman* (endurance). The Japanese pride themselves on their power of endurance, which has enabled them to achieve much in both peacetime and wartime. As a character-forming exercise, certain tradition-imbued Japanese don heavy layers of clothing in the sweltering heat of summer and thin cotton kimonos in midwinter. The Zen priest squatting under his icy waterfall, the martial artist battering his fist against a tree, the salaryman squashed up in a tube train, the young lady being married off to a family connection, the consumer paying double the world-market price for his food, the diplomat quietly nodding his head at the latest tirade from trading partners – all in their different ways are instances of Japanese *gaman* in action.

Many Japanese consider this ability 'to endure the unendurable', to quote the Emperor's speech of surrender, as not just a product of circumstances but an essential national characteristic, directly connected to the work ethic and social consensus. Yet whatever its spiritual virtues, as a guide to economic policy too much *gaman* is not always a good thing. Japan recovered from the recession of the late seventies more quickly than any of her trading partners through the efficiency of her export sector. Meanwhile the domestic economy remained stagnant, a combination of factors which resulted in the bloated current-account surpluses of the early eighties. By the middle of the decade Japan had become the largest creditor nation in the world, pumping out huge capital flows generated by her trade surplus, but the domestic sector of her economy proved unable to absorb any compensating flow of imports. The *gaman* appropriate to a nation with few natural resources facing a critical disruption in her terms of trade was not a sensible philosophy for the most powerful economy in the world. None the less, as far as policy-makers were concerned, low wage settlements, a tight fiscal policy, an undervalued currency and the preservation of inefficient processing industries remained the order of the day. Any attempt to channel high domestic liquidity into badly needed infrastructure or to stimulate consumer spending met with a decisive thumbs down. *Gaman* had become an addiction and the Japanese continued to sunbathe in their overcoats.

In the mid eighties, as worsening trade friction brought home the fact that export-led growth was no longer a realistic option, the national consensus began to shift in favour of a more expansive economic policy. The Japan Chamber of Commerce and the Doyukai lobbied accordingly – their members stood to lose most from domestic stagnation. However, the main momentum behind the change in direction was supplied neither by the bureaucrats nor by the business leaders, but by the politicians – a complete reversal of the events of 1955 and 1960. New leader Kiichi Miyazawa's 'asset-doubling plan' excited great public interest. Yasuhiro Nakasone, long committed to the *gaman* line, promulgated a number of 'big projects', to be financed by a combination of public and private-sector capital. Ordinary LDP dietmen, always in favour of expanded public works, meaning more pies for them to stick their fingers in, successfully exerted pressure on the government to ease its fiscal stringency. Meanwhile, the Doko-inspired programmes of deregulation and privatization were revitalizing the domestic economy.

The growth of the service industry, new businesses and new technologies was creating a different sort of dynamism.

Eishiro Saito, Inayama's successor, has shown himself to be more responsive to new ideas. As Chairman of JAPIC (Japan Project Industry Council), he promoted several long-term infrastructure schemes, including the plan to build a bridge/tunnel across Tokyo Bay. He is also more forthrightly critical of the US than is usual for a Japanese public figure. 'We should not be referred to as if we were culprits by a country which is suffering from years of loose economic management,' he stated in one of his first speeches. Previous Keidanren leaders had tended to view the periodic trade flare-ups as unpredictable events beyond the scope of human control. However, Saito's espousal of managed trade – equivalent to mopping up after the disaster, rather than trying to prevent its occurrence – revealed that little progress had been made. Internationalization of the Japanese economy, the need to open domestic markets and move from indirect to direct overseas investment, is the greatest challenge facing Japan in the remaining years of the century, but Keidanren has yet to formulate a coherent strategy to deal with it.

It will be no easy matter for Keidanren to recapture the economic initiative. Unifying the views of its own membership has become a complex, time-consuming task. Hard choices on interest rates, the balance of direct and indirect taxes, currencies and trade policy create a wider diversification of interests than ever before – between sectors and even between competing enterprises. Companies that have lessened their dependence on bank debt, increased procurement of components from overseas, and begun to invest in production within the foreign markets they serve will feel differently about these choices to those which have been slower to react.

In many cases the interests of light and heavy industry, retailers and producers, manufacturers of finished goods and manufacturers of components are directly opposed. None the less the more serious the tensions, the more important Keidanren's role in helping to resolve them. The Japanese economy has grown too big and boisterous to be led by the nose any longer, but the traditional Japanese method of balancing the scales of advantage and disadvantage will be as valuable as ever.

Keidanren's more active role, as a forum for launching new ideas and projects, still has its uses. It continues to lobby for fewer restraints on the armaments industry and greater government attention to aerospace, one of the few industrial sectors that has been neglected in post-war Japan. Its impact has so far been less than that of the US government, which is concerned both to encourage Japan's defence effort and to promote exports of its own armaments industry, but Keidanren support is slowly establishing the case for domestic or part-domestic development of new planes and weapon systems. Through his chairmanship of JAPIC, Saito has the opportunity to identify Keidanren with the futuristic mega-projects – artificial islands, greening of the deserts – which that organization is drawing up. These are of a scale which demands close co-ordination of interest between government and industry and between different industrial groups.

The Keidanren organization is a gerontocracy – twelve of its fourteen top executives are over seventy. In the Japanese business world greater age does not necessarily denote a lesser capacity to accommodate change. Indeed, men of that generation have an incomparably rich experience of historical transformations, both economic and social. They are now presiding over another upheaval, less traumatic than what went before, but still formidable in its challenge to the structures they have painstakingly assembled, and also to the code of behaviour on which Japanese business practices are based.

Bureaucrats in Heaven

When Prime Minister Nakasone convened his first cabinet meeting after the 1986 landslide victory he exhorted his new ministers to 'break through the wall of bureaucracy'. He was referring to the likely opposition from within the ministries to his programme of reform. What had happened to Japan Inc.? Suddenly Japanese bureaucrats, far from being extolled as masterful planners of the national destiny, were being treated as the villains of the piece.

It was a characteristic example of the Nakasone style, casting himself as the bold innovator opposed by an array of powerful interest groups wedded to the status quo. Rhetorical overstatement, no doubt, but not without a core of truth. Nakasone politics was about taking the initiative away from the bureaucrats and, in several instances, directly reducing their ability to influence events. The coming of Nakasone, combined with accelerating social and economic changes, means that over the remaining years of the century the role of the bureaucracy is likely to undergo a profound transformation.

Japan's bureaucrats are comfortable with power: they expect and are expected to wield it. Anyone meeting an official of the Foreign Ministry or the Ministry of Finance understands immediately that he is dealing with the very best that Japan has to offer. Intelligence, pragmatism and a keen patriotism, topped off with absolute confidence in the bureaucracy's problem-solving capabilities – it is a formidable combination of attributes. Educationally they are the élite, having passed through a gruelling series of examinations that, unusually for Japan, test analytical skills as well as memory. In other countries the top graduates may go into academic research, or law or finance. In Japan their natural destiny is administration. The rare scandal, such as the Yarntwisters incident, may temporarily knock a dent in their reputation for integrity, but their dedication to Japan's long-term interest is never seriously in doubt. As Prime Minister Ohira once stated, 'Bureaucrats devote their lives to working here [in government] – ministers are just temporary guests.' Bureaucratic influence permeates through the controlling heights of Japanese society. After their retirement from government service, usually at the young age of fifty, top civil servants move into advisory positions at major corporations, often those they dealt with in their official capacities. This process is known as *amakudari* (descent from heaven). Naturally they maintain their contacts in the bureaucracy, which enable them to secure favourable treatment for their new employers. Ex-bureaucrats are also prominent on the other side of Japan's equilateral triangle of power, the LDP. In the 1986 general election 25 per cent of all LDP candidates had backgrounds in government service. Of Japan's last ten prime ministers, eight have been ex-bureaucrats. The Ministry of Finance alone has forty ex-officials sitting in parliament. They may belong to competing factions, but when it comes to transmitting ministry policy they frequently act en bloc. Their presence contributes greatly to the close integration of the Japanese power structure, a quality which has been a vital factor in Japan's industrial success. Before any new policies are formulated, information passes back and forth between politicians, bureaucrats and industry leaders, enabling the balance of advantage to be gauged well in advance.

Within their own jurisdictions Japan's bureaucrats are accustomed to exercising considerable discretion. The Japanese see nothing unusual in the proposition that the Ministry of Education should screen (i.e. censor) all school textbooks. The Ministry of Agriculture manipulates food prices through its intervention buying. The Ministry of Finance's 'window guidance' lets the banks know what kind of loans they can and cannot make. MITI regulates everything from R & D subsidies to the type of ski equipment that should be used on Japan's 'especially wet' snow. Every year the Ministry of Health produces reports on how the nation's human stock is developing. If the tensile strength of fifth-graders is in a declining trend, appropriate remedies will be suggested. At a much humbler level the Japanese are willing to accept a degree of bureaucratic direction that would be unthinkable in the West. For example, all citizens must report a change of address to their local ward office within two months on pain of a fine. Yet Japanese bureaucrats can hardly be accused of empire-building. The budgets of the ministries are modest, MITI's being one of the smaller ones. Japan has only 44 civil servants per 1000 people, which compares with 101 in Britain and 77 in the United States. It is because the bureaucracy has been careful not to over-extend itself that it has managed to preserve its authority.

The Japanese civil servant has traditionally enjoyed a prestige unknown to his Western counterparts. The Confucianist ideal of the scholar–administrator came to Japan from China in the eighth century, and an extensive bureaucracy was soon devised, complete with entrance examinations, as a suitable employment for men of learning. In Tokugawa Japan both the Shogunate and the regional *daimyo* relied on specialist bureaucrats to handle the day-to-day business of administration. The samurai, deprived of their true *métier* by 200 years of peace, had developed into a class of civil administrators. It was the concentration of power in these men's hands that created the conditions for the Meiji Restoration. The Meiji leaders themselves believed that a strong centralized bureaucracy was an indispensable counterweight to the forces of factionalism and self-interest which, left unchecked, could weaken the nation in the face of the predatory Western powers.

The modern Japanese state did not evolve through centuries of conflict between different social groups. It was manufactured in a couple of decades. The Meiji government had a variety of models to work from, but none was exactly applicable to Japanese circumstances. The surest method of securing the economic and social developments it desired was to control directly the factors involved. The creation of a powerful industrial base was the main priority, but Japan had no capitalists equal to the task. Only central government had the funds and organization capable of establishing the factories, shipyards and railways that could build the 'rich nation, strong army'. Drawing on the savings of its citizens, the Meiji government immediately set about creating the capital stock required. Ex-samurai, who had the discipline, education and patriotism to be effective workers, were recruited into the labour force. These nationalized enterprises were run not according to the profit principle, but for Japan's long-term strategic benefit as construed by the Meiji leaders. Wage rates tended to be high, in keeping with the dignity of the purpose, and profitability was correspondingly low. After a series of financial crises had demonstrated that the burden was sustainable, the government sold off the businesses to friendly merchant houses, such as Mitsui and Mitsubishi, at bargain prices.

The relationship between government and industry was from the start one of mutual dependency, not confrontation. Even the radical nationalists who professed to despise mean-spirited merchants knew that they could not accomplish their military aims without a powerful industrial sector. Accordingly they built up groups of enterprises favourable to their own interests. The traditional merchant houses gradually extended their influence over parliamentary politics, until by the late twenties it was widely recognized that Mitsubishi and Mitsui each controlled one of the two main parties. Politicians ladled out the military contracts that were the lifeblood of the *zaibatsu* groups on the basis of prestige and personal connections. After the party politicians were discredited by the militarists the bureaucrats gradually imposed a command economy designed to serve the war effort. Major companies were encouraged to set up production in the new colonies for the sake of the national interest. As the chances of conflict with the West increased, the output of military hardware, especially warships, became an overriding necessity. Resources were directed away from the consumer sectors to heavy industry. The Ministry of Home Affairs, in which the young Yasuhiro Nakasone worked, became a monolithic instrument of control, its influence spreading into all areas of society.

It was not so much a radical change in structure as a reversion to type. Modern Japan had been a creation of the samurai, the bureaucrat-warriors. The two functions were now separated, but in combination had achieved a position of absolute dominance. Like the military, the bureaucrats were pledged to the Emperor, not to parliament. They conceived and drafted most laws, the politicians merely ratifying what was set before them. Additionally, through the use of imperial ordinances, the bureaucrats had an alternative method of legislation. Their prestige was high, in accordance with their dedication to the national good and their educational attainments – the civil service being one of the few employments where success was contingent on merit alone. Their great nation-building strategy appeared to have been successful. The authoritarianism that came with it did not seem unnatural to a people accustomed to having the minutiae of their daily lives regulated by government fiat.

After the defeat of 1945, Japan was once more manufactured by bureaucrats and soldiers, this time of foreign origin. The occupation authorities broke up the *zaibatsu*, purged 50,000 businessmen and politicians, reformed land tenure, education, parliament, the legal system and the financial system. To accomplish all this, however, they needed the help of experts, so the bureaucracy was left intact. When, with the coming of the Korean War, the strategy of the occupation authorities changed from cultivation of a model democracy to the rapid creation of a powerful economy, the Japanese bureaucrats were ready to take up the challenge. The methods they used were little different from those applied in the pre-war years. Foreign trade was strictly controlled. Resources were directed away from the consumer sector to strategic heavy industries. A select group of internationally competitive companies was nurtured with subsidies and tax credits and supported by a plethora of low-wage, low-productivity suppliers. Once again the results were brilliantly successful.

In the fifties and early sixties, when Japan's industrial infrastructure was being built up, the bureaucrats continued to play an all-important role in shaping the nation's economy. The most influential ministries – such as Finance, Construction, and Trade and Industry – had power of life and death over the sectors under their control. They could virtually shut down an industry, as MITI did to coal, or expand or cartelize it by 'administrative guidance', a system of directives which were not legally binding but which no businessman in his right mind would consider disobeying. Mergers could be enforced in the interests of economic rationality; prices controlled; both domestic and foreign competition kept at arm's length; imported technology directed to the companies that could use it best. Blessed by an undervalued exchange rate and an open and booming world economy, the authorities concentrated resources in the industries where Japan had strong international competitiveness. These were not all that difficult to identify. In steel, shipbuilding and heavy chemicals, Japan had made enormous progress in the wartime years. Once the plant was in place there was no reason to doubt that equivalent success could be achieved again. In most of these industries the technological parameters had already been set. The main determinants of competitiveness were scale merits and the cost of capital. Japan had a naturally large home market to cultivate the former and the right sort of financial institutions to ensure that the latter was as favourable as possible.

If that were the complete story of the Japanese economic miracle, then the bureaucracy would be justified in taking the lion's share of the credit. However, it is not even half the story, and although the bureaucrats helped to create the conditions for what followed, it was far from being an inevitable consequence of their actions. In autos and electronics, the two sectors which did most to create the leap in prosperity, the bureaucrats had little control over developments. Men like Soichiro Honda, who once returned from a foreign trip weighed down with smuggled motorbike components, did not need MITI to tell them how to run their businesses. The bureaucrats were expert at directing the factors that powered the steel industry. They were less at home with the dynamism of the consumer-goods sectors which have driven Japan's post-oil crisis growth. Indeed, MITI once attempted to force a merger between Toyota and Nissan on the magisterial assessment that Japan needed only one large auto maker. Today there are eight Japanese manufacturers of standard passenger cars, easily the largest number in any country. Not coincidentally, their competitive power has proved irresistible.

The role of the bureaucrat had shifted from director of events to facilitator of economic change. No amount of administrative guidance could produce a rotary engine or a radio that would fit in your breast pocket. As ever, Japan's bureaucrats were fully aware of the responsibilities that confronted them. Export credits were phased out and the number of cartels reduced, but import restrictions continued to promote domestic industry at the expense of the consumer. The Ministry of Finance's tight fiscal policies continued to foster the growth of personal assets which were then channelled into private-sector capital accumulation. Financial institutions did not compete for investors' deposits, so interest rates could be kept at artifically low levels. Sound financial management and the adroit nudging of technological innovation provided a fertile environment for the growth of Japan's new export sector. When the oil crisis demonstrated that Japan could no longer rely on her energy-guzzling heavy industries, their natural replacements were already to hand.

Apart from co-ordinating defensive responses to the change in industrial structure, MITI identified specific technological goals and encouraged companies to work together for their achievement. This has proved one of the most controversial aspects of Japanese industrial policy, both criticized and imitated by Western governments. Yet the actual scale of the resources committed to projects by government agencies belies the fuss that has been made. The proportion of research and development funded by government is much lower in Japan than in her main trading partners – only 22 per cent, against 50 per cent in the UK and 46 per cent in the US. The famous VLSI (Very Large-Scale Integration) programme, which laid the technological groundwork for Japan's IC industry, had a budget of Y29 billion over its five-year life span – roughly one-sixth of what Matsushita's R&D spend for a single year. In the United States the equivalent of Y70 billion was disbursed on a VHSIC (Very High Speed Integrated Circuit) programme and a further Y45 billion on related semiconductor projects.

More significant than the financial resources involved is the attitude of mind that makes Japanese inter-industry research projects feasible and successful. Although the electronics business in Japan is one of the most fiercely competitive areas of the economy, companies that had been rivals for decades were willing to pool resources for the sake of a government-defined priority. Then, once the basic technology had been established, it was back to the free-for-all of the market-place. The next leaps in circuit integration and breakthroughs in manufacturing techniques were achieved in the jealously guarded secrecy of the company laboratory. Again, the programme could not have been undertaken at all without faith in the wisdom of its organizers.

Government-sponsored programmes exist in aerospace, energy conservation, ocean development, computer science, nuclear power and several other areas. Although their scale is small they define national objectives just as the VLSI programme did. Yet official programmes do not of themselves create any technological breakthroughs. Those are the result of the hard work of teams of well-trained company researchers. The exchange of information between them is a useful method of ensuring that research efforts are not duplicated, but no more than that. Since the VLSI programme, and partly due to its success, the Japanese electronics industry has reached a new stage of evolution. The amount of funds that companies like Hitachi, NEC and Toshiba are pouring into R & D dwarfs anything the government can provide. In other industries too – in biotechnology, robotics, opto-electronics and new materials – the important discoveries will be made quite independently of bureaucratic direction. In the most exciting technologies there can be no setting of objectives, since no one knows the objective until it has been achieved.

Just as technological developments are growing less susceptible to bureaucratic control, so is the organic growth of the economy itself. Japan is changing from an export-reliant capital-investment-driven economy to one with a better balance of demand factors. The movement of consumer spending, traditionally sacrificed to the interests of industry, will be vital to the future health of the economy. The service sector is expanding rapidly – from 46 per cent of GDP in 1973 to 53 per cent in 1986 – but only the market can decide which services it wants. Video-game software, graphic design, head-hunting, fast food, investment consultancy, house removals –

the success of these enterprises depends solely on the entre-preneurial wit of those involved.

At the other end of the industrial structure Japan's most powerful corporations are in the process of turning themselves into true multinationals. Already, companies like Canon, Sony and Honda derive 70 per cent of their revenues from overseas. The realities of trade politics and a strong currency are forcing them to move production into the markets they serve, where they will come under the control of a different set of bureaucrats. Already, Matsushita has fifty-five plants overseas. By 1990, 35 per cent of Sony's revenues and 30 per cent of Honda's will come from overseas production. In finance the tremendous growth of the Euro markets has enabled Japanese companies to fund their investment pro-grammes with foreign capital. Japanese banks and trading companies have established subsidiaries in overseas financial centres which can undertake types of business forbidden to their parent companies by Ministry of Finance regulations.

Strangely enough, Japan's trading partners, usually so ill-disposed towards her industrial policy, have worked directly against the lessening of bureaucratic control. When the US imposed 'voluntary restraints' on Japanese passenger cars and the EEC on videos, it was left to MITI to parcel out quotas company by company. In anticipation of increases or reduc-tions in the overall limits, individual companies were forced to lobby the bureaucrats in order to preserve their market shares. Similarly, in semiconductor trade, the US demanded that Japan raise its usage of American-made chips from 8 per cent of the market to 20 per cent. The imposition of that kind of target, out of the question in the US domestic market, inevitably means transferring the power of decision from the businessman to the bureaucrat.

Politically, there has been a subtle evolution in the role of the ministries. Until the mid seventies they dominated the legislative process, not only drafting new laws but suggesting their enactment to LDP policy committees and managing them through the various stages of the Diet. The mass of uncontroversial and highly technical legislation needed skilled attention. Lower-ranking bureaucrats used to work in the same sections for their entire careers, which preserved a level of expertise within the ministries far superior to that of the politicians. However, in 1975 a new personnel policy was established that required bureaucrats to change postings every two years. The subsequent rise of the *zoku* (tribe) dietmen, politicians who specialize in representing a particular interest group, means that the LDP now has its own pool of expertise to draw on. These men often remain on the same LDP policy committee for ten years or more, building up their range of contacts and understanding of specific industries. For example, members of the telecommunications *zoku* are funded by the telecommunications industry, and know exactly what political and bureaucratic levers have to be pulled to assure it of the most favourable treatment. If necessary they will go to war against anyone, other *zoku* included, who seek to promote conflicting interests. Bureaucrats, the most able of whom are fishing for political and business appointments after retirement, no longer have the authority to stand against them. It used to be said that Japanese bureaucrats controlled the politicians who controlled the businessmen. Now the relationship has grown more complex. Businessmen control politicians who control bureaucrats, who in turn control businessmen.

The nature of legislation itself is changing. It is no longer enough for bureaucrats to promote the interests of the sectors they control. There are too many complexities involved, too many trade-offs that have to be made. The appropriate level of defence spending cannot be decided by the usual tug of war between the Defence Agency and the Ministry of Finance. Almost all decisions affecting the domestic economy are now foreign policy decisions as well. When the Ministry of Construction decides to promote the building of a new airport or bridge, foreign governments will be keen observers of how the bidding, if there is any, progresses. The Ministry of Agriculture may be supremely skilful at judging what is best for the nation's farmers, but it has no mechanism for setting that off against the interests of food manufacturers and consumers, let alone the likely reactions of trading partners. The necessary adjustment of interests can only be performed by an institution sensitive to the entire range of pressures – which is parliament, or, in the Japanese context, the LDP.

The Nakasone approach was to nominate specialist committees – composed of businessmen, scholars, media figures and, of course, some bureaucrats – to discuss controversial issues. In education, defence and internationalization of the economy, he relied on the recommendations made to push forward his own policies against the prevailing balance of vested interests. Those organs that already existed have been adroitly manipulated. Appointments to the Tax Advisory Council were traditionally made from a list supplied by the Ministry of Finance, but, much to the disgruntlement of the bureaucrats, Nakasone chose to pack the committee with his own 'special appointees'. In keeping with the tide of events in other major economies, the policies adopted often involved reductions in government control – sweeping away import restrictions, privatizing the national railways, breaking the telecommunications monopoly, creating an offshore banking market free of ministry supervision. Many of the large-scale construction projects formerly doled out by the Ministry of Construction will in the future be planned and financed by Nakasone's pet 'third sector' method. That involves using a combination of public and private funding to establish special corporations expected to make a profit and, one day, to be listed on the stock exchange.

Unsurprisingly, Nakasone is not the bureaucracy's favourite politician. Under the Ohira government he served as Chief Administrative Secretary, charged with carrying out the Doko line on administrative reform. As prime minister he followed it through against the resistance of the ministries. Within his own province he reorganized and strengthened the cabinet secretariat, creating what opponents called a mini White House. The powers of the reformed secretariat are far from presidential, but they do enable the prime minister to exercise a greater degree of supra-bureaucratic control. The new

Internal Affairs Office, staffed by eighteen senior officials recruited from five different ministries, will formulate integrated policies on trade friction, overseas aid, market access and other sensitive issues that had previously been handled separately by the responsible agencies.

Nakasone represented the triumph of politics. After five successive one-term prime ministers, all of whom were limited in their decisions by the LDP's internal balance of power, he managed to win six years in office. His 'settlement of the post-war account' was an ideologically based programme, of a different order from the careful mechanical legislation which is the bureaucracy's forte. Furthermore, the way he presented it implied that there had been something lacking in the government of Japan to date, a government in which the bureaucrats had been proud to play a leading part. In 1986 Nakasone went to the country on his own record and personality and won the largest LDP victory ever, securing a clear mandate for more leadership from the front. The scale of the landslide reduced any objections the opposition parties might have had to utter insignificance. It also shifted the initiative decisively from the bureaucrats to the politicians. The guests were beginning to look more at home than the staff.

The bureaucracy still exerts enormous power, but its ability to set new directions has probably gone for ever. Prosperity brings a completely different set of problems from adversity. The bureaucratic instinct for protection and control is in inevitable conflict with the natural vigour and animal spirits of a wealth-generating economy. By the mid eighties Japanese companies had come of age, were confident that their own judgement would bring the best results. Indeed, whether by cause or effect, the most thriving industries are those, such as consumer electronics, autos and office equipment, where regulation is minimal. By contrast, in cement manufacture, retailing or sugar-refining, Japan has little to teach the world.

Co-operation between politicians, businessmen and bureaucrats will still be vitally important over the years ahead. Japan's economy is undergoing a massive structural change that many industries will not survive. They will be voluble in their demands for protection, subsidies and special treatment, just as their counterparts in other countries have been. Japan cannot afford to heed them because, more than any other country, she depends on the development of new higher-value-added industries for her future growth. Politicians will have to take decisions that may be unpopular, and bureaucrats will have to find methods of enacting them that create the minimum of economic and social strain. Gradually and as painlessly as possible, Japan's bureaucrats will have to set about undoing their own handiwork of the sixties, when the structure of heavy industry was so carefully established.

With their usual application and thoroughness Japan's bureaucrats continue to produce frameworks, five-year plans, and 'visions' of the future, but the need for them is no longer obvious. Perhaps one day some committee of the great and the good will consider a modest proposal that would revive past glories – privatization of MITI and the Ministry of Finance and the rest, and their hiring out to the many countries, both developing and developed, that would benefit from their expert guidance.

Labour Pains

Protest action – wearing blue armbands to work. Strikes – carried out in the lunch break. Wage negotiations – settled before they start. Union leaders – who go on to become company presidents. In structure, function and influence, Japanese unions are quite unlike their Western counterparts. There are 75,000 of them altogether, the vast majority being 'enterprise unions' which comprehend the entire work-force of a particular company, both blue-collar and white-collar. Trade unions, horizontal alliances of workers performing the same class of job, are rare. It is an arrangement which has had a profound effect on the pattern of Japanese labour relations.

The unionization rate of Japanese workers is low by European, though not by American, standards and, in common with trends elsewhere in the world, has declined markedly in recent years – from 35 per cent in 1970 to 28 per cent in 1985. This is not due, as in Britain's case, to an absolute fall in membership, but to the rapid growth in service-sector and small-company employment. In small companies with less than 100 employees, where most of the new jobs have been created, union membership is only about 5 per cent.

Japan's union movement is poorly centralized and lacking in political influence. There are two large and two small umbrella organizations to which most, but not all, of the individual unions are affiliated. The largest of the four, Sohyo (the General Council of Trade Unions of Japan), has 4.5 million affiliated members, or barely 10 per cent of the total work-force. The second largest, Domei (the Japanese Confederation of Labour), is half the size. Even if they were able to agree a unified strategy their combined leverage would still be small compared to, for example, Britain's TUC.

Of the two, Sohyo is the more radical, having in the past conducted 'political struggles' on such issues as the US–Japan Security Treaty. It supports the left wing of the Japan Socialist Party and draws on the public-sector unions for most of its membership. Domei, which is made up almost entirely of company unions, is pledged to the centrist Democratic Socialist Party. Since the JSP has not held power since 1948 and the DSP never at all, Japan's union movement has had no direct influence over the country's economic management. In most other developed economies, union-backed parties, or at least coalitions of interests including the unions, have had their turns in government. Not so in Japan, where the unions have never set foot in the corridors of power.

The umbrella organizations have little to do with day-to-day labour–management relations. Traditionally their main role was to co-ordinate the annual *shunto*, the spring labour offensive which was once such a noisy feature of the industrial scene. Apparently endless processions of workers would wend their way through the centre of Tokyo, holding up the traffic even more than it is usually held up and bull-horning out their demands to the world in general. The implication was that if something wasn't done about those demands, then drastic measures would be necessary. The private railway workers, one of the few industry groups which act effectively en bloc, would frequently display their dissatisfaction with whatever increase was offered by withdrawing their labour for a day or two. This provided a fine opportunity for other workers to display their indomitable company spirit, either by bedding down in their offices or by rising before dawn to make the long trudge to work.

The eighties version of *shunto* is a pale shadow of what used to be. On the rare occasions when rail strikes take place, they last only for a matter of hours. The other group which once formed the vanguard of the offensive – the steelworkers – have grown even more mild-mannered. Continuing recession in the steel industry has kept their attention firmly on job security. Consequently the role of the umbrella organizations and the cross-industry federations has been considerably diminished, a trend which is likely to continue. The large gaps which are opening up in the business performance of companies from the same industrial sector and the unquenchable appetite of Japanese businessmen for diversification means that horizontal alliances will soon make less sense than they do now. The Federation of Iron and Steel Workers will have plenty to think about in ten years' time when the large blast-furnace companies, if all goes to plan, will be obtaining 30 per cent of their revenues from new ventures, such as software development and marine parks.

While Japanese unions have never held or aspired to hold much political influence, it would be a mistake to conclude that their members' interests have been sacrificed. Unemployment has stayed low, while the rise in consumer prices exeeded the annual wage increase only once in the ten years from 1977 to 1986. There have been no gruelling drawn-out strikes, no ructions about closed shops, no absurd demarcation disputes. Measured by results, the Japanese unions have performed a valuable service, both for their members and for the economy as a whole. In the turbulent period between 1976 and 1983 the wage increases of Japanese workers consistently outpaced the cost of living, while inflation was held down below 3 per cent.

The union structure has reinforced the inherent Japanese distaste for useless forms of conflict. It is a structure that corresponds closely to industrial reality. According to Japanese thinking, solidarity with those doing similar jobs in different companies is illogical, since they are rivals, working to take your market share, reduce your profits and, if possible, put you out of business. The union, the mechanism for maximizing wages, has no existence separate from the organism that generates the profits to pay them. It is merely the company in a different avatar, including all company employees, and excluding everybody else. Since there is little mobility of labour in the large-company sector, male union members will stay with the same employer for all their working lives, and the top union officers will hope to progress to management positions. Strikes or other forms of industrial action which harm the corporate organism are a desperate last resort. Much better to come to an amicable arrangement which might not be the very best that could be squeezed out, but at least presents no threat to future security. Japanese workers, like Japanese managements, think long term.

In the large companies all employees without management titles, except perhaps those in the wages department, are usually union members. Line workers, computer programmers, filing clerks, salesmen – all are defined, not by the restricted function they perform, but by their membership of the whole. Top executives, including the board of directors, were probably once union members themselves, which makes it easier to establish the community of interests in salary negotiations. It is worth noting that the differential between executive remuneration and the average wage is low on an international comparison. According to a Nikkeiren survey, the average company president receives 7.5 times the salary of a new recruit, against 30–50 times in the US and Europe. Workers know that money foregone in current salary will not find its way into the pockets of the directors or, for that matter, of the shareholders, but will be ploughed back into the business, thus contributing to future prosperity.

Japanese labour relations do not always live up to this

idyllic picture. Public-sector unions behave much the same as public-sector unions everywhere – though the right to strike is denied to civil servants, power workers and certain other groups. Nikkyoso, the teachers' union, spends its time quarrelling over abstruse points of Marxist dialectic. The old Japan National Railway contained several unions of different ideological hue, the most radical of which is very radical indeed, having close links with the murderous urban guerrilla movement. In 1986 leaders of groups co-operating with the government's privatization plan were viciously attacked in their homes, one man being beaten to death with steel pipes. Together, the JNR unions were successful in keeping out automatic ticket barriers and preserving spectacular levels of overmanning. The case of Japan Airlines is rather more worrying. Cabin crew belong to three different unions which are in a perpetual state of discord. In 1981 a pilot who had for months been slowly going round the twist decided to land his plane in Tokyo Bay. As a result of this experiment twenty-two people died. His co-pilot had long sensed that something strange was afoot but, since they belonged to different unions, had decided not to take up the matter.

Not all Japanese company unions are sweethearts either, as the management of Nissan is painfully aware. No important decision could be taken at Japan's second-largest auto maker without the approval of union 'Don' Shioji, with the result that productivity fell way behind Toyota's. At most other large companies the union is more self-effacing, but the unspoken trade-off is strictly maintained – co-operation in return for job security. As a result, even Japan's best-managed corporations contain squads of unwanted employees, usually estimated to make up 5–10 per cent of the total payroll. Members of the 'by-the-window tribe', often men in their forties who, through illness or lack of ability, have failed to keep up with their fellows, present a forlorn spectacle as they conduct their daily 'research' into newspapers and magazines. Japan's surplus workers are at their most visible in the major department stores, each one of which contains dozens of crisply-uniformed elevator and escalator girls whose only function is to bow and murmur courtesies at the stream of shoppers.

At times of crisis, lay-offs may be inevitable. Under such circumstances the government and the company will usually top up wages to 50–80 per cent of the average, and some form of rotation may be devised to share the burden equitably. In the major structural readjustments which Japan carried out so smoothly in the seventies the production capacities of the shipbuilding, aluminium, steel and petrochemical industries were reduced dramatically without any serious labour disputes arising. Huge enterprises like Mitsubishi Heavy Industries were able to redeploy their workers in new business areas, such as aerospace and special machinery. Many other companies, being members of large industrial groupings, transferred unwanted personnel to subsidiaries and affiliates.

Life was not always as peaceful as it is today. In the twenties Japan was racked by violent labour disturbances, and in the early post-war years there were several politically motivated strikes, culminating in the abortive general strike of 1947. Over the next few decades, protracted stoppages tended to be rare, but those that did occur brought violent clashes, sometimes leading to deaths, between pickets and police. Until the mid seventies the number of days lost in industrial disputes was higher in Japan than in most European countries (excepting Britain) and ten times the West German level. There is no truth at all in the theory that the currently harmonious state of labour relations is somehow genetically determined. However, Japanese workers, like Japanese managements and macro-economic policy-makers, responded swiftly to the changing circumstances of the stagflation years. The number of days lost began to decline dramatically after 1975, whereas in the USA, for example, the fall-off did not come until after 1980. Not coincidentally, over the same crucial period Japan also mastered inflation and kept her cost of capital well below Western levels. As a result businesses were able to take full advantage of the new technologies then coming on the market and build up a devastating competitive advantage.

Japanese workers and their unions were quick to appreciate that wage increases unaccompanied by job losses could only be financed by improvements in productivity. It is a starkly obvious proposition, but it failed to gain recognition in most Western countries. One of the reasons for that is the difference in history of the various labour movements. In the West, workers have traditionally regarded union militancy as a redistributive mechanism which raises their living standards at the expense of bosses/shareholders/other overpaid groups of workers. Wage increases can always be prised out of employers if enough force is applied. Post-war Japan started off with hardly any wealth to redistribute. Quite evidently there could be no gains in living standards without corresponding rises in productivity. The union movement could play its part in smoothing out relative levels of remuneration and ensuring that managements behaved themselves, but few workers could imagine that it was primarily responsible for the rapid rise in their incomes.

Moderate wage demands, like low dividends, contribute to the build-up of resources within the enterprise. Still more valuable, however, is the attitude of the work-force to technological innovation, the main generator of productivity growth. Unlike their Western equivalents, Japanese unions have co-operated with managements in rationalization and productivity-enhancement programmes. Indeed the Toyota union has even bestowed membership on some assembly robots. In return, managements have agreed to refrain from making involuntary redundancies unless faced with a desperate plight, and those have been relatively rare. Companies have adopted whatever labour-saving devices and strategies are available in order to stay competitive. At the same time they have had to think up new ventures to absorb the energies of displaced workers. The result has been to create an inherent growth momentum in every well-managed company, regardless of existing patterns of demand.

Enterprise unions grew up haphazardly in the chaotic post-war years, in many cases carrying on from the patriotic employee organizations which had been devised by the militar-

The World of Work

	Japan	US	UK	WG
Robots installed	41,265	9,400	1,753	4,800
Rise in productivity (1975–85)	+55%	+38%	+30%	+30%
Days lost in disputes (av. 1978–84 ,000 man-days)	744	15,013	10,372	723
Unionization	29%	19%	53%	28%
Net weekly working hours	40.3	36.3	36.4	32.8

Source: Keizai Koho Centre, Japan Institute of Labour

ists. There was nothing inevitable about their formation and development, but they have now become an integral part of the Japanese industrial structure. Over the next fifteen years they will be faced with a new set of challenges. Specifically, the trade-off between wage restraint and job security will come under increasing strain. The strength of the yen combined with the enduring problem of trade friction is forcing Japanese companies to shift production overseas, creating, according to one MITI survey, 650,000 job losses at home by the end of the century. Since the total number of unemployed in 1986 was only 1.6 million, the scale of the problem can be readily appreciated. At the same time the expected surge in imports of manufactured and semi-manufactured goods, such as textiles and petrochemicals, will force retrenchment in some of Japan's largest companies. If it is to remain competitive the steel industry will have to shed one-third of its 300,000 workers, and chemical and shipbuilding companies will be forced into similarly drastic rationalization. The pace of economic change and the ferocity of the competition from the NICs (Newly Industrializing Countries) make the old solutions of retraining and redeployment no longer viable.

How will the Japanese unions respond? A revival of militancy would be one way, but it could hardly turn back the macro-economic tide. Japanese workers, being pragmatists above all else, understand that prosperity is best maintained by adapting to change, not resisting it. Their record of success so far should give them every confidence in their ability to meet the challenge.

The Profit Clubs

Japanese companies, like the individuals who work in them, have an inherent tendency to cluster together in groups formed to promote 'mutual benefit'. It is a sort of homing instinct. Foreign businessmen often complain, with some justification, of the exclusiveness of the Japanese industrial structure. They may not realize that conditions are just as tough for independent Japanese companies, which is why there are so few of them. Membership of a group means security in hard times, reliable markets and suppliers, opportunities for collecting information and sharing resources. It provides access to the network of personal connections on which Japanese business relationships are based. It gives every deal a context, a history and a future.

The archetypal Japanese power groups were the *zaibatsu*, the great family-owned conglomerates which dominated the pre-war economic landscape. After the war the *zaibatsu* were broken up and most of their executives purged – the idea being to prevent the wealth concentration that had enabled the militarists to develop their command economy so smoothly. The occupation succeeded in reforming many areas of Japanese life, but the Japanese method of doing business proved itself stubbornly resistant to change. The companies so rudely sundered soon drifted together again, and have now settled into a looser version of the old configuration. The six modern groupings – Mitsui, Mitsubishi, Sumitomo, Fuyo, D K B, and Sanwa – are mammoth accumulations of financial, commercial and manufacturing power. Together, they have 650 member companies, including the leaders of most industries in scale, technology and prestige. They employ 1.8 million people, or 6 per cent of the Japanese work-force, and generate 18 per cent of all corporate revenues and profits. That does not compare with the dominance of the old *zaibatsu*, ten of which used to account for 40 per cent of private-sector output, but the Japanese economy itself has grown vastly more powerful. The groups now control more than 2 per cent of the entire world economy.

The chief executives of the twenty or thirty 'nucleus companies', usually the oldest and largest in the group, meet once a month to co-ordinate strategy on financial management, participation in big projects, joint research and development, political contributions, and other long-term issues. All the members of the 'Presidents' Councils' have equal voting rights, but, in true Japanese style, agreements are reached through consensus. Naturally the more prosperous members have a higher consensus quotient than those heavily in debt to the group bank. Since no details of the proceedings are ever released to the public, it is impossible to evaluate the significance of decisions taken. The participants themselves, still smarting from the media criticism they suffered in the mid seventies, play down the extent of group co-operation, preferring to describe the Presidents' Councils as social and study meetings. None the less it is hard to believe that the presidents of Mitsubishi group companies discuss, for example, Japan's defence policy out of an academic interest in the subject. Thanks to the role of political contributions in the shaping of government decisions, they have the power to enforce their conclusions at the highest possible level.

The extent of inter-group favouritism is difficult to judge, but obviously considerable. Mitsubishi companies pay their wages through Mitsubishi Bank, rent their head offices from Mitsubishi Real Estate, and their storage space from Mitsubishi Warehouse. By choice they use air-conditioning systems made by Mitsubishi Electric, machinery made by Mitsubishi Heavy, trucks made by Mitsubishi Motor, and fuel supplied by Mitsubishi Oil. Their factories are insured by Tokio Marine and Fire, the group insurance company, and the beer for their 'forget-the-year' parties is supplied by Kirin, the group brewer. Altogether, group members make 15–25 per cent of their sales to fellow members, the bulk going to the large general trading firms. Cohesion is further strengthened by the practice of executive transfer, usually from key financial institutions to junior members. Over two-thirds of the member companies of the six large groups have at least one executive who has been transferred from within the group, and one-third have executives who are holding posts in two member companies simultaneously. The purpose is to improve the flow of information within the group, to ensure that no conflicts arise in financial strategy, and to upgrade managerial quality in weaker members. Since mid-term career shifts are still a rarity in Japanese corporate life, intra-group transfer is one of the few methods available of introducing fresh thinking at senior levels.

Group identity is formalized in a complex pattern of interlocking shareholdings. Typically, one-fifth of a group company's equity is spread amongst fellow members. Whereas the old *zaibatsu* were controlled by family-owned holding companies, the modern groups are structured like complex molecules, each component binding with several others. No single company dominates the rest, but, as in social relationships, cumulative lateral pressure can match the sort that comes from above. In the early seventies, just before the liberalization of capital inflows into Japan, crossholdings were rapidly built up, the idea being to stave off foreign predators. This strategy has been highly successful. As customers, suppliers and friendly financial institutions also hold shares on a semi-permanent basis, contested takeovers are almost impossible to bring off. The few to occur in recent years have been shrewdly aimed at companies lacking group support.

The Japanese word for takeover is the same as that for hijack – which gives some indication of the disfavour in which the activity is held. Japanese executives would view a hostile bid for their company in much the same terms as they would an attempt to wrest control of their homes and families. They consider the shenanigans on the American and European capital market to be yet more evidence of hopelessly short-term industrial and financial strategies. None the less some of Japan's most respected businessmen – such as Noboru Goto, power behind the Tokyu group and chairman of the Japan Chamber of Commerce – owe their success to the voracious appetite for acquisition they demonstrated in the years of post-war upheavals. Takeovers were quite common until the mid sixties, before Japanese industry set into its present physical and ideological structure. Firms which carry on the practice in contemporary Japan are considered decidedly non-kosher. When Minebea, a good example of the breed, was itself threatened by the ultimate horror, a foreign raider, the business establishment looked on with ill-concealed satisfaction before finally coming to the rescue. The Japanese are now cautiously stepping up acquisition activities in the West, but that, of course, is a different matter.

Japanese industrial groups enjoy merits of scale without the most obvious demerits. Unlike typical conglomerates they are loose enough in structure to allow their individual components to respond quickly to market opportunities and technological change – each member company being locked in competition with its counterparts from other groups. Financial, technological and marketing resources can be shared. Sumitomo Electric and Nippon Electric can conduct their research into gallium-arsenide semiconductors without running the risk of inventing the same thing twice. For weaker members the cost of funds can be reduced by borrowing on the guarantee of the group trading firm. When Japanese companies were beginning their assault on foreign markets, membership helped companies to achieve results well beyond their natural scope. A machinery maker with no knowledge of overseas conditions, perhaps with no member of staff able to communicate in a foreign language, could make licensing agreements with top foreign makers through the services of the group trading company, obtain the necessary financing through the group bank, order custom-made electronic parts from other group firms, then use the trading company again to handle overseas marketing.

The groups have also specialized in large 'turnkey' projects, such as the export of petrochemical plants. An experienced consortium can quickly be assembled including all the necessary expertise to take the project from the blueprint stage to shipment – a bank, an insurer, a machinery maker, a plant engineer, a petrochemicals company to provide operational know-how, a trading firm to sell the output, a shipper to move it, and even, perhaps, a textile company to buy it. Given the growth of countertrade, now believed to comprise 8–10 per cent of total world trade, the ability to guarantee markets for the produce of a plant is becoming as important as provision of the hardware.

For the smaller manufacturing companies unsure of their international competitiveness, membership of one of the large groups has meant security – not just from foreign predators but from the hazards of the market. It is no coincidence that the major bankruptcies of recent years – Sanko Steamship, J. Osawa – have been of non-group companies. However, continual poor performance is not tolerated for long. Companies unable to stand on their own feet are likely to find themselves subjected to 'voluntary restructuring', often under the guidance of management drafted in from outside. In the worst case a merger can be arranged, such as that between the two shipbuilders, Ishikawajima and Harima, in 1962.

A simpler but, in Japanese terms, even more drastic remedy is the ouster of existing management. The best-known instance in recent times was the forced resignation of the president of Mitsukoshi department store in 1982 after an emergency meeting of the leaders of the Mitsui group. President Okada had been involved in all kinds of malpractices, the details of which were transmitted to the public by the weekly magazines in their usual lurid style. Mitsukoshi's imported fashion goods, it was reported, had mysteriously trebled in price after passing through a small wholesale company owned by Okada's mistress – a mark-up extravagant even by the generous standards of the Japanese retail industry. Such is the weakness of shareholders' rights in Japan, and so ingrained the habit of deferring to autocratic leaders, that the only way of getting rid of him was through pressure from above. If Mitsukoshi had not been a member of a powerful industrial group, Okada would have stayed and consumers would still be financing his high-value-added love life.

Japan's giant industrial groups are the product of a particular set of economic circumstances. They performed a vital role in the bureaucrat-directed establishment of heavy industry in the sixties and in the subsequent export drive. After the oil crisis many of the sectors on which they relied – chemicals, ship-building, steel, cement, paper and pulp – fell into structural recession from which there is still no sign of recovery. Turn-key exports slumped with the economies of the raw-material producers, and Japan's market share was eroded by the advances of the NICs. The whole Mitsui group suffered from the prolonged fiasco of the Iran Japan Petrochemical Company, a project started during the Shah's reign, inter-rupted for several years while the mullahs haggled over terms, then finally abandoned after repeated use for target practice by the Iraqi air force. The problems the major groups have been experiencing can be gauged by the feeble profitability of the two largest and oldest. In 1985 Mitsubishi and Mitsui recorded net profit margins of 0.8 per cent and 0.5 per cent respectively, well below the 2–3 per cent standard for listed companies. Far from leading the economy, the heirs of the old *zaibatsu* are having difficulty in keeping up with the competition. There is a danger of their becoming agglom-erations of the least dynamic elements in the Japanese econ-omy.

Gradually, cracks are appearing in the mighty monolith of group identity. Japanese companies are fighting for elbow room in the most competitive and dynamic market in the world. They cannot afford to let static conceptions of loyalty hamper their ability to respond. When Mitsubishi Corpora-tion decided to move into lap computers, it chose the best model on offer, which happened to be made by Toshiba, not Mitsubishi Electric. All the large groups contain unprofitable aluminium smelters, relics of MITI's import substitution policy, but their customers are increasing purchases of foreign ingots from the group trading houses. As the divergence in performance between different industries grows wider, the set of compromises and barters which holds the group together becomes more difficult to maintain. Inter-group co-operation may prove one of the most sensible ways of mediating the tensions. Already, Mitsui and Sumitomo have merged their shipping lines, and Mitsui Toatsu Chemical has set up joint ventures with Mitsubishi Petrochemical and Sumitomo Chemical.

Companies like Sony, Toyota, Matsushita, Honda, Ricoh, and Sharp have succeeded in transforming themselves into major presences in the world markets without affiliation to any of the major groups. In general, high-technology companies do not have much to gain from group membership. They are not interested in stable supplies of raw materials since they require so little. Usually they are sound enough financially to raise their own funds on the capital markets and, as major exporters, possess their own overseas distribution channels. Even if nominally group members, their degree of affiliation tends to be weak. For example, Hitachi, one of the largest employers in Japan's private sector, is a member of both the Fuyo and DKB groups. Of the forty-five members of the Presidents' Councils of the two oldest groups, only half a dozen could be described as either high-growth or high-technology companies.

That is not to say that Japan's most successful companies have gone it alone, without the benefits of structured business relationships. Many have set up small vertically integrated groups of their own. The classic example is Toyota, which with a labour force one-third the size of Ford's turns out nearly double the number of cars. The secret is not merely Japanese production efficiency. Toyota has a tightly structured group of 1200 parts manufacturers all competing for work, and behind them 38,000 tiny backyard enterprises that survive on wage levels roughly half those of the parent organization. As marginal producers they face large fluctuations in earnings according to the business cycle, with price squeezes at times of slack demand or currency appreciation, and prosperity when operating levels are high. Toyota owes a great deal of its success to their rigorous quality control and constant upgrading of productivity. The famous 'just-in-time' system of inventory management depends utterly on the ability of parts manufacturers to deliver exactly the right goods at exactly the right time. Without that guarantee, Toyota would be forced to carry the same fat inventory as any Western manufacturer.

The relationship between the large assemblers and their family of suppliers is often characterized in terms which suggest either disinterested paternalism or unscrupulous exploitation. The truth is more mundane – it is a relationship which has proved its worth to all parties involved. Under normal conditions the parent company must allow its suppliers a fair profit to encourage them to invest in productivity-enhancing equipment. On the other hand the bonuses and jobs of its own workers, who are all unionized, will inevitably take priority. For both sides of the transaction the advantages of doing business with a familiar partner have out-weighed the attractions of taking the best price available on an open market. The stable relationship between buyer and seller enables products to be adjusted to the manufacturer's detailed requirements and long-term investments to be made that would otherwise be outside the supplier's financial range. The competitive mechanism is preserved by the existence of hundreds of other small suppliers all jostling for an increased share of the business. Just as long as wage levels, equipment quality and material prices are roughly similar, any competitive advantage achieved is likely to be temporary.

The snag comes with the intrusion of an outsider, a foreign company for example, which has a wholly different and unmatchable combination of input factors. It remains to be seen how Toyota will respond when tempted by a supply of Taiwanese and Korean components 30 per cent cheaper than the products of its own long-nurtured 'family'. Profit or traditional Japanese virtue – which is it to be? The conflict did not even exist until the steep appreciation of the yen in 1985–6 handed a decisive cost advantage to the NICs. It will become even sharper over the remaining years of the century, subverting all sorts of relationships and assumptions.

The changing character of the traditional groups is reflected in developments amongst the core companies, particularly the large banks and trading firms which provide the financial glue that binds the organizations together. Both types of institution are massive in scale and miserable in profitability, having sacrificed their own interests for the good of their group and the economy as a whole. Both have excellent human resources, and consistently feature amongst the most popular employment choices of the nation's top graduates. Both are beginning to apply their obvious strengths with more imagination and purpose.

Japan's *sogo shosha* (integrated trading houses) are unique entities. In both scale and range of activity they dwarf every other trading enterprise in the world. Together the Big Nine *shosha* handle 70 per cent of Japan's imports and 44 per cent of her exports, and their combined revenues are equivalent to 30 per cent of the gross national product. Mitsubishi Corporation, the largest of the *shosha*, boasts annual turnover greater than the GNP of most of the countries it trades with – including Belgium, Indonesia and South Africa. As well as dealing in all kinds of commodity, from pigfeed to precious metals, the *shosha* act as investors, consultants, distributors, and planners of giant projects. They are by far the most 'internationalized' of Japanese companies, with over one thousand overseas offices between them and squadrons of experts in the languages and economies of Japan's trading partners.

The trading-house employee, the *shosha*-man, is a figure of great respect in the Japanese business world. He comports himself as a samurai devoted to the collective prosperity, and myriads of small enterprises depend on him for credit, market information and paternal advice. During his long, lonely postings in foreign lands, he tirelessly promoted the wares of unknown, unpronounceable Japanese companies, preparing the way for an era of export-led growth. He sifted through the foreign technologies and business ideas and brought the best ones home. He established Japan's raw-material bases in Australia, the Middle East and South-East Asia. He cultivated the third-world and communist markets where Japanese companies now have an important edge. All through the postwar period the *shosha*-man has worked to facilitate the efficient interaction of Japan's economy with those of other countries. Simultaneously he has acted as a buffer, removing the necessity for direct cultural contact. His endeavours have been invaluable to the great decontextualization process that has enabled the Japanese to absorb so much while staying the same.

The trading houses, like the groups they serve, reached the apex of their power in the sixties. After the oil crisis they fell into a slump popularly known as the *sogo shosha* winter. Japan's previously insatiable appetite for raw materials was suddenly dulled, and energy-intensive heavy industries made drastic cuts in capacity. Furthermore the political mood turned sharply against the *shosha* and their relentless pursuit of economic interest. To South-East Asian nationalists they became the symbol of Japan's second wave of colonization. At home the Lockheed scandal blew the gaff on their less orthodox marketing techniques. When economic recovery finally came the *shosha* were left behind, wedded to the wrong half of Japan's two-tier industrial structure. The leaders of the next growth stage, the auto and electronic companies, had their own overseas sales networks and could manage quite nicely without any help. Tight money played havoc with the *shosha*'s highly geared financial structure, and the plunge in commodity prices sent many of their resource projects sliding irretrievably into the red.

The *shosha*'s traditional business is unlikely to recapture its former lustre. The surging value of the yen – caused by the success of the mostly non-group exporters – has done lasting damage to the competitive power of Japan's heavy industries, pricing them out of overseas markets and creating new opportunities for imports from the NICs. Within the domestic economy the trend towards services and high-value-added manufacturing is gathering pace. The *shosha*'s response has been to move away from group business, indeed to reduce dependence on the Japanese economy altogether. The three largest *shosha* now derive one-quarter of their massive revenues from transactions outside Japan – such as selling Chinese textiles in Australia, or African bauxite in South America. Japanese trading companies already play a vital role in promoting the efficiency of the world-trading system. In future they could become as important to some of the less developed nations as they have been to members of their own groups.

The greatest challenge facing the *shosha*, offering the greatest potential rewards, is diversification of their business within Japan. As organizations they are superbly equipped to ride the next wave of economic change. They are highly adaptable, knowledge-intensive enterprises, with no factories or line workers. All their personnel, in terms of education the best that Japan can offer, are information workers, many of them with rare specialized skills. Indeed, a study by the Japan Socialist Party concluded that Mitsubishi Corporation was the most effective information-gathering organization in Japan, well ahead of the media and governmental bodies. Information equivalent to 7000 pages of the *New York Times* is transmitted within the company every day. In the industrial structure of the future, data will be the ultimate asset, and the ability to understand and use it the main criterion of profitability. If the trading companies can transform themselves into information clearing houses, they should recover their leading position in the Japanese economy.

When the possessors of the finest business skills in Japan finally start using them on their own account, a formidable competitive force is created. The shape of things to come can be discerned in the vast array of businesses to which the *shosha* have turned their attention. Hundreds of subsidiaries have been set up, covering the range of high-growth industries – hybrid seeds, urban redevelopment, ocean-bed mining, pharmaceuticals, artificial intelligence, microprocessors, aerospace and old-age homes. Finance is home territory, since the *shosha* are already major factors in world currency and commodity markets. Between them the five largest – Mitsubishi, Mitsui, C. Itoh, Sumitomo, and Marubeni – have twenty subsidiaries solely involved in procuring and managing money. Ultimately of much greater significance is their move into the telecommunications industry. Consortia organized by the *shosha* are powerful contenders in Japan's newly deregulated telecommunications market. Using their own satellites, digital networks and under-sea optical cables, they plan to control the Tokyo end of what is to become the world's most important information axis – that linking the United States with the dynamic Far Eastern economies.

At first sight Japan's 'city banks' do not give the impression of being the largest financial institutions in the world. The customer at a busy Tokyo branch may find himself waiting forty-five minutes to perform some simple transaction such as paying a bill. Because personal cheques are rarely used in Japan, every sizeable purchase requires a separate visit to the bank and a separate wait. Fortunately the customer is provided with a good selection of scandal magazines to while away the empty minutes. If that diversion proves insufficient, he can observe the complicated activities of the dozens of staff behind the counter as they struggle with heaps of hand-written documents and ferry large bundles of notes from one desk to another.

The well-being of the consumer has never featured prominently in the calculations of the large 'city banks'. Since Japan's interest-rate structure is fixed by the Ministry of Finance, there has not been any need for them to compete for his custom. The interest paid out to depositors has always been kept low, reaching a nadir of 0.26 per cent on an ordinary savings account in 1986. Overdrafts are extremely difficult to arrange, a situation which has driven many unfortunate individuals into the clutches of loan sharks who charge interest rates of 50 per cent per annum and use gangsters to collect overdue debts. Until the authorities finally cracked down in 1982 these unscrupulous operators were being financed by the respectable banks, both Japanese and foreign.

The banks have merely been reflecting the strategic priorities of Japan Inc. – investment for the future, not current consumption. The dramatic rise in living standards and the naturally high savings rate of Japanese households has guaranteed a steadily improving cash flow. The role of the banks has been simply to channel the money received into the appropriate capital-intensive industrial sectors. By the usual criteria of banking efficiency, their record has been abysmal. In terms of assets, the four largest banks in the world are all Japanese, but in terms of profitability not one comes within the top ten. However, in the performance of their designated function Japanese banks have been brilliantly successful. The capital provided has enabled client companies to grow into giant multinational enterprises that now generate enough funds to stand on their own two feet. The inevitable result has been a weakening of the relationship of dependence on which the power and influence of the banks was based.

Traditonally almost every Japanese company, whether formally attached to an industrial group or not, was served by a 'main bank', an exclusive provider of financial services. The relationship would often be cemented by mutual shareholdings, and the borrowing company would maintain 'compensating balances' at the bank in order to make the balance sheet ratios of both parties look less scary. If employees of the borrowing company wanted to receive any salary, they would have to set up personal accounts at the main bank. Until the mid seventies even the most famous of Japanese companies were so heavily in debt that the preservation of good relations with the main bank was management's prime goal. Debt-to-equity ratios of several hundred per cent were the rule rather than the exception, and bankers had the final say on all major investment decisions.

Many heavy industrial companies remain utterly dependent on the ministrations of their bankers, but Japan's corporate sector as a whole is now healthy enough to survive without the financial dripfeed. Between 1973 and 1988 the equity ratio – the proportion of assets financed internally – of Japanese manufacturers improved from 16 per cent to 34 per cent. That is still well below the 40–60 per cent standard in the West, but if so-called latent assets are taken into consideration Japanese companies have at least as great internal resources as their foreign competitors. Since Japanese accounting practices do not require assets to be revalued, land and securities acquired shortly after the war can be held on the books at the purchase price, usually a tiny fraction of current market value. Instead of being paid out in dividends, wages or taxes, the appreciation in value stays within the firm, a massive invisible reserve that provides excellent protection against inflation.

During the export boom of 1982–6 retained profits increased dramatically, while the growth of the international capital markets enabled Japan's top companies to obtain most of the financing they required directly. Toyota, Matsushita and their equals became so massively cash rich that they are sometimes referred to as banks in their own right. In 1976 only one listed company in eleven had a positive financial balance – that is to say, received more money in investment income than it paid out on borrowings. Ten years later, half were cash positive. Indeed, it was income from 'financial engineering' that enabled the exporters to survive the rapid appreciation of the yen. Meanwhile the Ministry of Finance was proceeding, albeit painfully slowly, with its programme of interest-rate liberalization. The result would be that the banks would have to compete amongst themselves for the custom of the companies they had reared.

Even within the ambit of the financial world the banks found that their position was threatened, mainly by the hard-driving securities houses, who were prospering from the very same economic trends. Traditionally the Japanese securities industry, with its door-to-door salesmen and flashy marketing, had been regarded with strong public suspicion. Off-course gambling is prohibited in Japan, and the natural impulses it might have satisfied seem to have gravitated towards the stock market. However, nothing succeeds like success, and there could be no cavilling at the magnitude of what was being achieved. In 1985 Nomura Securities made more money than Sumitomo Bank, previously Japan's most profitable financial institution. The following year three more securities houses managed the same feat. Just four years previously Sumitomo Bank had made almost twice as much as Nomura and more than the other three put together. It was a reversal in the terms of power that accurately reflected an important shift in the Japanese economy. The banks are highly regulated asset-oriented businesses, solemnly pledged to the greater national good. The securities houses are innovative, comparatively free of restrictions and affiliations, and dedicated to the most rigorous application of the profit motive. Like other parvenus – indeed, like Japan herself – they tend to provoke a peculiar mixture of envy and distaste, not least amongst those they have bested. By 1987, that included almost everyone. Nomura had become easily the top-earning company in Japan. Its various brokerage and underwriting activities were generating more profit than Toyota and Nissan combined.

Further deregulation of the financial markets offers the banks their best chance to make up lost ground. At present the Japanese version of the Glass–Steagall Act – which keeps banks out of the securities business – is enforced more strictly than the American original. If the rules were relaxed, Japanese banks could become the major forces in the global securities market that is now developing. They have the staff for the job and, of course, they have the money. If the barriers remain in place the banks will be forced to concentrate on the internationalization of their main business, already progressing at a rate of knots. Japanese banks account for one-third of all international lending, against an American share of under 20 per cent. They are firmly entrenched as suppliers of capital to the booming East Asian economies, having half of all banking assets in Hong Kong and some 70 per cent of the Singapore off-shore market. Within the United States, they make 10 per cent of all corporate loans, and in the highly competitive guaranteeing of municipal bonds their share is over 50 per cent. They are especially strong in California, where five of the eleven largest banks are Japanese owned. In Britain the Japanese have just under one-fifth of all lending, and make 40 per cent of loans to the public sector. Loss-making nationalized industries, hard-left local authorities, channel-tunnel syndicates – all are hungry for Japanese cash. In contrast, the impact of foreign banks in Japan has been negligible. Returns are too low, the commitment too heavy.

Can the Japanese do the same to financial services as they have done to the car and camera industries? Sceptics cite the need for high-level political contacts, sophisticated risk-management and fast, imaginative decision-making, none of them obvious Japanese strengths. Yet the Japanese have been confounding breezy assertions about the extent of their aptitudes ever since their pilots appeared in the sky over Singapore. There is nothing especially complex about the banking and securities business. New financial products, unlike new electronic gadgets, cannot be patented: once developed, they are available to be copied by everyone. The essential ingredients of success are power, organization and ambition, qualities that the Japanese have in abundance. Political influence and experience can both be bought. Japanese financial institutions number amongst their consultants former high officials of the Bank of England and the Federal Reserve and an ex-chancellor of the Federal Republic of Germany. They have recruited a succession of top traders and strategists, all of whom receive salaries far above those of their new bosses.

The Japanese are showing that the time-honoured tactics of undercutting competitors and maximizing market share can be just as successful with money as with goods. In underwriting and selected-loan business, margins have been driven down to nothing. Taking their usual long-term view, Japanese companies are quite prepared to risk substantial losses on deals if they believe that their reputation and power in the market will be enhanced. Since Japan's banks and brokers, unlike their predecessors in manufacturing industry, are already the world's largest in their own fields, they can tough out any profit slump with equanimity, indeed use it to increase their dominance. They are funded by the world's most scrupulous savers. They have a near monopoly on the financial flows of the world's largest exporter of capital. In addition the vast majority of their assets are denominated in a currency whose dollar value has doubled since the Group of Five meeting in September 1985. If the Japanese exploit these enormous advantages with their usual intelligence and determination, they will soon control the central nervous system of the world economy.

Both the massive structural strength and the peculiarly inbred quality of the Japanese financial system are reflected in the workings of the Tokyo Stock Exchange, which now accounts for over 44 per cent of world stock market capitalization. At the beginning of the 1980s, it accounted for just 15 per cent. The largest Japanese company, NTT, has a market capitalization greater than the entire German stock market, and treble that of IBM, the largest company in the United States. Japanese stocks have also been one of the best long-term investments around. $1000 invested across the Dow Jones Index in 1973 would have been worth $2300 at the end of 1988. A $1000 stake in the Tokyo Stock Exchange Index would have grown to $17,000 over the same period.

It might be supposed that investors all over the world would have been scrambling aboard this bullet-train ride to riches. In fact, foreigners own just 3 per cent of the Tokyo market and have been net sellers of Japanese stocks every year from 1984 to 1987, thus spurning a near trebling in the market index and a doubling in the currency. Overseas investment gurus and financial journalists complained continually and vociferously that Japanese stock valuations were way too high, and forecast that the inevitable collapse would precipitate a world-wide shakeout. In fact, the epicentre of the quake that did bring down markets everywhere was Wall Street, which plunged 23 per cent on one very black Monday in October 1987. The market that fell the least and recovered the quickest was Japan's. Within six months, it was back at its all-time high – a feat which befitted the world's most prodigious generator of capital.

The experts were wrong because they brought foreign preconceptions to a market which looks the same and sounds the same, but is governed by radically different principles: where strategic cross-holdings create a permanent shortage of stock; where the high savings ratio creates a permanently rising flow of funds into the investing institutions; where hostile takeovers never happen, and neither do prosecutions for insider trading; where competitive fund management and its destructive pressures are almost unknown; where the Big Four securities houses control half the market turnover and, with the active connivance of the authorities, use every trick in the book to keep stock prices moving in the direction that everybody wants – upwards.

By international standards, the Price-to-Earnings Ratios (PER) of Japanese stocks are extraordinarily high. Just before it collapsed, Wall Street was trading on a PER of about 20 – meaning that the market value was equivalent to twenty years of corporate earnings. At the same time, the PER on the Japanese market was 70. However, the ability of the Japanese to generate liquidity – through their savings, through their trade with the outside world – is also extraordinarily high by international standards, and that has powered the tremendous dynamism of the stock market. The other vital factor is confidence, which today's Japanese have in good supply.

Share markets have a better record as forecasters of economic change than all the pundits and politicians put together. Japan's long bull run, culminating in the spectacular lift-off of 1986–7, describes a sea change in power relationships, the full impact of which has yet to work through to everyday affairs. As legendary fund-manager George Soros put it, 'In 1929 the United States was superseding Britain as the world's predominant economic force. In 1987 the power was flowing from the United States to the Asian superpower, Japan ... The crash of 1987 revealed Japan's strength and made the transfer of economic and financial power clearly visible.'

10

War and Peace

We Japanese have made the gravest mistake in our history.
I fully believe this was because our culture was of a poor
quality, and the public had an inadequate understanding of
the essence and meaning of culture.

Hitoshi Ashida, Japan's third post-war premier, 1946

A nation is still a nation whether it wins or loses a war. A
nation must shed all sense of ignominy and move forward
seeking glory.

Yasuhiro Nakasone, at a factional seminar, autumn 1985

The sixth of August is the anniversary of the first of the so far
only two occasions on which a nuclear weapon has been used
in human conflict. Every year on that date solemn services of
commemoration are held in a bustling provincial city in
western Japan. Hiroshima was once a key staging point for
the Japanese Imperial Army. Now it is a prosperous, rather
characterless place of concrete and glass, notable chiefly for
the Mazda car company, its powerful baseball team and
superlative oysters. The only reminders of that terrible
moment of heat and light and naked energy are the mangled
dome of the old Industry Promotion Hall, and the 11,000
surviving *hibaku-sha* (victims of the bomb).

At 8.15 a.m. sharp, when the sun is already high and the
skyline hazing over, a siren wails through the network of
loudspeakers which connects every neighbourhood to the city
hall. On the early shift, on street corners, in homes, shops and
schools, people stop what they are doing and bow their heads
in prayer. A minute of perfect silence, then back to money-

making and breakfast and cars. Afterwards there are municipal ceremonies attended by government ministers and assorted bigwigs. There are rallies held by the stridently competitive groups of the fissiparous left. There are petitions, resolutions and denunciations.

Media interest is high, not just in Japan, but all over the world. The mayor of Hiroshima usually makes impassioned pleas to the leaders of the superpowers to halt the arms race. 'Hiroshima days' are observed in European and American cities. In Japan, schoolchildren weave together long chains of paper cranes, the bird that symbolizes peace and prosperity, and send them to be draped around the monuments of Peace Park. Hundreds of thousands of brightly coloured cranes, each one a tiny exercise in the art of Japanese manufacture, hang still in the heavy summer heat.

A visit to the museum in Peace Park is a harrowing experience. The photographs and artefacts on display together summon up an eschatological vision of ruin – paralysed clocks, human forms burnt into the pavement, hideous wounds and tumours. Crowds of tourists and Japanese school-children flood through the hall every day, most of them struck silent by the carefully catalogued assemblage of horror. 'No more Hiroshimas'; 'Never again'; 'The evil must never be repeated' – these are slogans with which few people are likely to disagree. In the modern consciousness, that gross blossom in the sky exists outside the particular context which created it, a symbol of the Faustian pact powered up to the ultimate.

Hiroshima is also the spiritual capital of Japan's peace movement, a force which has little direct political clout, but tremendous psychological influence. In spite of the martial traditions on which so much of their culture is based the Japanese have proclaimed themselves a 'peace-loving people'. In Hiroshima schools 'peace studies' – one of the few subjects outside the examination syllabus – are taught with the high seriousness that the British reserve for sex education. All politicians, whatever their real attitude to the defence issue, have to pay lip service to 'peace diplomacy'. The Matsushita group has established the PHP (Peace, Health and Prosperity) foundation, devoted to demonstrating the intimate connection between the three concepts. Mass-market newspapers such as the *Asahi Shimbun* espouse an idealistic pacifism absent from the mainstream of Western political thought since the thirties. They regularly carry gruesome accounts of the wartime suffering and relate it to Japan's efforts to strengthen her defences. The message is simple, but effective: 'look, this is where military spending leads'. It is also highly pragmatic. In the thirties, military expansion appeared the most sensible way of securing national advantage. Japan's post-war experience has shown that pacifism can bring far greater rewards.

Peace – the word is chanted by monks, sung by schoolchildren, bellowed by masked demonstrators, solemnly invoked by industrialists and politicians. It has come to denote an abstract quality, like heat or cold, entirely separate from, indeed opposite to, the real world of disputes and alliances and compromises. In the mind of a certain type of intellectual it is one of the features that distinguishes Japan from all other nations. It was once her manifest destiny to lead Asia to a new era of prosperity, free from the white colonialists. Now the only country to have experienced the horror of the bomb must present the world with a new model of international relations, a Pax Nipponica based not on arms but on technology and financial flows.

It wasn't so simple then, of course, and it isn't so simple now. If the passage of time is measured not by numbers of years, but by the speed and extent of change, then Japan is already further than any other country from the series of events that led to the flash in the sky over Hiroshima. If it is measured by the hold of the past over the present, then she is still too close for comfort.

Nine days afterwards, a number of elderly men in morning dress appear at a large Shinto shrine in central Tokyo. Amidst a phalanx of press and security people they pay their respects in the traditional Japanese manner, clanging the bell to summon the deity, clapping their hands in prayer, then passing a small donation to the head priest. Every detail of their behaviour is reported at length in the national press, together with much impassioned debate about its propriety. Foreign newspapers then take up the story and argue what it portends for the future of the civilized world, and their governments criticize any aspects of the ceremony of which they disapprove. For their part, the Japanese people view the whole business with stoic indifference.

The shrine is Yasukuni, meaning 'peaceful country'. The men are members of the Japanese cabinet, attending a service of remembrance for Japan's war dead. The day when the Emperor broadcast his recognition of Japan's only defeat in war was 15 August 1945. The technical reason for all the fuss is that the constitution enforces a separation of religion from matters of state which all in public office are required to uphold. However, if the shrine were one of the many dedicated to fertility or money-making, few would demur at Japan's leaders making as many visits as they liked. The real reason is the nature of the shrine itself.

Despite the name and the flocks of pigeons which strut across the gravel, Yasukuni's associations are far from peaceful. It enshrines the 2,400,000 Japanese killed in action since 1853, two million of them in the Second World War. 'See you at Yasukuni' was the parting phrase of the kamikaze pilots as they clambered into their Zeros. Before and during that war Yasukuni was the second most important shrine in the apparatus of State Shinto, its dignity bested only by the great shrine at Ise which holds the imperial regalia. Compulsory worship at Yasukuni was used to enforce loyalty amongst Christians, Buddhists, and members of other ideologically suspect groups. For ordinary citizens travelling past by bus, not to bow down in reverence was to risk interrogation by the secret police.

In modern times the shrine is used as a rallying ground by the right-wing extremist groups who so noisily advocate a return to pre-war values. Reputedly, no foreigner has ever set foot within its inner precinct. At the back of the main building is a small park containing a tank, some cannons and two *kaiten*, the manned torpedos launched at the US fleet in the last desperate stages of the war. Put simply, Yasukuni's history ensures that it will always be more than a shrine of remembrance and condolence.

In 1979 the spirits of General Hideki Tojo and several other Class-A war criminals were collectively enshrined. It was one year previously that then Prime Minister Takeo Fukuda had begun the custom by which LDP leaders worship at the shrine on the anniversary of Japan's defeat in the Second World War. Mindful of public sensibilities, both Fukuda and his successor, Ohira, maintained that they were worshipping in their private capacities and not as public officials. Zenko Suzuki, who took over the reins after Ohira's untimely death, made the carefully confused statement that he was worshipping neither as a private individual nor as a public official. In each case the media, the opposition, and non-Shinto religious groups kicked up a storm of protest, echoed in several neighbouring countries. Symbols are vitally important in Japanese politics, often more important than their point of reference. Official worship at Yasukuni, like the breaching of the 1 per cent of GNP limit on defence spending, has long been treated as a kind of leading indicator.

The next prime minister, Yasuhiro Nakasone, approached the subject in his usual confident style. In the first two visits of his term he paid his respects as 'Yasuhiro Nakasone, the prime minister of Japan'. In 1985, repeating a favourite ploy, he established a special advisory commission to look into the issue and stacked it with friendly academics. The conclusion they arrived at was ambiguous but essentially favourable to his wishes. Article Twenty of the constitution mandates that 'the state and its organs shall refrain from religious education or any other religious activity' but, as with the non-aggression clause, the facts of life suggest that the prohibition should not be taken too literally. Whenever a government representative attends the state funeral of a foreign leader he is taking part in a religious ceremony. The Imperial family conducts many traditional Shinto observances, all funded from the general account. Japan's institutions and customs, unlike those of the people who framed her constitution, have evolved over the centuries from an ancestor-worshipping culture, and the proper limits of religion are not so easily defined.

Nakasone made the first professedly official visit in 1985, signing his name in the worshipper's book as 'Prime Minister Yasuhiro Nakasone'. Domestic reaction was muted, most ordinary people being thoroughly fed up with the whole controversy. Only the Chinese, who were suffering from a huge and sudden bilateral trade deficit, sought to exploit the issue, with anti-Nakasone demonstrations springing up in several major cities. Partly to avoid their recurrence, in 1986 Nakasone cancelled his visit altogether, a move which only added to the confusion. Critics from both the left and the right assailed his lack of consistency. This was rather unfair. Nakasone had broken the taboo once and for all in 1985, and any further controversy would have served no useful purpose.

Why are Japan's political leaders so intent on stirring up memories of national disaster? Firstly and most simply, because there are votes in it. The 1.5 million-strong Bereaved Families Association is a powerful lobbying organization whose support no ambitious conservative can afford to alienate. In contrast the mild distaste that most Japanese feel for the airing of controversy will have little permanent effect on a politician's rise up the ladder. More important, many patriotic Japanese believe that the visit is proper. Nakasone gave this opinion at a factional seminar in 1983:

America has its Arlington Cemetery; the Russians and many other countries have their Tombs of the Unknown Soldier, or other places for people to give thanks to those who died in battle. That is quite natural. If there is no such place, who will be prepared to give their lives for their country?

The last sentence was typically rash, a gift to those on the left who had labelled Nakasone as the promoter of militarist revival. Still, the point being made is a reasonable one. When a country's leaders pay their respects to the war dead they are not endorsing the political aims of all the wars the country has ever fought, nor the manner in which they were fought.

Nor, of course, are they necessarily planning the next one. They are celebrating a national integrity which extends beyond the merely political – the association of values for which people have died.

The question remains – why Yasukuni? It would be more sensible to hold the ceremony elsewhere. In fact there already exists a secular ceremony, held every year on 15 August and attended by the Emperor as well as the cabinet. That, however, does not satisfy LDP right-wingers. The most important reason why they are so insistent on the Yasukuni visit is a development of the second. It is part of the general roll-back of what they consider to be misguided leftist attitudes towards Japan's proper position in the world.

The connection was spelled out by Masayuki Fujio, a prominent hawk who briefly held the post of education minister in the third Nakasone cabinet. The Yasukuni allergy, he claimed, was the result of the 'twisting and distorting' influence of the occupation education policies. As for the Tokyo War-Crimes Trial, 'Who gave the victors the right to judge the losers?' – the implication presumably being that Tojo and the other late arrivals at Yasukuni should have been allowed to carry on regardless. He also regretted that the number of public officials critical of the occupation had declined, a tendency that revealed a lack of political courage. The occupation had ended thirty-four years before Fujio spoke, but clearly, as far as he was concerned, its legacy was a living factor in contemporary politics.

Fujio's stint at the education ministry, a more sensitive posting in Japan than in most Western countries, made up in liveliness for what it lacked in length. Evidently hoping to capture the high ground for the forces of reaction, he delivered several blasts of provocative opinion which made Nakasone's nationalistic musings seem very feeble stuff. His first complaint, that not enough schools were flying the Rising-Sun flag, had some substance. All countries, capitalist, communist and non-aligned, have their symbols of nationhood, and the aversion of the teachers' union to the proper use of Japan's is abnormal. However, his demand that parents should fly the flag at home as well was equally abnormal. In democratic countries, government ministers do not advise citizens about the correct method of patriotic displays. The crowning achievement of his period in office was an interview given to a monthly magazine which contained a sort of handy compendium of his most uncompromisingly reactionary remarks. The Nanking 'incident', in which, depending on your choice of historian, 80,000–200,000 Chinese civilians were massacred, did not contravene international law. Most inflammatory of all, the Japanese annexation of Korea in 1910 was as much the fault of the Koreans as of anyone else. Coming just before Prime Minister Nakasone's official trip to Seoul, that little remark almost created a serious diplomatic rupture between the two countries. After only two months in office, Fujio was unceremoniously dismissed, only the third government minister to receive that treatment since the war.

The long-running controversy about school textbooks exemplifies the contradictions in Japan's relationship with history and with the outside world. It is strange enough that the Ministry of Education should feel it necessary to screen all textbooks, stranger still that, according to cabinet guidelines, the opinions of foreign governments should be taken into account. After all, France does not attempt to regulate the contents of Italian textbooks, nor vice versa. Furthermore, the country loudest in its criticisms, China, is hardly noted for rigorous devotion to objective scholarship. Yet such is the radical uncertainty about the war experience within Japan, and so removed is the Japanese perception of it from those prevalent elsewhere, that some process of adjustment is unavoidable.

The first censorship of textbooks in post-war Japan was conducted under the orders of Occupation GHQ: children were told to black out items of ultra-nationalist propaganda from their history books. Under the current system the ministry panels 'suggest' emendations to objectionable passages, often mandating the inclusion of sentences or phrases. Left-wing historian Saburo Ienaga waged a twenty-year court battle against its constitutionality. In 1986 the Supreme Court rejected his contention that the screening process infringed freedom of expression and, in the course of its decision, affirmed the ministry's objections to passages in his *New History of Japan*. The following quotations give a flavour of the way the argument went.

Ienaga original: 'The war was beautified as a "holy war", and since the Japanese Army's defeats and atrocities were covered up, the people were placed in a position where, not knowing the real facts, they had no choice but to co-operate in the meaningless war.'

First instance decision: 'That the war was beautified and that atrocities occurred are, unfortunately, facts. Nowadays, it is accepted as common sense that the "just war" was meaningless.'

Supreme Court decision: 'Some atrocities took place, but they were not limited to our army. In addition an extremely complex process led to this war. To categorize it sweepingly as "meaningless" creates problems.'

For decades the main point of the screening process was to air-brush out the opinions of leftist writers of the Ienaga species, a process that went fairly smoothly until foreigners started poking their noses into what was happening. In 1982 Japan's textbook methods suffered a diplomatic pummelling. In an astonishing feat, the Ministry of Education managed to line up the Taiwanese, the mainland Chinese and the North and South Koreans all on the same side. It was not trying to stir up controversy, still less to inflame latent ultra-nationalism. It wanted treatment of the war to be brief, dull and devoid of any analysis or interpretation. Instead of debating the whys and wherefores, students should be encouraged to view the whole unpleasant business as a morally neutral series of events with little connection to what happened before or afterwards. If this meant glossing over or omitting some of the harsher details, then so be it. Thus, the now classic instruction to replace the word 'invade' with 'advance' in accounts of Japan's conquest of China, the deletion of references to 'aggression', and the downplaying of the Korean resistance movement.

In 1986 an organization of nationalist intellectuals headed by a former ambassador to the United Nations produced a rightist textbook that had to be emended in 800 places, possibly a world record. The furore it created required the personal intervention of the prime minister, who was forced to order an additional review of its contents. The writers favoured 'Japanizing' the constitution and greater respect for the Emperor, his renunciation of divinity being one of the many historical events that they decided to omit. On the consequences of the war they were quite upbeat:

Through this war the control of Europe, which had long dominated Asia, quickly collapsed. Asian peoples through various means became independent and a new era in history began.

Thus, as *1066 and All That* might say, the war was ultimately A Good Thing. After the bureaucrats had finished with the passage, it read as follows:

Through this war the control of Europe, which had long dominated Asia, quickly collapsed. Asian peoples had also suffered through the serious actions of the occupying Japanese forces, but they achieved their independence while undergoing various transitions.

Japan is hardly unique in touching up her historical record, nor in glorifying rapacity and conquest. Yet there is a qualitative difference between offering partisan interpretations and obscuring or omitting events of tremendous importance and formative influence. In the first case, debate may flow and, as a result, some sense of historical proportion may be achieved. In the second case, there can only be blank incomprehension. It is impossible to understand the attitudes of Korean residents in Japan today without knowing the history of relations between the two countries. It is impossible to maintain a stable relationship with the Chinese, in diplomacy or business, without being at least aware of their interpretation of wartime events. Ultimately it is to the benefit of the Japanese themselves that they have a close understanding of their own recent past. Unfortunately, with the fostering of Japanese identity becoming accepted as a legitimate educational goal, 'fact friction' is likely to join trade friction as one of the regular manifestations of Japan's uneasy relationship with the outside world.

The historical experience itself is something which most Japanese do not care to dwell on. It still creates a polarization of opinion that could be extremely damaging to national unity. There is not even any agreement about what the war should be called. The Second World War, the designation standard elsewhere, is seldom used outside newspapers and reference books. Rightists tend to favour 'the Great East Asian War', a phrase which implies recognition of the ultra-nationalists' professed aims. More common is 'the Pacific War', which severs the US–Japan conflict from the years of military adventure which brought it about. The term which gives the clearest insight into what the experience has meant to the Japanese is 'the Lost War'. What exactly was lost in the Lost War, and how can what preceded it be reconciled with what came after? That is the great unspoken question in Japanese politics, laying bare a fault line in the national consensus that stretches from the surrender down to the present day. Yasukuni, the textbooks, the teaching of ethics, the status of the flag, the anti-spy law, and the other minor wrangles which, taken in isolation, seem hardly worth the energy expended – all are variations on this one great theme.

To generations born afterwards, the actual events are of only the remotest interest. Ninety-nine out of one hundred young Japanese have no idea who was Japan's prime minister at the time of the surrender, nor do they care – the subject never comes up in examinations. Perhaps the rapid post-war recovery could not have been effected without some such act of forgetting, just as Meiji industrialization required the erasure of Tokugawa feudalism from the national consciousness. Much went straight under the carpet, where it has since been dispersed by decades of regular treading. The Japanese could not understand the Kurt Waldheim affair at all. Within five years of the occupation's end, they had chosen a Class-A war criminal as prime minister. Members of the 731 Division who conducted germ-warfare experiments on prisoners of war and civilians are not skulking in South America or being hunted by a Chinese Simon Wiesenthal. Thanks to the generosity of the American intelligence service they are pillars of the pharmaceutical and academic establishment.

What is left in the racial memory is an image of extraordinary suffering, the causes of which are far less important than the scale. The atom bombings serve to confirm in the minds of many Japanese that their country has been war's supreme victim. Leftist commentators, who make most of the running in the media, ascribe the wartime disaster to the militarist clique who, according to the Marxist interpretation, led an unwilling nation into imperialist aggression. In the view of historians like Shinichi Arai of Ibaragi University, Hiroshima was bombed not in order to bring the war to a speedy end but as a signal to the Russians to watch their step. According to one best-selling theory, the work of another former UN official, the instrument-bearing parachutes dropped just before 'Little Boy' were intended to draw curious people out into the open and thus to increase the death toll. Rightists sympathize with the view of the war promulgated at the time – that it was motivated by a disinterested desire to clear the European colonizers out of Asia. Less extreme nationalists take the view that Japan was forced into war by the 'ABCD encirclement' (American, British, Chinese, Dutch) and the fuel embargo imposed by the Western powers. Her aggression against China was no more than an imitation of what the European powers had been up to half a century previously. The war was a terrible mistake, but not something that the Japanese need feel ashamed of for evermore.

Few people take any notice of what historians have to say, but most cannot help unconsciously absorbing the attitudes embodied in visual entertainment. Japanese war films do not regale their audience with acts of superhuman strength and valour, motorbike jumps to safety, assaults on snowy citadels, or any other of the confident images of victory. They are preoccupied with death, destruction and defeat. Indeed, 'defeat films' might be the more appropriate term. Although the works may be 'political' in that their directors have strong left- or right-wing opinions, they rarely display any understanding of either the domestic or international political context. The modern German cinema has repeatedly examined the processes that took the country to war, while paying relatively little attention to the actual experience of the conflict. Japanese cinema has followed the opposite course, accurately reflecting the interests and knowledge of its audience. The memory of the war, meaning the suffering, is overwhelmingly intense, whereas its background is vague and confusing.

The cinematic consensus has generally followed the political consensus, the sanctimoniously pacifist mainstream being occasionally disturbed by outbreaks of atavistic belligerence. Typical of the former genre is Kon Ichikawa's classic *Burmese Harp*, which tells of the post-surrender wanderings of a lugubrious, lyre-twanging Japanese soldier. Like his grimy-faced but noble comrades in arms he behaves as if he could hardly contemplate pushing his way on to a tube train, let alone sweeping through South-East Asia. Originally released in 1958, the film was remade in 1985 and scored a notable success, which suggests that the tastes of the 'new humans' are not so remote from those of their parents.

More controversial, and thus more profitable, were the rightist effusions of *The Great Japanese Empire*, one of the strongest box-office draws of 1982. Despite its title the film devotes little time to the actual formation of the empire in the thirties, or to the brilliantly executed series of attacks which, within a matter of months, destroyed half the American fleet and snatched all European possessions east of India. Instead, it dwells on, almost revels in, the empire's collapse. In pseudo-documentary style a narrator repeatedly emphasizes the imbalance in military strength and casualties, comparing the US retaking of Guam to 'one hundred cats attacking a small mouse'. The point is reinforced by a scene in which a swim-suited GI and his girlfriend are shown playing catchball with a Japanese skull. Cherry blossom swirling in the wind, death leaps, the doomed bravery of the kamikaze pilots, news clips of Tokyo burning, Hiroshima destroyed, then bogus war-crime trials and brutal beatings – the audience is regaled with an almost cosmic version of *ijime* (bullying) in which the Japanese are plucky and innocent victims of malign, vastly superior external forces. It is a vision shared by nearly all Japanese war movies, whatever the ideological orientation.

War films are crudifications of popular sentiment, and *The Great Japanese Empire* is a crudification of a crudification. None the less the world view it articulates does emerge in more intelligent form in books and magazines, in the remarks of politicians, and in the occasional alcohol-lubricated private conversation. According to the philosopher, those who cannot remember the past are condemned to relive it. The textbooks, the movies, the shrine visits – together could they presage a revival of the supremacist ideology which brought the world the East Asian Co-prosperity Sphere? Such an outcome is extremely unlikely. Although the Japanese may be confused about what happened forty years ago, and although they are growing less and less reticent about expressing their fierce sense of nationhood, they are unwilling to countenance anything that would damage their hard-earned prosperity. Japan has gained more than any other country from the current balance of power in the world, and is at pains to do nothing that might disturb it. Since markets in the West are near to saturation with Japanese exports, good relations with the countries that bore the brunt of Japan's wartime aggression – like South Korea and, especially, China – are vital to future growth. That is why the reactions of foreign governments to textbook content and memorial ceremonies are monitored so closely. That is why a government minister can be fired for giving a private opinion about the circumstances surrounding an event which took place in 1910. The Japanese have seen enough foreign-made war films to know what the rest of the world is thinking.

Undoubtedly many Japanese of the pre-war generation feel a powerful need to read some higher meaning into the national experience. Leftist intellectuals have adopted a fervent pacifism according to which morally pure Japan should remain aloof from the world of necessity and compromise. The nationalists hanker after a justification of the absolutist values of their youth. Both are bitterly opposed to American influence – the left politically, the right culturally. Both celebrate a vision of Japan as a nation apart. Neither understands the exuberant mess of lifestyles and values that their country has become. The exchange of opinion between the two is so immoderate and shrill-toned that a casual observer might be forgiven for supposing that the Japanese are wavering between communism and neo-nationalist revival. In fact the raised voices and exaggerated poses are vain attempts to attract attention to a debate entirely lacking in substantiality. The vast majority of people, quite content with Japan's political and cultural orientation, are simply not interested. As the years pass and memories fade, the views of the ideologues are growing more remote from the concerns of ordinary people, which makes the whole debate even shriller, but increasingly irrelevant.

The Defence Mechanism

There is one important issue in Japanese politics that is framed in the confrontational terms which Westerners would recognize from their own systems as 'political'. The question of national security cannot be handled by the consensual, problem-solving mechanism applied to all other policy choices. The division of opinion it provokes is too profound and bitter: about ends, not means. It relates directly to sensitive matters of pride and dependence, kindles the images of disaster, and provokes hard thoughts about Japan's place in the world. Here too, outside pressure and internal dynamics are combining to wreak a profound transformation, but history still governs the terms of the discussion.

Japan is not New Zealand. Wandering through the bleeping cornucopia of an Akihabara electronics store, or sipping one's Suntory Royal in the cosseted comfort of a Ginza nightclub, it is difficult to register the isolation and vulnerability of Japan's strategic position. She is adjacent to two heavily armed and mutually hostile superpowers, both of which espouse an ideology radically opposed to her own systems.

Nagasaki, the fourth-largest city on Kyushu island, is nearer to Shanghai than to Tokyo; Sapporo, the largest city on Hokkaido, is nearer to Vladivostok than to Tokyo. The other superpower, on which Japan depends for her security and 30 per cent of her trade, is an ocean away. A dozen of her Asian neighbours suffered from her depredations in the recent past and view her present intentions with deep suspicion. The nearest is an ex-colony, now divided into two military regimes that glare at each other across a cease-fire line drawn thirty years ago. Japan herself has a major territorial dispute to the north, and minor ones to the south and west. It is a complex, disturbingly dynamic situation, requiring the utmost flexibility of response. Unfortunately the whole subject is a tangle of contradictions, taboos and semantic confusion.

The imbalance between Japan's industrial and military might is one of the most extraordinary features in modern geopolitics. Despite her uncomfortable place in the world, her total reliance on imported energy and the rapid growth in her overseas interests, the free world's second-largest economy spends half as much on her defence as does Britain. In money value the Japanese defence budget is amongst the six largest in the world, but that position is largely due to the sky-rocketing of the currency in which it is denominated. Relative to GNP or the national budget, Japanese defence expenditure is still by far the lowest of the rich countries. In per capita terms, the Japanese are still spending only half as much as the Dutch. Of the total, only one-quarter, extremely low in comparison with NATO countries, is spent on weaponry, the rest being absorbed in salaries, supplies and overheads. In manpower the Japanese army is by far the smallest in the region, its 160,000 troops comparing with 330,000 in Taiwan, 540,000 in South Korea, 700,000 in North Korea, and 370,000 in the forty well-equipped divisions of the Soviet Far Eastern Army. In terms of soldiers per head of population, the Japanese are only one-third as militaristic as the British and one-quarter as the Swedes. Quality has yet to be tested, but sustainability (ability to resist in terms of ammunition and supplies) is believed to be under two weeks. Not a single serving member of any of the three forces has seen action. Participation in UN peace-keeping forces, even in disaster relief efforts, has long been a political taboo.

Altogether Japan's forces are far from negligible. Her army boasts 1000 tanks; her air force 50 F-15s, one of the most advanced fighters in the world. Her navy has 50 destroyers and frigates, and an anti-submarine capability second only to that of the United States. She has deployed large numbers of conventional missiles, such as the Hawk and the Patriot, and developed some sophisticated types of her own. Furthermore, in the age of C3I warfare (command, control, communications, and information), her prowess in electronics is a source of great potential strength. One-third of the cost of a modern jet fighter is in the electronics, one-tenth of the cost of a destroyer. In such specialist areas as phased array radar, the Japanese are believed to be several years in the lead already. Although Japan's defence budget is still hardly adequate to her needs, the growth in spending has been consistently strong, far ahead of the increases achieved by Western European countries. Between 1975 and 1985, a period in which the LDP held an absolute majority for only two years and pacifist sentiment was dominant, spending on defence rose by 240 per cent. With the LDP now firmly in the saddle and perceptions gradually shifting, further improvements in relative strength should be easily accomplished. The problem is not so much with the armed forces themselves, but with the confusion about what defence means, which is part of the larger confusion about Japan's role in the world.

Any moves to boost Japan's security have to be taken quietly and carefully. The press is sternly anti-militarist, and the main opposition party is committed to 'unarmed neutrality', meaning the disbandment of the army, navy and air force. According to opinion surveys taken by the Defence Agency, only 14 per cent of the public supports increases in defence spending, slightly less than the proportion that supports decreases; only 20 per cent has a favourable impression of the self-defence forces; only 5 per cent would join up in the event of an invasion. The pacifist impulse has declined from the days when most Japanese favoured abolition of the

U S–Japan Security Treaty and soldiers had trouble in finding partners for *omiai* (arranged marriage). None the less it is still orthodoxy amongst the intelligentsia and has powerful sentimental attractions even to people worried about the regional balance of power. Most Britons identify military spending with the capacity to defend national interests against an aggressor, the great lesson being the unpreparedness of the thirties. The Japanese have the same example etched into their national consciousness from exactly the opposite perspective.

The starting-point for the domestic debate is the American-drafted constitution adopted by Japan in 1948. Article Nine states flatly that 'land, sea and air forces, as well as other war potential, will never be maintained' since 'the Japanese people for ever renounce war as a sovereign right of the nation, and the threat or use of force as a means of settling international disputes'. Academic lawyers and left-wingers have taken this to mean what it says, a notion which runs against all the traditions of Japanese politics. Ironically it is now the U S which is most impatient with the pacifist tendencies that Article Nine has nurtured, and the anti-American left which is most vociferous in upholding its sanctity. Rightists, the sort of people that the drafters of the constitution were out to dish, agree that stronger military forces are required and demand that the document be amended accordingly. The official line, backed by popular sentiment and a number of court decisions, is that the constitution does not alienate the right of self-defence, only the ability to wage wars of aggression.

The distinction between aggression and defence is replete with the sort of vagueness with which the Japanese feel most comfortable. Technological developments and the concept of deterrence have reduced its value even further. Although long-range bombers, inter-continental missiles and aircraft carriers are still frowned upon, most other types of conventional weapon can be stockpiled in whatever quantities are required to meet the perceived threat. When the Air Self-Defence Force introduced F-4 Phantoms in the early seventies the nozzles for in-flight refuelling were removed, thereby restricting them to a 'defensive' range. The F-15s now in use have not been doctored, and the Defence Agency is considering deploying tanker aircraft. In 1978 Prime Minister Fukuda went so far as to claim that 'Japan can possess any type of weapon if it falls within the necessary minimum for self-defence purposes, even if this means nuclear or bacteriological weapons'.

It is not only the definition of defensive weaponry that has proved usefully elastic. What exactly is being defended? Firstly, the Japanese islands and the 200-mile territorial limit around them. But to protect the islands properly it is necessary to scan the waters outside the limits as well. Furthermore, if war did break out, Japan would need to secure her supply routes to the south. In 1981 Zenko Suzuki prompted a storm of protest when he agreed to American suggestions that Japan should take responsibility for 'sea lanes of communication' (S L O Cs) stretching 1000 miles. Measured from the tip of Kyushu, that would reach almost to Luzon in the Philippines. Yasuhiro Nakasone took an even more expansive view of Japan's role, affirming that she should have the capability to blockade the straits around the home islands, thus bottling up the Soviet Pacific Fleet in Vladivostok. Every year, Japan has played an increasingly prominent part in the R I M P A C (Rim of the Pacific) multinational naval exercises held off Hawaii. Despite a 1969 cabinet decision forswearing the militarization of space, she has decided to join the Star Wars project on a private-sector basis.

Japan has come a long way from 'trusting in the justice and faith of the peace-loving peoples of the world', as her constitution proposes. The first step came at the start of the Korean War when, in response to U S requests, the police reserve was converted into the Self-Defence Forces. That allowed American forces stationed in Japan to concentrate on the war across the water. Since then Japan's security, like her economic health, has become increasingly dependent on the policies of the United States. The core of her defence is the security treaty between the two countries, once the subject of huge 'Yankee go home' disturbances, now supported by an overwhelming majority of the public.

The treaty, as revised in 1960, empowers the United States to maintain several important bases in Japan, in return for which she promises to come to Japan's aid in the event of an attack. Until the late seventies the arrangement suited both sides pretty well. From the American point of view it fixed Japan in the Western camp, and provided an important capability physically close to the Soviet Union. From the Japanese point of view defence costs were saved, and the high-minded pacifism dear to the national consensus remained unquestioned. Japan worked hard making cars and VTRs. American consumers gobbled them up. Japan poured the proceeds into the US money markets, thus financing the budget deficit. America was able to build more missiles and submarines the better to defend her ally. Japan carried on churning out cars and VTRs, in peace and safety. It was a beautiful relationship, only spoiled by the inevitable shift in the balance of economic strength.

The extent of Japanese reliance on the US, much greater than that of any European country, can be gauged from the wording of the National Defence Programme Outline, the document which defines basic strategy. Japan's aim is the re-pulsion of 'limited and small-scale aggression, in principle, without outside assistance'. If that doesn't work, she will 'continue unyielding resistance by mobilizing all available forces until such time as co-operation from the United States is introduced, thus rebuffing such aggression'. The most likely kind of attack on Japan is very far from 'limited and small-scale', but to acknowledge that would be to reveal what lies behind the *tatemae* of pacifism – the US nuclear umbrella. Since the constitution bars collective defence, Japan is theoreti-cally incapable of becoming a regional power, either in partnership with the US or as part of a larger alliance. None the less, as Pentagon planners are well aware, if Japan would take full responsibility for her own defence as broadly con-strued – SLOCs included – the US Sixth Fleet could operate with infinitely greater flexibility in, for example, the Persian Gulf.

Many Japanese, not just those on the left, are extremely

wary of being drawn into the American geopolitical strategy. They fear that in an outbreak of hostilities between the two superpowers Japan's geographical position would put her first in the line of fire. Suspicion about the true motives of her former conqueror, now her one and only ally, are never very far from the surface. Gradually, however, the priorities of the two countries are drawing closer together. 'Interoperability', joint manoeuvres and data exchange make sound economic as well as strategic sense. Japan is to install an OTH (Over The Horizon) radar system with a range of 3200 kilometres, far enough to scan the heart of Siberia. She has also procured an AEGIS cruiser and is considering the deployment of AWACs. Official guidelines about what can and cannot be done in time of war are being modified. It is now accepted, for example, that Japanese ships could come to the aid of US ships on the high seas in the event of a threat to Japan. Closing the straits around the Japanese islands would be the most valuable contribution, since the current generation of Soviet submarine-based missiles would not be able to hit the United States from within the Japan Sea. They would, of course, be able to hit Japan without any trouble at all.

Japan's attitude to military matters is akin to that of an ex-alcoholic towards a drinks cabinet. While finding ways around the absolute prohibition imposed by the constitution, successive Japanese administrations have devised their own arbitrary restraints, nearly all of which have also been breached in the end. The most serious has been the restriction of defence spending to below 1 per cent of GNP, a cabinet-level decision reached by the Miki administration in 1973 and treated for a decade like holy writ. Any proposal to break through that limit was regarded by the press and the opposition and, indeed, some sections of the LDP, as if it were tantamount to a call for rearmament. In the late fifties when Japan's economy was one-fifteenth of its present size, defence spending often exceeded 1 per cent. In the mid eighties, as the ratio teetered at the brink, the difference between hawks and doves was 0.001 per cent of GNP.

There is, of course, no necessary connection between the

growth in a nation's output and its security requirements. When the limit was promulgated, Japanese GNP was growing at 14 per cent, and the Nixon–Kissinger détente policies were encouraging a relaxed view of the superpower confrontation. Seven years later Japan was struggling with recession, the Russians were in Afghanistan, and the US was agonizing over the Iranian débâcle, but 1 per cent was still 1 per cent. On a NATO-basis calculation, which factors in pension payments and coastguard expenses, the limitation had been exceeded soon after its establishment. Still, the consensus held that some sort of commonly understood, fixed ceiling was essential. Many Japanese in positions of authority remembered how, in the pre-war period, defence spending had risen to an awesome 17 per cent of GNP, a weighting of national resources that had created its own irresistible momentum. Implicitly, they could not trust themselves with the power that they were wielding, nor did they trust the Japanese public to check its abuse.

That consensus, like many others, was shattered by Yasuhiro Nakasone, who regarded the 1 per cent formula as not just an impediment to stronger defences but also a symbol of Japan's spiritual defeat. His first attempt to junk the limit received the thumbs down from factional rivals who resented his cocksure attitude. His second attempt, which coincided with tremendous pressure from the US on trade issues, proved unstoppable. Finally, the Japanese could arrange their defence policy in reference to the present, not the past.

Or not quite. Other, more ambiguous restrictions remain in force. The 'three non-nuclear principles' are one of those triads, like the 'three famous gardens' and the 'three beautiful sights', which appeal strongly to the Japanese imagination. Foreigners have appreciated this one too, as was demonstrated by the award of the Nobel Peace Prize to its originator, Eisaku Sato. The first two principles, not to manufacture or use nuclear weapons, are straightforward enough. The third, not to 'introduce' them, is more problematic. With over one hundred SS-20s well within range of her major cities, Japan is utterly reliant on the deterrent effect of US nuclear might.

US policy has always been neither to confirm nor deny the deployment of nuclear missiles on ships and aircraft, which permits the solemn fiction that warships visiting bases in Japan are mysteriously relieved of their Cruises and Tomahawks somewhere in mid-ocean. Ex-ambassador Reischauer's well-publicized revelation that this is not the case created the embarrassment that usually results when *tatemae* is rudely breached, and New Zealand's refusal to permit visits without a clear denial showed the left what might be achieved. Now, every time the *New Jersey* sails into Sasebo, she is greeted by a flotilla of dinghy-borne radical groups, all of whom can fairly claim to be enforcing government policy.

The prohibition of the export of weapons was another brainwave of the doveish Miki. Previously, Japanese policy had followed Sato's second set of 'three principles' – those forbidding the sale of arms to communist countries, UN-embargoed countries, and countries currently or likely to be at war. The Miki administration extended that ban to all countries, which may have been good for the national conscience, but has seriously inhibited the development of defence capability. Without the economies of scale that come from supplying export markets, the Japanese defence industry remains a high-cost producer, giving poor value for the money invested. The F-15s that Japanese companies make under licence cost double the McDonnell Douglas price, and most other types of 'front-end equipment' are similarly uncompetitive. In order to cultivate the domestic industry the Defence Agency has consistently favoured licensed production over imports, which means that the budget has much less buying power than appears to foreign eyes. As with the household budgets of ordinary citizens, the money value soars with the yen, but so do the costs.

In the seventies the ban was taken very seriously. The press waxed gleefully wrathful when some steel pipes made by a small machinery firm turned up in the guise of South Korean mortar tubes. Any proposal to lift the ban was immediately shouted down. At the same time, however, ways around it were being found with the usual ingenuity. In the definition game, what exactly are 'arms'? 'Dual-purpose' equipment – having both military and civilian applications – was not subject to restriction. Computers, integrated circuits, trucks, even helicopters, anything that did not have direct lethal potential, could be freely exported. It is believed that over 70 per cent of the ceramic packages that wrap the IC chips in US weapon systems are produced by a single Japanese company. In 1983 the US and Japan signed an agreement for the transfer of military technology (not products) from Japan to the US, thus bringing the one-way flow to an end. The Americans were interested in Japanese achievements in opto-electronics, fast-switching gallium-arsenide ICs, voice recognition and control, artificial intelligence, and other leading-edge technologies, all developed for ordinary commercial applications but vital to the next generation of defence systems.

Japan's defence industry is roughly the same size as her bakery industry, and the Japanese are not great consumers of bread. One important section of economic thought holds that she has gained tremendously from this weighting of resources. None of her great companies depends for more than a quarter of its business on cosy 'cost-plus-margin' military contracts. Technological breakthroughs do not end up squatting in desert silos never to be used. They are immediately channelled into consumer goods or productivity-enhancing industrial equipment and tested in the market-place. Yet, as Japanese business leaders and politicians are only too aware, developments in satellite and other technologies are fast invalidating the distinction between military and civilian applications, and also those between aerospace, communications and computing. The decision to participate in the Star Wars scheme was prompted not by recognition of its strategic merits – from the Japanese point of view, there aren't any – but fear of being left behind by the next wave of technologies.

At the outbreak of the Second World War Japan was producing the world's finest fighter planes. Today aerospace is one of the few industries where she badly lags behind Europe and America, a condition that will not be remedied without some further affronts to pacifist sensibilities. Since

most of the companies involved are large employers that are
suffering badly from the shipbuilding recession, the pressure
on government is intense. It is highly likely that by the end of
the century Japan's defence industry will have been allowed
to go international.

The authorities have got away with stretching, sneaking
around, and reinterpreting the rules to death because public
attitudes have gradually changed. Pacifism, like the anti-
Americanism that came with it, was all very well when
American power ruled the waves and skies. The Japanese are
more conscious than most of America's economic decline,
since they have made a sizeable contribution towards it. They
fully understand the long-term strategic implications. Jimmy
Carter's plan to pull out of South Korea rattled nerves badly.
Since then the Reagan administration's military build-up has
bolstered credibility, but the plunging dollar and massive
internal and external deficits do not inspire confidence in
America's ability, or will, to continue shouldering the defence
responsibility for her largest industrial competitor. Would the
Americans really risk their own cities for the sake of Japan?
Doubts were strengthened by an interview given to a Japanese
newspaper by Admiral Stansfield Turner, ex-chief of the
CIA. He explained that the nuclear guarantee, the basis of
Japan's whole defence policy, is not part of the US–Japan
treaty or any other understanding between the two countries
and, in his view, did not exist.

American resentment at Japan's 'free ride' on defence will
escalate as the shift in economic power becomes more pro-
nounced. At the same time the Japanese will become increasingly concerned about American trustworthiness, increasingly
confident in their ability, and right, to manage their own
destiny. The only realistic options are French-style independence, perhaps with a domestically developed *force de frappe*,
and greater assertiveness within the current framework. The
former would put tremendous pressure on the domestic consensus and send regular shivers down the spines of Asian
neighbours. The latter would offer less security in psychological terms, since it entails continued faith in American

intentions, but it would closely reflect the pattern of Japan's economic interests. Ultimately it could lead to a formal or, more likely, informal alliance with the NATO countries, offering Japan an important stabilizing role in a multi-polar world.

Public opinion is some way from approving Japan's transition into a military power. Many commentators, especially those featured in the national press, still support 'omni-directional' diplomacy – smiling nicely to everybody from under the shade of the nuclear umbrella. Some who have made their accommodation with reality favour a 'comprehensive security policy'. This involves holding down military expenditures while boosting overseas development aid for agreed strategic purposes, thus pleasing the Americans and preserving consensus and moral purity at the same time. An unkinder description would be trading cash for the potential risk to youthful lives. Still, it might be a useful *tatemae* procedure to cover this complicated intermediate stage in Japan's recovery from the trauma of defeat. She is now too rich and too important for the ostrich position to work. Again, it was Nakasone who put the matter most succinctly: 'since Japan has become a big house, the insurance premium is also large'.

Traditionally, the Japanese have felt the greatest threat to come from the Soviet Union, the country which, according to opinion polls, they fear and loathe above all others. The history of relations between them has been short, but packed with incident. Russia was the first of the Western powers to make serious efforts to force an opening of Japan in the nineteenth century, eventually being pre-empted by the Americans and British. As her imperial ambitions spread eastwards she participated with increasing vigour in the round of the great game being played in Manchuria, China and Korea. Japan won her first cap with a resounding victory over the Czar's forces in 1905, less than half a century after her emergence from feudalism and isolation. During the Russian revolution, Japanese expeditionary forces roamed through Siberia, ostensibly to aid the whites, actually to force territorial concessions. They stayed on until 1922, and in Sakhalin until 1925, long after the Western powers had withdrawn.

Fourteen years later the hubris of the Japanese military was dented for the first time, albeit temporarily, when its attack on the Red Army in Mongolia was repulsed with heavy losses. That incident strengthened the hand of the 'strike south' faction in military command, leading to a peace treaty with the Soviet Union and war with the Americans. The treaty was broken three days after the destruction of Hiroshima. In accordance with the Potsdam agreement, Soviet forces stormed into Japan's Manchurian puppet state, overwhelming the demoralized and exhausted defence. Although the two countries were at war for less than a week, the Japanese suffered several hundred thousand casualties, mainly prisoners of war who never returned from Siberia.

Technically they are still at war. The Soviet Union did not participate in the San Francisco Conference, and no peace treaty with Japan has ever been signed. The main outstanding issue is the fate of the Northern Territories, a string of fog-bound islands to the north of Hokkaido seized by the Russians shortly after the surrender. At Potsdam, Roosevelt had granted Stalin the whole of the Kurile chain without knowing how or when Japan had obtained it, or even, according to some sources, where it was. In fact the four southernmost islands, the ones under dispute, had never been Russian property. The Japanese had held them for the previous ninety years, before which the original owners, the Ainu, had been free to pursue their uncomplicated bear-worshipping ways. It was on the largest, Eterofu, which means 'snot-place' in the Ainu language, that the Japanese fleet assembled for the assault on Pearl Harbor. That island is now home to a Soviet military base stacked with MIG-23s, attack helicopters and long-range cannon. It guards the vital strait connecting Vladivostok to the Pacific. In the event of another conflict it would probably be the staging-point for an assault on Hokkaido, which is just three miles away from Habomai, the closest of the four islands.

The Soviets show no inclination to do the decent thing and

hand back the islands, refusing, in typically granite-faced style, even to acknowledge the existence of a territorial dispute. The Japanese government, preoccupied with national honour, and with one eye on the fishing grounds that are home to some of the tastiest morsels on the *sushi*-shop menu, takes a different view of matters. In all textbooks the islands are marked as Japanese territory. The main political parties, including the communists, are united in demanding their return, and the authorities have striven to keep the issue alive with poster campaigns, television advertisements and a Northern Territories Day. The results have been mixed. Although most ordinary Japanese feel that the islands should be returned, the sense of outrage, indeed interest of any sort, is at a low ebb.

The Tanaka–Brezhnev meeting of 1974 was the high point of détente from the Japanese angle. The Soviet side even admitted that outstanding issues had still to be settled, an implicit reference to the Northern Territories dispute. Since then relations between the two countries have deteriorated sharply. In Japanese minds, the invasion of Afghanistan revived the image of a huge predatory force to the north, always ready to expand its interests through cunning and brute force. The concept of 'separating economics from politics' – or doing business with the devil – was abandoned. Following the American lead, Japan cut trade links, giving up some large industrial projects in Siberia. She was the only major ally of the United States to enforce an official boycott of the Moscow Olympics. Three years later a Soviet fighter shot down a Korean jumbo jet over Sakhalin, an act that provoked world-wide outrage. Of the 269 people who died, twenty-eight were Japanese. Communications between the Soviet pilot and ground control were monitored, recorded and translated by Japanese military personnel. Wreckage, including human remains, was washed up on the shore of Hokkaido. Suddenly, East–West tension was no longer an abstract political issue. It was specific and emotional; quite beyond the scope of the usual jargon of peace diplomacy and mutual understanding.

Over the same period, Soviet military activity in the area around Japan showed a powerful increase. Between 1970 and 1980 the divisional strength of the Soviet Far Eastern Army doubled; large numbers of nuclear-armed SS-20s and Backfire bombers were deployed, both weapons capable of targeting Japan. Most remarkable of all was the boost in naval power. The Soviet Union's Pacific Fleet more or less doubled in size to 1.8 million tons, which compares with the combined 0.9 million tons of the US Seventh Fleet and the Japanese Maritime Self-Defence Force. By far the largest fleet in the world, it possesses two aircraft carriers (one of which is kept on station by a dry-dock built in Japan), over thirty nuclear submarines, and appropriate numbers of amphibious assault ships and landing-craft. Soviet warships pass through the straits around the Japanese islands, the ones that Yasuhiro Nakasone wants to block, an average of 500 times a year. They pass through the Tsugaru straits, the narrow strip of water that separates Honshu from Hokkaido, about once a week. Japanese fighter pilots scramble to meet threatened incursions into Japanese airspace by Soviet planes twice a day. In 1987, one of these cat-and-mouse games almost turned into a serious international incident when Japanese pilots fired on a Soviet bomber that ignored all attempts to communicate. The Soviets were quicker than most to spot Japan's potential, and made their investments accordingly.

The Soviet posture towards Japan has ranged from smiling blandishments to the crudest of threats. When Yasuhiro Nakasone talked of turning his country into 'an unsinkable aircraft carrier', Tass warned of a national disaster worse than Hiroshima, and the Soviet trade minister stated that Japan would stay afloat for less than twenty minutes. Yet, Soviet embassy personnel are known as the best Japanese linguists amongst the Tokyo diplomatic corps, skilled enough when smooth words are required. In that both countries have something to trade – the Northern Territories and raw materials on one side, American bases and high technology on the other – the possibility of a rapprochement can never be entirely dismissed. Imaginative pragmatism in the Kremlin; trade barriers raised by Congress; recession in Japan, reviving old attitudes towards the perfidious Yankee; a prime minister anxious to win a place in history by reclaiming a piece of the fatherland. It would take exceptionally bad policy by the United States and exceptionally good policy by the Soviet Union, a combination unlikely, but by no means impossible.

In the détente years Japan was the Soviet Union's top supplier of construction machinery and seamless steel pipe, and initiated ambitious projects for the exploitation of gas, coal and timber resources. If Mr Gorbachev is serious about doubling GNP by the year 2000, he will need Japanese machine tools, chemical plants and IC technology as well. Japan has always been astute in using foreign policy to maximize economic advantage, which is why she is the second-largest trading partner of both South Africa and Vietnam. Another relaxation of the superpower confrontation would enable her to get back to business. Fundamentally, however, relations between the two countries are likely to remain hostile, since their political systems and goals are so strongly opposed. As Japanese interests become more closely involved in the development of China, additional strains are certain to appear.

The opening of China is important to Japan both economically and strategically. In the long term it offers the Japanese an opportunity to adjust the mutually over-dependent 'odd couple' relationship with the United States and, of course, to make a great deal of money. China and Japan have known about each other for 2000 years. Despite the bloody events of the past 100 years, a great deal of respect remains on both sides. The Chinese, attempting to separate Western technology from the political and philosophical context that created it, are naturally drawn to the Japanese example. Japan will always be the favoured choice as economic partner since she brings with her no military threat or disruptive cultural influences. From the Japanese point of view China is both the home of civilization, rather as Italy and Greece are to the rest of Europe, and a new billion-unit market. The match is good. On one side, severe capital shortage, unexploited raw materials, and an immense fund of cheap labour. On the other, capital outflows the like of which have never been seen before, the highest-quality production technology, and a powerful appetite for foodstuffs, fuels, and minerals. China has, for example, some 80 per cent of the world's estimated reserves of 'rare earths', the mysterious elements vital to the strategic technology of superconduction.

Patience will be required. China is still one of the poorest countries in the region, and her internal convulsions and stop-go economic policies are disastrous to business confidence. At the best of times negotiations are tortuous and trading margins wafer thin. However, the men steering the relationship are thinking in terms of generations, not quarterly profits. The great trading houses have been in China for decades, gradually accumulating contacts and business opportunities regardless of the political climate. C. Itoh, for example, employs over one hundred Japanese speakers of Mandarin. Major Japanese banks have established themselves in Peking and have started to channel money into the special economic zones. When China decided to float her first foreign bonds in forty years, Tokyo was the natural market-place.

The results are already starting to come through. Japan is China's most important trading partner by far, accounting for one-third of all imports and providing the second-largest export market after Hong Kong. From the other side, China is now Japan's second-largest trading partner, well ahead of Saudi Arabia. In the boom year of 1985 Japan's import and export business with China totalled $19 billion, more than her trade with Britain and West Germany combined. The Chinese bought 30 per cent of Japan's production of television sets, 20 per cent of her steel exports, and more automobiles than any country other than the United States. It was a remarkable, if ill-advised, shopping spree, drastically depleting foreign currency reserves and endangering the whole modernization programme. It also gave Japanese businessmen a tantalizing taste of the opportunities which a properly developed Chinese economy could offer.

The main danger is that forcing the pace could create the conditions for more radical backlash. In the cycle of Chinese politics, as incomprehensible to the Japanese as Japanese politics is to Westerners, liberalization is followed by repression and the imposition of centralized control as surely as night follows day. Yet there is evidence that the relationship is being stabilized within commonly understood parameters. It was significant that immediately after Nakasone sacked Education Minister Fujio, he rushed to Peking to smooth ruffled sensibilities. Six months later, when Hu Yaobang fell from grace, Chinese statesmen rushed to Tokyo to reassure the Japanese that all was still hunky-dory. No doubt the Chinese path to development will contain many more swings and switchbacks all deeply unsettling to relations with Japan and other trading partners. It will take stern attention to mutual profit, rather than mutual understanding, for the great potential to be fulfilled.

What does security mean for Japan in the age of *perestroika* and mammoth US deficits? The superpowers appear to be moving from confrontation to an uneasy three-cornered accommodation, brought about not by a solution to the basic conflicts, but by the greater urgency of internal problems. Over the past ten years there has been a dramatic decline in the relative strength of all three of the superpowers – politically, economically, and culturally. In the case of the two communist states, their now revealed backwardness disqualifies them from superpower status in all except the purely military sense. Their attraction as ideological role models has evaporated. The relative decline of the United States is less comprehensive, but potentially more significant in its long-term implications. American society is the latest and currently the most powerful expression of values which have evolved over centuries of political and philosophical debate. If this tradition is seen to be economically unsuccessful, then the Darwinism of ideas will replace it with something else.

The decline of the superpowers has been accompanied by a decline in the strategic value of brute military force. The lesson the US learned in Vietnam has been relearned by the Soviets in Afghanistan. The Chinese had their own débâcle in Vietnam, and the US has since been successfully defied by ramshackle regimes in the Middle East and Central America. With direct intervention becoming a less attractive option, the use of surrogates has spread. In South America, South East Asia, the Middle East, and Africa, wars have been going on for nearly twenty years, and will probably continue for the rest of the century. The use of terrorism by political groups and states, one phenomenon that is certain to increase over the coming years, means that obscure regional conflicts can now be fought in the world's major capitals. Military power, religion, finance, and the competition for raw materials are becoming increasingly intertwined in a geopolitics that is less susceptible than before to ideological analysis, but just as combustible. In this complex world of shifting alliances and rapidly transmitted tensions, security will lie in the skilled exercise of every type of influence, including force and the threat of it. It will also require comprehensive information-gathering and the ability to manipulate friends and others.

The 1980s have been a deflationary decade, of collapsing commodity markets and excessive supply of almost everything. The set of circumstances which plunged the Third World into chronic indebtedness made Japan into the world's largest creditor. That process has itself created tremendous strains and, of course, extended Japan's interests all over the world. The 1990s will probably see a swing of the pendulum away from the commodity user and back towards the producer. This may well coincide with the increasing reluctance of the United States to defend the interests of richer allies. It is unlikely that the next decade will be any more peaceful than the current one, which will mean some tough choices for the Japanese. It is not hard to envisage a crisis which the Japanese would have to manage directly. That would create an unprecedented challenge to Japan's diplomatic and political maturity, and require a swift goodbye to the complexes of the past.

Since the end of the Second World War, superpower confrontation has been the major factor in world security. Its manifestations have been many and various, but the underlying conflict has been simple and therefore susceptible to control. Tensions have escalated and relaxed and then escalated again, but a rough balance of power – or balance of terror – has been effectively maintained. Now that the influence of that balance is in decline and the threat of an apocalyptic MAD (Mutually Assured Destruction) recedes, the potential for a sudden eruption or a rippling-out of regional conflicts is growing. In military technology the apple cannot be put back on the tree. New types of delivery system now enable nuclear weapons to be used as devastating versions of ordinary battle-field missiles. Several countries in areas of semi-permanent turmoil already possess nuclear capability, and the number is sure to rise over the coming years.

Perestroika itself could result in heightened risk. Failure would mean the overthrow of the current leadership and a return to hard-line Stalinist policies. Success would create a richer, more powerful Soviet Union, not as ideology-driven as before, but probably just as hostile to Western interests as was Imperial Russia. A less clear-cut outcome would be economic progress at the expense of political control, leading to the gradual destabilization of Eastern Europe, perhaps even of regions of the Soviet Union. In those circumstances, the leadership might be tempted to assert its mastery over everything new and complicated through some bold strategic gamble. As in pre-war Japan, another outstanding example of economic weakness coexisting with massive military power, social dislocation could create the conditions for expansionism. Whatever happens, the situation will remain unpredictable and highly volatile, and the most desirable outcome – a genuine reconciliation of values and objectives – will remain the least likely.

Japan is an island of stability and wealth in a world of violence and poverty. Her interests have now grown to such a scale and complexity that the characteristic head-below-the-parapet attitude will no longer suffice. The old traumas are slipping further into the past. The confidence that comes with industrial success is combining with the demands of allies to effect a gradual, but hugely significant change. How Japan manages her relations with the two struggling communist giants, how she adjusts her dependency on the United States, how she copes with the challenge of power second time round – these are questions on which depend not just her own, but also world security.

Epilogue

The relationship between tradition and change in Japan has always been complicated by the fact that that change itself is a tradition

Edward Seidensticker

octopuses in jars
transient dreams
under the summer moon

Basho

The most deeply venerated institution in Japanese religious culture is the great shrine at Ise, repository of the imperial regalia of sword, mirror and jewel. Set in a glade of noble cedars, many of them several hundred years old, it represents the prehistoric style of Japanese architecture, untouched by any Chinese or Buddhist influences – tall sloping roofs, straight eaves, unpainted cypress wood. In keeping with the primitive austerity of the buildings, the sacred rituals that take place within use fire made by rubbing stick on stick. Since time immemorial it has been the custom to raze the whole shrine every twenty years and erect an identical replacement. The structure has remained exactly the same for nearly two millennia, but the materials are always clean and new. The building was last put together in 1974.

Contemporary Japan is perpetually being knocked down and put together. Houses are constructed over weekends, six-storey office blocks in a couple of weeks. Small companies go under, new ones thrive in their stead. Messages are replaced. The 256k RAM yields to the 1 Megabit, which in turn gives way to the 4 Megabit. Catchphrases, scandals, ideologies – all blow away with the pinky-white blossom. Japan is the most truly modern of countries because she has learned to live with the disorientation of the modern world, indeed to respond to it profitably, without losing her sense of structure. It is a talent which allows the Japanese to look ahead to the next set of transformations with an enviable confidence.

In the West, awareness of Japan remains at a lamentably low level. Surveys published in the Japanese press indicate that numbers of Europeans and Americans believe her to be a communist country located somewhere on the Asian mainland. Perceptions will sharpen with the growth of direct Japanese involvement in the Western economies. Over the coming decades more and more people will find themselves striving to please Japanese clients, turning out products to Japanese specifications, taking orders from Japanese bosses. It should prove an educative experience for all concerned. Local companies and properties, indeed whole tracts of the economic landscape, will pass into Japanese ownership. Japanese factories and offices will become prominent, highly valued features of the business scene. Company directors and government ministers will have to explain their plans to Japanese financiers. Japanese tourists will become the new innocents abroad, the highest-spending, longest-suffering, most conspicuous of all foreign consumers. The delicate nuances of the Japanese defence debate will be recognized as having decisive influence in the global balance of power. The Japanese language will become an increasingly popular field of study. The influence of Japanese culture will follow, not immediately to the richer countries, but first to the peoples searching most eagerly for models of success.

Wealth also brings responsibilities, not all of them welcome. It means pouring capital into ill-fated development schemes in the third world. It means working to hold together the various international institutions which attempt to order the welter of conflicting interests. It means having one's own institutions and customs held up to critical scrutiny by foreigners, not all of whom are well intentioned. Most difficult of all, it means developing a moral outlook that transcends the maximization of economic gain, which has been the guiding light of post-war Japan. It would be pleasant to report that the Japanese understand what is demanded of them and are adjusting their attitude to the outside world. Unfortunately evidence of that has yet to appear. Progress is still made only in grudging response to outside pressure. Many young people view the problems of other countries with apathy, or, more worrying, dismissive arrogance. The few bureaucrats, businessmen and politicians with a sophisticated appreciation of Japan's international role stand well outside the mainstream of public opinion. The Japanese too have been taken by surprise.

Collective prosperity poses a different set of challenges from collective effort and collective suffering. Within Japan, the age of homogeneity is gradually giving way to particularization and complexity, making the country less easy both to govern and to categorize, but much more fun to inhabit. The bureaucratic centralism of Japan Inc. is being replaced by a dynamic, market-driven economy in which service and knowledge-intensive industries play the key role. Unemployment is rising, and so are salaries. Creativity and specialized skills are being rated above loyalty. The sense of solidarity is fading as economic inequities and contradictions become more apparent. Politically, the old consensus-building style of leadership no longer suffices. Consumers, farmers, high-tech exporters, depressed heavy industries, mammoth financial institutions – all have different priorities, which are becoming increasingly difficult to reconcile. Socially, young people are drifting away from the mass conformity which is the outside world's abiding image of modern Japan. New wealth and the gradual growth in leisure time offer them the chance to develop hobbies and personal interests that their parents never enjoyed. Women and old people are slipping out of their assigned roles. Profound changes are occurring in attitudes towards money, privacy and duty.

Japan is in flux, as usual. The outcome will affect us all.

Index

China (*cont.*)
  relations with, 225, 234, 264,
    328, 336, 352–4
  war with (1894–5), 25, 163, 166
Christianity, 21, 25, 326
chu (loyalty), 190
Chun, President Doo-Hwan,
    171, 197, 253
cinema, 335–6
class structure, 21–2, 55, 192, 269
cleanliness, 59
climate, 8–9
Columbia Top, 180
comic magazines, 5, 60, 141–3
Communist Party, Japanese,
    175, 195, 196, 198–200, 206
companies, *see* corporations
competitiveness, 13, 18, 56, 256,
    290, 291–2, 304, 310, 314
computers, 64, 292, 310–11
Confucianism, 52, 287
  commercial, 110
  filial piety, 126
  women in, 123
conglomerates, see *zaibatsu*
Constitution (1889), 162
Constitution (1947)
  Article Nine, 80, 340
  Article Twenty, 327
  defence, 80
  occupation, 168
  reform, 239–41, 246, 255,
    340
construction industry, 89
consumer goods, 48, 290
corporations
  accommodation for staff,
    102–3, 110
  accounting practices, 318
  competition, *see* competi-
    tiveness

conglomerates, see *zaibatsu*
consensus process, 55–6, 79
  employees identity with, 108–
    11, 119
  equity ratio, 318
  financing of, 48, 283, 317
  meetings, 88–9
  multinationals, 293
  paternalism, 102–3
  profit margins, 310, 318
  public/private, 295
  shareholders, 53, 88
  small, 109–10, 121
cosmetics, 41
countertrade, 309
cost of living, 270
crime, 82–91, 101
culture
  Asian influence, 7, 19
  insularity of, 38–43
Jomon, 19
  Western influence, 14–15

DKB, 305, 311
daimyo (regional lords), 22–3
de Gaulle, General Charles, 235
debt, personal, 52, 211, 316
defence, 240–41, 246–7, 251,
    255, 337–57; *see also* Air
    Force, armaments industry,
    Army, Navy
  electronic, 339
  industry, 346
  manpower, 338–9
  spending, 294, 343–4, 338
Democratic Party, 183, 223, 236,
    238–9, 277
Democratic Socialist Party, 177,
    194, 200–201, 298
developing nations
  aid to, 1, 30, 43, 359